"This thoroughly up-to-date and church-shaped commentary breaks new ground by rendering its message over and over through the critical filters of an Anabaptist understanding of how Christians ought to live in a complicated, violent, and insensitive world. Pastors and professors as well as students and Bible study leaders will benefit from the rich assortment of offerings for each passage in this noble study. This commentary will become one of the first I consult whenever I turn to the book of James."

—***Scot McKnight***, *professor of New Testament and author of* The Letter of James

"Sheila Klassen-Wiebe offers a gift to readers of James in both the church and academy. Paying careful attention to textual details and intertextual connections between James and other parts of the biblical canon, and rich in explorations of historical interpretations of James among Anabaptists, this commentary brings the biblical text to life for modern audiences."

—***Melanie Howard***, *associate provost and dean of the College of Arts and Sciences at Simpson University and author of* Twelve Biblical Characters

"This clear, accessible, and engaging volume addresses a range of thorny issues that arise in what is probably the most puzzling document in the New Testament. Anabaptist readers in particular will find the commentary useful as they grapple with the message and meaning of James."

—***Alicia Batten***, *professor of religious studies and theological studies at Conrad Grebel University College*

"The little letter of James has begun to receive long-needed attention from commentators in the last twenty or so years. Klassen-Wiebe further pursues this important trajectory with a commentary that is very readable, thorough but not overly technical, up-to-date with scholarly literature, well within the Anabaptist tradition out of which this series flows, and conversant with the history of the letter's interpretation. Especially valuable are her insights for contemporary Christian living. It's a real one-stop-shopping cart item for the preacher or teacher of James."

—***Craig L. Blomberg***, *Distinguished Professor Emeritus of New Testament at Denver Seminary*

"Klassen-Wiebe's brilliance lies in her willingness to take the Scriptures seriously, making this commentary on James a rich well for theologians, church practitioners, and everyday followers of Jesus. She does not give into the temptation to box James in, but rather uses a wholistic approach that confronts our entire being—head, heart, and hands. More than a tool for understanding James, this commentary is a guide to the gospel. In a time when Christianity's failures push people to search for Jesus apart from the church, Klassen-Wiebe's faithful encouragement, challenge, and hope in God's grace are a gift we must pay attention to."

—***Moses Falco***, *operations manager for Mennonite Disaster Service Canada and ordained pastor in Mennonite Church Manitoba*

"Klassen-Wiebe does a service to the church in bringing the practical insights of James into direct conversation with Jesus, revealing how both together give unified witness to the countercultural wisdom of God."

—***Meghan Larissa Good***, *author of* Divine Gravity *and* The Bible Unwrapped

"With the heart of an Anabaptist and the head of an educator and scholar, Klassen-Wiebe skillfully demonstrates how James's letter is, at its core, a pastoral message to the church as relevant today as the day it was written. The work outlines James's approach to relevant themes of unity, faithfulness, judgment, and church healing, among others, as he shares his theology of God's grace, goodness, and generosity. Pastors, scholars, educators, and folks in the pews will all find this work an engaging and useful resource as they dive into this work and discover (anew) James's conviction that faith is a matter of both heart and hands."

—***Cheryl Braun***, *Mennonite pastor and moderator of Mennonite Church Manitoba*

"Klassen-Wiebe has produced my new go-to commentary on James: grounded in sound scholarship yet eminently readable, filled with both theological insight and practical wisdom. Her years of teaching experience and engagement in church ministry are evident throughout. What a tremendous gift to the church!"

—***Michael Pahl***, *executive minister for Mennonite Church Manitoba and author of* The Word Fulfilled

Douglas B. Miller and Loren L. Johns, Editors

BELIEVERS CHURCH BIBLE COMMENTARY

Old Testament

Genesis, by Eugene F. Roop, 1987
Exodus, by Waldemar Janzen, 2000
Leviticus, by Perry B. Yoder, 2017
Numbers, by Jackie Wyse-Rhodes, *forthcoming*
Deuteronomy, by Gerald Gerbrandt, 2015
Joshua, by Gordon H. Matties, 2012
Judges, by Terry L. Brensinger, 1999
Ruth, Jonah, Esther, by Eugene F. Roop, 2002
1–2 Samuel, by David Baker, *forthcoming*
1–2 Kings, by Lynn Jost, 2021
1–2 Chronicles, by August Konkel, 2016
Ezra–Nehemiah, *forthcoming*
Job, by Paul Keim, *forthcoming*
Psalms, by James H. Waltner, 2006
Proverbs, by John W. Miller, 2004
Ecclesiastes, by Douglas B. Miller, 2010
Isaiah, by Ivan D. Friesen, 2009
Jeremiah, by Elmer A. Martens, 1986
Lamentations, Song of Songs, by Wilma Ann Bailey and Christina A. Bucher, 2015
Ezekiel, by Millard C. Lind, 1996
Daniel, by Paul M. Lederach, 1994
Hosea, Amos, by Allen R. Guenther, 1998
Joel, Obadiah, Micah, by Daniel Epp-Tiessen, 2022
Nahum, Habakkuk, Zephaniah, by W. Derek Suderman, *forthcoming*
Haggai, Zechariah, Malachi, *forthcoming*

New Testament

Matthew, by Richard B. Gardner, 1991
Mark, by Timothy J. Geddert, 2001
Luke, by Mary H. Schertz, 2023
John, by Willard M. Swartley, 2013
Acts, by Chalmer E. Faw, 1993
Romans, by John E. Toews, 2004
1 Corinthians, by Dan Nighswander, 2017
2 Corinthians, by V. George Shillington, 1998
Galatians, by George R. Brunk III, 2015
Ephesians, by Thomas R. Yoder Neufeld, 2002
Philippians, by Gordon Zerbe, 2016
Colossians, Philemon, by Ernest D. Martin, 1993
1–2 Thessalonians, by Jacob W. Elias, 1995
1–2 Timothy, Titus, by Paul M. Zehr, 2010
Hebrews, by Debra J. Bucher and Estella Boggs Horning, 2024
James, by Sheila Klassen-Wiebe, 2026
1–2 Peter, Jude, by Erland Waltner and J. Daryl Charles, 1999
1, 2, 3 John, by Jay McDermond, 2011
Revelation, by John R. Yeatts, 2003

James

Sheila Klassen-Wiebe

HERALD PRESS
Harrisonburg, Virginia

Herald Press
PO Box 866, Harrisonburg, VA 22803
www.HeraldPress.com

Library of Congress Cataloging-in-Publication Data
Names: Klassen-Wiebe, Sheila author
Title: James / Sheila Klassen-Wiebe.
Description: Harrisonburg : Herald Press, [2026] | Series: Believers church Cible commentary ; volume 38 | Includes bibliographical references and index.
Identifiers: LCCN 2025026195 (print) | LCCN 2025026196 (ebook) | ISBN 9781513805993 paperback | ISBN 9781513806006 ebook
Subjects: LCSH: Bible. James—Commentaries | LCGFT: Commentaries
Classification: LCC BS2785.53 .K53 2026 (print) | LCC BS2785.53 (ebook) | DDC 227/.9107—dc23/eng/20251119
LC record available at https://lccn.loc.gov/2025026195
LC ebook record available at https://lccn.loc.gov/2025026196

 Other versions cited briefly are listed with Abbreviations. Quotations of James are in italics. Quotations of other texts are roman and within quotation marks.

Library of Congress Control Number: 2025026195
International Standard Book Number: 978-1-5138-0599-3 (paperback);
978-1-5138-0600-6 (ebook)
Printed in United States of America
Cover by Merrill Miller
Interior design by Merrill Miller and Alice Shetler

30 29 28 27 26   10 9 8 7 6 5 4 3 2 1

To my parents,

George and Anita Klassen,

who modeled for me a lived and living faith

Abbreviations and Sigla

*	*see* TBC, Text in Biblical Context
+	*see* TLC, Text in the Life of the Church
×	times, as in 2×, two times
/	or
//	is parallel to
[. . . , p. 000]	italic brackets for cross-reference to an essay
A . . . A′ . . . A″	parallel lines or phrases
ASV	American Standard Version
AT	author's translation/paraphrase
BCBC	Believers Church Bible Commentary
BCE	before the Common Era
BDAG	Danker, F. W., W. Bauer, W. F. Arndt, and F. W. Gingrich. *Greek-English Lexicon of the New Testament and Other Early Christian Literature.* 3rd ed. Chicago: University of Chicago Press, 2000.
c.	century, centuries
ca.	circa, approximately
CE	Common Era
CEB	Common English Bible
cf.	*confer*, compare
chap(s).	chapter(s)
CWMS	*The Complete Writings of Menno Simons, c. 1496–1561.* Translated by Leonard Verduin. Edited by John C. Wenger. Scottdale, PA: Herald Press, 1956.
DLNT	*Dictionary of the Later New Testament and Its Developments.* Edited by R. P. Martin and P. H. Davids. Downers Grove, IL: InterVarsity Press, 1997.
ed(s).	editor(s); edition; edited by
e.g.	*exempli gratia*, for example
esp.	especially
ESV	English Standard Version, 2001
ET	English translation
GAMEO	Global Anabaptist Mennonite Encyclopedia Online. https://gameo.org/index.php?title=Welcome_to_GAMEO.
Gk.	Greek
GNT	Good News Bible Translation
GW	God's Word Translation
HBD	*HarperCollins Bible Dictionary.* Edited by M. A. Powell et al. 3rd ed. San Francisco: Harper One, 2011.
i.e.	*id est*, that is
KJV	King James Version, 1611
lit.	literally
LW	Luther's Works. American ed. 82 vols. Saint Louis: Concordia Publishing, [1955]–2022.
LXX	Septuagint (the Greek OT, cited with NRSV chapter and verse numbers)
Message	*The Message*, by Eugene Peterson
MM	*Martyrs Mirror: The Bloody Theatre, or Martyrs Mirror . . .* , by T. J. van Bracht. 2nd English ed. Scottdale, PA: Herald Press, 2001. https://www.ccel.org/ccel/vanbraght/mirror.iv.v.html.

MSG	*The Message*, by Eugene Peterson
MT	Masoretic Text (of the Hebrew Bible)
n(n).	note(s), footnote(s)
NASB	New American Standard Bible
NCV	New Century Version
n.d.	no date
NET	New English Translation
NIDB	*The New Interpreter's Dictionary of the Bible*, edited by Katharine Doob Sakenfeld, 5 vols. (Nashville: Abingdon, 2006–9).
NIDNTTE	*New International Dictionary of New Testament Theology and Exegesis*, edited by Moises Silva, 5 vols., 2nd ed. (Grand Rapids: Zondervan, 2014).
NIV	New International Version
NKJV	New King James Version
NLT	New Living Translation
NRSV	New Revised Standard Version, 1989
NRSVA	New Revised Standard Version, Anglicised, 1989, 1995
NRSVue	New Revised Standard Version Updated Edition, 2021
NT	New Testament
OT	Old Testament
𝔓	symbol for an ancient papyrus, such as $𝔓^{46}$
par.	parallel(s)
pl.	plural
p(p).	page(s)
rev. (ed.)	revised (edition)
RSV	Revised Standard Version
sg.	singular
TBC	The Text in Biblical Context
TEV	Today's English Version
TLC	The Text in the Life of the Church
trans.	translator(s)
v(v).	verse(s)

Contents

Series Foreword

The Believers Church Bible Commentary Series makes available a new tool for basic Bible study. It is published for all who seek to more fully understand the original message of Scripture and its meaning for today—Sunday school teachers, members of Bible study groups, students, pastors, and others. The series is based on the conviction that God is still speaking to all who will listen and that the Holy Spirit makes the Word a living and authoritative guide for all who want to know and do God's will.

The desire to help as wide a range of readers as possible has determined the approach of the writers. Since no blocks of biblical text are provided, readers may continue to use the translation with which they are most familiar. The writers of the series use the New Revised Standard Version or its Updated Edition and the New International Version on a comparative basis. They indicate which text they follow most closely and where they make their own translations. The writers have not worked alone, but in consultation with select counselors, the series' editors, and the Editorial Council.

Every volume illuminates the Scriptures; provides necessary theological, sociological, and ethical meanings; and in general makes "the rough places plain" (Isa 40:4 KJV). Critical issues are not avoided, but neither are they moved into the foreground as debates among scholars. Each section offers Explanatory Notes (comments), followed by focused articles, "The Text in Biblical Context" and "The Text in the Life of the Church." This commentary aids the interpretive process but does not try to supersede the authority of the Word and Spirit as discerned in the gathered church.

The term *believers church* has often been used in the history of the church. Since the sixteenth century, it has frequently been applied to the Anabaptists and later the Mennonites, as well as to the Church of the Brethren and similar groups. As a descriptive term, it includes more than Mennonites and Brethren. *Believers church* now represents specific theological understandings, such as believers baptism, commitment to the Rule of Christ in Matthew 18:15-20 as crucial for church membership, belief in the power of love in all relationships, and willingness to follow Christ in the way of the cross. The writers chosen for the series stand in this tradition.

Believers church people have always been known for their emphasis on obedience to the simple meaning of Scripture. Because of this, they do not have a long history of deep historical-critical biblical scholarship. This series attempts to be faithful to the Scriptures while also taking archaeology and current biblical studies seriously. Doing this means that at many points the writers will not differ greatly from interpretations that can be found in many other good commentaries. Yet these writers share basic convictions about Christ, the church and its mission, God and history, human nature, the Christian life, and other doctrines. These presuppositions do shape a writer's interpretation of Scripture. Thus this series, like all other commentaries, stands within a specific historical church tradition.

Many in this stream of the church have expressed a need for help in Bible study. This is justification enough to produce the Believers Church Bible Commentary. Nevertheless, the Holy Spirit is not bound to any tradition. May this series be an instrument in breaking down walls between Christians in North America and around the world, bringing new joy in obedience through a fuller understanding of the Word.

The Editorial Council

Author's Preface

Ever since I was old enough to read and study the Bible on my own, the book of James has been important to me. I vividly remember a time in my early teens when I read James 4:17 and was moved to do something that I knew was the right thing to do, even though it was unpleasant and hard. This short, practical letter appealed to my desire to "get it right," to be a "good Christian," and to live out the faith I professed. It taught me how to follow Jesus in everyday life.

The letter lost some of its shine in adulthood, when I needed to hear a message of grace and compassion more than I needed instructions on how to do better. My graduate studies led me into a career of teaching, preaching, and writing on the Gospels and Jesus. In particular, I loved the Jesus I met in the Gospel of Luke, with his message of compassion for the outsider, extravagant hospitality, and resurrection hope. My love for James became a distant memory.

It was with some mixed feelings, then, that I accepted the invitation to write the Believers Church Bible Commentary on the Letter of James. There was not enough Jesus in the letter—or so I thought. Jesus' name is mentioned only twice, and nowhere does James say anything about his life, death, or resurrection. The more I studied the letter, however, the more I realized that Jesus is everywhere. Not in stories or direct references but in the teachings of Jesus that James passes on so faithfully and creatively. I also realized that James is more than instructions for getting it right and living as a good Christian.

James's teachings on how to live faithfully as a follower of Jesus are deeply embedded in a theology of God's grace, goodness, and generosity (1:17; 4:6). Teachings about how to live are grounded in the good news that God has given us birth by the word of truth, making us first fruits of his creatures (1:18). James is calling Christians to live out that identity with integrity. When my teenage self went out with friends, my parents often said, "Remember who you are!" James is calling us to remember who we are. We cannot claim to have faith in the Lord Jesus Christ if we do not speak and act and live accordingly. Following Jesus, according to James, involves speaking kindly and truthfully, sharing generously with others, caring for the vulnerable and marginalized, being humble and not arrogant or envious, resisting temptation, repenting of sin, making peace, not showing partiality to those with status and money, being patient in suffering, and much more. This was the same Jesus whom I knew from the Gospels.

Studying James has also reminded me that this letter is not only for me personally as I strive to live out my faith. It is also for the church. James is calling the church to remember its identity and to live with integrity. We need each other—to pray for each other when we suffer, to hold each other accountable and forgive each other when we sin, to remind each other what the love of Jesus looks like when it is embodied and lived. The Letter of James is primarily a pastoral message to the body of Christ, not a list of rules for individual Christians.

An unexpected blessing while studying James was learning how important this little letter has been for Anabaptist expressions of Christian faith. This should not have surprised me. The Sermon on the Mount has always been highly valued by Christians for its teachings on discipleship. Since the Letter of James echoes so many of Jesus' teachings in the Sermon, it makes sense that my Anabaptist Mennonite church tradition has also used and loved the Letter of James. It was a delight to read James through that Anabaptist lens.

So I have come full circle. James has once again become a good friend. As a result of writing this commentary, my understanding of the letter has deepened and my appreciation and, yes, love for James has become richer. I have met Jesus in James and have been challenged and encouraged in my desire to follow Jesus in all of life.

Many people have accompanied me on this journey with James, some knowingly and some not. I am indebted to the work of many scholars throughout time and space who have influenced and sharpened my understanding of James and whose contributions are evident throughout the commentary. Some of these are included in the list of "Selected Resources" at the end of the commentary.

I am grateful to my professors and mentors at Canadian Mennonite Bible College, who whetted my appetite for ongoing study of the Bible; and for professors at Associated Mennonite Biblical Seminary and Union Theological Seminary in Richmond, Virginia, who taught me to read biblical texts closely and carefully. Canadian Mennonite University has provided several sabbatical leaves, without which I would not have been able to complete the commentary. It has also provided me with a supportive community of colleagues and students, who must surely be getting tired of me saying, "That reminds me of something in the book of James!" I am immensely grateful to the students who have taken my course "James and the Sermon on the Mount" and to the many church groups who have heard me preach and teach about James over the last decade or so. They have challenged me, offered new insights, asked thought-provoking questions, and inspired me. Although they are not quoted in the commentary like published scholars, their influence is everywhere.

Several people have offered feedback on drafts of the manuscript and have made it stronger. In particular, I wish to thank Valerie Smith and Bruno Dyck, fellow members at Charleswood Mennonite Church and excellent readers of Scripture. The Editorial Council and my New Testament editor, Loren Johns, have offered invaluable feedback and advice along the way and have been incredibly patient as I have slowly worked at the commentary alongside the demands of teaching. Many thanks also to S. David Garber for his careful and thorough work as copy editor.

Finally, I wish to thank my family. I am grateful to my parents, George and Anita Klassen, who first taught me to love Jesus and modeled what it means to follow Jesus with lives of service and generosity. My husband, Vern, and my daughters, Megan, Rebecca, and Nicolien, have been my greatest cheerleaders. They have encouraged me, given hugs, and listened patiently to my ramblings about James. I am profoundly grateful for their constant love and the joy they bring to my life.

My hope and prayer, dear reader, is that you will be as blessed by studying James as I have been. But I have learned from James that looking into the mirror of the word of God (1:22-24), even diligently studying it, is of no value if it does not impact how we live, if it does not urge us on to greater faithfulness and love. May it be so.

Introduction to James

Many people are disillusioned with the institutional church because of the hypocrisy of Christians who do not practice what they preach, people who claim to be motivated by love but act in unloving ways. James is concerned about this as well. To be sure, James has not given up on the church. In fact, it is because he cares so deeply that he is perturbed by how his *brothers and sisters* are living. The message of this relatively short New Testament book (only 108 verses) is quite straightforward. It is not about providing new information or about correcting false doctrine. It is not a checklist of things to do or about organizing committees. Rather, it is about living with integrity. James reminds the church that God has birthed its members into a new existence (1:18) and that they profess to follow Jesus Christ as Lord (2:1). The problem is that they are living as *double-minded* people: what they hear and say and what they know and believe are inconsistent with how they act. James seeks to change such a clash by writing a letter that prods them to deeper faithfulness.

This message continues to be relevant for the church two thousand years later. The problems James addresses are problems that the church in the twenty-first century continues to face. Disparities between rich and poor have not disappeared. Discrimination persists. Inflammatory speech continues to wound and divide. Although the letter is rooted in a first-century, Hellenistic (Greek) Jewish context, its intensely practical nature and the lack of specifics about context give it a timeless quality.

It is not surprising that this short letter continues to appeal to so many people today. The most difficult aspect of the letter is not a matter of understanding what the author means but putting into practice what he writes.

What Is This Book Called "James"?

At first blush the answer to the question "What is James?" seems obvious. It is part of a collection of letters from early church leaders to fledgling Christian communities. James 1:1 does sound like the typical prescript or opening of a Hellenistic letter: sender to receiver, greetings. But after that, it differs markedly from most other New Testament letters. It contains no thanksgiving or opening prayer and no final greetings, news, or farewell. In his influential commentary, Martin Dibelius argues that there is no obvious situation being addressed. The person writing the letter remains hidden and makes "no epistolary remarks of any sort," leading him to conclude that "it [is] impossible to consider [James] as an actual letter" (Dibelius: 2). Rather, Dibelius maintains that the book is paraenesis (advice or exhortation) in the literary form of a letter, "a text which strings together admonitions of general ethical content" (Dibelius: 3). Other scholars have also questioned the genre of James. Ben Witherington, for example, argues that it is a sermon simply using an opening epistolary form to deliver its message (2007: 533). Others have likened it to wisdom literature, such as Proverbs *[The Wisdom Tradition and James, p. 376]*.

Although the question of genre has not been resolved, many scholars argue that James is a genuine letter, as do most Christians who read it today. Although it does not target a specific ecclesial community, such as Paul's Letters to the Corinthians, it does address real, concrete issues, such as socioeconomic discrimination. The frequency with which the author addresses his audience as *beloved brothers and sisters* lends the letter a personal tone that implies it is more than a literary fiction. Since the genre of ancient "letter" was elastic and other letters end equally abruptly (e.g., 1 John), the lack of features typical of a Pauline letter does not disqualify it from being a real letter. Some scholars view James as conforming to the category of Jewish Diaspora letters. Such letters were typically written by a religious leader in Judea to Jewish communities outside the land about how to live faithfully as the people of God (Cheung and Yu: 90–91; Bauckham 1999: 19–21). Examples of such letters are found in Jeremiah 29; 2 Maccabees 1:1-9; 1:10–2:18; and 2 Baruch 78–87. James shares many features with them (Allison 2013: 90–91).

Why is the question of genre worth asking? Does it matter whether James was a letter? Identifying the literary genre of a piece of writing can help us know how to read something correctly. We would not read a fairy tale with the same expectations that we would bring to a newspaper article, for example. By adopting a specific literary genre, a writer is in effect making an implicit contract with the reader and following certain "rules" so that readers and hearers can better understand the message (Cheung and Yu: 87). This commentary assumes that the writer of James was penning a real letter intended for a real audience, though not necessarily one specific community. The book is not merely a collection of generic bits of advice but gives pastoral counsel from a trusted leader, wisdom intended to mold the church toward greater faithfulness.

The Message and Central Themes of James

The message of James is relatively straightforward: a commitment to Jesus as Messiah and Lord must be evident in how one lives. Specifically, both individual disciples and faith communities must strive to embody the will of God as revealed in the life and teachings of Jesus. Genuine faith is not an intellectual exercise or a theoretically good idea but has a profound impact on every aspect of life. James is calling the church to faithfulness, integrity, and wholeness—in short, to live out who they are.

Because of the danger of the church *not* demonstrating such coherence in their life together, James may sound like a teacher scolding or sternly lecturing his students on how to behave. More positively, James can come across as a rule book for being a "good Christian." This would be a misreading of the letter, however. Although it is not a systematic theological treatise, James's ethics are firmly embedded in convictions about who God is and what God is doing with and for the people God created. In this, the letter is consistent with the entire biblical story, in which right living is always a response to God's saving action.

Theology, Christology, and Eschatology

Grounding James's theology and ethics is the story of God's actions in the past, present, and future. Although not written to teach explicitly about God, the letter indirectly has much to say about the character of God. As Luke Timothy Johnson notes, it is "first order religious language, rather than second-order reflection on such language" (2002: 212). In this context, "first order" refers to the original language of sacred texts and traditions, while "second order" refers to later interpretations or doctrines built on the former. At the heart of James's theology lies an understanding of God as an abundantly generous, ungrudging Giver of gifts (1:5, 17) and a bestower of grace (4:5-6). This God is inherently good and never tempted by evil (1:13). The Creator, *the Father of lights* (1:17), fashioned people in *the likeness of God* (3:9). Like a mother, God birthed the church through God's word, making them the *first fruits* of God's new creatures (1:18). Knowing that people are torn by conflicting desires and trials, God generously grants wisdom to help them live congruent with God's desires (1:5; 3:17). God implants the divine word in God's creatures for their salvation and gives them the law of the kingdom to help them live freely in accordance with God's will (1:21, 25; 2:8). God is supremely compassionate and merciful (5:11), healing the sick and forgiving those who sin (5:15-16); God draws near to those who seek God and gives grace to the humble (4:6-10).

God is also the *Lord of hosts*, who will not tolerate injustice (5:4). By raising up the lowly and hearing the cries of the oppressed, God demonstrates that God is on the side of the poor and weak (1:9; 2:5; 4:10). Those who see the book of James as simply a compendium of moral instruction have not looked closely enough to see the profound theological convictions and expansive grace undergirding the letter.

Although the letter only mentions Jesus' name twice (1:1; 2:1), it does have an implicit Christology. God and Jesus are named in intersecting ways, such that the work of one appears to be the work of the other. Jesus is the Messiah (Christ), God's anointed agent to carry out God's will, and James identifies himself as the slave of both (1:1), implying a unity of purpose and status. Both God and Jesus are the object of his fealty and are to be obeyed. Jesus is also Lord, a title that connotes authority and invites worship. Interestingly, the word *Lord* (the translation of "Yahweh" in the Old Testament) is used fourteen times in the letter, sometimes to refer to God and sometimes to Jesus. Several times the referent is ambiguous, resulting in an interesting blurring of the two. For example, *the coming of the Lord* (5:7-8) almost certainly refers to the parousia (coming) of Jesus; but a few verses later (5:10-11), the referent is surely God. The *coming . . . Lord* (Jesus) is also the *Judge . . . at the doors* (5:8-9), but previously the *one lawgiver and judge* is likely God (4:12). Finally, the Lord in whose name the sick are anointed and who raises them up could refer to either Jesus (who raised the sick during his earthly ministry) or God or both. Jesus is most present in the letter in the form of his teachings, which James has passed on.

Eschatology is also integral to James's theology and ethics. How James conceives of God's actions in the future impacts how followers of Jesus must live now. God is a Savior who will raise up the lowly (1:9; 4:6, 10) and bestow on them a crown and a kingdom (1:12; 2:5). God is also a Judge who will bring down the rich and powerful, a Lord of hosts who hears the cries of the oppressed and enacts justice (1:9-11; 5:1-6, 9). James reminds the church of when they are living and who they are: *The coming of the Lord is near* (5:8), and they are the *first fruits* of God's creatures (1:18). The ingathering of God's people in the last days has begun. The reversals that God will bring about in the future are already beginning now in the church, as they refuse to curry favor with the rich (2:1-9), care for the most vulnerable (1:27), practice patience in the face of suffering (5:7-11), and refrain from judging and speaking evil of others (4:11-12; 5:9).

Faith

Beliefs about the grace and goodness of the creator God mean little if they remain only in the head. For James, faith includes belief, but since *even the demons believe* (2:19), faith is not primarily head knowledge. Faith is more: it is a matter of the heart and the hands. It is both trust in God and faithfulness, demonstrated in a desire to do the will of God. All these words—*belief*, *trust*, and *faithfulness*—are legitimate translations of the Greek word for faith (*pistis*) and are encompassed by it, but James emphasizes the latter two aspects. The poor are *rich in faith* and inherit a kingdom because they *trust* and love God, not only because they believe certain things about God (2:5). To *ask in faith* (1:6) means to ask with a basic trust that God is consistently good and generous. Faith is also *loyalty* or allegiance to the one true God and to Jesus the Messiah (1:1; 2:1). Unless such loyalty is demonstrated in action, it is dead, empty, and useless—not really faith.

To be clear, it is not one's works that save, but a genuine saving faith *will* have works. For James, any cleaving apart of faith and works (or justification and sanctification, to use terms foreign to James) is inconceivable. James's teaching on the inseparability of true faith and works is concentrated in 2:14-26, but this emphasis pervades the entire letter. For example, genuine faith is evident in rejecting patronage systems that favor the rich and sideline the poor (2:1-9) and in caring for the most vulnerable (1:27).

Integrity and Being "Perfect"

At the heart of the Letter of James is a call for congruency of head, heart, and hands. Sometimes this appears as an admonition to be perfect (1:4), but that word does not capture James's intention well, since it can imply "perfectionism." It is helpful to think about the opposite of what James means. Twice in the letter he warns against being *double-minded* (1:8; 4:8), the idea that people can walk two divergent paths at the same time. Followers of Jesus Messiah cannot be both *friend[s] of God* and *friend[s] of the world* (2:23; 4:4), for example, nor can they pursue both *wisdom . . . from above* and counterfeit, *unspiritual wisdom* (3:13-18). Although modern sensibilities may consider such dualistic language too uncompromising, James is drawing on Old Testament ideals by calling his readers and hearers to loyalty to the one true God. Just as Joshua urged Israel to "choose this day whom you will serve" (Josh 24:15; cf. Deut 11:26-28; Jer 21:8), so also James calls the church to align itself with God and God's Messiah, Jesus. In so doing, James echoes the words of Jesus, who is similarly uncompromising in his call to discipleship and single-minded faithfulness (Matt 5:48; 6:24; 7:13-14). Instead of compartmentalizing life into things that are "spiritual" or "religious" and things that are "ordinary," "economic," or "political," James invites his audience to live as *whole* people—followers of Jesus in *every* aspect of life. If indeed God has *given them birth* and made them *first fruits of his creatures* (1:18), they should live out that identity with integrity. They must hear *and* do (1:22-25), speak *and* act (2:15-16), know *and* live (4:17).

James is not telling his readers something they do not already know: he packages the teachings of Jesus in language and images of their faith tradition, their Scriptures. Jesus himself identified the essence of the law as loving God and neighbor (Mark 12:31-33 and par.). James's ethic is grounded in this same double love command (1:12; 2:5; 2:8). However, he is adamant that such love must not be merely an emotion. Rather, it must be expressed in concrete deeds of compassion, peacemaking, and obedience.

James is realistic about human sin and does not expect perfection: he knows that everyone stumbles (3:2) and assumes the need for mutual correction and forgiveness of sins (5:15-16, 19-20). In fact, he writes the letter for this reason: to call his *brothers and sisters* to a more faithful expression of their commitment to Jesus.

Personal and Communal Faithfulness

This call to a lived faith is both personal and communal. Christians today tend to read the letter as moral instruction for individuals. To be sure, James's teachings *are* relevant on a personal level. Disciplining the tongue, for example, is something each person must do. However, the letter is even more concerned about community formation. It is addressed to gathered bodies of believers for the purpose of shaping their life together in the world. As Patrick Hartin says so well, "The individual is addressed only insofar as he or she is part of the community" (2009a: 4). Individuals must learn to rein in their tongues because failure to do so leads to division and *death* (1:15; 5:20) for the whole body. When someone strays, it is the whole community's responsibility to bring that *brother or sister* back. Liberation of the oppressed is also liberation of the rich.

James's perspective on lived faith, grounded in theological and ethical convictions, comes to concrete expression in various themes and emphases. The following are five key ones:

Perseverance through Trials and Suffering

The question of how Messiah followers should respond to suffering and hardship is a significant aspect of faithful living for James. This is evident in the fact that the letter begins and ends with this theme (1:2-4; 5:7-11). At least some of the letter's recipients were suffering at the hands of rich oppressors and were victims of social injustice (2:6; 5:1-6). The scope of hardships is broader than this, however, for the letter begins with *whenever you face various trials* (emphasis added). Some are suffering because of illness (5:13-16). Entire communities are suffering because of divisions, conflict, and sin (4:1-2; 5:19-20). Sin is not unrelated to suffering (5:15-16), yet not all suffering is the result of sin. James does not try to explain theologically why people suffer. His concern is how to respond faithfully.

Although suffering is not redemptive nor to be sought out, followers of Jesus can choose to view hardship as an opportunity for growth and even joy (1:2-4). James encourages the church to respond to trials with patient endurance (5:7-11). He implies that they should not resist injustice violently (3:18; 5:6) and says that anger will not bring about the justice of God (1:20). When times of testing come, even faithful believers may succumb to temptations and sin. James urges them not to be led astray (1:16) and to resist the devil (4:7). When they encounter hardship, the church must pray for wisdom to respond faithfully (1:5) and for healing and forgiveness (5:13-18). They must remember that, above all, God is compassionate and merciful (5:11).

Wealth, Poverty, and Social Justice

According to James, faithful living demands attention to economic and social justice. For wealthy Christians, the letter raises the uncomfortable question of whether it is possible to be both rich and Christian. For Christians in the global South, the letter has proved to be liberating good news (Maynard-Reid; Tamez 2002).

Followers of Jesus must care about how they use material resources and how they treat the poor because God cares. Like Jesus in the Gospels, James testifies to a God who turns the status quo upside down. God raises up the lowly and brings down the rich (1:9-11); God opposes the arrogant and exalts the humble (4:6, 10); the Lord of hosts hears the cry of the oppressed and judges the rich (5:4). The glory of wealth is ephemeral, but the rich in faith will inherit a kingdom (1:11; 2:5; 5:2-3).

James is unrelentingly critical of the wealthy for several reasons: their accumulation and hoarding of wealth, their opulent living, their exploitative labor practices, and the arrogance and boasting that signal reliance on self rather than on God (4:13-16; 5:1-6). Although the recipients of his letter are likely not the wealthy oppressors of 5:1-6, James's words come both as a warning to the church about the perils of wealth and as comfort to the oppressed.

The message of James is also more than that, however. Knowing about God's action on behalf of the poor should influence how followers of Jesus act in situations of economic disparity. In fact, knowing the right thing to do and not doing it is sin (4:17). Speaking comfort to the poor without lifting a finger to feed and clothe them implies that one's faith is empty and dead (2:16-17). True religion provides concrete care to the most vulnerable in society (1:27). Perhaps the greatest danger for James's church, which is neither egregiously wealthy nor living in abject poverty, is the temptation to align themselves with the powerful and the privileged to benefit themselves and to sideline those of no consequence or social value (2:1-9). James subverts all the social and cultural values of patronage and honor and calls the church to follow the royal law, that is, to *love your neighbor as yourself* (2:8).

Speech

Throughout the letter but especially in the substantial discourse on the tongue (3:1-12), James is adamant that Christian faith must impact how one speaks. What he says about speech echoes commonsense wisdom in Jewish writings and Greek moral philosophy. James's admonitions on this topic, however, are firmly grounded in religious commitments. Because believers are given birth by the *word* of truth and because the saving *word* of God has been implanted in them (1:18, 21), their own words must reflect the divine word. To hear God's word without doing it—without allowing it to impact one's speech—lacks integrity (1:22-24). James even says that if someone cannot control their tongue, *their religion is worthless* (1:26) and they are liable to judgment (5:9).

The tongue is a powerful force that can be used for good or ill, but James foregrounds the perils of speech and its potential to wound. The concerns of the letter cluster around five main problems: First, the tongue is impulsive and undisciplined, even untamable (3:7-9). To temper this, James counsels, *be quick to listen [and] slow to speak* (1:19). Second, the tongue damages relationships when it judges and speaks evil of others (4:11), complains against others (5:9), curses people (3:10), and dishonors the marginalized (2:3). In short, it is *full of deadly poison* (3:8). James explicitly and repeatedly warns against such behavior. Third, speech is sometimes untruthful (3:14). Since people sometimes think oaths will bolster their claims, James admonishes, *Let your "Yes" be yes and your "No" be no*; in other words, simply speak the truth (5:12). Fourth, James warns against speech that is hypocritical, inconsistent, and lacking corresponding action (2:16; 3:9-10). He urges his audience to "walk the talk." Fifth, speech can be arrogant and boastful, self-centered and self-aggrandizing (3:14; 4:13, 16). Instead, James urges his readers and hearers to be humble and submit to God's desires (4:7, 10, 15). Aligning one's speech with God's will and Jesus' way of love is no easy task but one to which James thinks the church *must* attend if its faith is going to have integrity.

Although more muted, James does recognize the tongue's power to do enormous good. Just as a small rudder can turn a large ship, so can the tongue return a sinner from wandering (3:4; 5:19-20). Praise, confession of sin, repentance, and prayer are all positive forms of speech that can bring a community closer to God and to each other (5:13-18).

Arrogance and Humility

According to James, arrogance results in actions inconsistent with a life of faith and contrary to friendship with God. Arrogant people act as if their plans and opinions take priority and as if they, rather than God, have ultimate control over their lives (4:13-14). Together with envy and selfish ambition, arrogance results in false boasting about one's own accomplishments. Such boasting is essentially an attempt to elevate oneself above the neighbor and is not only unloving but also evil (3:14; 4:16). Arrogance also results in judging and tearing others down. When people speak evil of others and judge them, they are putting themselves in the place of God, who alone knows the full story and who alone is *Judge* (4:11-12; 5:9). Making distinctions based on appearance or status is also a form of judging and thus arrogance (2:1-9).

James calls his readers and hearers to humble themselves and to discern and submit to God's will (4:6-10). Being humble means acknowledging that they do not know what tomorrow will bring and that their life ultimately belongs to God, who gave them life and breath (3:9; 4:14-15). Rather than elevating themselves over others by making false distinctions and judgments, they are to love their neighbors (2:8). This means treating everyone, even outcasts, with dignity and honor (1:27; 2:1-9). In this, believers defy societal and cultural norms, where deferring to the wealthy can benefit oneself. All this is based on the eschatological reality that God will exalt the humble and judge the haughty (1:9-10; 2:5; 4:6, 10).

Prayer

In the Letter of James, prayer consists primarily of intercession for spiritual and physical health, confession, and petition (1:5; 4:2-3; 5:13-18), yet it also includes blessing (3:9) and praising God (5:13). Although the letter does not have a well-developed theology of prayer, James is confident that God hears and responds to prayer. Because God gives generously and ungrudgingly, people should freely ask God for what they lack (1:5; 4:2). In particular, James urges them to ask for wisdom (1:5). Like Elijah, they should pray with trust and confidence, with persistence and patience (5:17-18), instead of being constantly unsettled, like the wind-tossed sea (1:7-8). James recognizes that people sometimes ask wrongly out of greed and envy (4:3); this comes from being *double-minded*, not from having friendship with God. Instead, prayer should be characterized by submission to God (4:7) and discernment of God's will (4:15). Such prayer is *powerful and effective* (5:16).

Structure and Coherence

When I teach the Letter of James, I often begin by asking students to create an outline of the book and observe organizational patterns. Usually there are as many outlines and rationales as students in the class. In this, they mirror the scholarly discussion of the structure of James.

In 1921 (English translation, 1976), the German scholar Martin Dibelius wrote an influential commentary in which he argued that

James is not a letter but a potpourri of wisdom and ethical teachings, loosely strung together with catchwords. In his view, it has no coherent structure, no specific audience, and little to no theological content. Although scholars have largely abandoned this view of James, all have had to seriously engage Dibelius's important contributions. Although many today argue that James is indeed a coherent letter addressed to a real audience, no clear consensus about structure has emerged.

Some have found rhetorical markers to be a helpful structuring device; for example, each new segment might begin with *brothers and sisters* and close with a pithy aphorism (McCartney 2009: 63–67). Others have suggested that the main body (2:1–5:6) is a chiasm embraced by an introduction (1:2-27) and conclusion (5:7[13]-20). Some scholars organize the letter around key topics such as trials, wisdom and speech, and wealth and poverty (Blomberg and Kamell: 26; Davids 1982: 22–28). Another detects seven subsections, with each contrasting negative and positive behavior (Elliott 1993: 720). That such an array of proposals exists suggests that the letter does not have an obvious organizational logic.

Three things can, however, be said about the structure of the letter. First, it resembles Proverbs and other wisdom literature in its loose structure and organization. Second, the letter contains several distinct units, each with a main focus: 2:14-26 on faith and works, 3:1-12 on the tongue, and 4:13—5:6 on wealth. Third, as many scholars have noticed, the first chapter functions as a preview of the rest of the letter: all the main themes and key theological terms introduced here emerge again later:

• endurance and testing	1:2-4, 12-16	5:7-11
• being complete or "perfect"	1:4	2:22; 3:2
• wisdom	1:5	3:13-18
• prayer	1:5-8	4:2-3; 5:13-18
• double-mindedness	1:8	4:8
• wealth and poverty	1:9-11	2:1-7; 5:1-6
• desire, sin, and death	1:14-16	4:2; 5:15-16, 19-20
• truth	1:18	3:14; 5:19
• speech	1:19-21, 26	3:1-12; 4:11-12; 5:9, 12
• faith and works, hearing and doing	1:22-27	2:14-26
• law	1:25	2:8-12; 4:11-12

Although not a formal table of contents, one quickly gets a sense of what the letter is about by reading the first twenty-seven verses.

In short, the letter is not a random assortment of disparate ideas but has coherence and unity of purpose. Careful study reveals how interconnected the ideas are and how seemingly untethered sentences acquire meaning in the wider context. For example, comments about prayer (5:13-18) must be read with statements about God's goodness and generosity (1:5, 17). Accusations about war and murder (4:1-3) gain clarity in the context of earlier words about disordered desire (1:14-16) and the destructive potential of the tongue (1:19; 3:5-8). In the commentary that follows, I assume that the author has loosely connected ideas by means of shared vocabulary, rhetorical markers, and common themes without having a careful, clear structure in mind.

The Letter of James is more like a musical composition than a systematic argument. Melodies emerge, recede, and then reappear with a slightly different rhythm or in a different key; the same notes are used throughout the letter but in different combinations to produce different sounds. Sometimes a musical phrase slides harmoniously into the next one. Other times a new thought sounds dissonant. The overall effect is a composition with a distinctive voice and tone, offering a coherent perspective on Christian faith and life.

This commentary will use the following outline of the letter, not because it is the best or only way to structure the letter, but because it is one way to try to hear what James is saying.

1:1	Address and Opening Greeting
1:2-18	Becoming First Fruits of God's Creation in Times of Trouble
1:19-27	Hearing, Speaking, and Doing
2:1-13	Favoritism and the Law of Love
2:14-26	Unity of Faith and Works
3:1-12	Faithfulness in Speech
3:13–4:10	The Two Ways of Wisdom and Friendship
4:11-12	On Judgment—God's and Ours
4:13–5:6	Warnings about Arrogance and Wealth
5:7-12	Living Patiently and Speaking Faithfully
5:13-20	The Church as a Healing, Confessing, and Forgiving Community

Author, Date, Provenance, and Audience

Historical information such as authorship, date of writing, audience, and provenance can be helpful for understanding ancient literature. Unfortunately, with respect to the Letter of James, none of this information is uncontested; because the questions are interconnected, resolving them is like untangling an enormous, knotted bundle of yarn. (See *Authorship and Date, p. 343* for a more thorough discussion.)

Authorship, Date, and Provenance

The letter claims to be written by someone called "James" (1:1), which is the English equivalent of "Jacob" in Greek and Hebrew. (The adjective "Jacobean" is used to describe things related to James.) The letter does not specify which James, however, since it was quite a common name. Indeed, there are several in the New Testament. Because he must have been known well enough not to require further identification, the author was probably James the brother of Jesus. This James was the leader of the Jerusalem church in the first decades after Jesus' ascension and, according to church tradition, died a martyr's death in 62 CE *[James the Brother of Jesus, p. 357]*. Origen (ca. 185–253 CE), the first Christian writer to cite the letter explicitly, called the author "the Brother of the Lord" (Johnson 1995: 93).

For various reasons, however, scholars throughout history have questioned whether the brother of Jesus actually wrote the letter. Authorship is also closely tied to date and provenance. The three main positions and arguments are summarized here.

1. The letter was written in the late first or early second century by an anonymous Christian and attributed to the apostle James. The location could be anywhere in the Greek-speaking Diaspora, likely not at Jerusalem, especially if it was written after the (second) rebellion against Rome in 135 CE.
2. The letter was written by James the brother of Jesus, probably in the 50s but certainly before his death in 62 CE. It was written from Jerusalem, where James was a "pillar" apostle (Gal 2:9).
3. A mediating position posits that the letter reflects two stages. Someone wanted to pass on the teachings and traditions of James and thus adapted them for a new context sometime after James's death (Martin: lxxvi–lxxvii). Though perhaps still written in Jerusalem, a location such as Antioch is more probable after 70 CE.

The first position maintains that the letter is pseudepigraphy; that is, "tradition coming from an eminent person is written up by another person in a new and later situation and presented straightforwardly as the work of the eminent person" (Painter and deSilva: 21). Such a practice was not uncommon in the first century and would not necessarily have been considered deceitful. The main reasons are as follows: First, to many it seems implausible that a Galilean peasant could have composed the sophisticated, literary Greek of this letter. Second, the letter is not quoted by early church leaders and did not have authoritative status until late in the process of canonization. Third, if 2:14-16 was deliberately written to counter Paul's theology of justification apart from works, the letter would likely have been penned later than 62 CE. Fourth, some scholars argue that the lack of reference to the inclusion of Gentiles, to the temple (destroyed in 70 CE), or to matters of ritual purity suggests a period later in the history of the church and a writer other than the leader of Jerusalem-based Jewish Christianity.

Many scholars argue for the authenticity of Jacobean authorship for the following reasons. First, almost all church tradition associates the letter with the brother of Jesus. Second, given the degree of Hellenistic influence in first-century Galilee and Judea, especially Jerusalem, James may well have acquired proficiency in Greek or could have been assisted by an educated Hellenistic Jew in composing the letter (Bauckham 1999: 24). Third, the letter contains strong echoes of Jesus' teaching but does not directly quote the Gospels. This suggests that the letter was written early, using pre-Gospel traditions. Fourth, it seems unlikely that a pseudepigraphal letter would have circulated while James was still alive or even shortly after his death. Fifth, although the sluggish canonical acceptance of the letter is puzzling, James may not have been quoted much because it was not useful in the theological controversies and christological debates of the early church. Sixth, the fact that the author seems aware of Paul's writings on faith and works does not mean the letter was written decades later. James could well have been addressing a misunderstanding of Paul since already during Paul's lifetime people were misconstruing what he was saying (e.g., Rom 3:8; 2 Pet 3:15-16).

The third view of authorship offers a mediating perspective on the above two divergent positions. It maintains that the letter draws on tradition (oral and written) coming from James the brother of Jesus in Jerusalem but that its current form was the work of a later editor. This allows for someone else with proficient

Hellenistic Greek to be responsible for the good Greek and makes it possible that the letter was written considerably later, accounting for its slow reception and use.

This commentary leans toward the second or third view, while recognizing that there are sound arguments for each position and the evidence is ambiguous. Substantial content likely originated from James in the mid-first century even if it was edited later.

One might ask if it matters who wrote the letter. That is a valid question. On the one hand, the theological and ethical contributions of the letter, its authority, and its value for the ancient and modern church does not depend on certainty about who wrote it. It did become part of the Christian canon and has been a beloved and influential part of Scripture through the centuries. On the other hand, authorship was important in the early church, since apostolic origin was a key criterion for inclusion in the canon. In addition, historical information about the author and date contributes to a fuller understanding of the history of the early church, the development of its theology, its relation to its Jewish roots, and its key leaders. For example, authorship and date affect how one interprets James's relationship to the Jesus tradition. In the end, though, appreciation of James's teachings on the importance of lived faith and his creative recapitulation of Jesus' teachings do not depend on one specific view of authorship.

Audience

Little can be known definitively about the recipients of this letter. The somewhat cryptic address to *the twelve tribes in the dispersion* locates them within a larger biblical story. "The twelve tribes" refers to all Israel, the descendants of the twelve sons of Jacob. As a result of the Assyrian and Babylonian conquests (722 and 587 BCE respectively), the twelve tribes were dispersed in lands outside Israel and Judah. By the time James was writing, Jewish communities existed in major centers around the Mediterranean, such as Rome, Athens, Ephesus, and Antioch in the west; Alexandria in Egypt; and Babylon and Susa further east. After the Jewish revolts against Rome in 70 and 135 CE, the Jewish population in Palestine declined drastically.

It is therefore difficult if not impossible to know precisely to which communities in this widespread Diaspora James was writing. Almost certainly the phrase refers to people literally living outside the land of Palestine and is not a metaphorical, spiritual designation for people exiled from a heavenly home (as it is in

1 Pet 1:1, 17). Although large communities of Jews existed in both the Roman and Persian Diasporas and the mission of the early church spread both west and east, the fact that James is written in Greek suggests that it went primarily to communities in western and central regions of the Roman Empire, rather than the easternmost provinces. "It was mainly on the Mediterranean coast and in the ancient Syrian capital of Antioch that Greek was the first language, otherwise Aramean-Syriac was the first language of most people all the way [eastward] to the Persian Gulf" (Skarsaune: 761).

The address to the *twelve tribes* implies a Jewish audience. More, the whole letter seems to presume its recipients were steeped in the Scriptures, traditions, and stories of Israel. Were they exclusively Jewish, or might these gatherings of Messiah followers have included Gentile believers also? Some Gentiles were attracted to the ethical lifestyle of the Jewish people and to the Greek Scriptures, even though they did not always fully convert. The church's mission to the Gentiles probably began with these "God-fearers," and we know that Jewish and Gentile believers intermingled in the synagogues outside of Israel (Skarsaune: 753, 767). Consequently, the *twelve tribes* addressed by James may have included Gentile followers of Jesus. At the same time, the letter contains no hint of the controversies between Jewish and Gentile believers evident in other New Testament writings or any other indication of Gentiles among the addressees: on the surface they appear to be mostly or even solely Jewish.

Scholars have sometimes questioned whether the letter necessarily assumes a Christian audience. Some nineteenth-century scholars suggested that it was originally a Jewish wisdom writing, with 1:1 and 2:1 added later by an editor wishing to "Christianize" it (Hartin 2009a: 50). Although most would not adhere to such views today, the idea that James was written by a Jew for Jews has not disappeared. For example, Dale Allison argues that the author was a Jewish Christian but deliberately avoided anything explicitly Christian in his letter in order to maintain irenic relations with nonmessianic Jews in the synagogue, to which he and other believers still wished to belong. The letter is then a kind of apologetic, emphasizing what Jews and Christians have in common and not pushing uniquely Christian beliefs (2015; 2013: 32–50).

Such proposals make an important point: at least for the first century of the church (and probably longer in places) the boundary between Jews who believed Jesus was the Messiah and those who did not was often porous or even nonexistent. The first followers of Jesus were Jewish and continued to see themselves as Jewish. The book of Acts portrays the apostles meeting with fellow Jews in synagogues and worshiping at the temple. As Oskar Skarsaune notes, the border region between Judaism and Christianity "was, at a grassroots level, a rather peaceful border in many places and most of the time. There was much border traffic, probably in both directions. . . . Jewish believers in Jesus would think of themselves as good Jews, no less good because of the fact that they believed the Messiah of Israel had appeared" (753). Moreover, scholars believe the parting of ways happened later and was messier than previously thought (Elkins and Bolin: 337–38). In all probability, the parting of ways did not happen in a clean once-for-all separation, but likely in fits and starts and at different paces in different parts of the Roman Empire.

In the end, our conclusions about the religious and cultural background of the letter's recipients must be held lightly. Nevertheless, this commentary will proceed on the basis that they were *primarily* of Jewish heritage and *primarily* people who confessed Jesus as Messiah. The most obvious evidence for the latter is 2:1, which I take to be authentic and not a later addition to the letter. Although more ambiguous, references to new birth (1:18), elders of the *ekklēsia* (church or *assembly*; 5:14), blasphemy of *the excellent name invoked over you*, and the *parousia* (*coming of the Lord*; 5:7-8) also seem to imply that the *twelve tribes in the dispersion* consisted of followers of Messiah Jesus.

Finally, James's letter was probably not written to a single synagogue or assembly but to several communities of Messiah followers. Perhaps it was an encyclical of sorts. If so, it was not primarily addressing specific situations but dealing with the kinds of challenges they might face as followers of Jesus. Nevertheless, it does sound as if the recipients consisted of people in the lower socioeconomic bracket who were experiencing economic oppression at the hands of the rich (1:2-4; 2:6-7, 15; 5:1-6). Such hardships caused suffering for these fledgling faith communities and tested their faith. If 2:1-9 and 4:13-17 refer to specific situations, these churches may have also included people with resources.

In summary, then, the audience of the Letter of James consisted primarily of Jewish believers in Messiah Jesus, many of whom were not well off and were suffering hardship and injustice. The letter was intended to circulate among these faith communities and was addressed to people who needed encouragement and practical guidance about how to live faithfully.

Hellenistic Jewish Character of the Letter

The Letter of James is a Hellenistic Jewish writing. It was written in Koine Greek and incorporated Greek rhetorical features. It is also deeply rooted in the Scriptures, story, and faith of Israel.

Jewish Heritage and Faith

As noted in the preceding section on audience, James, by identifying his audience as *the twelve tribes in the dispersion* (1:1), draws from a deep well of Jewish history and identity. Though scattered throughout the Mediterranean world, the Jewish people continued to hope that one day God would reunite the descendants of Jacob and free them from foreign domination.

That the recipients of James's letter were primarily Jewish and not Gentile followers of Jesus is implied by the fact that they were meeting in a *synagogue* (2:2 ASV), something obscured in many English translations (*assembly* or *meeting*), though the New Jerusalem Bible uses the word *synagogue* at this point. Old Testament characters are named as exemplars of faithfulness, patience, and perseverance: Abraham (2:21-23), Rahab (2:25), the prophets (5:10), Job (5:11), and Elijah (5:17-18). James explicitly quotes the Old Testament several times (Lev 19:18 in James 2:8; Gen 15:6 in 2:23; Exod 20:13-15 and Deut 5:17-18 in 2:11; and Prov 3:34 in 4:6), and there are many more allusions (e.g., Isa 40:7 in 1:11) as well as resonance with other Jewish literature (e.g., Sirach). As Eric Mason states, James "uses images drenched in Scripture and interpretative tradition that prod, shape, evoke, remind, and illustrate" (28). Luke Timothy Johnson makes a strong case that James intentionally incorporated several elements of Leviticus 19:10-18 to support his teaching against partiality, swearing falsely, and holding back a worker's wages (1982). James also uses distinctive phrases such as *Lord of Sabaoth* (5:4 ASV; NRSVue: *Lord of hosts*), a title for God only comprehensible in the context of its Old Testament usages.

James is often compared to Jewish wisdom literature *[The Wisdom Tradition and James, p. 376]*, but the letter also has strong connections to the Law and the Prophets. Thus, all three parts of the Hebrew Bible are represented in James (the Law, the Prophets, and the Writings). James refers frequently and positively to the Law, by which he likely means the Torah (Wall: 83–98). The law is *perfect* (1:25), a *law of liberty/freedom* (1:25; 2:12 NRSVue/NASB), and a *royal law*, the law of God's kingdom (2:8). Like Jesus, James highlights the commandments against adultery and murder (2:11; cf. Matt 5:21, 27) and the love commandment (2:8). His emphasis is entirely on the moral law, for he never refers to purity laws or circumcision, which proved so contentious in the church's mission to the Gentiles. God gave the law (4:12) to help God's people do God's will and stay in right covenant relationship with God and each other. For James and for his readers, then, the law is extremely positive and not burdensome nor abolished by Christ's coming.

The letter has echoes of the prophets in its strident condemnation of the rich and its advocacy for justice for the poor and oppressed (1:9-11, 27; 2:1-9; 5:1-6). In fact, James has sometimes been dubbed "the Amos of the New Testament." James points to the prophets as an example of suffering and patience (5:10) and to Elijah as a model for fervent prayer (5:17-18).

Like Jewish wisdom literature, James contains many short aphorisms, admonitions, similes, and metaphors. This letter draws on human experience, reason, and observations from life to give practical advice on how to live well in this world. It assumes that creation is inherently orderly and purposeful and can yield insights about God and the world. James touches on many themes common in wisdom literature, such as speech, wealth and poverty, testing, and suffering. It evinces an ethical dualism, with two paths—one leading to folly and destruction and one to wisdom and the good life. Like other wisdom writings, James extols wisdom as desirable and ultimately from God (1:5; 3:13-18; cf. Prov 9:10). Interestingly, although James contains many Greek words found seldom or not at all in the rest of the New Testament, many of these distinctive words do appear in the wisdom literature of the Septuagint (McCartney 2000: 53).

The Letter of James has a strong eschatological orientation, which differs from the older, classical wisdom traditions that focused on rewards in the present life and God's truth discerned in creation. Like Jewish apocalyptic literature, James looks to the future for redemption and judgment (1:12; 2:5; 5:3-5, 7-9) and understands truth to be revealed by God in the word (1:18, 21). Such an intertwining of wisdom and eschatological perspectives is characteristic of Jewish theology from the second century BCE onward (Bauckham 1999: 32–35).

Hellenistic Features

With Alexander the Great's conquest in the fourth century BCE, Greek language and culture spread throughout the Mediterranean world. Judaism was deeply influenced by such Hellenization, necessitating the translation of the Hebrew Scriptures into Greek (the Septuagint). The Jewish Letter of James was written in polished, literary Greek. It uses an array of Greek rhetorical devices and contains images and ideas prevalent in Greco-Roman philosophy and ethics.

Ancient oral and written persuasive communication generally took one of three forms. Of these, James has qualities of deliberative rhetoric, designed to influence an audience's behavior (McCartney 2009: 41). The preponderance of imperative verbs suggests that James was not persuading them to *believe* something as much as he was persuading them to *act* on their beliefs. One of the main Greek rhetorical devices he uses is the diatribe. In a diatribe an author argues with an imaginary interlocutor, using rhetorical questions, irony, strong vocatives (examples of direct address), and rapid-fire statements. A prime example of this is 2:14-26, where James argues for the importance of works in true faith. He also uses alliteration, catchwords, rhymes, and wordplays for rhetorical effect, something evident in Greek but not in English.

James resembles Hellenistic moral literature in ways that go beyond mere formal elements, however. Many of the metaphors and ideas in the letter appear also in the writings of Greco-Roman moral philosophers: for example, the mirror as a tool of self-reflection (1:23-24) and the wave of the sea as a metaphor for someone in mental turmoil (1:6). Comparisons of the tongue with a horse's bridle, the rudder of a ship, or a raging fire (3:3-6) are all stock images in Greek speech ethics. Unusual phrases like the *cycle of life* (3:6) resonate more with Greek philosophical thought than Hebraic thinking. Speech ethics and friendship are prominent topics in the work of Greco-Roman moralists; James's words about desire giving birth to sin and death are reminiscent of the attention to "disordered desire" in Greek discourse. The "insistence on the unchanging nature of God is particularly characteristic of Greek philosophy" and Jewish thinkers influenced by it, such as Philo (Jackson-McCabe: 52). Greek moral instruction frequently made use of *topoi*, as does James. Luke Timothy Johnson defines *topoi* as "standard treatments of a subject, usually consisting in a loose agglomeration of clichés, propositions, examples, and other statements organized around a central theme and frequently drawn together by a process of association" (1995: 28). He argues that James 3:13–4:10 is built on the *topos* (singular of *topoi* defined above) of envy (Johnson 2004b).

The Letter of James thus grows from the soil of a first-century Judaism thoroughly immersed in its Hellenistic environment.

Many texts from the first century evince such a synthesis of Jewish and Greco-Roman culture and thought (Jackson-McCabe: 45). It is not always possible to determine whether James's vocabulary, literary style, images, or ideas rely more on Hebrew Scriptures or his Greek cultural context, but such identification is unnecessary for an appreciation of the letter's contribution to the Christian canon and to the church today.

Place in the Canon and Early Reception

James is the first of seven catholic epistles (James; 1 and 2 Peter; 1, 2, and 3 John; Jude), so called because many of them are addressed to a universal, or "catholic," audience. Although sometimes disparagingly dubbed the "junk mail" of the New Testament, these letters give a valuable non-Pauline glimpse into the early church. The order of the books follows the sequence of the "pillar" apostles Paul names in Galatians 2:9: James, Cephas (Peter), John (Lockett 2020: 128). The collection begins and ends with letters attributed to Jesus' brothers, both of which conclude with admonitions about redeeming an errant believer.

Although the Catholic epistles follow Paul's letters and Hebrews in our Bibles today, several major early Greek manuscripts and canonical lists place them directly after Acts and before Paul's letters. It is interesting to consider how our interpretation of James might be affected if we read the letter right after reading Acts. As William Baker suggests, this would make it "more apparent that James showcases concerns of the church in its earlier, pre-Gentile days, as seen in the earlier chapters of Acts" (2005: 349).

One of the puzzling questions about James is its sluggish recognition in the early church and its relatively late acceptance into the canon. This plays a role in debates about authorship and dating. In brief, if the letter was indeed written by the brother of Jesus before 62 CE, why was it not deemed authoritative right away, and why did early church leaders not use it more? The earliest explicit reference to the letter is in the writings of Origen (ca. 184–251 CE), who referred to the letter as "Scripture" and attributed it to James the apostle. The letter may have been used earlier, perhaps by the authors of writings such as Shepherd of Hermas and 1 Clement, but without direct citations it is difficult to determine. James apparently found acceptance in the Eastern churches (e.g., Alexandria) earlier than in the West (e.g., Rome) *[Reading James through the Centuries, p. 362]*. By the mid-fourth century, James appeared in many important canonical lists, and its presence in Jerome's

Vulgate and in Augustine's writings helped solidify its place in the Christian Scriptures.

It is difficult to know why the acceptance and use of the Letter of James was as slow as it was. Perhaps its focus on practical Christian living made it less useful for the intense doctrinal controversies over such matters as Christology. Perhaps its distinctive Jewish flavor made it less friendly to an increasingly Gentile Christianity. Perhaps uncertainty about authorship slowed its acceptance into the canon. In the end, the Letter of James is part of our Christian canon and provides an invaluable glimpse into one stream of the early Christian tradition.

Where Is Jesus in the Letter of James?

James almost never refers to Jesus by name (only in 1:1 and 2:1) and says nothing about the events of Jesus' life nor his death and resurrection. No wonder Martin Luther relegated James to the periphery of the New Testament for failing to "preach Christ." Still, Christians who read the letter today often do not notice this absence of Jesus and instinctively or unconsciously associate the letter with the teachings of Jesus. Why is this?

Although James never quotes the Gospels explicitly, the letter contains many striking parallels with the synoptic teachings, especially in the Sermon on the Mount. The clearest echo is the prohibition of oaths in James 5:12 and Matthew 5:34-37, though the verses lack direct verbal correspondence in Greek. Other noteworthy similarities include teachings about asking and receiving (James 1:5; Matt 7:7), hearing and doing (James 1:22-23; Matt 7:24-26), the poor inheriting the kingdom (James 2:5; Matt 5:3), making peace (James 3:18; Matt 5:9), and storing up wealth (James 5:2-3; Matt 6:19-20).

Although scholars have noticed the affinity between James's and Jesus' teachings, many disagree about the number of parallels, whether the allusions are deliberate, or the nature of the relationship between the letter and the Jesus tradition. (For a fuller discussion, see *James and the Jesus Tradition, p. 353.*) The parallels are significant enough that some kind of interdependence seems likely. Richard Bauckham has compellingly argued that James was so immersed in the teachings of Jesus that they became his own. He did not simply repeat them but was inspired by them, creatively reformulated them, and adapted them for the needs of his own audience (1999: 74–93). Whether James's readers would have recognized them as Jesus' teachings cannot be known, but perhaps it does not matter. In some ways, this is what the church continues to do and should do. Followers of Jesus even today need to become so soaked in the teachings of Jesus that they too can become creative performers of and improvisers on Jesus' teachings in ever-new contexts.

Interpreting James Today

With almost every thorny exegetical question in the Letter of James, one encounters a diversity of scholarly opinions and enough data to support more than one argument. Commentators pay attention to various factors to resolve the issues, such as sociocultural dynamics, historical context, literary and linguistic factors, and economic and political realities, with each interpreter weighing some things more heavily than others. Not to be ignored is how the commentator's own social location influences interpretation.

Reading and interpreting the Bible is always a dance in which the interpreter's prior assumptions, beliefs, and experiences are confronted by and intertwine with the "otherness" of an ancient text, rooted as it is in a foreign culture, language, and history. The challenge is to recognize how what we bring to the text influences our reading even as we remain open to hearing something new, to encountering a word from God that is different from our own word. Joining the dance are the many interpreters through time and space—both scholarly and lay readers—whose insights and questions swirl around with our own. Each interpreter pays attention to some kind of hermeneutical community, whether intentionally or not.

In the history of interpretation of the Letter of James, much attention has been given to the relationship between James and Paul and the question of faith and works, specifically whether *works* are necessary for salvation or whether salvation is by grace through *faith alone* (cf. James 2:24; Rom 3:28, Luther Bible). This perspective on James traces back to Reformation leaders like Martin Luther, whose personal experience of God's grace and his critique of the Roman Catholic church colored how he read the letter. But this is not the only question or even the most important one that the letter raises. Indeed, the apparent tension between James and Paul was not problematic for most patristic and medieval interpreters (Batten 2017a: 538). Christians in rural communities of the global South and in poor urban neighborhoods today pick up on James's condemnation of the rich and his good news for the poor much more quickly than do Christians in comfortable middle-class suburbs, who have been swift to claim that James does not really condemn *all* rich people. Over and over, social context influences a community's or an individual's reading of James. In his study of reception history, Dale Allison has shown how "the history of the interpretation and reception of James reveals the plasticity of texts, . . . how easily and thoroughly they succumb to interpretive agendas" (2014b: 12).

This commentary stands in the believers church tradition in which discipleship, community, peacemaking, and service are core expressions of a life transformed by Christ. In this tradition, God's gift of salvation through Christ's life, death, and resurrection is received in adult baptism and demonstrated by a commitment to follow Christ in all of life, even when that leads to suffering. In view of James's emphasis on lived faith, it is no wonder that the letter has been a favorite among Anabaptist and Mennonite Christians. Although early Anabaptist writers did not quote James extensively, phrases and ideas are woven seamlessly into their work, especially in relation to the new birth and hearing and doing God's word. Because my own faith home is in this tradition, it cannot help but influence interpretive choices I have made, even as I have tried to be attentive to the text and have tried to listen to dance partners that challenge my own perspective.

One concrete way that my tradition has informed the commentary is in regard to how "Christian" the Letter of James is. It is possible to read the letter as written entirely for a Jewish audience by someone who may or may not have been a follower of Jesus (on the assumption that references to Jesus in 1:1 and 2:1 are later additions). For example, *[God] gave birth to us by the word of truth* (1:18) and *the implanted word that has the power to save your souls* (1:21) need not have anything to do with new birth in Christ or with the word of the gospel, nor does *the coming of the Lord* (5:8) necessarily refer to the parousia of Christ. On the other hand, if one begins with the belief that James and his readers and hearers were followers of Jesus, these words resonate with the good news of Jesus found in the rest of the New Testament. In this commentary I have chosen to read James as a Christian letter circulated by the early church because it helped them better understand and live out their identity as followers of Jesus. I also read it like early Anabaptists did, who consistently understood 1:18 and 1:21 in terms of *new birth* as Christians and the *word* of the gospel.

Like others in the BCBC series, this commentary reads James in the context of the biblical canon, not as a stand-alone letter. Such a context makes it impossible not to hear echoes of Jesus' teachings in the words of James and makes it easy to hear phrases such as *the coming of the Lord* (5:8) and *heirs of the kingdom* (2:5) as expressions of Christian hope. This too was how Anabaptist writers read James. I once asked my students what we would gain or lose if the Letter of James were the only New Testament writing we had. All agreed that we need to hear James in the context of the rest of the Bible, since Jesus' death and resurrection, so glaringly absent in James, are essential for Christian faith. Yet the Letter of James has an important place in the canon and in Christian faith. It reminds the church of its Jewish heritage and calls us to an active and living faith, demonstrated in deeds of mercy, justice, and peace and aligned with Jesus' own life and teachings. It shows us how the church has, since the first century, interpreted Jesus' teachings for its own context.

The Letter of James appeals not only to Anabaptist-minded believers but to all Christians who have no use for religion that does not speak into the urgent crises of our world or for a church that walks with its head in the hereafter. Even though it is deeply rooted in a story that began long ago and exhibits a robust hope in what God will do in the future, James calls followers of Jesus to live their faith in the here and now. In a world of hypocrisy and inflated words, it calls for integrity of faith and life. In a world of immense social and economic disparities, it insists that followers of Jesus eschew privilege and act with justice and compassion for all people. In a world of false news and pernicious speech, James calls followers of Jesus to speak truthfully and with kindness. In a world that seeks to avoid suffering, James invites believers to embrace hardship as an opportunity for growth. In a world of individualism and "you do you" (do what's best for yourself), James calls people to confess their sins and pray for each other, to admonish one another, and to *love your neighbor as yourself* (2:8). Although it is difficult to pin down exactly to whom James was writing or when or in what situation, this imprecision has the advantage of giving the letter a timeless quality and ongoing broad appeal.

This commentary is written from the perspective that the Letter of James was written by a follower of Jesus for the church and that it continues to speak to Christians today. It has also been influential in organizations less directly connected to Christianity and has gained a hearing in interreligious dialogue, perhaps because of its practical nature and less overt Christian theologizing. Dale Allison's research into reception history is illuminating. For example, the Letter of James "was of key importance to the founders of Alcoholics Anonymous" and "was so popular among early members of A.A. that some wanted to call their fellowship 'The James Club'" (2014b: 23) *[Reading James through the Centuries, p. 362].*

James and Bible Translation

The Letter of James was written in literary Koine Greek; several striking features are evident only when one reads it in Greek. One of the translation challenges is that it contains so many words not found anywhere else in the New Testament. Dale Allison counts 67 of these *hapax legomena*, 49 of which occur in the Septuagint (Allison 2013: 85). Several words do not appear in any extant Greek writings before James, prompting the question of whether James coined them himself (e.g., *dipsychos*, "double-minded," in 1:8; 4:8; *chrysodaktylios*, "gold-ringed," in 2:2; and *thrēskos*, "religious," in 1:26). Despite being written in polished Greek, the letter also includes Semitic idioms and grammatical constructions. It is evident that the writer was steeped in the Scriptures of Israel, likely in their Hellenistic form (LXX). Sometimes word order makes translation difficult (e.g., "of glory" at the end of 2:1), and English versions vary considerably. James regularly makes strong rhetorical moves in his effort to be persuasive and uses literary devices such as alliteration, wordplays, and rhymes, which are evident in Greek but difficult to replicate in English. In the commentary I will pay attention to James's skillful use of language.

This commentary uses the New Revised Standard Version Updated Edition (NRSVue) as a basis but regularly compares this translation with others. Where my own translation differs from standard English versions, this is noted as "author's translation" (AT), with the rationale for translational choices given in the Explanatory Notes. In the commentary I tend to use phrases like "followers of Jesus" or "Messiah followers" or simply "believers" to refer to the recipients of the letter, since "Christians" implies a separation from "Jews" that was not yet solidified when James wrote. I do use the word "church" to refer to the body or assembly of such believers. I have also chosen to translate the Greek *adelphoi* most often as "brothers and sisters." Although it is possible that only the males gathered for worship and teaching in the synagogues, more likely both men and women were present in the early gatherings of Messiah followers and the letter was directed to all.

Every translation from one language to another involves interpretive choices. Sometimes it is impossible to capture the nuance of the original succinctly. Translating from an ancient language to a modern one poses additional challenges because of the great cultural, historical, and linguistic divide between original readers and us. Discussion of Greek words and phrases in this commentary attempts to bridge that divide, at least in part. Still, as noted in a previous section, we always bring our preunderstandings to the text, including two thousand years of Christian theology. What we understand by words like "law" and "world," for example, may be different from what James intended. Learning to read the Bible is learning to listen for the questions the text wants to answer, even when those questions are different from our own.

James 1:1

Address and Opening Greeting

PREVIEW

Reading the first words of the Letter of James is like opening someone else's mail. Although in letters today the signature appears at the end, in this one we discover immediately who wrote the letter and to whom. Beyond the basic information about sender and receiver, we also discover something about the tone of the letter and the identity of the different parties. To the extent that modern-day readers see themselves as living within the same overarching story as those original recipients—the story of God's relationship with the people God created—the letter also becomes relevant for us. In that sense we are not only reading someone else's mail; we are also reading words that speak to the church today.

OUTLINE

Sender, 1:1a
Recipients, 1:1b
Greeting, 1:1c

EXPLANATORY NOTES

James begins with a salutation typical of letters in the ancient world: sender to recipients, greetings. However, apart from these opening words, James does not sound like most of the other letters in the New Testament. Its style is quite different from Paul's letters. It lacks an opening thanksgiving and prayer, it contains no personal greetings, and it ends rather abruptly, without a closing benediction. As a result, some scholars have argued that James should be seen as a sermon or compendium of teachings rather than a genuine letter (see the Introduction on genre). If one does not take Paul as the standard for all letter writing in the early church, however, there is no reason for not reading James as a real letter addressed and sent to real communities. After the formal opening, the body of an ancient letter could, in fact, conform to different genres, depending on its purpose (Johnson 1995: 22–24). Although letters often concluded with greetings and a blessing, these were not mandatory. In the New Testament, 1 John is an example of a letter that ends as abruptly as James. Similarly, Revelation is an apocalypse even though it begins with a letter salutation. We will assume, then, that the first verse of James is the opening salutation of a real letter.

Sender 1:1a

The author of this letter identifies himself only as *James, a servant of God and of the Lord Jesus Christ.* The English name "James" derives from the Latin "Jacobus" and Old French "Jaimes" (Johnson 1995: 93), but in both Hebrew and Greek the equivalent is "Jacob." In the Old Testament, Jacob was the father of twelve sons and at least one daughter. English readers are thus liable to miss the fact that the letter's first words bind author and audience to the foundational story of Israel: "Jacob" is writing to the scattered twelve tribes.

Apparently the James of 1:1 was known well enough in the early church that the original recipients would have recognized the sender without further identification. Unfortunately for contemporary readers, James was a common name in the first-century Jewish and Christian world, so his identity is no longer obvious to us. The New Testament contains references to many people with the name, including James the son of Zebedee (Mark 1:19), James the son of Alphaeus (Mark 3:18), James the father of Judas (Luke 6:16), James the son of Mary (not Jesus' mother; Matt 27:56), and James the brother of Jesus (Mark 6:3; Acts 12:17). Of the various possibilities, James the brother of Jesus is mostly likely the James of James 1:1. As one of the pillars in the Jerusalem church, James would have been widely recognized as an authoritative voice; thus it is plausible that he could have written such a letter to the communities of Messiah followers *[James the Brother of Jesus, p. 357]*.

For various reasons, scholars throughout history have questioned whether the brother of Jesus wrote the letter himself or whether someone wrote in his name decades after his death. There are weighty arguments both for and against Jacobean authorship. They have to do with the high quality of Greek, the letter's slow acceptance into the canon and sparse use by early church writers, and its relationship to Paul's writings, particularly on faith and works *[Authorship and Date, p. 343]*. Whether the brother of Jesus wrote it himself or with the aid of a scribe skilled in Greek, or whether a Jewish believer wrote on James's behalf after his death, the church has received the letter as reliably representing the teachings that James the brother of Jesus passed on.

From the Gospels it is unclear whether James was a follower of Jesus during his lifetime, although it seems unlikely. Texts like Mark 3:20-21, 31-35; 6:1-4 imply reluctance to associate with Jesus. John 7:5 explicitly says, "Not even his brothers believed in him." Whatever Jesus' relationship was with his brothers during Jesus' lifetime, after the resurrection James became a prominent leader in the Jerusalem church, perhaps at least in part because of Jesus' special appearance to him after he rose from the dead (1 Cor 15:7). James was one of a few people with whom Paul met during his first visit to Jerusalem, and Paul acknowledges him as one of the "pillars" of the church, together with Cephas and John (Gal 1:19; 2:9). James played a conciliatory leadership role in the Jerusalem Council (Acts 15:13-21), voicing the church's final decision to accept Gentiles as fellow believers without requiring circumcision. According to the Acts of the Apostles, when Paul met with James in Jerusalem on his last visit, James exhorted Paul to take a vow that would make explicit his commitment to the Torah (Acts 21:18-26). Paul's Letter to the Galatians recounts how a visit from Jewish believers associated with James (though not necessarily sent by him) prompted Peter and other Jewish Christians to stop eating with Gentiles because they were afraid of the "circumcision faction" (Gal 2:11-14).

In general, New Testament references portray James as consistently associated with Torah piety and faithful adherence to the Jewish law. As leader of the church in Jerusalem, the center of the Jewish religious world, he would have been an apostle with some stature and authority—not only in the Jewish Christian community in Jerusalem but also beyond. Known in the writings of the early church as James the Just or the Righteous, church tradition recounts that he died a martyr's death in Jerusalem, possibly by stoning, in 62 CE (McKnight: 20–23).

If the letter were written by James himself, it is curious that he does not identify himself as Jesus' brother. Why would an early church leader not want to highlight this special relationship? As the next phrase shows, James's authority was based on his spiritual calling, not biological connection. Instead of capitalizing on his family connections, James identifies himself as *a servant of God and of the Lord Jesus Christ*. The Greek word *doulos* could be translated *servant* (NRSVue, NIV) or *slave* (CEB, NLT). For contemporary readers, the word "slave" undoubtedly calls to mind the horrific history of slavery in North America and its ongoing devastating effect for African American people. In the ancient world, as in modern times, slaves were the legally owned property of their masters (that is, chattel slaves) and were completely subservient to them. They would have been considered essential to the economy. In other respects, ancient slavery differed considerably from slavery in the American South. In biblical times slaves had various roles, ranging from manual labor to responsible positions as managers, educators, and physicians. They represented a variety of socioeconomic positions and were not identifiable by race or ethnicity. Still, slaves had no power, were totally at the mercy of their owners, were separated from all kin, had no legal protection, and had no identity of their own (Bartchy; Harrill). In such respects, ancient slavery was as morally reprehensible as modern slavery.

Nevertheless, the phrase *slave of God* (CEB) has positive connotations in the biblical context. In the Old Testament, the people of Israel are sometimes called God's slaves/servants (cf. English versions and *doulos* in LXX: Deut 32:36; Pss 119:38; 143:12), as are Christians in the New Testament (Acts 4:29; 16:17; Rev 1:1). The expression communicates loyalty to God and a willingness to serve and obey God. By calling himself a slave or servant of God, James is also associating himself with other illustrious servants whom God called to speak and act on God's behalf: Moses (Deut 34:5; 1 Kings 8:53), Joshua (Josh 14:7), David (2 Sam 3:18; 7:8, 25), and the prophets who spoke in the name of the Lord (Jer 7:25; Dan 9:10; Joel 2:29; Amos 3:7).

Other New Testament writers identify themselves as slaves in their opening addresses: Paul (Rom 1:1; Phil 1:1), Titus (1:1), Peter (2 Pet 1:1), and Jude (1:1). In this they are following the example of Jesus, who taught his followers, paradoxically, that anyone who wishes to be first must be slave of all (Mark 10:44) and that he himself came not to be served but to serve (Mark 10:45). By introducing himself to his readers as *a slave of God and of the Lord Jesus Christ*, (CEB) the author of this letter is saying that he is owned by and is subject to the higher authority of God and of God's Messiah Jesus. He is expressing his allegiance to this higher authority and his commitment to serve this authority. In so doing, James highlights his humble status (slave) on the one hand, but also his authority (answerable to God), both of which serve his purpose in the letter. The fact that he calls Jesus *Lord*, which could also be rendered "Master," reinforces his humble and subservient status and makes explicit his loyalty. Perhaps such a self-identification was important for James at the outset of a letter in which he would chastise his readers for being boastful and envious, giving preferential treatment to the rich, and acting with selfish ambition.

Whom is James called to serve? First of all, God. Even though this is a practical letter, it is profoundly theological. As was true for all Jews, central to James's theology is the belief in and loyalty to the one true God, evident in 2:19, which echoes the Shema of Deuteronomy 6:4: "Hear O Israel: The LORD is our God, the LORD alone." The God of James is the Creator: the *Father of lights*, who created the heavenly bodies (1:17) and the one in whose image human beings are made (3:9). God is also a personal Being, namely, a *Father* (1:27; 3:9). In the patriarchal ancient world, the father held primary authority in the family and was responsible for protecting and providing for his household. In addition, James speaks of God in feminine terms: like a mother, God gives people birth by the word of truth (1:18). God is supremely generous, the Giver of every good and perfect gift (1:4, 17). The God whom James serves is extraordinarily compassionate (5:11), pays attention to the plight of the poor and the vulnerable (1:27; 2:5; 5:4), heals the sick and forgives sin (5:15), and lifts up the humble (4:6, 10). At the same time this God is also a Judge, who holds God's people accountable on the last day and opposes the arrogant and oppressively rich (1:9-11; 4:12; 5:9).

Second, James is a slave of the *Lord Jesus Christ*. This is one of only two references to the name of Jesus in the letter (also in 2:1). Although James references God often, he says little about Jesus explicitly. To be sure, the letter is thoroughly soaked in the wisdom and teachings of Jesus, but there is no mention of Jesus' life, healing ministry, death, or resurrection. Thus, it is significant that in the very first sentence of the letter, James openly acknowledges his loyalty to Jesus as Lord and Christ. Since the nouns do not have articles in the Greek, it would be possible to read the phrase as "a servant of Jesus Christ, God and Lord." Such an explicit equating of

Jesus and God is rare in the New Testament, however, and unlikely in this letter. Although we should not read too much into the conjunction *and*, by associating Jesus and God so closely (he is a slave to both), James is also making some interesting christological assumptions. He is saying that God and Jesus the Messiah both have claim to his fealty and service. "The God whom James serves is made known in the person and teaching of 'Lord Jesus Christ'" (Painter and deSilva: 50). In acknowledging Jesus as both *Lord* and *Christ*, James reflects early Christian preaching about Jesus (e.g., "God made him both Lord and Messiah, this Jesus whom you crucified," Acts 2:36) and uses language frequently found in other letters of the New Testament (e.g., Rom 5:1; 1 Cor 1:7-8; Gal 1:3; Phil 2:11; 1 Pet 1:3; Jude 1:21).

In the Old Testament *Lord* (Greek *kyrios*) is the name for God; in this letter James also identifies God as *Lord* (1:7; 5:4, 10). At the same time, sometimes *Lord* in James seems to refer to Jesus (5:7, 8) and sometimes the referent is ambiguous (5:14). This seemingly interchangeable usage of the title *Lord* for both Jesus and God implies a conflation of the two that James may or may not have intended but points to later developments in the church's reflection on the identity of Jesus. As Peter Davids suggests, "Perhaps they are so closely associated for James that he is not concerned about clear differentiation or simply does not notice the ambiguity" (Davids 2019: 125). Naming Jesus as *Lord* also has implications at a time when Caesar was Lord of the Roman Empire and demanded allegiance from his subjects. At the outset of this letter, James confesses his ultimate allegiance to a higher authority, above all other lords.

The word *Christ* is not a personal name for Jesus, as it has come to be used, but a title. *Christos* is the Greek translation of the Hebrew *mašiaḥ* (Messiah), which means "anointed." Although priests and prophets were "anointed" for service to God, the word is used most often in reference to the kings and especially to Davidic kingship. Jewish hope after the exile included the expectation that God would send an "Anointed One," a Messiah from the line of David to deliver God's people. By the time of the New Testament, however, there was no homogeneous, monochromatic expectation of who the Messiah would be. For example, Psalms of Solomon 17 speaks of a human Davidic Messiah-king, while the Testament of Levi 18 envisions a priestly messiah figure who would cleanse Israel. The Dead Sea Scrolls speak of both a priestly Messiah and a royal Messiah. By giving Jesus the title *Christ* (Greek) or *Messiah* (Hebrew), James is acknowledging him as the fulfillment of Israel's hopes and God's promises in Scripture. The opening words of this letter, therefore, situate the author and the contents of what follows squarely within the Jewish-Christian tradition. This will be important to remember as we explore the rest of the letter.

Recipients 1:1b

James addresses his letter to *the twelve tribes of the dispersion*, a designation that is as evocative as it is enigmatic, as theologically significant as it is informationally vague. *The twelve tribes* makes sense only within a particular story, namely, the story of Israel as told in the Hebrew Scriptures. In that story "the twelve tribes" refers to the whole people of God, descended from the twelve sons of Jacob and his wives. Each of these tribes was allotted a portion of land after the people fled Egypt and settled in the land of Canaan. God made a covenant with all Israel on Mount Sinai, calling them to be God's people and giving them the law to help them live in covenant relationship with God. At the outset of this letter, then, the recipients are reminded that they belong in this same story and are part of the same covenant. Just as their ancestor Jacob addressed his twelve sons in Genesis 49 at the end of his life, so now another "Jacob" writes to the descendants of those twelve tribes, teaching them how to live faithfully.

By the time James wrote, however, the twelve tribes were no longer intact but were dispersed outside the land of Israel. The ten northern tribes were scattered in the eighth century BCE during the Assyrian conquest, and many inhabitants of the southern tribes of Judah were exiled to Babylon in the sixth century BCE. By the first century more Jews were living outside the land of Palestine than in it, many of them in major cities like Alexandria, Rome, Ephesus, and Antioch in the west; and Babylon, Susa, and Ecbatana further east. After the Jewish revolts against Rome in 66–73 CE and 132–136 CE, no significant population of Jews remained in Palestine. To identify his audience as *the twelve tribes in the dispersion*, then, not only places them within a specific story but also acknowledges them as a people displaced from their historical and religious homeland.

Since the twelve tribes were no longer intact, James uses the phrase metaphorically rather than in a strictly literal sense. Undoubtedly the language is more about memory and hope than physical identity. But to say that James is simply addressing all

Christians, including Gentiles, as the "new Israel" does not adequately consider how deeply and firmly embedded such language is in the Jewish Scriptures and story. To be sure, the church did appropriate language from the Old Testament to define its new identity (e.g., "Abraham's offspring," Gal 3:29; "royal priesthood," 1 Pet 2:9). The letter of 1 Peter, written to suffering Gentile Christians, uses the word *dispersion* in a spiritualized sense to refer to Christians' sojourn here on earth as aliens and exiles, away from their true home in heaven (2:11).

Given the Jewishness of the rest of the letter, it is unlikely that James uses *twelve tribes in the dispersion* with a similar metaphorical meaning only. The only other place *dispersion* appears in the New Testament outside of James and 1 Peter is in John 7:35, where it literally refers to Jewish people living outside Palestine, intermingled with Greeks. James sent this letter to people from the house of Israel who were living outside the land of Palestine, perhaps as close as Antioch, perhaps farther west or east. These dispersed Jewish believers may have included those who were "scattered" because of persecutions described in Acts (Acts 11:19). They may even have included some Gentile believers, "God-fearers," who had been drawn to the Jewish Scriptures and story, but there is nothing explicit in the letter to suggest this.

By addressing his words to *the twelve tribes of the dispersion*, James not only calls to mind a rich heritage and history but also situates "his writing within an eschatological framework" and taps into deep theological yearnings (Hartin 2009a: 51). After the Assyrian and Babylonian exiles, the prophets and later Jewish writers gave expression to the enduring hope that God would one day reconstitute Israel, gather the scattered people of God, and restore the land. Ezekiel 37:21-22 is but one such example: "Thus says the Lord GOD: 'I will take the people of Israel from the nations among which they have gone and will gather them from every quarter and bring them to their own land. I will make them one nation in the land'" (see also Deut 30:4; Isa 11:11-16; Jer 31:8-14; Ezek 47:13-23; Zech 10:6-12; Psalms of Solomon 17.26-28).

This vibrant eschatological expectation is captured also in Jesus' promise to his disciples that in God's end-time reign they would sit on thrones ruling the twelve tribes (Luke 22:29-30; Matt 19:28). The brief phrase *twelve tribes in the dispersion* need not carry all this theological freight; yet when set in the context of the rest of the letter, which offers suffering recipients hope for what God will one day do in the future (1:12; 2:5) and for the coming of the

Lord to judge and to save (5:7-9), it reverberates with such eschatological overtones.

Additionally, when the word *Diaspora (or dispersion)* appears in the Septuagint and other Jewish literature, it is often in the context of punishment or tragedy. To be scattered from one's homeland has negative connotations (Verseput: 100–101). Such literature offers consolation, calls for repentance, and looks forward to a time when God will bring restoration and return God's people to the land (e.g., Jer 29:1-23; 2 Macc 1:1-9; 1:10–2:18; 2 Bar [Syriac Apocalypse] 78–87). James's use of the word *dispersion* seems apropos in this context since some in his audience are also suffering (1:2-4; 5:13), he is calling them to repentance (4:7-10), and the letter has an eschatological outlook, even if not envisioning a physical return to the land of Israel (2:5; 5:7-8).

In summary, then, when *James, a servant of God and of the Lord Jesus Christ*, addresses *the twelve tribes in the dispersion*, he is writing not to a specific congregation but to communities of primarily Jewish followers of the Messiah Jesus outside Palestine. These messianic communities probably were intermingled with Jewish brothers and sisters who were not convinced of Jesus' messiahship and may even have included some Gentiles attracted to the Jewish faith and to the Messiah Jesus. These dispersed Jewish believers saw themselves as a continuation of the story of Israel and believed that through the Messiah Jesus the eschatological ingathering of the scattered people of God had begun and would be fulfilled at the coming of the Lord (5:7-8). In the meantime, though, they were living a displaced existence, away from their spiritual home, and needed guidance. James is not merely writing to those individual Christians about how to live ethical lives (though that is often how modern Christians read the letter). Rather, he is shaping a peoplehood, a community firmly rooted in a story and living into a future hope. That past and future impinge on how they live faithfully together in an uncertain present.

Greeting 1:1c

The salutation closes with the single word *Greetings*. This is a common secular greeting found in many Hellenistic letters (1 Macc 10:18, 25; Josephus, *Life* 217, 365; Letter of Aristeas 41) and occasionally in the New Testament (Acts 15:23; 23:26). More often in New Testament letters, we find the "greeting" in an expanded, Christianized form, including words such as "grace," "mercy," and "peace" (Rom 1:1; Gal 1:3; Phil 1:2; 1 Tim 1:2; Philem 1:3; 1 Pet 1:2;

Jude 1:2; 2 John 1:3; Rev 1:4). In comparison to these, James sounds simple and to the point. Whether deliberate or not, James's single word *greetings* (*charein*) creates an alliterative link to the word *joy* (*charan*) in the next verse. Such linking of sounds and catchwords is especially evident at the beginning of this letter.

The opening salutation of the Letter of James gives only the sparsest information to readers two thousand years later, who might be hungry for more details and context. The fact that it does not address as many particular issues in the readers' immediate context as some of Paul's letters makes it more difficult to interpret some aspects of the letter. At the same time, the imprecise circumstances help make it more widely applicable to Christians today.

James 1:2-18

Becoming First Fruits of God's Creation in Times of Trouble

PREVIEW

Contemporary readers of the introduction to this letter may feel as though they are being led down a meandering path, without any clear direction. Catchwords hook the first eight verses together, guiding us along from one thought to the next, but thematic coherence is difficult to discern:

> Find joy in *trials.*
> The *testing* of faith produces *endurance.*
> Let *endurance* do its *complete* work
> so that you might be *complete* and *lack* nothing.
> If you *lack* wisdom, *ask*
> the *giving* God
> and it will be *given* to you.
> *Ask* in faith and don't *doubt.*
> The one who *doubts* is like a wave of the sea.

By the time we reach verse 12, we are back at the subject of testing and trials, with which verse 2 began. Although the rest of the letter contains larger units of thought, the rather disjointed nature of this first subunit is to some extent characteristic of the entire first chapter and even the letter as a whole. In the first chapter, James introduces virtually every topic that appears later, which gives it an episodic quality. For example, endurance during times of trial appears in 1:2-4, 12 and again in 5:7-11; wisdom is introduced in 1:5 and reappears in 3:13-18; James's harsh critique of wealth shows up in both 1:9-11 and 5:1-6; the word "double-minded" occurs only in 1:8 and 4:8; the topic of desire, sin, and death is introduced in 1:14-16 and resurfaces in 4:2; 5:15-16, 19-20; and so on. The first chapter could thus be considered a kind of table of contents. Although the letter does not develop a coherent linear argument (like Paul's letters) or have a narrative structure (like the Gospels), in its own unique way it does have a theological coherence and a clear and forceful message. That message already begins in the first subunit.

In these introductory verses James's intention in the letter is already evident: to help his Christian brothers and sisters live with integrity and faithfulness amid the ordinary and exceptional challenges of life. James encourages them to live out their identity as the first fruits of God's new creation, having been given birth by a God who is consistently faithful and abundantly generous in giving gifts to God's people. These gifts include wisdom, justice, wholeness, and ultimately the *crown of life*. The road to wholeness will not always be easy, since it will require endurance in difficult times, trusting God in turbulent waters, and resisting the temptation to indulge disordered desires that lead to sin. James knows this and so begins this letter full of ethical exhortations with both warnings and good news.

OUTLINE

Character Formation through Testing, 1:2-4
Seeking Wisdom in Trust and Not Being Double-Minded, 1:5-8
God's Promises of Blessing and Reversal for the Poor and Rich, 1:9-12
Two Birthing Processes, into Death and into God-Given Life, 1:13-18

EXPLANATORY NOTES

Character Formation through Testing 1:2-4

How should Christians think about the troubles they encounter in a life of faith? What kind of person does one need to be in order to embrace such trials wisely? These are the questions James addresses in the opening of his letter to the dispersed communities of Jewish Christians. They are questions specific to his audience while also relevant to believers at any time.

James addresses his audience as "brothers (and sisters)" fifteen times in the letter, often in combination with the pronoun "my" (2:14; 3:10) or the adjective "beloved" (1:16, 19) or both (1:19; 2:5). Although the Greek word in verse 2 is "brothers," it is unlikely that James was speaking only to the males in the community. The fact that he includes "sisters" among the hypothetical poor in the community (2:15) and is mindful of the "widows" (1:27) suggests otherwise. This commentary uses the phrase "brothers and sisters" when the original simply has "brothers" and will translate words like "man" (e.g., in 1:8 ESV) in a way that includes the presence of women in the church.

Although the use of family language to refer to disciples is common in the literature of the New Testament (Matt 18:15; Luke 6:42; Acts 15:7; Rom 12:1; 1 Cor 1:10; Phil 3:1; 1 John 3:13), its frequency and concentration in this short and otherwise somewhat impersonal letter is striking, in particular in conjunction with the added intimacy of "beloved." Where wisdom literature often couches instruction in parent-child language (e.g., Prov 1:8; 6:20; 31:1-9) or envisions a master-pupil relationship (Prov 5:13), James eschews any such hierarchical relationships in favor of the language of mutuality. Even though he is a teacher (3:1-2), he does not speak down to his readers but addresses them as brothers, as one who is concerned for their well-being. They are all part of the same household of faith.

James's first concern in this letter has to do with how they respond to adversity, that is, how they *face various trials*. The Greek verb translated "to face" (NRSVue, NIV) or "to meet" (ESV) is rare in the New Testament but is used elsewhere in contexts of people "falling into" dangerous circumstances (Luke 10:30; Acts 27:41). Among James's readers are those who have been plunged into adverse situations.

Various questions arise when one considers what kinds of trials might be envisioned here. For one thing, the word *peirasmos* (trial or temptation) can refer either to testing that arises from inside a person as a "temptation" or to "trials" that arise from external pressures. Which meaning is more appropriate depends on the context. In James 1:2-4 and 12, the notion of external trials is in view, whereas 1:13-16 is about temptations arising from internal desires. In the end, however, these two aspects of testing are not far apart, especially not in this letter. As they are "tested" by oppressive circumstances, James's readers may be "tempted" to respond angrily with harsh speech or violent actions (1:19-21; 2:9-10; 4:1-12; 5:9). Endurance is the response James encourages in the face of both trials and temptations.

Commentators disagree about whether the letter has in view particular experiences in specific communities or whether James is writing to all believers in general, who are likely to experience challenges of some kind in their lives. The fact that he says *various trials* suggests a fairly open-ended and widely applicable situation. The word *trial* does not necessarily imply suffering, since faith can be tested in many different ways, nor is there any hint of persecution for their faith (as in 1 Peter). James is particularly concerned with issues of poverty, wealth, and social inequality: his audience is likely experiencing some socioeconomic oppression at the hands of the powerful, wealthy elite (2:6-7, 15; 5:1-6). Perhaps James also thinks of discord in the community, caused by favoritism (2:1-6), envy (4:1-2), anger (1:19-20), and hurtful speech (3:9-10; 4:11). Possibly the trials to which he refers are illness and physical suffering (5:13-16). The fact that the whole letter is framed by references to endurance (1:2-3; 5:10-11) and to trials or suffering (1:2-3; 5:10, 13) suggests that what is testing their faith is some experience of suffering. Whatever is troubling the church, when they encounter such challenges, says James, they should consider it as *all joy*.

Modern readers would surely think this a strange way to begin a letter: "Be happy when you suffer hardship!" How can hardship and even suffering possibly be a source of joy for anyone? Moreover, considering suffering as inherently redemptive is downright dangerous when used to legitimate abuse or oppression (see TLC below). What James is referring to here is not a superficial happiness nor the power of positive thinking nor a misguided desire to inflict pain on oneself or others. In verse 12 he comes back to the subject and says, *Blessed is the one who endures testing* (AT). The kind of joy James commends to his readers is one that arises out of divine blessing (cf. Matt 5:10-12). It is not an emotion but a "theological perception of trials" (Wall: 48). James urges his readers to *consider* their trials as joy, to *choose* to see them in a certain way, rather than gritting their teeth to get through them or avoiding them at all cost.

Endurance is not merely a resigned passive acceptance of trouble but an act of will and an act of faith. It is resistance against the power of suffering to destroy a person or a community. James does not answer the question of why good people suffer, nor is he saying that God inflicts pain to teach people a lesson. People *fall into* (AT) trials. Trials happen. To cry out against God and question "Why?" is an understandable reaction: lament is an appropriate and even faithful response to adversity, as the Psalms show. In this letter, though, James advocates an alternative: believers can choose to meet trials and tribulations with joy.

Why, then, should believers *consider it all joy* when they encounter trials? The New Testament offers various perspectives on the role of testing and suffering in Christian faith but consistently assumes that followers of Jesus should expect to suffer because of their allegiance to a crucified Lord (Mark 8:34-35; Col 1:24; 1 Pet 4:12-16). According to the author of James, Christians should meet trials with an attitude of joy for two reasons: (1) character formation and (2) eschatological reward. In 1:2-4 it is mostly the former that predominates, and in 1:12 (also 5:7-12) the latter is preeminent, but both reasons are equally important for understanding James's theology of suffering.

James 1:2-4 suggests that enduring trials produces moral fiber and strengthens character. The word *testing* in verse 3 (*dokimion*) is a different word than the word for *trials* (*peirasmoi*) in verse 2 and refers to establishing the genuineness of something, as when precious metals are tested and refined by fire. The idea that hardship can have a refining effect on character appears also in Jewish writings. For example, Sirach 2:1-5 says,

> My child, when you come to serve the Lord, prepare yourself for testing. Set your heart right and be steadfast, and do not be impetuous in time of calamity. . . . Accept whatever befalls you, and in times of humiliation be patient. For gold is tested in the fire, and those found acceptable, in the furnace of humiliation.

James holds up some Old Testament heroes as models of faith: Abraham (2:21), the prophets (5:10), and Job (5:11) steadfastly endured testing. When believers *face various trials*, the test is whether their faith will grow stronger or be destroyed. James exhorts his hearers to consider the testing of their faith as positive because of its ability to produce endurance and, beyond that, integrity of character.

Neither suffering nor endurance are themselves the goals, then; rather, believers must let endurance *do its complete work* (AT). The chain of effects that James establishes, as well as the language he uses, sounds similar to Romans 5:3-5 and 1 Peter 1:6-7, where enduring suffering is also seen as a stepping stone to something greater. In those texts the logic moves more explicitly toward eschatological hope and glory than in James. For the latter, when endurance is allowed to run its course, it results in growth in faith and character, both of the individual and the community.

Perfection—or better, "wholeness, integrity"—is an important theological theme in the letter, perhaps even the coherent center, as some would argue (Hartin 1999). The adjective *teleios* appears no less than five times in the letter (1:4 [2×], 17, 25; 3:2), along with two related verbs, *teleioō* ("to complete, make perfect" in 2:22) and *teleō* ("to finish, fulfill" in 2:8). No other New Testament book has such a high concentration of this word group as James, an indication of its importance for the letter's message and theology. As elsewhere, James's words resonate with Jesus' words in the Sermon on the Mount, when he urges his disciples to "be perfect (*teleios*), therefore, as your heavenly Father is perfect (*teleios*)" (Matt 5:48; cf. 19:21).

But does the translation "perfect" adequately communicate what *teleios* means? Is "perfection" not a futile and even pernicious goal? The NRSV and NIV translate the word as *mature* in 1:4 (as in 1 Cor 2:6; Phil 3:15; Col 4:12; Heb 5:14), suggesting that it refers to the full development of a person. Many other translations and commentaries render it as *perfect* (RSV, NASB, NKJV, NET, TEV), which is how the NRSVue and NIV translate *teleios* elsewhere in the letter (1:17, 25; cf. *mature* in 3:2). A literal translation of 1:4 would be something like this: *Let endurance do its perfect work in order that you might be perfect and whole, in no way lacking anything.* The problem with the translation "perfect" is that it is associated too easily with perfectionism—unrealistic expectations, hypercriticism of self and others, and demanding, unachievable standards (consider, for example, societal pressure for perfect test scores, perfect bodies, and perfect relationships). This is not what *teleios* means.

In the Septuagint, *teleios* is sometimes used to translate the Hebrew words *tāmîm* and *šālēm*, meaning "blameless, whole, unblemished, undivided, or completely loyal." This begins to get at what the word means in James. Noah was "blameless" before God because he was devoted to God and walked in God's ways (Gen 6:9), even though he was not perfect in every respect. The Israelites were to offer a lamb "without blemish" in their sacrifices—that is, a lamb that was whole (Exod 12:5). Moses exhorted Israel to be undivided in their loyalty to God (Deut 18:13). The Deuteronomistic

History evaluates Israelite and Judean kings as to whether their hearts were "true" or "whole" in their commitment to God, not whether they were perfect (1 Kings 8:61; 11:4; 15:3, 14; 1 Chron 28:9). This range of meaning for the Hebrew equivalent of *teleios* in the Old Testament gives us a fuller sense of what James means in 1:4 (Hartin 1999: 23–24).

James's concern is with wholeness and integrity, with being a complete human being and becoming fully what God intended. This is something other than perfection in the sense of sinlessness or flawlessness. The letter, in fact, recognizes that such perfection is impossible *since all of us make many mistakes* (3:2). To be sure, being *mature and complete, lacking in nothing* (NRSV) has ethical implications and requires a certain kind of behavior. Faith, for example, cannot be perfected or whole unless it is accompanied by action consistent with that faith (2:2-4), and loving one's neighbor "completes" or "perfects" the royal law (2:8). However, the goal here is something more than individual human achievement. Being "complete" or "whole" in 1:4 has to do with character, with the kind of person one is becoming when one endures testing and remains faithful to God. It means having integrity instead of being divided in one's loyalty, being "double minded" (1:8; 4:8).

The integrity or wholeness that James envisions is dependent on a God who gives *perfect gifts* (1:17) and is guided by the *perfect law, the law of liberty* (1:25). It characterizes those who are already now the *first fruits of [God's] creatures* (1:18), even if they still sin. James's words about being whole and having integrity pertain not only to his readers as individuals but also to the community. As a church their corporate faith is being tested ("your" in v. 3 is pl.) by painful experiences in the community. Yet these trials can be a source of joy if they choose to consider them opportunities to mature as the body of Christ. Such wholeness can and will be fully realized only at the future *coming of the Lord* (5:7-8) when the blessed who have proved faithful in testing *will receive the crown of life* (1:12).

Two synonyms at the end of 1:4 reinforce the idea of *teleios* as wholeness or integrity. When endurance has done its perfect work, they will be *whole* or intact (like "unhewn stone" [Deut 27:6] or a healthy body [Acts 3:16]) and will be *lacking in nothing*. In this context, *lacking in nothing* cannot mean that one will have all the material things one could ever want. Rather, it has to do with character that conforms to God's original intention. In the rest of the letter, this concern for integrity comes to the fore again and again, often in the form of warnings against the opposite. James warns against those who are *double-minded* (1:8; 4:8) and whose friendship with God is compromised by *friendship with the world*. He encourages his audience to have integrity in hearing and doing (1:22-24), in speaking and doing (3:9-12), and in believing and doing (2:14-26).

In summary, James begins his letter by exhorting his fellow believers to embrace hardship joyfully because of its potential to help them grow more fully into people with integrity, who embody the *first fruits of [God's] creatures* (1:18) and who, on the last day, will receive the *crown of life* (1:12).

Seeking Wisdom in Trust and Not Being Double-Minded 1:5-8

The connection between 1:5-8 and what precedes is not immediately obvious, other than that the verses are chained together with the catchword "lack." A closer look, however, reveals that verses 5-8 build on and further develop James's concern for steadfast faith in times of trial. In verse 4, James assures his beleaguered readers that the long-term gain of staying the course would be mature faith, however difficult it may be to do that in the midst of trying times. Adversity is experienced as testing of faith rather than a cause for joy. Even though eventually they may *lack in nothing*, that is not now. James suggests what they lack now is wisdom. As Patrick Hartin says, "The gift of wisdom enables people to act in the midst of trials and suffering in such a way that their actions lead to wholeness (perfection)" (2009a: 66–67).

As noted earlier, the first chapter of James introduces virtually all the themes that appear later in the letter. Wisdom is one of those themes, reemerging explicitly in 3:13-18. The Letter of James finds its home in the rich wisdom tradition of Israel in part because of its explicit references to wisdom but also because of the many other features it shares with books like Proverbs, Sirach, and the Wisdom of Solomon *[The Wisdom Tradition and James, p. 376]*. But wisdom is more than a genre of literature. It is also more than intellectual knowledge or theoretical reasoning. Wisdom (*sophia*) is the divinely given ability to live in conformity with God's will. It is the capacity to move beyond theoretical knowledge about God's purposes to the practical embodiment of those purposes in life. Later, in 3:13-18, James will expand on what such wisdom looks like in a community of Jesus followers: it bears fruit in justice and peace and is expressed through mercy, gentleness, and holiness.

The association of wisdom with adversity and integrity of character is part of this scriptural tradition. In Jewish wisdom literature, trials serve a disciplinary and teaching function for those who seek wisdom. James lifts up Job as someone who demonstrated integrity of character when he remained steadfast in suffering (5:11). The deuterocanonical wisdom book Sirach (Ecclesiasticus) speaks of the refining value of testing (2:1-6) and portrays a personified Wisdom disciplining and testing her followers, bringing joy to those who endure (4:17-18). The Wisdom of Solomon says that a person cannot be perfect or whole (*teleios*) without God's gift of wisdom (9:6), and throughout Israel's history, "Wisdom rescued from troubles those who served her" (10:9). Like his forebears, James links seeking wisdom (1:5) with persevering through troubles (v. 3) and integrity (v. 4). Similarly, the church will need wisdom to perceive their testing in a way that strengthens faith.

Also present in the Jewish wisdom tradition is the conviction that wisdom cannot be gained by human effort or perseverance but always has its origin in God: "For the LORD gives wisdom; from his mouth comes knowledge and understanding; he stores up sound wisdom for the upright" (Prov 2:6-7). "But I perceived that I would not possess wisdom unless God gave her to me" (Wisd of Sol 8:21; see also Prov 9:10; Sir 1:1). King Solomon stands out as the scriptural model of someone who asked for and was granted wisdom by God (1 Kings 3:5-15). James is on solid ground, then, when he exhorts those who lack wisdom to ask God for it; he assures them that God will generously grant it (1:5).

At the end of the letter, James returns to the theme of petitioning God in time of trouble as he exhorts the church to pray for the sick (5:13-18). A letter addressed to believers whose faith is being tested in adversity is thus bracketed by the encouragement to ask God for help in such troubling times. As Luke Timothy Johnson says, "Prayer is the essential conversion for one unable to 'perceive' or 'calculate' life's testings in the appropriate way" (1995: 184).

In this subunit (1:5-8), then, James urges his readers to ask God for wisdom in order to become whole people, able to prevail against trials and tests of faith. In what follows he (a) gives a glimpse into the character of God, who responds to such requests (v. 5); and (b) offers counsel on the appropriate stance with which to approach God when making such requests (vv. 6-8).

According to James, the notion of "gift" is integral to the very nature of who God is. He will reiterate this when he says that every good gift and every complete gift comes from above (1:17). Here he uses two parallel adverbs to describe *how* God gives: God gives to *all* people *generously and ungrudgingly* (v. 5). The word that the NRSVue translates as *generously* (*haplōs*) appears only here in the New Testament and is difficult to translate. In addition to "generously" (like the cognate noun in Rom 12:8; 2 Cor 8:2), it can also mean "without reservation," "with single intent," "straightforwardly," or "sincerely" (like the cognate in Matt 6:22; 2 Cor 1:12; Eph 6:5). The latter fits the context of James better, since a contrast is being made between a person who vacillates and is unstable and double-minded (vv. 6-8), and God, who is single-minded, gives without hesitation or duplicity, and responds to entreaties with genuineness. The second adverb is a synonym: God gives without grudging or obligation, without reproaching the one who asks. In one succinct sentence, James offers a picture of God, who graciously invites God's people to ask for what they lack and who gives without reservation and without reproach.

The promise that *it will be given you* recalls Jesus' words in Matthew 7:7-11//Luke 11:9-13: "Ask, and it will be given to you; search, and you will find; knock, and the door will be opened for you. For everyone who asks receives, and everyone who searches finds, and for everyone who knocks, the door will be opened." Matthew's version promises "good things" to those who ask, Luke assures supplicants of receiving "the Holy Spirit," and James tells his readers that God will supply "wisdom" to those who ask. Some scholars have drawn parallels between God's gift of wisdom in James and the Spirit (who is never mentioned in the book). Both are given by a generous God, and both bear fruit in peace and justice (e.g. Kirk: 24–38; Davids 1982: 52–56; but cf. Baker 2008: 293–315, who argues against too close an association). Just as God gave Solomon wisdom when he asked for it, so God continues to give wisdom ungrudgingly to people who ask God for it today.

James moves from speaking about God to instructing readers on how they should approach God with their requests. Verses 6-8 are often troubling for readers of Scripture today: Who does not, at some point in life, have doubts? If God does not grant a request, is it because the person praying did not have enough faith? These verses have been both a deterrent to honest critical questioning and the source of guilt for faithful Christians. To be sure, James is not one to mince words, and he often says things intended to provoke readers, both ancient and modern, to critical self-reflection and more faithful Christian living. We cannot squirm away too quickly from the sharp prodding in verses 6-8. Yet, these verses require more careful interpretation than a quick read affords.

James exhorts all those who bring their requests to God to *ask in faith, never doubting* (v. 6a). He goes on to characterize "doubters" in three ways: They are (1) *like a wave of the sea, driven and tossed by the wind* (v. 6b); (2) *double-minded* (v. 8); and (3) *unstable in every way* (v. 8). Such people should *not expect to receive anything from the Lord* (v. 7). These descriptors help us to understand further what James means when he speaks of one who "doubts."

First, we need to look at what the words "faith" and "doubt" mean in the context of the whole letter. The noun *pistis* (faith, belief) appears sixteen times in James (1:3, 6; 2:1, 5, 14 [2×], 17, 18 [3×], 20, 22 [2×], 24, 26; 5:15) and the verb *pisteuō* ("have faith, believe") three times (2:19 [2×], 23). Clearly, most of what James says about faith appears in chapter 2, in his argument about faith and works. The relationship of faith and works will be treated in more detail in that part of the commentary. In brief, James speaks of two kinds of "faith." There is faith that consists only of head knowledge, which even the demons have (2:19, 24). This is not a true, living faith, but barren, dead, and empty; it is not a faith that "saves" (2:14). Real faith is not mere intellectual assent but actual trust in God and loyalty to God, manifested in corresponding actions and virtues. Abraham and Rahab are paradigmatic of real faith because their trust in God was evident in what they did. Thus, when James says in 1:6 that believers must *ask in faith* he does not mean that they must simply believe that God will do what they ask. Rather, asking in faith means placing oneself in the hands of a God who desires one's well-being and is generous and ungrudging; it is lived allegiance to such a God.

The verb that is often translated "doubt" in verse 6 can have a range of meanings. In its active form it can convey the following: "to distinguish, differentiate, evaluate, judge, separate." This range is reflected in classical Greek literature and the Septuagint, and it is how the word is used in 2:4, its only other occurrence in the letter. In the passive voice the verb can signify "to dispute, take issue with, contend" and, perhaps, "to be at odds with oneself," that is, "to doubt or waver." The problem with the definition "to doubt" is that it would be unique to the New Testament and subsequent Christian writings. This prompts some scholars to argue in favor of a meaning more consistent with extrabiblical sources, thus avoiding the need to come up with a new definition. Peter Spitaler, for example, maintains that the one who should not expect to receive from God is a "debater," that is, someone who quarrels with God and also stirs up interpersonal controversies (2:4;

3:8-4:8) (560–79; also Batten 2017b: 113–14; cf. Allison 2013: 179–81, for a counterargument). The problem is not internal doubt and insecure faith, according to such an interpretation, but opposition to and separation from God.

Defining the problem as "debating" with God instead of "doubting" God helpfully unsettles unsatisfactory interpretations of this verse but is ultimately not convincing. The same word (*diakrinomai*) appears in Matthew 21:21; Mark 11:23; and Romans 4:20; 14:23 as antithetical to "faith," and it is hard to see it meaning anything other than "doubt" in those verses. If it means "doubt" in the Gospels, it could also mean "doubt" in James, whose language often echoes that of the synoptic Jesus. Moreover, in the New Testament and early Christian literature, *diakrinomai* is sometimes used synonymously with *distazō*, which does mean "to doubt." For example, in Matthew 14:31 Jesus reprimands those with little faith, who doubt (*distazō*); and in 21:21 Jesus commends having faith and not doubting (*diakrinomai*; Allison 2013: 180–81). It is also difficult to see how the meaning of "contending with God" fits into the context of James 1:2-8. What would the "debater" be arguing about with God? Why introduce this idea here? On the other hand, it makes good sense that those whose faith is tested (1:2-4) might at times waver or doubt.

Looking at the three ways in which James characterizes the one who doubts in 1:6b-8 also illumines what James is saying. First, *the one who doubts is like a wave of the sea, driven and tossed by the wind* (v. 6b). This is the first of many vivid similes and metaphors in the letter. It is a popular image used by other ancient writers, both Jewish and Greek (e.g., Sir 33:2; Philo, *On the Migration of Abraham* 148). Isaiah compares the wicked to the "tossing sea that cannot keep still; its waters toss up mire and mud" (57:20). Like the waves of the sea, doubters are never settled; they are always in motion, always vacillating, affected by winds above and currents below. Both doubters and large bodies of water are not just uneasy in a storm but are also like this by their very nature.

Second, the person who should not expect to receive from God is *double-minded* (1:8). Here we get at the crux of what James means by the word "doubt"; once again, the word requires some unpacking. The Greek word for "double-minded" is *dipsychos*, literally meaning "two-souled." Because it appears only here and in 4:8 in the New Testament and is absent from Greek literature before James, some scholars posit that James coined the word himself. It does appear in early Christian writers, who either were familiar with the Letter of James or drew from similar sources (e.g., 1 Clement 11.2; 2 Clement 11.2; Didache 4.1-4; Shepherd of Hermas, Mandate, 9.1-6). Despite its rarity, the idea it conveys is firmly grounded in Jewish literature and theology. Psalm 12:2 (11:3 LXX) deplores those who speak with "a double heart," and Sirach 1:28 warns against approaching God "with a divided mind." At the heart of Israel's confession lay the commitment to love God with their whole heart and whole soul and whole mind (Deut 6:5; 26:16; cf. 2 Kings 23:25).

If James understands doubt to mean double-mindedness, then *not* to have doubt does not mean being certain about everything one believes. It does not mean never questioning God. And it does not mean believing that God will do exactly what one asks. Rather, to doubt is to be divided in one's allegiance and to distrust the Divine. It means to be fragmented instead of whole (James 1:4). It directly contrasts with the character of God, who gives with integrity and single-mindedness (v. 5). Later James claims that one cannot maintain both friendship with the world and friendship with God (4:4) and exhorts the "double-minded" faith community to purify their hearts, to get rid of all that compromises their commitments (4:8).

This sounds familiar because it is so similar to Jesus' words to his disciples: "No one can serve two masters; for a slave will either hate the one and love the other, or be devoted to the one and despise the other. You cannot serve God and wealth" (Matt 6:24// Luke 16:13). Individuals or faith communities who ask God for wisdom—or anything else—*and* are as turbulent as ocean waves in a storm in trusting God should not be surprised when they ask God for something and do not receive anything. They do not really expect to! Those who are *rich in faith* (2:5), on the other hand, will inherit the kingdom—not because they never question God or never doubt, and not because they believe God will give them whatever they desire, but because they trust and love God.

Third, individuals and communities whose loyalties are divided will be *unstable* (*akatastatos*) *in every way* (1:8). In chapter 3 James uses this same word to describe the "restless" (*akatastatos*) evil of an untamable tongue (v. 8) and the "disorder" (*akatastatia*) caused by envy and selfish ambition (v. 16). Such instability or disorder is antithetical to the wisdom that comes from above (3:17-18). In 4:3 James says, *You ask and do not receive, because you ask wrongly, in order to spend what you get on your pleasures.* The Greek words for "ask" and "receive" are the same words we find in 1:6-8. Just as the double-minded and unstable doubter should not expect to receive anything from God when he or she asks, so also one whose requests derive from desires more consistent with worldly friendship than with friendship with God should also not expect to receive. With the overlap in terminology between 1:6-8 and 3:8-4:8, we sense what James has in mind when he claims that *one who doubts . . . must not expect to receive anything from the Lord.* Doubters are not just people who have questions about God and faith, as many people do at some point in life, but include those who sit with part of their soul in the commitments and trappings of this world and give only part of themselves to God, those who cannot or do not trust God and foment instability and disorder. They should not expect to receive wisdom—or, for that matter, any of God's gifts—in the abundance that God always desires to give because they are unable to receive them.

God's Promises of Blessing and Reversal for the Poor and Rich 1:9-12

At first blush, James seems to switch to a new topic in verse 9, but when the broader context of these verses is considered, we see more continuity of thought than seems evident at first. Although verse 12 could be considered part of the next subunit (vv. 13-18), due to similar vocabulary of testing/temptation, it makes more sense as the culmination of verses 9-12. In verse 12 James returns to the subject of verses 2-4: the positive outcome of enduring trials faithfully. Verses 2-4 and verse 12 thus function as bookends around the topics of wisdom and faith (vv. 5-8) and poverty and wealth (vv. 9-11), nudging listeners to consider the intervening verses in light of what surrounds them. The churches to whom James writes include people for whom economic adversity is surely a test of faith, demanding endurance and wisdom. Because of the letter's strong emphasis on lived faith, the community's treatment of the poor and its relationship to wealth become central to what it means to have a vibrant faith and to seek wisdom.

Verses 9-12 contrast the long-term fates of the lowly and the rich: God will lift up and bless the poor, who suffer now, but will bring down the wealthy, whose fortunes are as fleeting as flowers in the hot sun. James will return to the topic of wealth and poverty several times in the letter (1:27; 2:1-7, 15-16; 4:13-17; 5:1-6). This theme gives the letter affinities with both wisdom literature and the prophets. Wisdom books like Proverbs include many sayings that contrast the rich and the poor as well as moral teaching about material possessions (e.g., Prov 10:4, 15; 11:24; 13:11). Like James, the prophets denounce social and economic injustice and warn of God's judgment on rich oppressors (e.g., Isa 3:13-26; Jer 22:13-17; Amos 2:6-9; 6:1-6).

What James is articulating here taps deeply into a conviction found throughout the biblical story: God delivers the oppressed, injustice will not be allowed to continue forever, and God's righteousness will prevail. The counterpart to God raising up the lowly is that God brings down the rich and powerful. Their power, wealth, and status will not—*cannot*—continue when God brings about justice. God is a God of reversal. In the exodus from Egypt, Israel came to know God as One who liberates the oppressed and removes tyrants from their thrones. Hannah celebrates this God when she sings at the birth of Samuel: "The LORD makes poor and makes rich; he brings low; he also exalts. He raises up the poor from the dust; he lifts the needy from the ash heap, to make them sit with princes and inherit a seat of honor" (1 Sam 2:7-8).

The refrain of God turning things upside down continues in the ministry of Jesus. In anticipation of Jesus' birth, Mary voices the convictions and hopes of her people when she says that God "has brought down the powerful from their thrones, and lifted up the lowly; he has filled the hungry with good things, and sent the rich away empty" (Luke 1:52-53). What James says in 1:9-11 resonates with Jesus' teachings that "all who exalt themselves will be humbled, and all who humble themselves will be exalted" (Matt 23:12// Luke 14:11; 18:14). Jesus also told stories that depict such reversal; for example, Lazarus, who sits at the rich man's gate begging for food and covered in sores, ends up being comforted by Abraham after he dies; the rich man, who wears expensive clothes and feasts sumptuously during his lifetime, ends up tormented in Hades (Luke 16:19-31).

Like Jesus, James turns upside down prevailing assumptions that wealth is a sign of blessing from God and a reward for upright living and hard work. Like Jesus, James bears witness to a God who cares for and brings justice to the lowly, the oppressed, and the marginalized. For James's readers, who know the despair of poverty, this is good news. For readers who are well off, it is a reminder not to trust in their material wealth but to join God in raising up the poor and to share generously with those in need (1:27; 2:15-16).

Who then are the "poor" and the "rich" that the letter is talking about? Do these terms refer only to economic status? Or do they have a broader scope? Are some rich people among those who *believe in our glorious Lord Jesus Christ* (2:1 NRSV)? Or are the "rich" not part of the church?

The word translated "humble" in verse 9 (*tapeinos*) certainly includes the economically poor since they are being contrasted with "the rich," but equally they are people with low social status. It is a word associated with the *anawim*, or "pious poor" in the Old Testament (e.g., Pss 10:18; 34:18; 138:6; Prov 3:34; 11:2) and describes people who are utterly dependent on God, often because they are destitute. In 1:9 *tapeinos* is used in direct contrast to *plousios* (v. 10), which uniformly means economically rich. In our context, *those of humble means* would be primarily those who are socioeconomically oppressed, not just the spiritually humble. James also specifies that he is writing about the lowly brother or sister, thus to fellow believers in Christ.

There is no agreement among scholars about the identity of "the rich." Some read James as saying that the faith communities he is addressing include rich Christians (e.g., Hartin 2009a: 69; Witherington 2007: 430; Blomberg and Kamell: 58; Ropes: 145–46); others think the "rich" must be outsiders (e.g., McKnight: 98–99; Davids 1982: 77; Sleeper: 54; Wall: 56; Martin: 26). In favor of counting rich people among the believers are the following factors. First, since the word "boast" is explicit in James 1:9 but only implied in verse 10a, the word "believer" could also be implicit in verse 10a: *Let the believer who is lowly boast in being raised up, and [let] the rich [believer boast] in being brought low* (NRSV). Second, there are hints elsewhere in the letter that not everyone in the assembly is destitute. In 2:2-4 the writer imagines someone in wealthy attire entering the meeting place, and 4:13-17 addresses people well off enough to travel on business. Third, some interpreters cannot imagine James exhorting rich unbelievers to glory (*boast*) in their own judgment. As one writer says, such bitter sarcasm would be "too twisted to be taken seriously" (W. Baker, quoted in Blomberg and Kamell: 58). If James is indeed addressing rich Christians, verse 10 could mean either that (a) they should not take pride in their transitory earthly riches but glory in their humble and dependent state before Christ; or (b) they should rejoice when hardships result in the loss of their material things or social status since those markers have no spiritual value anyway.

Although such readings are possible, arguments are stronger in favor of *not* seeing verses 9-11 as addressed to rich believers. The main reason for not taking "the rich" in verses 10-11 to be part of the community of faith is that every other occurrence of the word *plousios* (rich) in the letter is almost certainly a reference to nonbelievers. This is most explicit in 2:6-7, where James reminds his readers that "the rich" not only oppress them and drag them into court but also *blaspheme the excellent name invoked over [them].* If that name is Jesus, as seems probable, these "rich ones" cannot be believers. The severe judgment against the wealthy in 5:1-6 is probably a literary apostrophe, that is, rhetoric directed at an imaginary audience rather than actual believers. Elsewhere, when James refers to economically secure people, the term "rich" (*plousios*) is not used. For example, the elegantly dressed person in 2:2-4 is not necessarily part of the assembly, and the traveling merchants of 4:13-17 are not necessarily wealthy. We will look at each of these texts in more detail as we come to them.

The point of 1:9-11, then, is not to teach rich believers how to live, even though these words have ethical implications for Christians then and now. Nor is James sarcastically telling them to boast about their downfall. Rather, he is using vivid, extreme language to describe the eschatological reversal that God will effect. His point is that the flip side of God lifting up the lowly is the downfall of the rich and powerful and that material wealth is transitory and ephemeral. If his audience consisted primarily of humble, poor folk, who worked hard and still experienced hardships, these words would be especially encouraging and comforting. To the extent that wealthy people were part of the assemblies to which James wrote, these words were not only a sober warning and call for repentance, but also good news: their status rests not in their ephemeral wealth but in their identity as beloved children of God.

In today's world it sounds strange to encourage someone to "boast," since bragging is considered to be in poor taste. In the broader biblical context, however, "boasting" can mean "to glory in" or "to rejoice or delight in" something or someone. What makes all the difference is the object of the boasting. The Bible repeatedly warns against boasting in one's own accomplishments or merit but encourages the people of God to boast in what the Lord has done. Many scholars see an allusion to Jeremiah 9:23-24 in verse 9:

> Thus says the LORD: Do not let the wise boast in their wisdom, do not let the mighty boast in their might, do not let the wealthy boast in their wealth; but let those who boast boast in this, that they understand and know me, that I am the LORD; I act with steadfast love, justice, and righteousness in the earth, for in these things I delight, says the LORD.

Besides James, only Paul (and one reference in Heb 3:6 ESV) talks about boasting. One should not boast in one's own merit (1 Cor 3:21; Gal 6:13), but in God's exceeding goodness and faithfulness (Rom 5:11; Gal 6:14). Paul can "boast" in his own weakness because it ultimately points to the glory of God working in him (2 Cor 12:9). Later in his letter, James also warns against inappropriate boasting (3:14; 4:16), but here at the outset he encourages lowly believers to exult in the reversal that God is about to effect.

Perhaps it is helpful to think of boasting as similar to the attitude James encourages in 1:2-4. That is, just as believers can choose to view their trials joyfully, so also they can choose to exult in their lowliness. In verses 9-12 the reason for boasting is not the potential for personal and communal character formation, as in 1:2-4, however, but God's action on behalf of the poor and oppressed. Does this action lie entirely in the future? Or is there reason to boast in their status already now? The answer is both. In 2:5 James will remind his readers that God has chosen the poor to be *rich in faith*, which is a kind of upside-down wealth experienced already now. They already now are "heirs" of a kingdom that will only come to full fruition in the future. When God's reign comes in full, they will receive the *crown of life* promised to those who love God (1:12; 2:5). The words in 1:9 are similar to those in 4:10, where James exhorts his readers to *humble* themselves before the Lord, who will *exalt* them. On the last day, God will act decisively to raise up the lowly and strip the oppressor of power. In the meantime, when the rich generously share their wealth and act with justice toward the poor, they participate in God's raising the lowly and begin to make the kingdom a reality even now.

If the poor should exult in the great upheaval God will bring about, what about the rich? James is likely speaking ironically here when he says *the rich [should boast] in having been humbled* (1:10). We should remember that this is not instruction for rich believers in how to behave, but colorful rhetoric intended to drive home a point about God's upside-down justice. What the poor know as God's justice will be experienced by the wealthy as God's judgment. The colorful imagery James uses here is typical of the letter as a whole and makes his teaching memorable. Because of the extended comparison in verses 10b-11, this subunit emphasizes the negative outcomes for the rich more than the plight of the poor.

While such an emphasis might be reassuring for poor readers, for modern wealthy readers it is uncomfortable and even disturbing. Rich Christians today, who listen in on James's prophetic critique and are moved to share their wealth with the poor, may in the end find that they too can delight in the reversal God is bringing about: they are being freed from the tyranny of possessions and are part of a community where all have enough and all have status in the eyes of God.

James compares rich people to the flowers of field grasses. He begins and ends with an explicit comparison: like the flowers, the rich will disappear (1:10b) and wither (v. 11). Between these two pronouncements are four short clauses that detail their demise: the sun rises, with its burning heat; the grass dries up; the flower falls off; and its beauty perishes. The Greek word for *scorching heat* could be a reference to the seasonal hot desert winds of Palestine, but more likely James is referring simply to the intense rays of the sun. Either way, the result is deadly for the fragile flowers of the field.

The imagery here is not only memorable but also familiar to readers of Scripture, which elsewhere compares the transitory nature of human life to vegetation that is here today and gone tomorrow (Job 14:2; 27:13-23; Pss 90:3-6; 103:15-16; Zeph 2:2). James's language is closest to the Septuagint version of Isaiah 40:6-8, and he may even have this text in mind: "All flesh is grass, their constancy is like the flower of the field. The grass withers, the flower fades, when the breath of the LORD blows upon it; surely the people are grass. The grass withers, the flower fades; but the word of our God will stand forever."

First Peter 1:24 explicitly quotes these verses, but James's point is not Peter's. That is, James is not pointing to the constancy of God's word but to the inconstancy of earthly possessions. Actually, his point is even sharper: Not only will wealth disappear, but also, like flowers in the field, the rich themselves will be destroyed. His words echo the psalmist, who says the wicked and wrongdoers "will soon fade like the grass, and wither like the green herb" (Ps 37:1-2). In 5:1-6, where James again castigates the rich, both the transitory nature of riches and the judgment of the rich themselves are in view.

The word that the NRSVue translates as "busy life" (1:11, *poreia*) appears only here and in Luke 13:22. It can refer to a literal journey or road as well as metaphorically to a person's life activity. Some take this phrase to be a reference to the business trips of the merchants in 4:13-17, but this is probably too specific and distant an allusion. We should also not think of *a busy life* merely as the necessary tasks of daily life. James is thinking of the excessively absorbed and absorbing lifestyle of the affluent and their pursuit of wealth for the sake of gain. This is what God will radically interrupt.

Verse 12 functions as a transitional verse that wraps up 1:2-11 while also introducing a new concern in verses 13-18. It does this by means of the word *peirasmos*, which can mean either "testing, trial" (NIV, NASB, ESV, CEB), as in verses 2-4, or "temptation" (NRSVue, NKJV), as in verses 13-15. (The two words are related since "temptations" also function to "test" one's faithfulness.) In verse 12 *peirasmos* should be taken as referring to trials or testing rather than temptation. First, in both verses 2-4 and verse 12, James sees *peirasmos* as a potential source of blessing, not as an impetus to sin. Second, a notable overlap in vocabulary between verses 2-4 and verse 12 suggests that verse 12 is picking up the subject of the earlier verses. James's comments about being tested thus create a frame around and color interpretation of the intervening material about wisdom and economic hardship. Since "trials" can also become "temptations" and thus a cause of sin, verse 12 also introduces the topic of the next few verses, which address the source of temptation.

Verse 12 is a beatitude, a speech form found in the teachings of Jesus (Matt 5:3-12; Luke 6:20-23; 10:23) and throughout Jewish Scriptures, but especially in Psalms and Proverbs (Deut 28:4; Pss 1:1; 40:4; 84:5; Prov 3:13; Jer 17:7; Dan 12:12; Sir 34:17). It begins with the Greek word *makarios*, which is often translated as "happy" but has a much richer meaning. To be "blessed" is to be in right relationship with God and deeply favored or gifted by God. Frequently, however, those whom Jesus pronounces "blessed" do *not* seem to be in happy circumstances by the world's standards: the poor, the meek, those starved for justice, the persecuted. James follows in the tradition of Jesus when he says that those who endure trials are blessed (cf. Matt 5:10-11//Luke 6:22). The blessing derives not from what the recipient is currently experiencing but from what God has promised. In James, the lowly and the poor who endure various trials and whose faith is proved genuine through testing are blessed because they *will receive the crown of life*.

The phrase *crown of life* is uncommon in the New Testament and appears elsewhere only in Revelation 2:10, where it also describes the reward for faithfully enduring persecution (cf. "crown of glory" in 1 Pet 5:4 and "crown of righteousness" in 2 Tim 4:8, both of which are also eschatological rewards for faithfulness). The reward of a crown calls to mind the victory wreaths awarded to triumphant Greek athletes or a symbol of royal power. The image finds its home equally in Jewish literature, where it is often used metaphorically. For example, grandchildren are the crown of the aged (Prov 17:6), "the fear of the Lord is the crown of wisdom" (Sir 1:18), and Zion is called "a beautiful crown in the hand of the LORD" (Isa 62:3). In James 1:12 the image clearly means a reward given to the faithful, and *the crown* consists of *life* itself, God-given eternal life.

This is a blessing that is both "already" and "not yet." That is, those who endure trials faithfully and love God are blessed already now as they experience the abundant life God has promised them. At the same time, the dominant tone of the promise here is eschatological in that the full benefits of God's blessing of life will only be experienced fully in the age to come. We are helped in understanding what it means to *receive the crown of life* when we compare this verse with the parallel in 2:5:

> 1:12 The one who has stood the test
> *will receive the crown of life that* <u>the Lord has promised to those who love him</u>.
>
> 2:5 Those who are poor in the world but rich in faith
> *are heirs of the kingdom that* <u>[God] has promised to those who love him</u>.

The *crown of life* that lovers of God will receive is the *kingdom* or end-time reign of God. Comparing these two verses also clarifies that those who faithfully endure trials and testing are indeed the economically poor and lowly, supporting the link we made earlier between 1:12 and 1:9-11. It also reinforces the notion that God's promises are fulfilled partially in the present and fully in the future, just as the kingdom that Jesus proclaimed is both a present and future reality.

The idea that God makes promises and faithfully keeps them is found throughout the Scriptures, even though they do not explicitly speak of God promising a *crown of life.* At the heart of Israel's faith lay God's promise to show *ḥesed*, "steadfast love" or "covenant faithfulness," to those who "love me and keep my commandments" (Exod 20:6; Deut 5:10; 7:9). In turn, the commitment to love and obey God lies at the core of Israel's response to God's promise: "Hear, O Israel: The LORD is our God, the LORD alone. You shall love the LORD your God with all your heart and with all your soul and with all your might" (Deut 6:4-5). God stays true to God's promises even when Israel fails to maintain its part of the covenant relationship. The New Testament writings claim that, in Jesus Christ, all God's promises are fulfilled (e.g., Acts 13:23, 32; 26:6; 2 Cor 1:20; Gal 3:14-29; Eph 2:12; 1 John 2:25). James's words in 1:12 carry echoes of these commitments and reassure believers, who love the God revealed in Jesus, that they will surely experience the full blessing of those promises of life in God's end-time reign.

Two Birthing Processes, into Death and into God-Given Life 1:13-18

Any church or individual who has experienced hardships knows how severely they can test faith. For this reason, trials have the potential to strengthen character when successfully overcome, but they can also have the opposite effect. In times of crisis it is hard to remain faithful to what one knows to be true and to right relationships. Under stress, even the most faithful Christians may be tempted to lash out in anger, say things they later regret, or do what benefits themselves rather than what furthers God's justice. In short, testing can easily slide into temptation.

It is not surprising, then, that the Greek word *peirasmos* encompasses both meanings. The translation "testing" communicates more of the external pressure caused by a difficult experience; the translation "temptation" conveys the internal, subjective pull toward something harmful. In 1:13 James makes the transition from the former to the latter. He here enters into dialogue with an imaginary interlocutor who raises questions about the source of testing or temptation. Such imagined conversation is an ancient rhetorical style called a diatribe, which is used often by Paul and is the first of several in this letter (cf. 2:3, 16, 18; 4:13).

James's Jewish readers would surely remember occasions in their history when God did test them: Abraham's trust in God's promise was tested when he was asked to sacrifice Isaac (Gen 22:1-14); God tested Israel repeatedly during the wilderness wanderings, tests that the people usually failed (Deut 8:2; 13:3). God allowed Job to be tested severely (Job 1:12; 2:6) and the psalmist says, "Prove me, O LORD, and try me; test my heart and mind" (26:2). It is perhaps not surprising, then, that James imagines his readers saying, "If testing strengthens character and if God sometimes tests our faith and if we are thereby tempted to sin, is God the source of temptation? In other words, does God cause people to sin?" James's unequivocal answer is "No!" His words echo the declaration of the Jewish wisdom book Sirach: "Do not say, 'It was the Lord's doing that I fell away,' for he does not do what he hates. Do not say, 'It was he who led me astray,' for he has no need of the sinful. . . . He has not commanded anyone to be ungodly, and he has not given anyone permission to sin" (15:11-12, 20).

James also insists that God does not tempt anyone to sin or to do evil. This implicit dialogue in James reflects a tension and paradox within Scripture and in Christian history: On the one hand, the Bible does talk about God testing God's people, and sometimes good things can come out of suffering. On the other hand, there is a strong conviction, especially in postexilic and Hellenistic writers, that God is purely good and can have no association with evil. James does not resolve the tension. Testing of faith can produce good fruit, *and*, at the same time, God does not tempt people to do evil nor is God tempted by evil. Although the Greek of verse 13b has been variously translated, the point James is making is clear: God is not in league with evil in any form. In fact, in verses 17-18 James characterizes God as the opposite: God can be trusted to give only good gifts, and God consistently desires the well-being of God's creatures.

Before James expounds on the character of God, however, he addresses the question of the real source of human temptation and sin. His purpose is not to solve the problem of evil but to hold his messianic community accountable for their failings as part of a larger effort to teach them about genuine faith. The question of where temptations come from is age-old. The earliest biblical witnesses attributed all things to God, whether good or bad, because God alone was the one true God and was all-powerful. Later Jewish writings entertain the notion of an Opponent or Accuser, a being who embodies evil rejection of God's purposes (e.g., in the book of Job). The New Testament moves further in this direction when it speaks of Satan, the devil, or Beelzebul, the prince of demons (e.g., Matt 4:1-11; Mark 3:22-26; Acts 5:3; Rom 16:20; Rev 12:9). James knows about the devil and in 4:7 warns his readers to resist the devil.

However, in 1:13-18 James places the blame for giving in to temptation squarely on individuals. Like Jesus, James thinks evil intentions that defile a person arise from within the human heart (Mark 7:20-23). Such language does not sit well in contemporary North American society, where individuals quickly leap to blaming the government, their family, their teachers, the church, society in general—anyone but themselves—when things go wrong. "No," says James, *one is tempted by one's own desire, being lured and enticed by it.* God is not to blame when we fall into temptation. The words used to describe what happens when we allow desire to lead the way are fishing and hunting metaphors. Like fish caught by lures or animals enticed into a trap by bait, we are seduced by our own desire.

But is desire inherently evil? What kind of desire does James have in mind? Desire in itself is not intrinsically wrong, but remains neutral. Rather, it is the object of the desire, the motivation behind desire, and the general character of the one who is desiring that determines whether a desire leads to the positive or the negative. There are references in both Jewish and Christian writings to righteous desires of those who seek God (e.g., Pss 10:17; 37:4; Prov 10:24; 11:23; Sir 3:29; 5:2; 6:37; Wisd of Sol 6:17, 20; Luke 22:15; Phil 1:23; 1 Thess 2:17). In Hellenistic Jewish literature, however, the word "desire" (*epithymia*) tends to have a negative connotation, as also in the New Testament, where "desire" usually has to do with self-gratification and self-aggrandizement. Desire often harms others and runs counter to God's will for shalom and salvation for all (e.g., Num 11:4; Pss 112:10; 140:8; Sir 18:30-32; Mark 4:19; Rom 6:12; Gal 5:16; Col 3:5; 1 Pet 2:11). We catch a clue that James is referring to destructive desire in 1:14 by looking ahead to 4:1-4, where misguided desires for pleasure and friendship with the world give rise to hatred and violence.

Some interpreters think that Jewish *yēṣer* theology lies behind James's words about desire. The *yēṣer* refers to the inclination of the human heart: within a person the "evil inclination" (*yēṣer hārā'*) does battle with the "good inclination" (*yēṣer haṭṭôb*). Although such theology is more fully developed in later rabbinic writings, it may have served as a source for James's theology. Still, James's primary concern is to warn against temptations that find their origin in desire and that distract from faithful living rather than to philosophically address the conflict between such human impulses.

Desire in and of itself is not sinful, but it can lead to sin. Although James is talking here about desire in general, the imagery and language he uses implies sexual desire and seduction. He draws on an image common in wisdom tradition when he personifies desire as a foolish woman luring a righteous man (Prov 7:10-27). Contemporary readers will be dismayed not only by such harmful ancient stereotypes of women as seductresses but also by James's use of the metaphor of conception and birth to describe the outworking of disordered desire: *When that desire has conceived, it begets to sin, and that sin, when it is fully grown, gives birth to death* (1:15 AT). It is jarring to speak of sin and death in terms of the joyful, life-giving event of birth. What the birth metaphor does well, though, is highlight the slow, inexorable way in which human desire, when fed, can grow up to become sin and, when fully grown, can result in death. Disordered desire does not immediately kill but may gradually lead to sin and death.

The movement from temptation (*peirasmos*) to death contrasts with James's earlier words on enduring testing (also *peirasmos*). Faithfulness during testing produces endurance that leads to life (1:2-4, 12), but giving in to temptation stimulated by wrong desires produces sin, which leads to death (v. 15):

testing (*peirasmos*) → endurance → life
temptation (*peirasmos*) → desire → sin → death

James warns his *beloved brothers and sisters* not to be *led astray* (v. 16 AT). This is the first of three times (1:16, 19; 2:5) in the letter that James uses the word *beloved* together with *brothers [and sisters]*. These are words of warning to people whom he cares about in the family of faith. About what does he warn them not to be deceived or led astray? Does verse 16 point back to verses 13-15 (Do not be deceived by the desire that is enticing you to sin)? Or forward to verse 17-18 (Do not be deceived into thinking God tempts people or gives anything other than good and perfect gifts)? Perhaps it is both. That James does not want his readers to be deceived or to wander into sin is evident from the similar language we find in 5:19-20, where he talks about a sinner being "deceived" or "wandering" from the truth and being saved from death. At the same time, James does not want his readers to be led astray in how they understand God and God's saving purpose, the focus of the next two verses (17-18).

Having denied that God could tempt anyone to sin, James now asserts the opposite: God is the Giver of all good gifts (1:17). The poetic meter of the first part of the verse in Greek leads some scholars to suggest that James might be quoting part of a poem here, but there is insufficient evidence to know that with certainty. James uses two parallel phrases in verse 17, with different words for "gift" (*dosis* and *dōrēma*). The first can refer to the gift itself or to the act of giving, and the NRSVue chooses the latter when it translates the phrases as *every generous act of giving, with every perfect gift*. James could, however, simply be piling up synonyms to emphasize God's goodness and generosity. The more literal translation, *every good gift and every perfect gift*, captures the rhetorical impact of this better. The word "perfect" (*teleios*) is the same word used twice in verse 4 to describe how endurance, when it does its "perfect" or "complete" work, can make someone "perfect" or "complete" or "whole." Similarly, God's gifts are also "complete" or "perfect." James's words in verse 17 recall what he said in verse 5 about God granting wisdom generously and ungrudgingly to all who ask. They also point ahead to his description of wisdom that *comes down from above* in 3:15, 17. One of the "good and perfect gifts" that comes down from above is surely wisdom.

But wisdom is not all that God gives. *Every* good gift, *everything* whole/complete/perfect, comes from God. James is making some profound claims about the character of God in verses 17-18. Readers who think of James as simply dishing out practical advice for living would do well to pay attention to verses such as these, where we catch glimpses of the theology that undergirds his ethical instructions. Gift-giving lies at the heart of God's character; since God alone is truly good (Luke 18:19), God gives only what is good for God's creatures and God's creation. From the beginning of the biblical story, where God created the world and pronounced it "good," to the end of the story, when God will usher in a new heaven and a new earth, God is revealed as the Giver of all good. As he does in many other places in the letter, James echoes Jesus: "If you then, who are evil, know how to give good gifts to your children, how much more will your Father in heaven give good things to those who ask him!" (Matt 7:11; cf. Luke 11:13). God is always on our side, always giving generously, so that we might be drawn closer to God and so that God's purpose of shalom might be fulfilled. God is gracious, God is good.

We learn more about James's understanding of the character of God in 1:17. He calls God *the Father of lights*, an evocative but unusual phrase not found anywhere else in the New Testament or Septuagint. The title is probably a reference "to God as the creator of the sun, moon, and stars" and the source of all light (Gen 1:3, 14-17; Ps 136:7; McCartney 2009: 108). The rest of verse 17 is more difficult since James uses three Greek words that appear only here in the New Testament (*variation, shadow, change*). The manuscript tradition also includes a plethora of variant readings, suggesting that not only modern scholars but also ancient scribes had trouble figuring out exactly what James was saying. The words all have to do with astronomical phenomena, perhaps prompted by the characterization of God as the *Father of lights*. Although the movement of the heavenly bodies (the *lights*) is in one sense predictable and regular, their ever-changing nature makes them seem unstable. Jewish writings sometimes call attention to the inconstancy of sun, moon, and stars; for example, in Isaiah 60:19-20 the prophet says that although the sun will set and the moon withdraw its light, the Lord will be an everlasting light (cf. Sir 27:11). Dan McCartney captures the contrast in James: "Ordinary heavenly lights produce shadows, but God's light is shadowless. Ordinary lights wax and wane, shift, move around, go through phases and fade; even the sun is occasionally eclipsed. And all such lights cast shadows that are both inconstant and evanescent" (2009: 109). Despite the unusual vocabulary, the basic sense seems clear: God is stable, constant, and unchanging, unlike the heavenly bodies (Hartin 2009a: 93; Johnson 1995: 197). That is *not* to say that God cannot be moved to change God's mind. After all, Abraham's pleading influenced God's verdict on Sodom and Gomorrah. God also decided to spare Nineveh when the city repented, much to Jonah's chagrin. What James means is that God is consistently faithful, not capricious or unreliable. God is the opposite of the doubter and the double-minded, who are unstable, tossed to and fro like the waves of the sea (1:6-8). The classic hymn "Great Is Thy Faithfulness" incorporates a phrase from James 1:17 (in the KJV) and captures James's meaning well in poetry:

> Great is Thy faithfulness, O God my Father,
> There is no *shadow of turning* with Thee;
> Thou changest not, Thy compassions, they fail not;
> As Thou hast been Thou forever wilt be.

Verse 18 continues to affirm God's faithfulness by showing how God acts consistent with God's purposes. The contrast between God's actions and human behavior is striking. Where human desire gives birth to sin and death (v. 15), God gives birth to a new community, the first fruits of God's redeemed creation (v. 18). As McCartney says, "Standing opposite the unplanned pregnancy and birth of sin in 1:14-15 is the deliberate and intentional reproductive activity of God in 1:18: it is 'according to his purpose'" (2009: 109–10). The verb *gave birth* is the same one used in verse 15b with reference to sin birthing death. It is found only in these two places in the New Testament and only in 4 Maccabees 15:17 in the Septuagint, where it refers to a woman giving birth. This is an unusual mixing of masculine and feminine metaphors for God: the Father of lights is also a Mother who "gives birth" to the church. As Luke Timothy Johnson notes, this is "one of the most striking female images for God in the NT" (1995: 197).

The community is given birth by means of *the word of truth.* God's word is "true" in the sense of being truthful and faithful, and it is also a word *about* truth and *is itself* truth. The Bible is full of references to God's word and to God's speaking words of truth. So to what is James referring when he says that God *gave us birth by means of the word of truth*? Interpreters have typically suggested three possibilities (e.g., Johnson 1995: 197–98, 205):

1. It could be the word of God that spoke creation and, in this case, humanity into being (Gen 1:26-30; Ps 33:6; Isa 55:11). This picks up the creational imagery of *Father of Lights.*
2. *The word of truth* could be a reference to the Torah, which formed and shaped the people of Israel and is sometimes spoken of as "the word of truth" (Pss 119:43, 142). Deuteronomy 32:18 links the giving of the law with God's giving Israel birth.
3. James could have in mind the good news of Jesus, the incarnate Word, who brought the Christian community into being (Eph 1:13; Col 1:5; 2 Tim 2:15).

It is impossible to know for certain which of these James had in mind, and perhaps his readers would not have thought to ask the question or to limit *word of truth* to one meaning.

In the context of the rest of the letter and the New Testament canon, understanding the *word of truth* as the good news about Jesus makes sense. James is speaking to an audience that confesses Jesus as Messiah (2:1). He is not addressing them simply as created human beings, though they are that, nor only as Jews who honor the Torah, though they are that as well. Despite the sparse references to Jesus or use of salvation language when compared with what we find in other letters of the New Testament, James is addressing people who have been given a new identity and a new way of living because of Jesus Christ. The seed of the word of God has been planted in them and is bearing fruit (Luke 8:11-15).

The most compelling reason for understanding *the word of truth* as the gospel message is the way "word" is used in the following verses. In verse 21 James urges them to welcome *the implanted word that has the power to save your souls*, and in verses 22-23 he instructs them not only to hear this word but also to allow it to govern their actions. (For *implanted word*, see Deut 30:11-14, esp. v. 14; Jer 31:33-34; Ezek 36:26-27.) In short, "the word" brings about new birth and new identity (v. 18) and has the power to save souls when it takes root (v. 21). However, it also requires an active response: it must be received (v. 21) and obeyed, not only heard (vv. 22-23; Kovalishyn: 279). In a Christian context, such a saving, transformative word is surely the word that God spoke in Christ.

God birthed this faith community into being because it was God's will and so that it might be *a kind of first fruits of [God's] creatures* (v. 18). The term first fruits has its home in an Old Testament cultic context and refers to the first and finest of Israel's flock and fields, which would be set apart as an offering to God (Exod 22:29; 23:19; Num 15:20-21; Deut 18:4; 26:2). Even Israel's firstborn sons were called first fruits and were to be consecrated to God (Gen 49:3; Num 3:12-13). In the New Testament first fruits is used metaphorically for the beginnings of something that will be experienced or received more fully in the future, such as appetizers before a sumptuous banquet. In other words, first fruits becomes an eschatological word in the New Testament. The risen Christ is the first fruits of all who will be resurrected on the last day (1 Cor 15:20, 23), the Holy Spirit is given to believers as a first fruits of the redemption to come (Rom 8:23), and the church becomes the first fruits of God's new humanity (2 Thess 2:13; Rev 14:4).

In James 1:18 the word is also used metaphorically, as indicated by the phrase *a kind of.* The ecclesial community (note the pl.: *so that <u>we</u> would become*) is a harbinger of what is to come, a living sign of the redemption that God intends for all of God's creation. The word that James uses is actually *creatures*, not "creation." James's use of this word draws attention to the creatureliness of human beings, and the church as the first fruits of not only the new creation in general (though it is that too) but specifically of God's creatures. As first fruits of God's creatures, humans have a responsibility to care for *all* of God's creatures, not only the human ones.

To be called *a kind of first fruits of God's creatures* has at least two implications for James's church. First, it is a word of hope. In the present time, they may be experiencing trials that test their faith. They should remember, however, that they are the beginning of God's new humanity, given birth by the word of truth. They are the recipients of God's good and perfect gifts. The new life that God has given them is only the beginning of what God will one day do for all creation. They can live in the hope of what is yet to come. Second, it is a reminder of who they are and therefore how they should live now. As first fruits of God's creatures, given a new birth, their life together should be a representation, a sign of what God desires for all humanity. As such, they will not only profess their faith but also show in their actions what it means to live under

God's reign. As first fruits they are consecrated to God; their life together as the body of Christ should bear witness to this new reality, even as they live in a world of testing and temptation.

THE TEXT IN BIBLICAL CONTEXT

God's Transformative Work as New Birth

The work of transforming and renewing creation is central to the activity of God and is revealed most fully in Jesus, in whom the rebirth of creation has begun. James says it this way: *God gave birth to us by the word of truth, so that we would become a kind of first fruits of his creatures* (1:18). Paul's epistles, the Johannine literature, and 1 Peter all testify to this same good news.

The theme of God's transformative work as new birth appears in Paul's letters in various ways. First, Paul speaks about the "newness" of life in Christ. Through baptism, believers die to sin so that they may walk in newness of life now and be united with Christ in a future resurrection (Rom 6:3-11; Col 2:12). The old has passed away, and there is a whole new creation (2 Cor 5:17). Those who are "in Christ" have put off the old nature and put on the new (Eph 4:22-24). Second, Paul uses birth imagery to express eschatological hope. Although in Christ the new creation has begun and we have the first fruits of the Spirit, it is not yet here in full. Creation groans in labor pains while it waits for the final redemption of all things (Rom 8:22-23). Third, Paul uses the most explicit birth imagery when he speaks about his relationship with churches. Because Paul "birthed" these congregations, he considers himself to be their parent. In the NRSV, 1 Corinthians 4:15 says, "I became your father"; but literally the words are "I begat you" (ASV; also Philem 1:10; cf. 1 Thess 2:7, 11) or "I fathered you" (NRSVue).

The metaphor of birth is most explicit and pervasive in the Johannine literature and in 1 Peter. Jesus tells Nicodemus that in order to enter the kingdom of God, he must be "born anew" (ASV; or "from above," NRSVue; John 3:3-5). Those who receive the light that is Jesus become children of God and are "born of God" (1:12-13). The Johannine idiom "to be born of God" is a way of stating that the believer's origin lies in God. Jesus is also "of God" because he was sent from God (3:31, 34; 16:28). By being united with him, disciples gain abundant life that begins now and continues eternally.

First John is thick with characterizations of those who are "born of God." First, to be born of God has ethical implications. Since the Son is righteous, those who do what is right have been born of him and are children of God (2:29–3:2); conversely, those who are born of God do not sin (3:9; 5:18). Of course, the writer knows that believers *do* sin and so assures his readers that "if we confess our sins, he who is faithful and just will forgive us our sins and cleanse us from all unrighteousness" (1:9). Second, since love comes from God and God is love, everyone who loves is born of God (4:7). God's love was revealed in Jesus. Those who have received this love and have God's love abiding in them will love their brothers and sisters not just in word but also in action (3:16-18; 4:12, 16-21). Third, to be born of God is connected to what one believes or puts one's trust in. Those who believe that Jesus is the Messiah are born of God (5:1), and this faith is itself born of God.

The closest semantic parallel to James 1:18 is in 1 Peter. As in James, the recipients of the letter are suffering (1 Pet 1:6-7; 4:12-16). As in James, the new birth comes through the word of God, which in 1 Peter is characterized as "living and enduring," and as "the good news that was announced to you" (1:23-25). In contrast to James, 1 Peter attributes the new birth explicitly to the resurrection of Jesus (1:3). Because of the resurrection, Christians can have hope that will sustain them through their trials. This hope is for an inheritance that will not perish or fade but will be kept in heaven for them until it is fully revealed at the end of time (1:4-5, 13, 21). James, too, speaks of people inheriting a kingdom and receiving the "crown of life" (1:12; 2:5; cf. "crown of glory" in 1 Pet 5:4). Both 1 Peter and James talk about new birth resulting in transformed lives. The writer of 1 Peter urges his readers to live holy lives (1:14-15), to love each other deeply (1:22), and to do what is right and good (3:13-14). They have been given new birth, but like newborn babies, they need to grow into their salvation (2:2).

The New Testament bears witness to a God who gives new life to people through the living word/Word of God. The imagery of birth vividly expresses this new thing that God does when God creates and recreates God's people. In using this birth metaphor, James stands in good company with many other biblical writers.

A God Who Gives Birth

James 1:18 employs a noteworthy and even startling metaphor to capture the transformation that God effects in people. Using a verb that is rare in the Bible but more common in Greek literature, James says that God "gave birth" (*apokyeō*) to us. According to Luke Timothy Johnson, this is "one of the most striking female images for God in the NT" (Johnson 1995: 197).

Of course, all language for God is metaphorical and analogical, for God is transcendent and never fully knowable. All metaphors for God thus have an "is" and "is not" quality to them. At the same time, God is a God who desires relationship with God's creatures and has revealed God's self to people in history. The metaphors we use for God express aspects of our relationship with God and what we believe about God.

Since the Bible was written in a patriarchal and androcentric culture, the biblical metaphors for God are primarily masculine or inanimate: king, shepherd, warrior, father, rock, shield. At the same time, there are some striking and significant feminine images: Lady Wisdom, midwife, a woman seeking a lost coin, and mother, to name only a few. Because James uses the birthing metaphor, we will focus on the image of God as mother.

One of the reasons why Old Testament writers avoided maternal or birthing language to describe the relationship between God and Israel was because of a desire to dissociate Israel from the surrounding nations, whose male gods had female consorts and whose religions included fertility myths. "Israel is Yahweh's people not by natural procreation but by election" (*NIDNTTE* 1:560). Birthing metaphors in the Old Testament are all the more striking, then, when they do appear. With an interesting mix of metaphors, Moses accuses Israel of being "unmindful of the Rock that bore you" and forgetting "the God who gave you birth" (Deut 32:18). With intimate and evocative imagery, the psalmist speaks of his relationship with God in terms of a comforted, weaned child with the mother (Ps 131:1-2). The language of Hosea 11:3-4 is some of the most tender and compassionate in the Old Testament, and although it could apply to fathers, in ancient households early child-rearing was primarily the mother's domain: "Yet it was I who taught Ephraim to walk; I took them up in my arms. . . . I was to them like those who lift infants to their cheeks. I bent down to them and fed them."

Some of the maternal images for God use animal metaphors. Deuteronomy 32:11 compares God to a strong mother eagle (cf. Exod 19:4). Similarly, Jesus' lament over Jerusalem depicts him as a protective mother hen (Luke 13:34). We often think of maternal imagery as being comforting and gentle, but in Hosea the metaphor of God as a mother bear and a lioness is fierce, even violent: "I will confront them like a bear deprived of her cubs, And I will tear open their chests; I will also devour them there like a lioness" (Hos 13:8). Yes, God nurtures God's children, feeding them and caring for them. But God is also fiercely protective, strong, and powerful.

The second half of Isaiah contains especially vivid birth metaphors to express the intimate relationship between God and God's people. Arising out of a context of devastation, trauma, and loss, Deutero-Isaiah addresses the Babylonian exiles' longing for comfort and their hope that God has not abandoned them. The prophet combines imagery from Israel's past with rich new metaphors to interrupt their despair and to birth new life. In Isaiah 42:13-14 he juxtaposes the metaphors of God as Divine Warrior and as a Mother in labor, a startling contrast that highlights the strength and courage with which both warrior and laboring woman face what lies ahead. In Isaiah 45:9-10, the metaphor of a mother in labor is combined with that of God as a potter, working with clay, and a father, who begets a son. Here the images of bringing forth something new are used to challenge those who would question God. When the people of God feel abandoned, when they feel like a motherless child, the prophet assures them of God's unending compassion: "Can a woman forget her nursing child, or show no compassion for the child of her womb? Even these might forget, yet I will not forget you" (Isa 49:15). Strong birthing language is also present in Isaiah 46:3-4, reassuring Israel of God's constant care. Even after the return from exile, the prophet consoles them with maternal images: "For thus says the LORD: . . . As a mother comforts her child, so I will comfort you" (Isa 66:12-13).

Scholars offer different opinions about why so many maternal images appear in Deutero-Isaiah. Mayer Gruber suggests that the strongly monotheistic prophet "may have used both masculine and feminine metaphors for God to counter the goddesses of other religions" (Claassens: 46). Others think that during this time of upheaval and loss of temple and king, people took comfort in God's presence with them in the ordinary, domestic experiences of life, such as the familiar yet miraculous birth of a child. Whatever its origin, the image of a mother laboring and giving birth proved to be a hopeful one for a people that had experienced the trauma of exile. Like a mother, God would give birth to a recreated people after the exile.

There is no way of knowing if James had any of these maternal images in mind when he wrote to the church that God had given them *birth by the word of truth* (1:18). There is no evidence that he did, and he was not somehow immune from the thoroughly patriarchal culture in which he lived. Nevertheless, by using such striking feminine imagery for the work of God in their midst, James is part of a small but rich vein of scriptural tradition that portrays God as Mother giving birth. These images continue to be an important theological resource for the church today.

THE TEXT IN THE LIFE OF THE CHURCH

Doubt and Faith

James exhorts believers to *ask in faith, never doubting.* These words in 1:6-8 have troubled many Christians. They have even prompted people to blame themselves when their prayers seem to go unanswered. Who can honestly say that they have never had questions or been uncertain about matters of faith? To doubt is part of being human. Many Western philosophers and theologians have argued that doubt is not incompatible with faith but an important component of faith and even an ally of faith (Moore-Keish: 32; Boyd).

The Bible itself recognizes that doubt is part of the human condition. Although the psalms do not explicitly talk about "doubt," the psalmist at times questions God's goodness and God's promises, as in Psalm 77:7-9. Belief and unbelief, faith and doubt, sometimes reside in an individual and a community at the same time. In the Gospel of Mark, a father begs Jesus to help his suffering child. When Jesus says, "All things can be done for the one who believes," the man cries out, "I believe; help my unbelief!" (9:23-24). When the apostles meet the resurrected Jesus in Galilee, Matthew reports that "they worshiped him, but they doubted" (28:17; cf. 14:28-33). Apparently, followers of Jesus can both worship and doubt at the same time. In the Gospels the disciples are people of "little faith" who doubt and fail Jesus repeatedly, yet this does not stop Jesus from sending them out to participate in his work of healing and proclaiming good news.

So how should Christians today understand James's exhortation to ask in faith and not doubt, and his warning that the doubter should not expect to receive anything from the Lord? As explained above in the comments on 1:5-8, James is not referring merely to uncertainty when he uses the word "doubt," or to questions that inevitably arise in a life of faith, but to a far-reaching unsteadiness in relationship to God.

First, we must look at the word "faith," which James contrasts with "doubt." Of course, volumes have been written about the nature of faith in the history of Christian theology. At the risk of oversimplification, faith in James—and throughout the Bible—encompasses head, heart, and hands; as Martha Moore-Keish puts it, faith is "propositional, personal, and practical" (38–39). James is concerned about the whole person and the whole community and about integrity in all of life. So belief, trust, and faithful living are all important aspects of faith in God.

Even James would say that his readers should "believe" certain things. For example, they believe that *God is one* (2:19), they can *know the right thing to do* (4:17), and they can *wander from the truth* (5:19). Because we bring our intellect and convictions into a relationship with God, belief is part of faith. This does not mean belief is static and unchanging or constitutes dogmatic certainty. Although belief includes affirming some things to be true, faith that is *only* head knowledge is inadequate, for even the demons "believe" that God exists (2:19). Here is another way to say this: it is not enough to know *about* God; it is also essential to know God. One can know that the Canadian prairies are vast and beautiful, for example, but until one drives from Manitoba to Alberta under that great dome of sky, one does not really "know" the vastness of the prairies.

Second, then, faith must also encompass relationship. To have "faith" in God means to trust God, love God, and know God. The poor are *rich in faith* because they recognize their dependence on God and trust and love God (2:5). Abraham did not understand how God would fulfill God's promises, but he trusted God to keep those promises despite all evidence to the contrary. Third, faith is not only cognitive belief or tenacious trust in God's goodness: for James, faith *must* be evident in words and actions, in character and behavior. James develops this at length in 2:14-26, where he repeatedly insists that *faith without works is dead.* Faith that is not lived out is a false, empty faith that cannot save. Faith is ultimately in the *Lord Jesus Christ* (2:1), and it is by faith—this robust, whole-person, embodied faith—that we are saved (1:21; 2:14).

"Doubt," then, if contrasted with "faith" as in 1:6a, is a whole-person unsettledness. To doubt is not only to have questions and uncertainty, for these are natural and inevitable in a life of faith and may even lead to stronger, deeper faith. In James, doubt is a fundamental lack of trust in God—in the goodness of God, who gives generously and without grudging (1:5)—and an unwillingness (not just inability) to live according to God's desires. Just as faith involves the whole person (head, heart, hands), so also does the doubt that James has in mind. This kind of "doubter" is indeed as unstable as the restless waves of the sea and does "not stand still long enough to receive God's gifts" (Moore-Keish: 33).

Having said all this, a Christian might still protest, "But it's not only that I have questions about faith. My trust in God is also sometimes fragile, and I don't always live with integrity!" In other words, to use James's language, Christians *are* sometimes *double-minded and unstable*, and their doubt is more than intellectual uncertainty. Of course! That is what it means to be finite, imperfect, and human. Jesus knew that when he dubbed his disciples those of "little faith" and yet called them to follow him and participate in his ministry. James is writing precisely because hardships *are* testing the church's faith. He is encouraging them to have faith because they *are* doubting and *are* lacking wisdom and *are not* living faithfully.

Christians today are no different from Jesus' first disciples nor the believers to whom James wrote. Rather than blaming themselves for not having enough faith to have their prayers answered or unrealistically expecting that they will never doubt, followers of Jesus today can and should take James's words as encouragement in tough times to trust in God, who gives generously and ungrudgingly. Even to doubters!

Enduring Trials and Suffering with Joy

The Letter of James begins with a countercultural message about adversity: *Whenever you face various trials, consider it all joy*. These words undoubtedly sound strange or even masochistic in modern North American society, where people go to great lengths to avoid suffering. As Luke Timothy Johnson so aptly puts it,

> James' call for a perception of testing as a chance to grow in a commitment is certainly at odds with a world that conceives of life solely in terms of gratification and self-aggrandizement. In that worldview, anything interfering with pleasure is a source of "suffering" which must at all costs be avoided. The idea of "endurance" is not attractive to hedonism for it assumes an understanding of human character based on something more profound than pleasure, possession, or power. (1995: 183)

Even Christians who concede that hardship can strengthen character are tempted to abandon faith under relentless suffering.

Especially problematic for many is the idea that suffering should be viewed as positive or even redemptive. Dale Allison maintains that in regard to James 1:2-4, "the exegetical and homiletical traditions have been mostly blind to the ethical problem of exhorting those in difficult situations to rejoice" (2013: 138). Using these verses to valorize suffering or legitimate abuse because it is "a joy to suffer" or because God rewards those "who endure testing" is a blatant misuse of the text. The suffering of victims of domestic abuse, for example, is never redemptive: such persons should be empowered to leave rather than endure because that is the "Christian" thing to do (Moore-Keish: 24). Nor should James be read as advocating the status quo for people in poverty or promoting resignation about injustice, as though such conditions have intrinsic merit. People suffering under imperial occupation, victims of racism, workers being harassed on the job—all need liberation, not an admonition to suffer more.

Elsa Tamez, a New Testament scholar from Latin America, recognizes the potential difficulty of this text for the poor but advocates for a "militant patience" that resists injustice (2002: 43–44). In short, where one stands makes all the difference. People outside a situation of suffering or, worse, *causing* the suffering dare not impose this text on victims of injustice to maintain or justify the status quo. On the other hand, when victimized people use these verses to claim power and to encourage each other to have courage, James's message can be valuable. Although we cannot know James's circumstances (was he, for example, leading the Jerusalem church when it received famine relief?), perhaps he sees himself as standing *with* people in their misfortune when he addresses them as "brothers and sisters."

Although James's readers were probably suffering from economic injustice rather than suffering persecution for their faith, many Christians have drawn comfort and courage from James 1:2-4 and 1:12 in times of persecution. What follows are only a few examples from history.

The Czech reformer Jan Hus (1369–1415) quoted James in various writings after he was excommunicated and before he was burned at the stake. Citing James 1:2-4, 12, he urged fellow believers in Prague, some of whom had abandoned the movement for fear of the authorities, to be steadfast and count it as joy to suffer (Hus: 81, as cited in Gowler: 68). Anabaptist martyrs in the sixteenth century understood their suffering to be participation in the sufferings of Christ. For them, willingness to suffer for their faith was central to their understanding of discipleship (Dyck 1985: 15). Even though most early Anabaptists probably had limited formal education, their knowledge of Scripture was extensive. Sermons, hymns, personal communication, and other writings all incorporate Scripture passages seamlessly and extensively. James

1:2-4 and especially 1:12 were favorite Scripture verses for the Anabaptist martyrs, and James 1:12 is "one of the most commonly cited verses" in the *Martyrs Mirror* (Batten 2017a: 544).

The following excerpts are only two examples of the many letters in which Anabaptists encouraged family and friends to persist in faith despite their suffering. Thomas van Imbroeck was only twenty-five years old when he was beheaded in 1558. While in prison, he wrote to his wife: "And you have also asked Him to remove from your path everything that might be in the way of your salvation. Hence think that He is proving us both, and let us willingly take the yoke upon us, and count it all joy. Jas. 1:2" (*MM*: 581).

Jerome Segersz and his wife, Lijsken, exchanged several letters while in prison in Antwerp before their deaths in 1551 and 1552. In one letter he writes, "My dear wife, do remain faithful to the Lord until death, Rev. 2:10, for the crown is not at the beginning, nor in the middle, but at the end. If you remain faithful to the Lord he will not forsake you; he will give you the crown of eternal life, and lead you into his kingdom, James 1:12" (Dyck 1995: 150). The frequency with which 1:12 is cited suggests that these Anabaptists garnered hope from the eschatological promise of a "crown of life" at the end of all their suffering, perhaps more than from the reassurance that endurance would promote maturity and integrity of character, as James 1:2-4 promises. Jennifer Powell McNutt summarizes the significance of the Epistle of James for these early Anabaptists:

> James, in fact, was precious to a group increasingly caught between the tenacious assaults of persecution by magisterial Protestant and Romanist authorities alike. This was a book from which Anabaptists in particular could draw parallels between apostolic-era persecution and their own. For this reason, James importantly contributed to the development of an Anabaptist mindset that regarded trials and the testing of faith with joy despite the harsh realities of imprisonment, torture, exile, and almost certain death. (159)

Many churches around the world still experience trials of many kinds, including persecution, war, and economic injustice. Do James 1:2-4 and 1:12 continue to be encouragement for them? Although not persecuted, Christians in North America are not immune from *various trials*. Financial crises, mental illness, sudden tragedy, pandemics, natural disasters, and unemployment can test the faith of people today as much as persecution. James encourages the church today also to consider these trials as an opportunity for spiritual growth (1:2-4) and to find hope in God's promise to those who love him (1:12).

New Birth and Right Living

The Letter of James is a favorite of many Christians because of its down-to-earth, practical instructions on how to live. It would be inaccurate to see it as *only* about ethics, however. Despite accusations that it is theologically light and that James does nothing but scold his readers, the letter is firmly anchored in theological claims shared by the rest of the New Testament.

One of the key verses in the letter to do that is James 1:18. This verse, along with verse 17, speaks declaratively about the character and work of God in humanity. It professes that God is working out God's purposes, consistent with God's generous and faithful character. God's purpose includes giving birth to new creatures, *a kind of first fruits* of what God is doing with all creation. This happens through God's *word of truth*, which is implanted in us and has the power to save (1:21). James's exhortations to faithful living emerge from this profound truth.

Although James does not explicitly speak of this birth as new birth in *Christ* through *the word of truth*, the gospel, when one reads these words canonically or in the context of the rest of the letter, it not difficult to understand them as such. This is certainly how Anabaptist writers understood James 1:18, which—together with texts such as John 3:3, 5 and 1 Peter 1:3, 23—figures prominently in early Anabaptist writings about the new birth. References to James 1:18 appear in discussions of baptism, free will, sanctification, and the nature of the church. For Anabaptists, the conviction that people are justified by grace through faith was a given, as was the atoning significance of the death and resurrection of Jesus. In this, they were in full agreement with Protestant Reformers.

However, writers such as Balthasar Hubmaier, Dirk Philips, and Menno Simons were adamant that the work of justification was inseparable from sanctification, although they did not always use those words. Instead, they spoke more often about new birth and regeneration. God's saving action in Jesus Christ wrought a real change in people. That is, justification was not a "legal fiction" but had to result in a transformed life to be genuine. As Jennifer Powell McNutt states, "Overall, an Anabaptist emphasis on the necessity of rebirth was not merely a defining characteristic of belief but also a pointed critique of a perceived Protestant over-emphasis on *sola fide*" (166).

Anabaptist writers stressed that rebirth does not happen through human volition but is the work of God through the *word of truth*, always understood to be the good news of Jesus. For example, Dirk Philips writes, "We are also not born anew out of flesh and blood, nor out of any perishable things, but just as Peter, . . . and James . . . testify, . . . out of the Word of the living God" (Philips, Dyck, Keeney, and Beachy: 358). He then goes on to say the Word of God consists of the law and the gospel, and the gospel is "the word of grace, the joyful message of Christ Jesus" (359).

> The Holy Spirit also plays an essential role in new birth and ongoing growth in discipleship. As Dirk Philips stated in his argument against infant baptism, "But the new birth which takes place out of God the heavenly Father through Jesus Christ, as a transformation and renewal of persons through the Holy Spirit, applies to those who understand. . . . These must be washed through the bath of the new birth in the Word and be transformed through the renewal of the Holy Spirit, James 1:18" (Philips, Dyck, Keeney, and Beachy: 299).

For Hubmaier, the free will given by God at creation was destroyed in the fall, but something of God's Spirit remains in people. Through the new birth in Christ, the will is again freed to choose what is good and do what is right. He quotes James 1:18 in his work "On the Freedom of the Will" (1527):

> If we would again be free in the spirit, be healed in the soul, and also that this Fall be unharmful to us in the flesh, then such must, must, must take place through a new birth, as Christ himself says, or we will not enter into the kingdom of God. Now God, however, as James writes, gives birth to us willingly with the Word of his power, so that we become a new a [*sic*] beginning of his creatures, James 1:18. (Hubmaier, Pipkin, and Yoder: 445)

James 1:18 was significant in Anabaptist writings on ecclesiology and the pure church. In his "Reply to Gellius Faber," Menno Simons writes, "The bride of Christ, namely, the church, can bring forth no true children but from the legitimate seed of Christ, that is, from the unadulterated and rightly preached Word, through the Holy Spirit, and conceived in the heart of the believers. . . . James says, 'Of his own will he begot us with the word of truth'" (*CWMS*: 737; see also Dirk Philips, "The Congregation of God," in Philips, Dyck, Keeney, and Beachey: 357). From this small sampling of texts, it is evident that James 1:18 provided significant support for early

Anabaptist theology about the work of God in humanity and the new birth, which must bear fruit in righteous living.

What about in contemporary Anabaptist/Mennonite theology? While a thorough study of this question is impossible here, some general (and tentative) observations may be in order. First, contemporary Mennonite theologians are not as thoroughly saturated in Scripture as their Anabaptist forebears were: one does not find modern theological writings peppered with Scripture references. Second, the Letter of James is used more often as a source of practical moral wisdom rather than mined for its theological insights. Third, language of "new birth" is not prominent in Anabaptist and Mennonite theological discussion of the last generation. When it does appear, James 1:18 is not one of the go-to texts.

At the same time, James 1:18 is not entirely absent from current Anabaptist Mennonite theological writing. One significant work that does pay attention to "new birth" and refers to James 1:18 is *A Contemporary Anabaptist Theology*, by Thomas N. Finger (2004: 150, 176). He maintains that "rebirth or new birth . . . was the Anabaptists' chief metaphor for salvation" and arose from the preaching of the Word (176). It is still key to understanding Anabaptist soteriology today. "Ontological transformation" in both personal and communal life happens by divine initiative and is inseparable from a changed life and discipleship. For Finger, this way of understanding salvation circumvents some of the intractable debates about justification and sanctification in Protestant and Catholic theology. (For an accessible discussion of these different understandings of salvation with implications for congregational life, see Finger 2006: 22–30). Language of "new birth" also appears in contemporary denominational confessions of faith, but James 1:18 is not referenced (e.g., "Salvation" in *Confession of Faith in a Mennonite Perspective* [1995]).

In a letter that is heavy on oughts and shoulds, James 1:18 reminds the church today, as it did in the first century and the sixteenth century, that faithful Christian discipleship begins with the transforming initiative of God through the Word of truth.

James 1:19-27

Hearing, Speaking, and Doing

PREVIEW

Words can bring people closer. Hateful and harmful words can drive people apart. In short, words *do* things.

Throughout the Bible, God's word also *does* things. It does not return to God empty but accomplishes God's purposes (Ps 29:3-9; Isa 55:11). James too presents God's word as active and effective. After telling his readers that they have been born of God through *the word of truth* (1:18), he goes on to spin out the implications. God's word is *implanted* in God's people and saves (v. 21). When it is heard, it must bear fruit in action (v. 22). One of those actions is human speech. When human words are spoken hastily and in anger, they do not accomplish God's purposes (vv. 19, 26). The topic of speech is important in the letter and recurs often, most forcefully and colorfully in the excursus on the tongue in 3:1-12. Although the subject of words (divine and human) is what hooks this section to the previous one, in 1:19-27 James also introduces several other important topics that will reverberate throughout the rest of the letter: the law, hearing and doing, righteousness, humility (or meekness), and caring for the vulnerable.

In this unit, verse 19 functions loosely as an organizing agenda for the rest of the chapter. It is like a braid of three interwoven strands that get teased apart and combed out in the following verses:

1. In verses 20-21 James picks up the strand about anger, pointing out its ineffectiveness for furthering God's purposes and presenting an alternative.
2. In verses 22-25 he teases out the implications of genuine "hearing" that results in "doing."
3. Finally, in verses 26-27 he ties the strand of careful speech to proper devotion to God and love of neighbor.

The first two strands contain the word *logos* (word), referring to the word of God, and in the third, James raises the issue of human words, that is, controlling the tongue. In this unit, as in 1:2-18, James is not knitting together a tight argument but loosely connecting wisps of ideas to be developed later. In the end, all these wisps and strands add up to a substantial vision for what a Christian community looks like, a community that takes both its Jewish heritage and the teachings of Jesus with utmost seriousness.

OUTLINE

Behavior That Does and Does Not Serve God's Righteousness, 1:19-21
Being Doers of the Word and Not Hearers Only, 1:22-25
True Religion, Evident in Speech and Action, 1:26-27

EXPLANATORY NOTES

Behavior That Does and Does Not Serve God's Righteousness 1:19-21

Although it is possible to take the first clause of verse 19 as concluding the previous paragraph (*You [already] know this, my beloved brothers and sisters*), most English translations rightly render it as a command introducing what follows: *Understand this, my beloved brothers and sisters: be quick to listen. . .* (AT). The main reason is that almost every other occurrence of the vocative *brothers and sisters* in the letter introduces an imperative (as here) or a rhetorical question, rather than looking back. The clause thus parallels the opening clause of the previous section: *Consider it all joy, my brothers and sisters . . .* (v. 2). Both sections begin with an exhortation to perceive what follows in a particular way: *Consider . . .* (vv. 2-18) and *Understand . . .* (vv. 19-27).

The three directives in verse 19 are pithy, memorable, and interconnected: *Be quick to listen, slow to speak, slow to anger.* People who get angry quickly often speak too hastily, without listening to another's perspective. Those who are poor listeners often talk a lot themselves. And because they do not listen well, they jump into anger quickly. This is commonsense wisdom that, not surprisingly, is typical of both ancient Greek and Jewish literature. Here are a few parallels from Jewish wisdom literature:

- "When words are many, transgression is not lacking, but the prudent are restrained in speech." (Prov 10:19)
- "A soft answer turns away wrath, but a harsh word stirs up anger." (Prov 15:1)
- "Do not be quick to anger, for anger lodges in the bosom of fools." (Eccl 7:9)
- "Be quick to hear, but utter a reply patiently. If you understand, answer your neighbor; but if not, put your hand over your mouth." (Sir 5:11-12)

The words *quick* and *slow* in verse 19 are counterintuitive and give pause for thought. For one thing, listening is not a "quick" activity. To listen carefully, both to the spoken words and to what is being said underneath the words, requires patience and time. Listening well requires turning off the internal voice that quickly wants to formulate a rebuttal or dish out advice. If one wants to listen "quickly," one needs to be slow to speak. Of course, James is not saying one should never speak. He himself is a teacher who is "speaking" to the church. *Be slow to speak* is not an excuse to be silent in the face of injustice, to be hesitant about speaking truth to power, or to be limp in giving verbal testimony to one's faith. It is an admonition to pause and think carefully about what one wishes to say. For James, a key reason for hitting pause before one speaks is the tangled relationship between speech and anger. As a result, the final phrase in his sequence is *be slow to anger*.

Interestingly, James doesn't say, "Do not get angry." Such would be an impossibility, since anger is an emotion that comes unbidden. Rather, to be *slow to anger* means refusing to fuel anger with simmering resentment or bitterness. It also means choosing carefully what to do with anger so that it doesn't flame out in destructive words and actions. James's words call to mind Jesus' teachings in the Sermon on the Mount, that keeping the commandment "You shall not murder" is insufficient. Rather, anyone who is even angry with a brother or sister will be liable to judgment, and anyone who insults someone or calls someone "fool" will likewise be held accountable (Matt 5:21-22). Paul also recognizes the dangers of becoming angry: "Be angry, but do not sin; . . . and do not make room for the devil" (Eph 4:26-27). The problem with human anger is that even if it seems justifiable, it is so easily warped by sin, both in what motivates it (selfishness, greed, envy) and in how it is expressed (unkindness, violence). According to James, *human anger does not produce God's righteousness* (v. 20).

The language of "righteousness" is pervasive in the Bible. Its use is rich and diverse, and the meaning of phrases such as *the righteousness of God* cannot be packaged into a tidy theological concept. In each case, context is vital for understanding (Johnson 1995: 200). The Greek word for "righteousness" is *dikaiosynē* and can also be translated "justice." The verb form (*dikaioō*), with God as subject, refers to God's "right-making" (justifying) activity or God's saving action. It is used this way in 2:21-24, when James speaks about Abraham being *justified* (by God) when he demonstrated his faith in action.

Both humans and God can be characterized as "righteous" or possessing "righteousness" (1:20; 2:23; 5:16), although only God is truly righteous. The noun "righteousness" also appears in 3:18, where it refers to the fruit that results from sowing peace and the gift of wisdom from above. Righteousness (and cognate words) in James is thus not primarily an abstract quality of God but has to do with God's action on behalf of people (declares them righteous) or with how people act (with righteousness). In 1:20, James urges his readers to be *slow to anger* because their *anger does not produce God's righteousness.*

The Greek word that the NRSVue translates "produce" is literally "to work," the same word that appears in 2:9, "to work (commit) sin," and it is related to the word "works," which appears often in 2:14-26. Just as favoritism "works" sin, so also acting out of anger does not "work" the righteousness that comes from and characterizes God. In short, human anger is not part of God's "right-making" activity and cannot bring about the justice and the right relationships that God desires and is constantly working toward.

The Letter of James is addressed to people who are enduring trials and being oppressed by the rich. It would be understandable if their suffering erupted in anger against their oppressors and the injustices they were experiencing. Perhaps righteous anger could even assist God in raising up the lowly and bringing low the rich. Perhaps railing against or cursing or even using violence against the unjust oppressor would be justified under the circumstances.

James urges caution: *Be slow to anger*. In the heat of anger, people often act rashly to right the perceived wrong and end up escalating the violence and the injustice. In response to such an instinctive human desire to implement God's justice with anger, James says, "No, that is not how God's justice will come about."

We must be careful to attend to what James is and is not saying. Never once in the letter does James advocate passivity or indifference toward injustice. Faith in a God who is righteous and judges evil demands active participation. *Faith without works is dead*, James vehemently emphasizes in 2:14-26. Followers of Jesus must care for the poor and vulnerable (1:27; 2:15-16), harvest *righteousness* by sowing *peace* (3:18), and *resist the devil* (4:7). At the same time, participation in God's right-making activity will not be well-served by impetuous anger and hastily spoken words. *Be quick to listen, slow to speak, slow to anger, for human anger does not produce God's righteousness* (1:19-20).

Verse 21 begins with the conjunction *therefore* or *for this reason*, indicating that what follows is the logical consequence of what was just said. Instead of looking outward at what is causing anger, they should look at themselves. Because anger does not produce God's righteousness, followers of Jesus should instead do two things. The first requires letting go of something negative (*rid yourselves of*), and the second involves acquiring something positive (*welcome*).

The word translated *rid yourselves of* can mean literally to take off one's clothes, but in the New Testament it is more often used figuratively for stripping off old vices (Rom 13:12; Col 3:8-10; 1 Pet 2:1). What does James say his beloved fellow believers should strip off? As is typical of his style, James heaps up expressive and sometimes unusual words, which English translations variously strive to capture: *all sordidness and rank growth of wickedness* (1:21 NRSVue); *all moral filth and the evil that is so prevalent* (NIV); *all spoiled virtue and cancerous evil* (Message); *every evil thing and every kind of wrong* (NCV). The Greek noun for *sordidness* or *filth* is found only here in the New Testament, but in 2:2 James uses the adjective to describe a poor man's dirty clothing. Perhaps the image of stripping off soiled farm clothes after a day of mucking out the barns is appropriate for the kind of moral housecleaning that James has in mind.

The Greek word for *wickedness* (NRSVue) or *evil* (NIV) is frequently found in lists of vices, along with anger, slander, and envy, and is sometimes rendered "malice" (Rom 1:29; 1 Cor 5:8; Eph 4:31; Titus 3:3). In this context, James seems to be referring not so much to wickedness in general as to behavior that overflows from destructive anger. Anger that stains relationships with malice and abusive language does not help bring about the justice God desires. Followers of Jesus must strip off all such "dirty attire" and do some ethical laundry.

Having gotten rid of the negative, they should receive the positive: *Welcome with meekness the implanted word that has the power to save your souls* (v. 21b). This stance of gentleness and open receptivity to God's word is the opposite of an attitude of anger and malice. Such meekness is not weakness nor helpless resignation to injustice. Rather, it is willingness to listen and to be guided by God's agenda for righteousness. It is the posture of submission to God, which James will speak about in 4:7-10. God's word has no chance to be embedded in people when their lives are glutted with self-serving words, so they must be *quick to listen* and *slow to speak* (v. 19).

Although "stripping off sordidness" evokes laundry imagery, the phrase *implanted word* suggests the sowing of seed—even seed *that has the power to save your souls.* Readers today might recall Jesus' parable of the sower, in which the seed is explicitly identified as "the word of the kingdom" (Matt 13:19) or "the word of God" (Luke 8:11). The phrase *implanted word* also recalls James 1:18, which speaks of *the word of truth* by which God *gave birth to us,* forming us into the *first fruits of his creatures.* This is one and the same "word," the *implanted word* and the *word of truth,* the word that gives birth and the word that is able to save. Rejecting dangerous anger and welcoming God's word humbly opens oneself to God's life-giving power.

The phrase *save your souls,* in modern religious language, might sound exclusively spiritual and nonphysical. However, the Greek word *psychē* refers to the whole self, body and spirit, and could be translated "life" (cf. John 10:11). To be "saved" in James encompasses deliverance from sin, sickness, and death (1:15; 5:15-20) and the gift of life, both now and especially in the future age (1:12; 2:5).

If James's audience consisted mostly or entirely of Jewish believers, as seems likely, it might seem strange that James would exhort them to get rid of filth and malice and receive God's life-saving word. As we have noticed, James often uses vivid or extreme language for emphasis: verse 21 is another example of this dramatic style. If the churches to which he wrote were experiencing stress and disharmony and failing to live according to their identity as followers of Jesus, perhaps they needed to hear things said in a way that caught their attention. Perhaps James's words reflect that the Christian life is a dynamic process, not a static event. Believers in every age should periodically clean house (get rid of filth and malice) and with openness and humility receive afresh God's powerful, transforming word. God's work in us is never finished.

Being Doers of the Word and Not Hearers Only 1:22-25

The triad of advice introducing this section began with *Be quick to listen* (1:19). In 1:22-25 James picks up that thread about hearing. Now we learn that the listening James has in mind is about more than sounds entering the ears, about more than hearing. To listen means allowing the words to take root and have an impact on behavior. In verse 19, then, James was critical of acting and speaking without listening. Now he is critical of listening without acting. In this subunit, James introduces the important theme of putting faith into action, a topic he will develop further in 2:14-26. As happens frequently in this letter, James echoes the teaching of Jesus, recasting it in his own words (Matt 7:21-27; Luke 11:28). Verses 22-25 constitute a simple chiasm that emphasizes the importance of "hearing" and "doing" (McKnight: 146):

- Be *doers* of the word and not only self-deceived *hearers* (v. 22)
  - Mirror illustration (vv. 23-24)
- Be not forgetful *hearers* but be *doers* of work (v. 25)

The repetition of words, not only in verses 22 and 25 but also in verse 23, reinforces the importance of hearing and doing in James's message. As David Gowler states, "'Become doers of the word' is the heart of James's message, and much of the letter elaborates this central theme" (128).

In verse 22 James says that people who hear God's word without acting on it deceive themselves. The matter of being deceived or led astray comes up more than once in the letter. In fact, the first chapter contains three different Greek words for "deceive" (vv. 16, 22, 26). Perhaps this has something to do with being double-minded and unstable (1:8), making friends with the world instead of cultivating friendship with God (4:4, 8).

In what way, though, is not acting on what one hears a form of self-deception? About what is such a person being deceived? In verse 25 James says that people who gaze into, listen to, and act on God's word will be blessed. They do not immediately forget who they are. Conversely, those who hear without doing are people who look into God's word but on turning away immediately forget their identity as God's people. They are deluded about how the "word" is working in them, believing they are acting as "first fruits" of God's new creation when actually they are not. They think their anger might bring about God's justice when it actually does not. They are deceived about their salvation and their ethical behavior.

In verses 23-25 we find a series of contrasting parallels. The second column describes those who will experience God's blessing:

hearing and not acting	hearing and acting
looking at one's own reflection in a mirror	looking into the perfect law of freedom
looking into the mirror and immediately leaving	peering intently into the law and remaining
forgetting what the mirror shows and doing nothing	not forgetting what the law shows and acting on it

James uses one of his typically memorable similes to characterize the person who hears and does not act. In the Greek it reads like a mini-story about a man who looked into a mirror and forgot what he looked like after he left. Modern translations, however, tend to render it in more inclusive and general language: *They look at themselves and . . . forget what they were like.* Mirrors in the ancient world were usually made of polished metal (such as copper, tin, or an alloy), making the reflection somewhat distorted or unclear, unlike the sharp images that mirrors reflect today. James's point, however, is not the unclarity of the image (as in 1 Cor 13:12) but the fleeting reflection and whether it has any impact.

As with most metaphors, the analogy is not exact. And since this is not an allegory, it should not be pressed too hard. Some commentators argue that the image in the mirror (the Greek in v. 23 is lit. "face of origin/birth") refers to the "image of God" or, contrastingly, to one's sinful human nature. Both these interpretations seem to read too much into the image. Likely the phrase "the face of origin/birth" refers simply to one's "natural appearance"—one's "birth face," so to speak (so Johnson 1995: 207; McCartney 2009: 121).

Because mirrors are everywhere today, it is hard to imagine we could ever forget what we look like or that anyone would want to, given our culture's fixation on physical appearance. In the ancient world, not everyone had mirrors, and people did not go around glancing in mirrors to check their appearance. Still, it seems a little absurd to think that anyone who saw their reflection would, upon walking away, immediately forget what they looked like. James's metaphor, then, seems rather overstated. But therein also lies its impact. To hear words of truth, words that give life and save, and not be profoundly impacted, such that one's actions and way of life change, is altogether ludicrous.

In using the analogy of the mirror, James is drawing on a common trope in ancient Greek literature, particularly in moral instruction (Johnson 2004c). In this literature the mirror is more than just a means for inspecting one's physical appearance; it is a metaphor about moral self-improvement. Just as a mirror can give knowledge about a person's looks, so also contemplating a specific teaching or observing a model can foster self-knowledge and prompt an attentive learner to improve their character. The following excerpt from Plutarch's "On Listening to Lectures 8" (*Moralia* 42A–B) is only one of many examples (quoted in Johnson 2004c: 175):

> As a matter of course, when he [a student] rises to leave the barber's shop, he stands by the mirror and feels his head, examining the cut of his hair and the difference made by its trimming; so on his way home from a lecture or an academic exercise, it would be a shame not to direct his gaze forthwith upon himself and to note carefully his own spirit, whether it has put from it any of its encumbrances and superfluities, and has become lighter and more cheerful.

The metaphor is not as common in contemporary Jewish literature, but the idea would nevertheless have been familiar to James's readers. One finds it, for example in Wisdom of Solomon 7:26, where wisdom is a mirror reflecting God's goodness. For James, however, the proper object of contemplation is not the self: it is not self-knowledge that leads to higher morality. Rather, it is *the perfect law, the law of liberty* (v. 25).

This phrase, *the perfect law . . . of liberty*, is one of the most important but difficult features of this text, and each word requires attention. The word *perfect* (*teleios*) appeared earlier in 1:4 and 17; it means "complete, whole, having integrity, mature." Since every good and *perfect gift is from above* (v. 17), it follows that the *the perfect law . . . of liberty* must be one of God's complete and perfect gifts.

This is the first of several references to the law in the letter (2:8-12; 4:11-12). Later James will refer to the law as *the royal law*

(2:8) and *the law of liberty* (2:12). What is this *perfect law of liberty* in 1:25? In light of the Jewish tone and theology of the letter and its implicit Jewish Christian audience (1:1), the phrase *law of liberty* must surely refer to the law of Israel—that is, the biblical Torah, which "gives expression to God's moral will for God's people" (Hartin 2009a: 111). This is confirmed if we look at how "law" (*nomos*) is used elsewhere in the letter. In 2:8-12 it includes the commandment *Love your neighbor as yourself* (Lev 19:18) and the Ten Commandments, and in 4:12 God is referred to as the one lawgiver. Although *the perfect law of liberty* (1:25) does not refer narrowly to the Old Testament law, as we will see shortly, it must at least encompass it.

James's positive view of the law is consistent with how the law is portrayed in the Old Testament and with how his fellow Jews would have viewed it. The law of the Lord is extolled as "perfect, reviving the soul," and God's ordinances are "true and righteous altogether" (Ps 19:7-10). Psalm 119 expresses the psalmist's love for the law, which is a source of freedom (vv. 44-45), delight (vv. 47, 92, 174), life (v. 93), and light (v. 130). Throughout the Old Testament and also in other Jewish writings, we find an emphasis not only on hearing but also on doing God's law (e.g., Deut 31:12; 1 Macc 2:67). Josephus reports, "For thou oughtest not only to read [the laws], but [also] chiefly to practice what they enjoin thee" (*Jewish Antiquities* 20.2.4).

James's positive perspective on the law also resonates with Jesus' words in the Sermon on the Mount: "Do not think that I have come to abolish the *Law* or the *Prophets*; I have come not to abolish but to fulfill. For truly I tell you, until heaven and earth pass away, not one letter, not one stroke of a letter, will pass from the law until all is accomplished" (Matt 5:17-18). Paul in Romans 2:13 comes close to James when he says, "For it is not the hearers of the law who are righteous in God's sight, but the doers of the law who will be justified." For Jews, the law was not an onerous burden but God's gracious provision for God's people, given that they might remain in covenant relationship with God. The Jewish followers of the Messiah Jesus would have had this perspective on the law as well.

But more needs to be said about James's understanding of the *perfect law of liberty*. At the beginning of this subunit, James was talking about "hearing and doing" *the word*. In verse 25, however, the ones who "hear and do" are those who look into the *law* and remain there. What then is the relationship between "the word" (*logos*, vv. 18, 21, 22, 23) and "the law" (*nomos*, v. 25)? Although not explicit, the logic of the text suggests that James equates the two. A look at the four occurrences of the noun "doer" in the letter supports this: *doers of the word* (1:22); *not a doer but a hearer of the word* (1:23); *doer of work* (*doers who act*, 1:25 NRSVue); *doer of the law* (4:11). For Jewish Christians, who understood the Torah as the word of God to be obeyed and delighted in, this association of "word" and "law" would have been natural. If the two words function synonymously, however, the *perfect law of liberty* must encompass more than the Jewish Torah. Earlier we suggested that the *word of truth* is the good news of Jesus. By this *word*, God gave us birth, making us harbingers of God's new creation (v. 18), and this *word* implanted in us has the power to *save our souls* (v. 21).

For James and his primarily Jewish Christian audience, the word of God revealed in Torah and the word of God revealed in Jesus were part of one ongoing revelation of the will of God. The letter was probably written well before there was a sharp division between Jews and Christians and before Christianity became predominantly Gentile. James's addressees were Jews who believed the Messiah had come. God's sending of the Messiah to save them was consistent with God's gracious gift of the law, God's powerful word that made things happen, and God's liberating deeds in their past. For James and his community, Jesus did not come to abolish the law but to fulfill it (cf. Matt 5:17-20), so it is *Jesus'* interpretation of the law that is authoritative.

In this sense the law is "perfect" or "complete," for it has reached its *telos* (goal or completion) in Christ. This law is God's new covenant, which has been written on their hearts (Jer 31:31-34; Ezek 36:26-27), what James calls the *word of truth* implanted in them. Although the Jewish believers to whom James wrote may have continued various Jewish ritual practices of their faith (we have no way of knowing), the letter itself does not refer to the cultic laws but focuses entirely on moral and ethical matters of the law. The importance of the command *Love your neighbor* in the letter further hints that James is viewing the law through the lens of Jesus' teaching, which upholds love of God and neighbor as the most important commandments, a summary of the whole law (Mark 12:28-34; cf. Rom 13:8-10; Gal 5:14). In reading James on the "law," then, we ought not make a sharp distinction between the Torah, Jesus' teachings, and the liberating word about Jesus.

This law is the *law of liberty*, a law characterized by freedom and giving freedom. A popular perception today is that laws restrict freedom because they force people to do and not do certain things.

In reality, every society needs some rules (whether written or unwritten) to order life and to enable people to live together. Traffic laws, for example, give people the "freedom" to drive without getting ensnared in traffic jams and guard against accidents. Some scholars want to link James's *law of liberty* with Greek Stoic philosophy, which says that obeying the laws of nature, or the rule of reason, is what makes one truly free. However, James is solidly rooted in the soil of Jewish Christianity: Jewish influence is much more significant for shaping his view of the law than is Greek philosophy. In the Jewish perspective, living in accord with God's law gives one freedom. The first-century Hellenistic Jewish philosopher Philo wrote, "All whose life is regulated by law are free" (*Every Good Person Is Free* 45). For first-century Jewish Christians, Jesus the Messiah fulfilled the law, liberating people from sin and evil and setting them free to serve God and neighbor.

Those who gaze into this *perfect law of liberty,* remain there, and allow it to transform their actions *will be blessed* (v. 25). This is what James is exhorting his audience to do when he says, *Be doers of the word and not merely hearers, who deceive themselves* (1:22). The NRSVue renders the Greek in verse 25 *doers who act*, but literally the text says *doers of work*, which makes the connection to James's later words about faith and works more obvious (2:14, 17, 24; 3:13). The blessing is eschatological—like the *crown of life* given to those who endure trials (v. 12)—but it is not solely future, for God's blessing on God's faithful people begins already *in their doing* (v. 25). The kind of "work" James has in mind will become evident in what follows. It includes compassion and mercy to the vulnerable, love of neighbor, generosity to the poor, and control of one's speech. In this particular "doing of work," followers of Jesus Messiah will experience the blessing of God, both now and in the last day. Believers who do not allow the implanted word to bear fruit in such deeds, who do not live the saving word they have heard, run the risk of forgetting who they are: the redeemed children of God. They are like people who look in a mirror and forget what they look like when they walk away.

True Religion, Evident in Speech and Action 1:26-27

Although only loosely connected to the rest of the chapter, the last two verses function as both a conclusion and a transition to what follows. James identifies three crucial aspects of a vibrant, genuine faith, that is, true "religion": (1) control of one's speech; (2) care for the poor and vulnerable; and (3) not being tainted by the "world."

The first of these picks up the middle thread of the triad in verse 19 (*Be slow to speak*) while also introducing a major focus of concern in 3:1-12 (also 2:12-16; 4:11; 5:9, 12). The second picks up James's concern for the poor already mentioned in 1:9-11 but further developed in 2:1-7, 15-16; 5:1-6. The third topic indirectly relates to temptation and desires (1:14-16) yet also anticipates the antithesis between friendship with the world and friendship with God (3:13-18; 4:1-4). All three of these are integrally related not only to *hearing* the word but also *doing it*, a subject that James will address in 2:14-26 when talking about faith and works.

These verses address what it means to be "religious." Although the Bible is the book of a major world religion, the word itself is not found often in the Bible. In fact, the Greek adjective for "religious" (*thrēskos*, v. 26) is found only here in the New Testament. "Religion" could also be translated "piety" and "can be used positively and negatively depending upon the context" (Lockett 2007: 55). The adjective "religious" does not communicate well in modern society: it is often associated negatively with institutional or organized religion and specific doctrines and practices. To be "religious" can have negative connotations of shallow or inauthentic faith in contemporary North America, leading some people to claim they are "spiritual but not religious."

James's use of the word "religious" is more positive than this. "Religion" in 1:26-27 refers to a relationship with a divine being expressed in belief, worship, rituals, and service. Since James's context is Jewish-Christian, this relationship is specifically *with the God and Father* (v. 27 AT) of Israel, revealed in God's Messiah, the *Lord Jesus Christ of glory* (2:1 NRSV). Notably, although James no doubt assumes certain beliefs and rituals involved in this relationship, here he focuses on ethical behavior, perhaps because that is what he perceives to be lacking in his audience. In *these* verses, to be "religious" is not about going to a building to worship on a specific day of the week or believing certain doctrines or participating in traditional rituals or feeling something toward God. It is to live and act in a way that accords with God's will.

To make his point, James begins with an imagined possibility: *If any think they are religious . . .* This way of raising a problem, with a conditional sentence, is a stylistic technique that James uses frequently (1:5, 23; 2:2, 15; 3:2-3, 14; 5:19). Twice already in this chapter, James has talked about being deceived (vv. 16, 22). Those who give in to temptation, those who do not act on what they hear, and those who do not control their speech are all susceptible to thinking they are someone they are not. This fits with James's larger concern about integrity and not being double-minded. The religion of people who are self-deceived and talk indiscriminately is *worthless*, futile, or empty, says James (v. 26). The adjective used here sometimes appears in contexts of idol worship (e.g., Isa 2:20; Jer 8:19; 10:3; Acts 14:15; 1 Pet 1:18) and may seem exaggerated. Does failure to control our tongues really make worship of God as worthless as idol worship? As elsewhere, James uses sharp rhetoric to make his case that how we talk and what we say has everything to do with faith.

James introduced the matter of right speech with a positive command: *Be slow to speak* (1:19). Now he makes a similar point in negative terms: people are *not* religious if they cannot control their tongues, with "tongue" being a metonymy for speech in general and "bridle" a metonymy for control *[The Tongue, p. 370]*. (A metonymy is a figure of speech in which a related word or phrase is used in place of the actual name.) James uses the colorful image of putting a bit in a horse's mouth to control where it goes, an image to which he returns in 3:2-3. The subject of speech ethics surfaces repeatedly in this letter. This could be because the topic was popular in Jewish wisdom literature as well as in ancient Greek moral literature. Both Proverbs and Sirach, for example, contain many sayings about the wise controlling their tongues and the foolish speaking carelessly (Prov 29:20; Sir 4:29; 19:6-12; Eccl 5:2).

Greek writers also viewed brevity of speech as a virtue to be cultivated and silence as necessary for learning wisdom. As Luke Timothy Johnson says, "The ancient world agreed that the wise person was also taciturn. Silence was generally better, and always safer, than speech" (2004d: 155). James's interest in the topic is motivated by more than its popularity in contemporary literature, however, for it is one of the problems facing the churches to whom he writes. James's teaching about speech deals primarily with how it can and does negatively affect relationships in the community. Thus, James criticizes those who curse a brother or sister made in the image of God (3:9-12). Because they bless God, they may think they are religious, but their actions reveal how they are fooling themselves.

James also addresses other negative speech habits: complaining against others (5:9), boasting (3:14; 4:16), speaking untruthfully (3:14), swearing oaths (5:12), judging (4:11-12), and speaking without doing (2:15-16). All these failures to "bridle the tongue" create tears in the fabric of the community, which is already fragile because of the trials they are experiencing. Although most of James's words about speech are warnings, he ends the letter by encouraging several kinds of positive speech: praying for healing, singing, confessing, and forgiving sin (5:13-20).

When James turns to characterizing true religion, he uses adjectives often associated with cultic requirements of worship: *pure, undefiled,* and *unstained* (v. 27). Sacrifices to God in the Old Testament had to be pure and unblemished because God was holy, set apart, other. Likewise, those who entered the temple for worship had to meet the ritual requirements of the law. Although these aspects of Jewish ritual purity may have continued to be important for James and his Jewish Christian readers, in 1:27 he is talking not about the cultic aspect of worship but about moral behavior. The Septuagint and rest of the New Testament also use terms like *katharos* (pure) metaphorically for moral purity (Ps 51:10; Hab 1:13; Matt 5:8; 1 Pet 1:22) (Lockett 2007: 56). Service to and worship of God is *pure and undefiled* when it is oriented toward justice and mercy and away from selfish desires and greed. James does not list everything he could to describe ethical behavior that is pleasing to God but names two things that are especially pertinent for his audience. The first requires attentiveness to others, the second toward oneself.

First, faith communities that have an authentic relationship with God will *care for orphans and widows in their distress* (v. 27). The verb in this sentence means "to visit" someone with the intent of helping or bestowing care (BDAG 378). It is used often in the Septuagint for God "visiting" God's people to rescue them (e.g., Gen 21:1; Exod 3:16; Josh 8:10; 1 Sam 2:21; cf. Luke 1:68; 7:16; Johnson 1995: 212). James singles out widows and orphans because they were the most vulnerable in ancient, patriarchal societies, having no husband or father to protect or care for them. Because they were economically and socially disadvantaged, their chronic condition was one of *distress.*

This verse resonates with the Old Testament, where examples of God's compassion toward orphans and widows is ubiquitous (e.g., Deut 10:18; 24:17-22; Ps 146:9; Isa 1:17; Jer 22:3; Ezek 22:7; Zech 7:10). Psalm 68:5 speaks of God as the "Father of orphans and protector of widows." It is especially fitting, then, that James refers to God as "Father" in verse 27, reminding his audience that the orphans for whom they are to show compassion have the same divine Parent as they.

Although James does not make this explicit, in caring for *orphans and widows*, followers of Jesus are acting in the character of God the heavenly Parent. A verse in the Jewish writing Sirach captures well what is only implicit in James: "Be a father to orphans, and be like a husband to their mother; you will then be like a son of the Most High" (4:10). Of course, James's point here is not care for widows and orphans *only*, but also any who are dispossessed and vulnerable. Since widows and orphans may no longer be the most vulnerable in society, "religious" readers of James might be prompted to ask who the equivalent are today.

James also does not specify what constitutes "care" for such vulnerable people. As in James's day, it might include providing for their physical needs, but in the twenty-first century, care that embodies "true religion" might involve providing trauma healing to former child soldiers, working to change policies that create "widows and orphans," or offering resources and time to new immigrants and refugees.

Second, people whose religion is *pure and undefiled* will keep themselves *unstained by the world*. By this, James does not mean believers should become recluses or ascetics. Doing this would make it impossible to care for those who have been stained by that same world's injustice and pain. In his use of "world" and his exhortation to be different from society, James echoes other New Testament writings, especially the Gospel of John (e.g., 17:14-18).

We catch a sense of what James means by "world" (*kosmos*) by looking at his other main use of the word in 4:4, where friendship with the world is equivalent to enmity toward God. By "world," James does not mean the material as opposed to the spiritual or the human as opposed to the divine. Rather, the "world" is that which is incompatible with God and God's way of doing things. As Darian Lockett has argued, it refers to a broad cultural value system or worldview (2007: 58–59). The "world" tempts people to say, do, and be things that run counter to their identity as followers of Jesus. The "world" is the human context that is characterized by discord and enmity, cravings and coveting, selfishness and greed (4:1-4). Although James does not refer to the "world" in 3:13-18, those verses describe wisdom from above as opposed to earthly wisdom. The latter could also be called the wisdom of the "world" since it has the same qualities of envy, selfish ambition, falsehood, and so on. *To keep oneself unstained by the world* is related to (but not synonymous with) being "perfect" or, rather, having integrity and being whole (*teleios*, 1:4). To be *unstained by the world* is to refrain from being double-minded (1:8; 4:8). It is not trying to be friends with God and with the world at the same time.

Just as James does not spell out what it means to care for orphans and widows, neither does he give instructions on *how* to keep oneself from being corrupted by the values of the world. In a sense, the whole letter is an attempt to address that question. A major theme in the letter is the two ways that lie before his readers: friendship with God or friendship with the world. James persistently nudges his readers toward being friends of God, and he does so by pointing them back toward the will of God as expressed in Scripture (especially Torah) and in the teachings of Jesus. Although he never actually says this, perhaps his answer to the question of how to keep oneself "unstained by the world" would be to gaze into that mirror, the will of God. In the reflection one would come to see oneself as a member of the family of God, living in relationship with God and community.

The two things James identifies as authentic religion are only representative, of course, and prompt further reflection on what pleases God and what it means not only to think of oneself as devout but actually *be* devout. This is true not only for the individual believer but also for the church. James 1:26-27 suggests that a life of genuine faith is attentive both to the needs of others and to one's own holiness. It includes acts of compassion and mercy to others as well as resistance to greed and selfishness in oneself. The two are closely interrelated, and each serves as a corrective to an unbalanced focus on one at the expense of the other.

In the rest of the letter, James further addresses the topics he has raised in the introductory chapter. Always the focus will be on authentic faith in *God and the Lord Jesus Christ* (1:1), lived out in community, in the context of a world animated by different values and commitments.

THE TEXT IN BIBLICAL CONTEXT

Human Anger in the Bible

Anger is as common in the Bible as it is in our time. Hebrew and Greek words for anger appear hundreds of times, and anger is often evident even when not explicitly named. Although many of the occurrences of "wrath" or "anger" refer to God's response to sin, God is foremost "merciful and gracious, slow to anger, and abounding in steadfast love" (Exod 34:6). We will focus here on human anger, however, since that is James's concern.

The Bible recognizes anger as part of human nature, "a natural response on the part of people who feel wronged" (Goldingay: 156). In the Old Testament, people get angry both when they feel personally wronged and when other people or God are wronged. Examples of times when human anger is described in neutral terms or when it seems to be a positive response to wrongdoing include the following. Moses' anger "burns hot" when he finds God's people dancing around the golden calf (Exod 32:19). David gets angry at the greedy man in Nathan's fable, oblivious to the fact that he himself is that rich man (2 Sam 12:5). Jonathan is angry at Saul's jealous hostility toward David (1 Sam 20:34). Dinah's brothers are furious when they hear that Hamor has raped her, although their anger is likely motivated more by a sense of their own honor being violated than by compassion for their sister (Gen 34:7). Nehemiah gets angry when he hears about the injustices against people in the community (Neh 5:6).

Although in many of these circumstances the anger seems justified, the Old Testament also makes clear how dangerous anger is. Even when anger is understandable, the outworking of that anger often leads to greater harm and even violence. Esau is understandably angry at Jacob for stealing his birthright, but his anger prompts a desire to kill his brother (Gen 27:41, 45). Moses' anger at the people of Israel results in him breaking the stone tablets inscribed with God's words and inciting the Levites to fratricide (Exod 32:19-29). Although Dinah's brothers are justifiably angry about the rape of their sister, they indiscriminately kill all the men of Shechem, a degree of violence that Jacob condemns on his deathbed (Gen 49:5-7; cf. 34:30). Saul's jealous anger at David destroys relationships (1 Sam 20:30-34), and Balaam unreasonably beats his donkey out of anger (Num 22:27). Proverbs consistently associates anger with folly and emphasizes its destructive effects (e.g., Prov 14:17; 15:18; 22:24-25; 29:22). Psalm 37:7-9 eloquently counsels forbearance, even in the face of wrongdoing, and the forsaking of anger, which can only lead to more evil. The prophets condemn kings who rule with anger (Isa 14:5-6; Amos 1:11). Although people do get angry in the Old Testament, anger is dangerous because of what it can lead to.

The New Testament continues this critical trajectory on human anger. No text explicitly commends anger and many verses outright warn against it (see below on whether Eph 4:26 is an exception). (I am indebted to the work of Gibbs 2015 for what follows.) Herod the Great slaughters the children of Bethlehem out of anger

(Matt 2:16); the people of Nazareth are filled with rage and want to hurl Jesus off a cliff (Luke 4:28-29); the Sanhedrin is enraged at the preaching of the apostles and seeks to kill them (Acts 5:33; 7:54); and the Ephesians attack Paul because his message threatens their economy (Acts 19:28). When the disciples of Jesus get indignant, it always reflects their selfishness, their concern for status, or their failure to understand Jesus (Matt 20:24-28; Mark 14:4).

Many of the New Testament teachings portray anger as so dangerous that it leads to sin and is even equated with sin (Gibbs 2015). We might reasonably want to differentiate between the emotion of anger and what one does with it, but the New Testament does not seem to make such a distinction explicit. The apostle Paul lists anger among the vices that people redeemed in Christ must eliminate (2 Cor 12:20; Gal 5:20; Eph 4:31).

In the Sermon on the Mount, Jesus warns that those who get angry are as liable to eschatological judgment as those who murder (Matt 5:21-22):

> You have heard that it was said to those of ancient times, "You shall not murder"; and "whoever murders shall be liable to judgment." But I say to you that if you are angry with a brother or sister, you will be liable to judgment; and if you insult a brother or sister, you will be liable to the council; and if you say, "You fool," you will be liable to the hell of fire.

With these words Jesus intensifies the prohibition against murder by including matters of the heart that lead to killing. Whatever disrupts right relationships with a brother or sister is wrong, whether it be murder or anger or harsh words. The two illustrations in 5:23-26 make the point that disciples must take initiative to repair broken relationships as quickly as possible. The categorical nature of Jesus' words here has troubled interpreters throughout history. That at least one scribe added the phrase "without cause" after "if you are angry with a brother or sister" indicates the church's discomfort with prohibiting *all* anger.

Ephesians 4:26, "Be angry but do not sin; do not let the sun go down on your anger," quoting Psalm 4:4, seems to leave space for human anger if it does not lead to sin. However, the verb should probably be taken as a concessive rather than an imperative: "*Even though* you get angry, do not sin." Anger is dangerous precisely because it easily provokes harsh judgment, unkind speech, vengeful actions, or even violence. Not letting the sun go down on one's anger, similar to the illustrations in Matthew 5:23-26, suggests that one should not let anger fester and grow. Broken relationships should be quickly repaired. Many of those who have noted that *Be slow to anger* (James 1:19) does not prohibit all anger conveniently disregard the subsequent forthright assertion: *Human anger does not produce God's righteousness.*

People sometimes use the fact that Jesus and Paul got angry as justification for what they consider "righteous" anger. Paul certainly expressed anger toward those demanding circumcision for Gentile believers in Galatia (Gal 3:1-5; 5:12), but we do not know the outcome of his letter and whether God's righteousness might have been better served by a less caustic response. According to the Gospels, Jesus got angry at the religious leaders (Mark 3:5; Matt 23), and many people think Jesus' clearing of the temple was a display of violent anger (Mark 11:15-18 and parallels; John 2:13-17). However, Jesus' temple cleansing is more likely a prophetic sign-act against the temple and its abuses than a violent rampage (see Yoder Neufeld 2011: 57–72). Moreover, since Jesus was always fully aligned with *the righteousness of God* and humans are not, using Jesus to prop up one's own potentially flawed actions seems dubious at best.

From a biblical perspective, then, although human anger is understandable in situations of injustice, it is dangerous. It easily leads to sin rather than furthering the righteousness (or justice) of God. Such a conclusion does not address the many pastoral and practical questions that arise, and drawing out the implications requires nuance. Modern readers know that denying or repressing anger can be as harmful as reacting with anger and may wonder if the energy behind anger against injustice can be harnessed for good. These questions will be explored further below (in TLC).

The World

Some verses in the Bible, such as James 1:27, give the impression that the world is inherently evil and that one should stay as separate from the world as possible. This has led some Christians to choose a radically ascetic lifestyle or to withdraw from society. The Bible is much more nuanced in how it represents "the world" than such impressions warrant, however.

The Greek word *kosmos* (world, universe) does not have an equivalent in the Hebrew Bible. In fact, the Old Testament "lacks the Gk. concept of the cosmos. It never regards the world as an independent entity in itself, but always in its relation to God, the Creator" (*NIDNTTE* 2:732). In the Septuagint, *kosmos* has the sense of "world" only in the Apocrypha (e.g., Wisd of Sol 2:24; 2 Macc 13:14). In contrast, the word *kosmos* occurs some 186 times in the New Testament, over half of which occur in the Johannine literature.

Both the Old and the New Testament view the earth and its people as created by God and good. The Bible is not world-denying in the sense that physical creation is inherently corrupt, as some ancient Greeks thought. Frequently when the New Testament refers to the "world" (*kosmos*), it has a neutral sense and simply means the universe, the created earth, or the inhabited world. For example, "the God who made the world and everything in it" (Acts 17:24; cf. John 1:10b; Rom 1:20) or "before (or from) the foundation of the world" (Luke 11:50; John 17:24; Eph 1:4; 1 Pet 1:20; Rev 13:8). Sometimes the world is the sphere of human activity, as in Matthew 4:8; 13:38; and 26:13. Many of the Johannine references to Jesus being sent into the world (John 1:9; 3:17; 6:4; 10:36; 11:27; 12:46; 17:18; 18:37) or departing from the world (13:1; 16:28) would also fit in here. Sometimes "world" is a metonymy for the people who inhabit the world (John 1:10c; 3:16-17; Rom 3:19; 2 Cor 5:19). All these usages depict the world as neither good nor bad but simply the realm of creation and human activity.

The way the New Testament speaks about "the world" is governed by the dualistic framework of the Jewish apocalyptic worldview. "World," then, becomes not only a neutral, spatial concept but also a temporal, historical, and theological idea. First John 2:17 is only one example of this dualistic temporal perspective: "The world and its desire are passing away, but those who do the will of God abide forever." In Paul's letters "the world" is often synonymous with "this present evil age," in which there is sin, suffering, and death (1 Cor 2:6; 3:19; 7:31). In English translations the Greek *kosmos* (world) and *aeon* (age) are so closely associated that the words are used interchangeably. For example, although Romans 12:2 uses the word *aeon*, most English translations render it something like the NRSV: "Do not be conformed to this world."

In this present aeon, the "world" is alienated from God and in need of redemption. God loves this world so much that God sent Jesus to reconcile the world to God's self (John 3:16-17; 2 Cor 5:19-21). Salvation is not escape from this earthly existence but the restoration of all things in the new creation. Interestingly, "the future redeemed world is never called [*kosmos*]; the contrast to 'this world' is not 'that world' or 'the coming world,' but rather 'the age to come,' 'the kingdom of God,' 'a new heaven and a new earth'" (*NIDNTTE* 2:734).

It is within this dualistic, apocalyptic context that we must understand the references to the world as something Christians should *keep oneself unstained by* (James 1:27). As Robert Bratcher summarizes, the world is "a place which is hostile to God and to Christ, a source of moral corruption, a danger to the spiritual health and life of Christians" (433). This perspective is especially strong in the Johannine literature (e.g., 1 John 2:16). In the Gospel of John, the "world" is fundamentally alienated from God and in need. Jesus is bread that gives life to a hungry world (6:33); Jesus brings light to a world in darkness (8:12; 9:5; 11:9); Jesus is the Savior of a world that needs liberation (4:42; 12:47).

The problem with the world is that it rejects God's revelation in Jesus. It does "not know" Jesus or God (John 1:10c; 17:25), cannot receive the Spirit (14:17), and hates Jesus and his disciples (7:7; 15:18-19; 16:33; 17:14). This world is governed by "the ruler of this world," who personifies all the cosmic powers that are hostile to God (12:31; 14:30; 16:11; 1 John 5:19; Klassen-Wiebe: 12). The ruler of the world has no power over Jesus, however, and Jesus will conquer the world (14:30; 16:33). Jesus does not tell his disciples to withdraw from this world. They are not "of the world" because their origin lies in God and they belong to Jesus (15:19; 17:14, 16). At the same time, they remain in and are sent into the world (17:11, 18). While in the world, their calling is to bear witness (15:26-27) and to love one another (13:34-35; 15:12). Disciples of Jesus are not to be governed by the values of the world.

Although this characterization of the world as negative is strongest in the Johannine literature, it is also present in other parts of the New Testament. In Colossians 2:20 Paul berates his readers for living as if they still belong to the world. The nations of the world strive for material security, but followers of Jesus are to strive for God's kingdom (Luke 12:30-31). The verses in James about the world also fit in here (1:27; 4:4). Like Jesus in the Gospel of John (17:11) and Paul in 1 Corinthians (5:10), James does not expect his readers to withdraw from the world, for they will continue to do business (4:13) and interact with both rich benefactors and poor widows (1:27; 2:1-9). As Darian Lockett states, "These references to 'the world' in James refer to something more than the material world or humanity in general, but rather the entire cultural value system or world order[,] which is hostile toward what James frames as the divine value system" (2007: 58). It is this worldview that can "stain" the lives of followers of Jesus and must be guarded against. Christians must not be shaped by the commitments of this present aeon but by the reign of God.

Widows and Orphans in the Bible

Widows and orphans are often mentioned together in the Old Testament because, along with resident aliens, they represent the most vulnerable in society. Ancient Hebrew society was patrilocal (where married couples lived with or near the husband's family) and patrilineal. The whole extended family was under the leadership of the male head. Women and children who did not have the protection and support of the husband or father were thus in a more precarious situation economically, socially, and legally. They were not represented in the village legal assembly comprised of male landowners (Janzen: 308). Women were valued for their roles in bearing and raising children and managing the household but had less honor without those roles. A childless widow would return to her father's (Gen 38:11) or mother's (Ruth 1:8-9) house until she remarried.

The Old Testament speaks of God as the protector and refuge of widows and orphans (Deut 10:17-18; Pss 10:14; 68:5; 146:9; Prov 15:25; Jer 49:11). Even though human fathers and husbands could fail them, God would not. The covenant law included prohibitions against oppressing the widow and orphan (Exod 22:21-24) or taking a widow's garment in pledge (Deut 24:17). There were provisions for widows and orphans to glean in the fields during harvest (Deut 24:19-22; cf. Ruth 2). Every third year there was to be a special tithe so the aliens, widows, and orphans could participate in the blessings of the land (Deut 14:28-29; 26:12). The law of levirate marriage stipulated that a deceased man's brother should marry his widow if she had no sons to ensure that the family line would continue (Deut 25:5-10).

Despite these provisions, widows could still fall on hard times (1 Kings 17:8-24; 2 Kings 4:1-7). The wicked often acted unjustly toward the orphan and widow (Job 24:9, 21; Ps 94:6). The prophets of Israel and Judah condemn the nations for their oppression of the widows and orphans. They also condemn the kings for their failure to protect these vulnerable people (Isa 1:17, 23; 10:2; Jer 7:6; 22:3; Ezek 22:7; Zech 7:10; Mal 3:5). The widows and fatherless depended on God for protection, while the righteous *care[d] for orphans and widows in their distress* (James 1:27).

In the New Testament, orphans are not explicitly named as needing care and compassion, other than in James 1:27 (cf. John

14:18; 1 Thess 2:17). Widows, on the other hand, appear frequently, especially in Luke-Acts, which contains almost half of the occurrences in the New Testament. Because young women were often married off to older men and because life expectancy was low, there were more widows in the first century than widowers.

The Greek word for "widow" applied not only to women whose husbands had died, but also to "women who were divorced, separated, or abandoned" (Gench: 111). Women in general had less power than men, and widows continued to be vulnerable to abuse, legal exploitation, and poverty. This reality is evident in several Gospel stories and teachings (e.g., Mark 12:38-40; Luke 18:2-5; 21:2-3). Jesus had compassion on the widow of Nain, whose only son died, because of the vulnerable state in which this left her (Luke 7:11-17).

At the same time, the portrayal of widows in the New Testament is more complex and varied than commonly assumed. It is a misperception to think that all widows in this time were destitute, powerless, and dependent on male relatives (Hylen 2019b: 81–92). Legal and social norms varied, depending on time and place. "Under Roman law, widows were independent, legal parties who could inherit from their husbands and manage their own property" (Thurston 2009: 847). Information about Jewish widows is sparser. The Apocrypha contains the tale of Judith, a wealthy, independent, and powerful widow. Papyrus fragments from the Judean desert document a dispute between two women over property; other documents show that women could inherit property from their husbands or mothers (Hylen 2019a). The status and socioeconomic situation of women in the New Testament was also quite diverse. "Although the capacities of women varied a great deal, a woman's agency was affected by her social standing or legal independence more than by her marital status" (Hylen 2019b: 85–86). Widows had greater freedom than married women, especially if they had financial resources. In short, although there were many poor widows in the New Testament era, their poverty was not necessarily due to their marital status, nor were all widows poor and eager to remarry.

The New Testament and other early Christian writings suggest that the church took care of its widows. According to 1 Timothy 5:4, 8, 16, family members were to honor widows by caring for them. However, the church provided charitable support for widows who were truly destitute and without family connections.

Although Luke-Acts contains examples of needy widows, it also offers other possibilities. The prophet Anna, widowed after only seven years, is a paradigm of piety, faithfulness, and hope in God (Luke 2:36-38). The fact that Jesus could accuse scribes of "devouring widows' houses" suggests that they did own houses. The parable of the widow and the unjust judge (Luke 18:1-18) depicts a widow who is a persistent, assertive advocate for justice. The widows in Acts 6:1-6 are usually understood to be recipients of charity, but some interpreters have argued that the widows were involved in a ministry of hospitality and service and that a conflict arose because the Hellenist widows were being excluded from the diaconal work of *serving* food (R. Finger: 93–94, 246–75; cf. Schüssler Fiorenza: 165–66).

From the second century to the fifth century, there was an institutional "order" of widows that had special responsibilities in the Christian community, "a recognized ecclesial office for women devoted to ministries of prayer, charitable endeavor, hospitality, and instruction" (Gench: 111; see Polycarp's letter *To the Philippians* 4.3; Tertullian's *On Monogamy* 11; and the *Didascalia apostolorum* 14, among others discussed in Thurston 1989). Although parts of 1 Timothy 5:3-16 are concerned with charitable assistance for poor widows, this text also points to a possible early stage of such a ministry when it outlines rules for who should be on "the list" of widows: those who do good works, show hospitality, and help the afflicted.

While the Bible emphasizes widows and orphans as among the most vulnerable in society, in need of protection and care, it also offers a glimpse of the significant role some widows had in the early church. Both aspects are present in society and church today too and also pertain to widowers and young widows. In North America the elderly are often vulnerable to abuse and financial exploitation. Since women usually live longer than men, many of this older population are widows. At the same time, just as some widows in the early church held positions of responsibility, older single women in the church today often pursue vital ministries of service, hospitality, and pastoral care.

James calls the church to care for the "widows and the orphans," to act in the character of God, who comes to the aid of the most vulnerable in the community. Perhaps widows and orphans are not the only or the most vulnerable in society today. In North America, not only do orphans continue to need care but also children in foster care, who often become victims of neglect, or people experiencing homelessness, abuse, or mental illness. At the same time, these vulnerable groups may have strengths we do not see.

Indeed, the category of "vulnerable" may be as complex a category today as "widow" was in the first century.

THE TEXT IN THE LIFE OF THE CHURCH

The Power of Anger for Good and for Evil

Talking about anger in the life of the church requires care and sensitivity. Everyone gets angry, often for good reasons, and it is unhelpful to say someone should not get angry or that anger is a sin. Anger is an emotion that simply is. The challenge of James 1:19-20 is how to navigate the tension between the *reality* of anger and the serious warnings against anger in the Bible. Is it true that anger never produces God's righteousness, as James claims? And what should followers of Jesus do with their anger, especially when it is "righteous" anger at injustice and sin?

This is not a new tension, to be sure. The church has wrestled with the Bible's teachings against anger for centuries. The history of interpretation includes both those who argue that not all anger is sinful and those who insist that anger is categorically prohibited in the life of a Christian. Many find latitude for some anger in such texts as Ephesians 4:26 and James 1:19. The seventeenth-century English Puritan Thomas Manton (1620–77) wrote extensively about anger in his commentary on James and maintained, "All anger is not sinful" and "There is a necessary holy anger, which is the whetstone of fortitude and zeal" (120). He also outlines what makes anger sinful and under which conditions anger is acceptable. "Thomas Aquinas, in the *Summa*, said that if 'someone becomes angry for a good reason, then it is praiseworthy to become angry'" (II-II. Q158, "Anger," https://www.newadvent.org/summa/3158.htm; Allison 1999: 64). In contrast, the Venerable Bede, in his eighth-century commentary on James, wrote, "Even if anger seems justified in human terms, it can never be right in God's eyes" (Bray: 17). The monastic tradition consistently urges the forsaking of all anger, as this quote from Abba Agathon exemplifies: "A man who is angry, even if he were to raise the dead[,] is not acceptable to God" (Allison 1999: 65). Dietrich Bonhoeffer, commenting on Matthew 5:21-22, says, "Anger is always an attack on the brother's life, for it refuses to let him live and aims at his destruction. Jesus will not accept the common distinction between righteous indignation and unjustifiable anger" (Bonhoeffer 1959: 116).

The few references to James 1:19-20 in Anabaptist Mennonite writings largely view anger as negative. This is primarily for two reasons. First, Anabaptists took the teachings of Jesus on the Sermon on the Mount seriously and literally, including those on anger (Matt 5:21-26). Second, anger is often associated with violence, and Anabaptists and Mennonites believed that nonretaliation and nonviolence were central to discipleship. For example, Joost de Tollenaer wrote to his daughter Betgen while in prison in 1589, saying, "And do not hate [the enemy], neither avenge yourself, but . . . be slow to wrath, for the wrath of man worketh not the righteousness of God" (*MM* 1079). As a result of their historic refusal to participate in war, to not resist the enemy, and to practice nonconformity to "the world," Mennonites have sometimes been viewed (by themselves and others) as being passive and self-effacing in conflict, while suppressing anger (Krall: 145). The inability or unwillingness to admit and deal with conflict and anger has thus sometimes resulted in behavior that is unhealthy and harmful to self and others while also contrary to Jesus' way of love and peace. Failure to confront domestic violence and pastoral sexual abuse are only two such examples.

So how can Christians honor the New Testament teachings on anger while also dealing with the reality of anger in their lives? Anger is often a secondary emotion, a reaction to fear or grief, for example. It is an appropriate reaction to injustice, oppression, and cruelty. Ruth Krall, reflecting on her experience with anger as a feminist, states, "I have come to see anger as an emotional experience of responding to a moral perception that something is wrong" (Krall: 161). Anger can be an important and helpful signal to attend to what is wrong within oneself or one's context. Repressing anger can result in it being misdirected against others. It can lead to bitterness, judgmentalism, depression, or passive aggression. Since people's minds, emotions, and bodies are integrally connected, anger that is not dealt with in healthy ways can lead to mental or physical illness. Victims of patriarchy, racism, sexism, and other forms of oppression have too often been told not to be so angry by those who benefit from the status quo and their position of privilege. Suppression of anger then becomes yet one more form of oppression and marginalization. Anger can be understood simply as energy. As such, it can be channeled for good or for ill. It can be a motivating force for positive change, an impulse to correct what is wrong. Anger against egregious injustice and violence, for example, can motivate someone to choose to stand in harm's way, to work for systemic change, to find creative ways to love both neighbors and enemies.

The Bible warns that anger is also dangerous, and this too is something followers of Jesus must heed. Rarely is anger selfless and altruistic, even when motivated by injustice. As Craig Blomberg and Mariam J. Kamell say, "Too often . . . we appeal erroneously to the concept of righteous indignation to justify what are self-centered attempts to get our own way, disguised in pious language" (97). Although anger can motivate someone to address a wrong, anger also impedes judgment and can prompt one to react unkindly, without mercy and compassion, vengefully. This is true whether the anger is directed at a person or a situation, since an angry reaction to a situation invariably impacts people in the situation. In short, acting out of anger often exacerbates the wrong and is usually more destructive than constructive. Anyone who has sent an email in anger or has lashed out at a misbehaving child knows this, and these are only small, everyday occurrences.

Ruth Krall maintains that Christian peace movements are "filled with people who resist understanding their own violence" and rage (159). She refers to the work of Barbara Deming, who "documents the disruptiveness of that tucked-away, hidden, and non-aware anger to the goals of nonviolent social change" (Krall: 160). In our society "righteous anger" is ubiquitous and often assumed to be positive. Unfortunately, what is deemed "righteous" is often only that which is consistent with one's own opinions, politics, and values. Even "righteous anger" about an obvious injustice can lead to hurtful, violent, and, yes, sinful actions. "Righteous anger" becomes a problem as soon as one starts to see the target of one's anger as "other" and not as God's beloved. When anger erupts in words that bite and injure *people, made in the likeness of God* (James 3:9), it is sin. When anger lashes out in violence rather than furthering true and lasting shalom, it is sin. Anger that corrodes relationships and does not express love for the neighbor cannot grow God's justice.

Jesus and biblical writers like James and Paul knew of the reality of human anger and its potential to provoke sin. Their counsel is intended to help the church and individual followers of Jesus curb the toxicity of anger. Here are three examples of practical guidance they give: (1) Jesus urges his disciples to take the initiative to reconcile with the brother or sister who is angry with them and uses illustrations that underscore the urgency of such action (Matt 5:23-26). (2) James tells his audience to be *quick to listen, slow to speak, slow to anger* (1:19). Listening carefully and trying to understand the other's perspective is difficult but necessary work to slow down anger and curb destructive speech. (3) Paul warns against sinning when one is angry and urges his readers to attend to anger promptly rather than letting it fester and poison relationships (Eph 4:26-27).

One could add other suggestions for managing anger. Difficult but effective is simply to say or do nothing immediately. Taking the time to breathe and reflect opens space to consider what has prompted such strong emotion. Perhaps the reaction is out of proportion to the situation because of unrelated (or related) fear or grief. Talking to a friend who is more removed from the situation can help. Sometimes anger can become a way of being rather than a reaction to a specific situation because it grows out of a longstanding hurt or deep-seated, unacknowledged rage about a past event. Talking to a skillful and trained counselor or pastor can help one understand and overcome such anger.

James's advice to be quick to listen and slow to speak bears repeating and expanding. It can be incredibly difficult to put oneself in the shoes of someone with whom one radically disagrees and with whom interactions always seem to result in "seeing red." Yet taking the time to truly understand the other's perspective—why they believe what they do, why they did what they did, why they seem so opposed to your "right" opinion, and so on—can mitigate one's hot anger and press the pause button on rash and hurtful action. Finally, although it may sound simplistic, persistently praying for the person or situation can be a powerful way to manage one's anger.

Anger is a warning sign that something is wrong. When something is wrong, followers of Jesus will want to act to right the wrong, to further God's righteousness. Sometimes the wrong lies inside one's own spirit and mind. Sometimes the wrong resides in the world outside of oneself. Whatever action we choose, the teachings of the New Testament remind us to act first and only out of love for God and neighbor. To do that, we need to let anger take the back seat, not drive the bus.

Hearing and Doing

Mirrors are so ubiquitous today that we scarcely think about their purpose in daily life. Mirrors tell us if we have food stuck in our teeth or if our hair is windblown or if our shirt is on backward. We can choose to ignore what we see, but the implicit function of a mirror is to prompt action when such action is required. James uses the metaphor of a mirror to make the same point about God's word: we must allow it to have an impact on us if it is to fulfill its purpose. Although James speaks specifically about the law as a mirror (1:25), the whole of Scripture fulfills this function. The idea that hearing God's word must not be sundered from doing it is present elsewhere in the Bible (Ezek 33:31-33; Matt 7:24-27; Luke 11:28; Rom 2:13), but for James, it is absolutely essential in the life of faith. This letter has been a favorite among preachers who wish to emphasize the same.

Although James's concern is that hearing God's word should impact behavior, the reverse is also true: doing God's word has implications for how God's word is heard, read, and interpreted. To use the image of the mirror, looking in the mirror not only has an impact on subsequent action, but the actions we take also then affect what we see in the mirror. The metaphor of the mirror thus says something about our engagement with Scripture. We will look at only two examples of this.

The first chapter of James was a well-loved text for nineteenth-century Danish philosopher and theologian Søren Kierkegaard (Bauckham 1999: 1). In *For Self-Examination: Judge for Yourself!* he reflects on James 1:22-25 as a metaphor about reading Scripture. Kierkegaard envisions something that James probably did not—that someone might see only the mirror and not their reflection in the mirror.

Specifically, Kierkegaard took issue with scholars who treat Scripture only as an object of historical-critical study and fail to let it take hold of their hearts (Bauckham, 1999: 4–8). In his words, "In order to see yourself in the mirror when you read God's Word, you must . . . remember to say to yourself incessantly: 'It is talking to me; I am the one it is speaking about'" (Kierkegaard 1940: 39). Richard Bauckham rightly argues that Kierkegaard is too hard on biblical scholarship, for careful study of the text is of immense value for the church, not only the academy (Bauckham 1999: 8–10). Yet, Kierkegaard's complaint also rings true, since "both for scholars and those who read their books [there is] the temptation to substitute study for faith and action" (Bauckham 1999: 5). Kierkegaard also insists that what we learn from looking into Scripture must immediately be put into action; hearing and not doing is like looking into a mirror and walking away. Too often the complexity and strangeness of the biblical text become an excuse for not doing what it says.

> When you read God's Word it is not the obscure passages which bind you, but that which you understand—and with that you must comply at once. If there were only a single passage in the whole Bible which you understood—all right, you have to do that first. You do not have to sit down first and ponder over the obscure passages. God's Word is given in order that you shall act according to it and not that you shall practice interpreting obscure passages. (Kierkegaard 1940: 29–30)

In his reflections on James 1:22-25, Kierkegaard speaks also to the church today. First, when we look into the mirror of God's word, we must allow what we see to change us. This requires softening our defenses and temporarily laying aside the many legitimate questions the text often raises. Second, looking into the mirror of God's word should prompt us to act. Many things in Scripture are indeed unclear, . . . but many are clear.

Sixteenth-century Anabaptists were uncompromising about the importance of doing and not only hearing. Balthasar Hubmaier quoted James 1:22-24 when writing about the need for good deeds in his "Apologia" to King Ferdinand (1528; Hubmaier: 526; cf. 490). Menno Simons cited obedience to the Word (James 1:22) as a mark of the true church (*CWMS*: 743). This emphasis on lived faith and discipleship has persisted as a defining character of churches in the Anabaptist tradition.

Obedience to the teachings of Jesus was not only the *goal* of hearing God's word for Anabaptists but also the *prerequisite* for understanding Scripture (Murray: 189; Ollenburger: 49). Put differently, obedience was an epistemological principle and fundamental for the Anabaptist hermeneutic. Anabaptists distrusted the Reformers' interpretation of Scripture because too often they did not see it being lived out. They viewed the latter's obedience as constrained by loyalty to the state, the influence of secular authorities, and an unwillingness to disrupt the status quo. For Anabaptists, obedience to Christ was more important for the interpretation of Scripture than education, intellectual qualifications, or institutional credentials (Murray: 189). "Emphasizing the difficulties involved in interpreting Scripture discouraged obedience, they argued, for this put the focus on understanding instead of application. Uncertainties about the meaning of texts encouraged hesitation and caution, not bold and radical action" (Murray: 187). In this they sound remarkably like Kierkegaard several centuries later. Reading, interpreting, and applying the Bible was not only the responsibility of priests and theologians, then, but of all believers in community. It was in the church, with the guidance of the Holy Spirit, that God's word could be understood and lived.

Related to the hermeneutics of obedience was a hermeneutics of suffering. By following the way of the cross, the Word of God was opened up in new ways. All this can sound as though the Anabaptists were legalistic and works-oriented. Though such a charge might be legitimate for some, on the whole Anabaptists relied heavily on the grace of God and the divine empowerment that came from new birth and the indwelling Spirit. The goal was not slavish adherence to Scripture but a Spirit-infused following of Jesus, by whose life and death they had been given new life.

It is interesting to ponder the implications of the "hermeneutics of obedience" for churches whose feet are still planted in the streams of Anabaptism. The fact that the Believers Church has put out a Bible commentary series attests to the value placed on scholarship. Knowledge of original languages, historical and literary context, and intracanonical dialogue help Christians better understand what the Bible says and means. Passages that seem simple or straightforward can be misunderstood, misused, and even abused without careful attention to such matters. At the same time, although early Anabaptists were sometimes naive about their own blinders to interpretation, their insistence that methodology and scholarship are of little value if the word of God is not obeyed is worth pondering. To put it bluntly, reading this commentary on James is not nearly as important as gathering with other brothers and sisters in Christ to discern together how you will live what the biblical text is calling you to do. If we read James without allowing it to impact our actions, we are like those who walk away from the mirror with food still stuck in our teeth.

Nonconformity and Separation from the World

In 1526 Raphel van den Velde wrote to his wife from prison in Flanders, "For if we remain entirely faithful to Him, so that we keep ourselves unspotted from the world, He will be a faithful Father unto us" (*MM* 1031). The reference to being "unspotted from the world" comes from the Letter of James (1:27). A theme that runs through the writings of many Anabaptists and their descendants is that the church must be visibly distinct from its surrounding society. A text that is cited more often than James is Romans 12:2, which says Christians must not be conformed to this world. Convictions about nonconformity and separation from society, though not exactly the same, go hand in hand in historic

Anabaptism. What such beliefs actually look like in practice has varied widely among different groups and in different times and places. Although not unique to Anabaptists (it was also part of late medieval piety, for example), the struggle to negotiate the church's relationship to "the world" has characterized Anabaptist groups in various ways.

As Arnold Snyder notes, for Anabaptists "the world" did not mean the creation, which God created good. Rather, "'the world' is all that pleases Satan and a fallen humanity, and displeases God; the world is all that has been corrupted by fallen, disobedient human nature. . . . The world and the flesh are the locus of self-will, pleasure, self-seeking, and sin" (2004: 37–38). Anabaptists' understanding of "the world" was related to their belief that there were two kingdoms, one governed by Christ and the other by Satan. The idea that Christians were to remain radically separate from anything outside the lordship of Christ was especially robust in Swiss Anabaptism. It is exemplified in the Schleitheim Confession of 1527, where article 4 begins, "We have been united concerning the separation that shall take place from the evil and the wickedness which the devil has planted in the world, simply in this; that we have no fellowship with them, and do not run with them in the confusion of their abominations" (Klaassen 1981: 304).

For many Anabaptists, separation from the world included the refusal to participate in the state-controlled church, to swear oaths of allegiance, and to bear arms. For some, such as the Hutterites, radical nonconformity also included sharing possessions. Anabaptists' nonconformity to social and political expectations of their time often resulted in persecution, which further reinforced their separation from the "ungodly" and hostile world around them. Separation from the world and nonconformity were central to the Anabaptist commitment to take seriously the teachings of Jesus and to follow Christ in all of life. As Hans Denck wrote, "All who truly fear God must renounce the world" (Snyder 2004: 38).

Early Anabaptists were not uniform in their understanding of the church-world distinction, however. Menno Simons allowed for some participation of Christians in affairs of society and government. Yet he also wrote, "The entire evangelical Scriptures teach us that the church of Christ was and is, in doctrine, life, and worship, a people separated from the world" (*CWMS*: 679). Pilgram Marpeck also affirmed Christian participation in some beneficial aspects of government. Balthasar Hubmaier was one of the least separatist among the Anabaptists. He defended the Christian's use of the sword, for example, since we are "stuck in [this kingdom] right up to our ears, and we will not be able to be free from it here on earth" (497).

For the first Anabaptists, nonconformity to the world centered on separation of church and state, nonresistance, and the oath. In the centuries that followed, nonconformity in culture and lifestyle became important. This included matters of dress, language, transportation, entertainment, marriage, involvement in politics, and worship practices, to name only a few. In these areas, nonconformity to the world also meant uniformity in group practice. Differences in what nonconformity meant in practice resulted in many schisms in Mennonite history. Although an overstatement, H. S. Bender remarked in 1956, "It is notable that practically never has any significant Mennonite schism occurred over doctrinal questions. It was more often questions of discipline, particularly in relation to nonconformity, that led to breaks in personal and group relations" (Bender, "Nonconformity," GAMEO). The General Conference Mennonite Church was born in 1860, for example, when a group of Mennonites seceded from the Franconia Mennonite Conference over disagreements about nonconformity in dress and personal and social conduct (Fretz, "Nonconformity," GAMEO).

Since the mid-twentieth century, much has changed in the Anabaptist tradition regarding separation from the world. On the one hand, conservative groups such as the Old Order Mennonites, Amish, and Hutterites continue to remain distinct from mainstream society in visible ways such as dress, language, or transportation. Their separation from the world, however, is not only in externals. Economic sharing, radical forgiveness, and nonresistance are deeply embedded in a lived faith and mark these Christ followers as different from the wider society (as evidenced in the story of *Amish Grace*, by Kraybill, Nolt, and Weaver-Zercher). At the same time, many churches whose origins lie in the Radical Reformation have become so assimilated that there is no longer any obvious difference between them and broader society. Since the mid-twentieth century, forces such as urbanization, higher education, prosperity, business involvements, media, technology, and globalization have contributed to erasing external cultural distinctiveness. Theologically, the strict separation between "two kingdoms" that characterized early Anabaptists has also changed (Snyder 1995: 387). Mennonites run for political office, are part of "worldly" financial and economic institutions, and serve as police officers, to give only a few examples.

Although keeping *unstained by the world* means something different in post-Christian North America than it did in sixteenth-century Europe, and although Mennonite and Brethren churches are outwardly indistinguishable from "the world," many still practice an Anabaptist-grounded faith that does not conform to the values of wider society. One of these distinctives is a commitment to nonretaliation, love of enemy, and active peacemaking. Despite a weakened commitment to pacifism in some historic peace churches, this deeply held conviction remains nonnegotiable for many believers churches and sets them apart from "the world," especially in times of heightened militarism and nationalism, as in the aftermath of the 9/11 attacks in the United States.

A commitment to living simply, consuming less of the world's resources, and walking lightly on this earth, while not unique to descendants of the Anabaptists, is also one way the church today strives to remain unstained by the world's greed and overconsumption. The cookbook *More-with-Less* (1976), by Doris Janzen Longacre, was a small but powerful way this faith conviction found practical expression in an earlier time. The Mennonite Creation Care Network seeks to embody similar commitments today. Many more examples exist.

The goal of the church is not nonconformity itself, but following Jesus. The way of Jesus is inherently upside-down and counter to the ways of a world indifferent to Jesus. Faithful discipleship will thus inevitably clash with the values, priorities, and commitments of the larger society at times. In every age the church will need to discern anew what it means to follow this nonconformist Jesus and to *keep [themselves] unstained by the world.*

James 2:1-13

Favoritism and the Law of Love

PREVIEW

We have all seen examples of favoritism in our lives that have made our blood boil. It is the sin (2:9) of giving preferential treatment to those with more power, wealth, and status so that they benefit themselves while disregarding those with little worth in the eyes of the world. The problem is as old as time and yet takes on new flesh in every age. Yet it is precisely those with presumably little worth to whom God gives preferential treatment and who will receive the wealth of God's kingdom.

This section packs an emotional punch as it addresses this problem. The first seven verses, in particular, have a rhetorical force unparalleled by anything in the letter so far. James is clearly writing to effect change in the church. Any faith community shaped by the Scriptures, whether in the first century or twenty-first century, knows that loving one's neighbor as oneself is central to what God desires of God's people. Favoring those with influence does not show love to *all* one's neighbors. Claiming to be a follower of Jesus, obedient to God's law, is hypocritical if one still sins against the neighbor who counts for little in the world. James does not mince words.

In 2:1-13 James uses powerful tools of persuasion to provoke change in his audience, strategies that would have been compelling to ancient readers and are still effective. Some scholars argue that James is consciously using Greco-Roman rhetorical discourse to persuade his audience (Wachob: 154). He begins with a colorful illustration and vivid language to appeal to his readers' imaginations. The unit has features of the ancient diatribe, where a writer engages in conversation with an imaginary opponent. Perhaps the most forceful strategy James uses here is the barrage of rhetorical questions. Worded to presume assent, they nudge readers to indict themselves for unfaithfulness. James follows the accusatory questions with an argument from the Torah as to why their behavior is sinful. His reasoning leaves an implicit question hanging: Could it be that they are no better than adulterers and murderers?

Fortunately, mercy has the last word! The severity of James's rhetoric is also softened by the now-familiar identification of readers as *beloved brothers and sisters*. He is not speaking to his audience as a stern judge but as a loving brother in Christ and a servant of the same *glorious Lord Jesus Christ* (NRSV).

OUTLINE

Opening Exhortation and Theme: Do Not Practice Discrimination, 2:1

Illustration of the Problem and Implication, 2:2-4

Reasons for Incompatibility of Favoritism and Faith, 2:5-7

- 2:5-6a The Actions of God toward the Poor
- 2:6b-7 The Actions of the Rich toward the Church

Biblical Rationale: The Law of Love, 2:8-11

Concluding Reminder about Judgment and Mercy, 2:12-13

EXPLANATORY NOTES

Opening Exhortation and Theme: Do Not Practice Discrimination 2:1

As noted above, one noteworthy and puzzling feature of this letter is the paucity of explicit references to Jesus' name, which appears only twice in the whole letter, here in 2:1 and in 1:1. Because of the awkward Greek syntax of this verse and the dearth of references to Jesus, a few scholars (e.g., F. Spitta in 1896) have argued that the words *our Jesus Christ* are a later interpolation intended to "Christianize" an originally Jewish document. With some recent exceptions (e.g., Allison 2013: 382–84; Batten 2017b: 124), this proposal has garnered little support. There is no manuscript evidence for the absence of those words in the original text. Allusions to Jesus' teachings are sprinkled throughout (e.g., 1:22; 2:5; 5:12). And some verses refer to Jesus without naming him directly (e.g., *the excellent name* in 2:7; *the Lord* in 5:7-8). There are better ways to account for awkward syntax than eliminating words that have been in the text since the first Christians began reading it.

A host of interpretive questions concerning translation, historical context, and theology confront the careful reader at the beginning of chapter 2. The first is whether to translate 2:1 as a question (as NRSV does) or as a command (NRSVue). The main Greek verb is ambiguous, and a strong argument can be made for the imperative reading: *My brothers and sisters, do not with favoritism have faith in our glorious Lord Jesus Christ* (AT; cf. NKJV, ESV, NASB, NET, NIV). The problem with taking it as a question is that the Greek construction anticipates the answer "no," but everything that follows presumes a "yes" (that is, they *are* showing favoritism despite believing).

The end of verse 1 also poses contentious exegetical difficulties. The two main problems are (1) the relationship of "Lord Jesus Christ" to the noun "faith/belief," and (2) the relationship of the syntactically awkward "glory" to the rest of the sentence. The first of these is the more complex, with greater theological implications.

Although the NRSV translation uses the single verb "believe" (*Do you . . . really believe in . . .*), the Greek actually has two words, "have" (or "hold") and "faith" (or "belief, trust"), followed by a string of genitives. The NRSVue has *do not claim the faith*. The main issue is that this grammatical construction can mean either "have faith *in* our Lord Jesus Christ" (objective genitive) or "have the faith [or faithfulness] *of* our Lord Jesus Christ" (subjective genitive). There is no consensus among commentaries as to which of these best represents James's meaning, although the subjective genitive (that is, "the faith *of* Jesus") is more popular in recent commentaries. Attention to this interpretative issue in James has no doubt been sharpened by the debate about the meaning of the phrase "faith *of* or *in* Jesus Christ" (*pistis Iēsou Christou*) in Paul's writings over the last few decades (e.g., in texts like Gal 2:16; 3:22; Rom 3:22, 26; Phil 3:9).

What is at stake here and what is the supporting evidence? According to one perspective (represented by NRSVue, CEB, Johnson 1995: 220; Hartin 2009a: 117; Wall 107–110; Witherington 453; and others), James is telling his audience that being partial to the rich is incompatible with Jesus' faith in or faithfulness to God. The strongest argument in favor of this reading is that the verb "believe" (*pisteuō*) is used twice in James, both times with God as the object of faith, not Jesus (2:19, 23). Proponents of this position say that speaking of "faith in Jesus" does not fit the Christology of James. What is important for James is faithfulness to *God* and obedience to *God's* will, as expressed in Torah. Since Jesus models such faithfulness and is not partial to the rich, James exhorts the church not to show favoritism if they hold to this same faith that Jesus had.

The other way of interpreting 2:1 is more traditional and reflected in most English translations (NRSV, NIV, ESV, NET, NLT, NASB). In this view (represented by scholars such as Blomberg and Kamell: 106; McKnight: 176–77; McCartney: 135–36; Bauckham 1999: 139; and Wallace: 116) James is telling his audience that their favoritism is incompatible with their own faith *in* Jesus. The following arguments support this interpretation. First, since to confess Jesus as "Lord" and "Christ" (2:1) is already a strong profession of faith in Jesus, it is not inconsistent with the Christology of the letter to speak of "faith *in* Jesus Christ" (McKnight: 177). Second, the only other place in the New Testament where the words "have faith" (*echete pistin*) are followed directly by a genitive (as in James) is in Mark 11:22, where Jesus commands his disciples to "have faith in God." In this case the genitive is clearly objective not subjective (so also Acts 3:16, "by faith in his name"). Third, in this passage James is teaching his listeners about *their* faith: "You should not have the kind of faith that privileges the rich and discriminates against the poor." The faith *of* Jesus would, by definition, not do that. Claiming faith *in* Jesus while also pandering to the rich is precisely the kind of double-mindedness of which James is so critical (1:8; 4:8). Rather, as 2:14-26 emphasizes, they must show genuine faith by how they act.

Of the two interpretations, "faith *of* Jesus Christ" is increasingly popular in current scholarship. It has a strong appeal for Christians, such as those in the Anabaptist stream, who look to Jesus as a model for discipleship and an example of faithfulness. The second option, "faith *in* Jesus Christ," is a better reading of the Greek in this specific case, however (though not necessarily in Paul's letters), and conforms with the letter's broader emphasis on integrity of faith and action.

The other major interpretive problem in James 2:1 has to do with the words *of glory*, which appear rather clumsily at the very end of the sentence in the Greek. Although the text has many variant readings, the three most plausible renderings are (a) *our glorious Lord Jesus Christ*, (b) *our Lord Jesus Christ, the glorious one*, and (c) *our Lord Jesus Christ, the Glory*. The second and third options take seriously the emphasis on "glory" at the end of the sentence. More likely, "of glory" should be taken as modifying the titles for Jesus, that is, *glorious Lord Jesus Christ* (so NRSV, NIV, and others) or *Lord Jesus Christ of glory* (NRSVue), rather than in apposition to them, since this descriptive use of the genitive is stylistically common in the letter (Vlachos: 68). The translation "who has been resurrected in glory" (CEB) is an interpretation of what "glory" means and goes beyond what the text actually says.

Despite the many translation difficulties, the point of 2:1 is quite clear: showing favoritism is not Christian behavior. As the ensuing verses indicate, showing favoritism means giving preferential treatment to some over others on the basis of economic worth, social status, outward appearance, or influence. With this, James picks up an important theme in the letter, already introduced in chapter 1: the issue of wealth and poverty. He also echoes Old Testament laws, which instruct judges not to accept bribes and to make impartial decisions: "You must not be partial in judging: hear out the small and the great alike; you shall not be intimidated by anyone, for the judgment is God's" (Deut 1:17; cf. 10:17-18; 16:19-20). Leviticus 19:15 states, "You shall not render an unjust judgment; you shall not be partial to the poor or defer to the great: with justice you shall judge your neighbor." Since James quotes from this part of Leviticus elsewhere (Lev 19:18 in James 2:8), it is likely that he had this text in mind in 2:1 (Johnson 1982). Since God does not show partiality (Acts 10:34; Rom 2:11; Gal 2:6; Eph 6:9), neither should those who love God and trust in God's Messiah Jesus.

Illustration of the Problem and Implication 2:2-4

James follows his opening admonition with a vivid scenario illustrating the kind of prejudicial treatment he has in mind. Verses 2-4 consist of a lengthy "if" clause, followed by a rhetorical question that assumes an affirmative answer in Greek: "If such and such happens, then you have behaved thus, . . . right?" Scholars disagree as to whether James is presenting a purely hypothetical illustration or has in mind an actual situation. He paints the situation in such bold, dramatic colors because he wants his readers to "see, hear, and sense the event" (McKnight: 181). Thus, the description of the disparity and the egregious behavior of the host presents a caricature of what might happen. It calls to mind Jesus' parable of the rich man and Lazarus (Luke 16:19-21), which similarly describes both the clothing and the position of the two main characters in extreme terms. If this letter was to be circulated among Jewish Christian communities throughout the Diaspora (1:1), James may not have had one incident in mind. At the same time, blatant prejudice against the socially marginal and a bias toward the wealthy and powerful may well have been a recurring problem. The clearest indication of this is verse 6, which pointedly accuses, "But *you* [emphatic] have dishonored the poor." Whether or not verses 2-4 describe an actual situation, James seems to be aware that favoritism is a problem in the churches he is addressing.

The scenario envisioned in this unit raises several interpretive questions about the sociohistorical-religious setting: Why does James use the word "synagogue" to refer to the meeting and not "assembly" (*ekklēsia*)? Are the people who gather in this space followers of Jesus Messiah, nonmessianic Jews, Gentiles, or some combination? Are the rich man and the poor person regular attenders or visitors, followers of Jesus or interested bystanders? What is the relationship between the rich man and the gathered community? What power dynamics come into play? What cultural expectations are assumed? Finally, is the context a judicial setting, a worship service, a fellowship meal, or something else entirely?

These are fascinating questions for people curious about the social, cultural, economic, and religious context of the letter, and investigating them might shed light on the problems James was addressing and, by implication, analogous problems today. Having said that, the main point of the scenario is clear regardless of the precise answers to these context questions: Discriminating against the poor and privileging the rich are wrong in any situation, regardless of whether they are believers in Christ or what the precise setting is.

The setting for the situation is *your synagogue* (v. 2, *assembly*, NRSVue). Here the use of the Greek word for "synagogue" is noteworthy. In 5:14 James will use the more typical *ekklēsia* (assembly, church) to refer to the gathered believers. In the first-century Jewish world, "synagogue" could refer to a physical building or to an assembly of people, although the two are obviously related, since people gather in a particular place. Before the destruction of the temple in 70 CE, physical synagogues were often simply large rooms located in houses similar to private dwellings (*DLNT*: 1142). In later centuries they developed into larger, more elaborate structures, taking on features similar to the temple. Synagogues were prevalent throughout the Diaspora—in Egypt, Asia Minor, Rome, and Syria, to name only a few—as well as in Palestine. Synagogues served a variety of functions in the first century. Jews met in synagogues primarily for worship, prayer, and the reading and study of Scripture. They were also settings for the resolution of disputes and administration of justice, for the distribution of alms, and for gatherings of Jews socially. The fact that James says, *enters your synagogue* (AT), suggests that he has a physical space in mind.

More difficult to determine is the religious identity of the people meeting in this space, with implications for the makeup of James's audience. The relationship between Jews who believed in Jesus and Jews who did not in the first-century Diaspora was complex and varied in different settings, contexts, and times (Skarsaune: 745–46). In general, the borderline between Jews who believed that Jesus was the Messiah and those who did not was porous in the early decades of the church. Acts describes Paul regularly going to synagogues first when he entered a city, with some Jews believing the good news of Jesus and some opposing him. The Gospel of John's portrayal of "the Jews" reflects considerable tension and even division in some early messianic communities, probably reflecting the situation of a generation later than when the Gospel was written.

Archaeological and literary evidence suggests that Jews and Christians continued to interact with each other for centuries. Scholars such as Boyarin and Skarsaune suggest that the border region between the two groups "was, at a grassroots level, a rather peaceful border in many places and most of the time. There was much border traffic, probably in both directions" (Skarsaune: 753). So what does all this mean for how we interpret James's reference to a synagogue in 2:2? As noted previously, the letter assumes an audience thoroughly steeped in Jewish history, tradition, and Scripture. Likely the Messiah followers to whom James wrote were still meeting in synagogues. These gatherings likely included some Gentile God-fearers and perhaps even some Jews who were not convinced that Jesus was the Messiah. What is clear is that the believers in the Lord Jesus Christ who were gathering in these synagogues were not impervious to the polarizing social and economic tensions that characterized other associations in the ancient world. This is what James argues is incompatible with faith in Jesus.

Another interpretative question has to do with the context of 2:2-4, since ancient synagogues were used for various activities.

When Christians today read this text, most probably think of a modern church worship setting with pews or chairs in rows facing a pulpit; they envision a wealthy socialite and a homeless person being greeted in the foyer by ushers. This is not the first-century context in which James was writing. One common interpretation goes back to the seventeenth century but is often attributed to R. B. Ward (Allison 2000: 163–64). It argues that the setting of 2:2-4 is an ecclesial court and that the church is being called to render a legal verdict in a dispute between a wealthy member and a poor member (Ward: 87–97). Several factors favor such a view: First, judicial language is prominent in the context. For example, the rich drag people into court (v. 6), and transgressors are *convicted by the law* (v. 9). Second, rabbinic literature contains several similar accounts that warn against making unjust judgments in favor of the rich. Strikingly, these parallels mention not only the clothing of the rich and poor, but also the impropriety of one person standing and another sitting in court (e.g., Deuteronomy Rabbah Shofetim 5.6; Sifra Kedoshim Perek 4.4). Third, Leviticus 19:15, which informs James's letter, also speaks about impartiality in judicial contexts.

Although the judicial interpretation has merit, it is also problematic. First, although verses 6-7 use judicial language, the situation is different from that in verses 2-4. In verse 6 a rich nonbeliever (i.e., someone who blasphemes the name of Christ) takes a poor person to court, whereas the judicial interpretation of verses 2-4 requires that two people of faith go to a synagogue for dispute mediation. Second, the rabbinic literature comes from a time considerably later than James and the parallels are not as close as they at first seem. Third, verses 2-4 say nothing about a judge, nor is the problem an unfair verdict, as in Leviticus 19:15. Rather, the focus is on how the church welcomes newcomers. The favoritism has to do with seating, not with judgments rendered. In fact, the issue of the proximity to the speaker would not even make sense in a court.

Instead of a formal gathering of a Christian assembly for judicial discernment, James more likely has in view a meeting of Jewish Messiah followers, typically gathering for worship and study, prayer and fellowship. Daniel Streett has suggested a meal setting for 2:1-9, since communal meals were a regular part of early Christian assemblies. Such a context makes sense of the language of sitting and standing, the issue of proximity to the host (people of higher social and economic status typically were seated close to the host), the judgment of newcomers based on attire and economic status, and the values of honor and shame. Whatever the situation, modern interpreters who become fixated on determining the specific sociohistorical context of the scene run the risk of missing James's point: followers of Jesus must stop favoring those with influence and wealth over those who are economically and socially vulnerable.

Another ambiguity in the text is whether the two people who enter the assembly are visitors and whether they are followers of Jesus. That they must be told where to sit suggests that they are not regular attenders. Since the letter elsewhere implies that its recipients include the economically poor and associates piety with poverty (1:9; 2:5-7, 15; 5:4), we are likely to think of the person in filthy clothes as a believer. More than that is hard to say, though scholars have made various suggestions. David Edgar, for example, postulates that the poor were radical itinerant prophets of the Jesus movement (120–21). Craig Blomberg believes many were poor day laborers on estates owned by absentee landlords (152; cf. 5:1-6). What matters to James is that they are poor enough not to have adequate clothing and that they are given no regard in the community.

The question of whether the splendidly dressed man is a Messiah follower is not really germane for the problem James is addressing since he is concerned about how those in the assembly treat such a person, not the behavior of the rich man himself. For sociohistorical reasons, though, it is interesting to consider whether the churches to whom James wrote included wealthy people. Perhaps this was a source of some of the conflict we read about in the letter.

The question of the socioeconomic makeup of the church was raised already in 1:9-11 and will come up again in 4:13–5:6. On the one hand, if the gathering regularly included and was open to messianic Jews, nonmessianic Jews, and Gentile God-fearers alike, the wealthy man could have been a visitor who did not confess Jesus as Messiah. The fact that James describes only his attire and does not explicitly call him "rich" (*plousios*), a word he uses elsewhere for nonbelievers (2:6-7; 5:1-6), leaves open the possibility that he is a Messiah follower. The fact that he says, *Have you not made distinctions among yourselves* (v. 4), might also imply that the two people entering the assembly belong to the community, pointing to diversity in the church. Although James does not address the question, one wonders how the rich man treats the poor person in front of him. Although the affluent are not inherently wicked (nor the poor inherently righteous), such a display of wealth would have been deemed distasteful. Moreover, the rich were part of systemically unjust patronage structures that created power imbalances and economic disparity such as one finds in this text.

Even more important than the contrasting socioeconomic statuses of the two people entering the room is the reprehensible behavior of the church toward them. The physical appearance of the two who enter is dramatically portrayed, with the language itself prioritizing the wealthy man. He is named first and is identified as, literally, a *gold-fingered man with brightly shining clothes* (AT). The second person is not even given the dignity of being called a "man" but is simply "a poor one" with "filthy clothes." Perhaps the poor person is even one of the *widows in distress*, for whom they should care (1:27).

The writer draws the reader's attention closer to the wealthy man by saying, *If you take notice of the one wearing the fine clothes.* One takes greater notice just by reading the words *if you take notice*! Yet the text gives no such attention to the poor person, whose clothes are not worth mentioning again. The words of the host also draw the rich man spatially close, while distancing and demeaning the poor person: *Sit comfortably here* (AT) to the former but "'*Stand there' or 'sit at my feet*'" (lit., "*sit under my footstool*") to the latter. Slaves were required to stand; sitting at someone's feet indicated subservience or lower status. The whole tenor of the passage implies groveling before the rich while disdaining the poor.

The dynamics of the situation are illuminated more sharply when one understands the cultural values of shame and honor that prevailed in the first-century Mediterranean world. (The following comments rely heavily on Patrick Hartin's helpful summary of the "Cultural Scripts behind the Letter of James" [2009a: 140–48].) Honor is publicly acknowledged worth. To have honor, one conformed to the values esteemed by the group to which one belonged. The values that a minority group considered honorable were sometimes at odds with what the larger society valued. Since Jesus' way of life was often countercultural, followers of Jesus also espoused values that ran contrary to what the larger society considered honorable. This is especially evident in the realm of wealth and poverty. The society at large (the "world") honored those who had wealth, power, and social status. The poor were those who had lost honor or were vulnerable to losing honor. Those who were lower on the socioeconomic ladder would seek the patronage of the wealthy and, in return for favors and benefits, would be obliged to give them loyalty and service. In the larger society, then, acts of favoritism toward the wealthy were expected and even honorable.

One possibility for the scenario in 2:2-4 is that the rich man entering the assembly was a patron or potential benefactor (Batten 2017b: 129–31). The community would be obliged to flatter and give preferential treatment to him in exchange for benefits. Conversely, the poor man had nothing to offer and could be swept aside. James turns the expected social behaviors on their head. The church must be governed by different values than the society around it. To use James's earlier words, they must keep *unstained by the world* (1:27). Because James's readers put their trust in Jesus, their lives should reflect his way of life, a lifestyle that honors the poor and gives them dignity.

In the realm of the church, to lift up the lowly and act with justice toward the poor is the honorable thing to do. Jesus critiqued those who coveted recognition and chose seats of honor (Matt 23:6; Luke 20:46); he told parables in which the positions of the poor and rich were reversed (Luke 14:7-14). James chastises his audience for acting according to the values of the surrounding society by catering to the rich and dishonoring the poor (v. 6). James urges his readers to live by the alternate honor system of Jesus, their glorious Lord and Messiah (2:1), who relinquished his glory to become human. If the rich person were indeed a patron, James is exhorting them to engage in riskier behavior than just treating individuals equally. He is calling for active resistance against the system of patronage, which was inherently discriminatory. Such an act of protest ran the risk of impoverishing the community further if the patron perceived their refusal to privilege him as dishonorable treatment and retaliated. In other words, in 2:2-4 James is not just exhorting the church to be nice to the poor but also to take the risk of publicly questioning cultural mores and resisting systemic injustice.

In verse 4 we finally come to the end of the long "if . . . then" sentence that begins in verse 2. The apodosis of the sentence (the "then" part) is framed as a pair of rhetorical questions that expect the answer "Yes." As a result, they function more as accusations than genuine questions. Implicit in these questions is the charge that, yes, they have *made distinctions among [themselves]* and, yes, they have *become judges with evil thoughts* (v. 4). First, by discriminating among people on the basis of their appearance and economic status, they have fractured the community, something that ought not to happen among those who were given birth *by the word of truth* and are the *first fruits of God's creatures* (1:18). The Greek word for *made distinctions* (*diakrinesthai*) is the same word that is translated "doubt" in 1:6. It could also be translated with a passive force, "to be divided" (Spitaler: 576). Just as double-minded, doubting individuals are divided within themselves, so a community that discriminates among people on the basis of outward appearance is also divided within itself.

Second, making distinctions among people requires making judgments. If they judge by standards inconsistent with their identity as followers of Jesus, they are evil-minded judges (2:4). They are no better than corrupt judges who rule in favor of rich clients and justify their unjust practices with false reasoning. Later, James will admonish them not to malign each other, which is another way to judge each other and fracture the community (4:11-12). Instead of judging, they should love their neighbors as themselves (2:8). Moreover, there is really only one Judge, and that is God (4:12), whose agent is Jesus Christ (5:9). Through these rhetorical questions, James implicitly criticizes the church for being judges whose thoughts and motives have been corrupted by worldly standards of wealth and power.

Reasons for Incompatibility of Favoritism and Faith 2:5-7

James follows up the scenario in verses 2-4 with the first wave in his argument against favoritism. This short subunit is rhetorically crafted to have a powerful impact on its audience. A terse command to pay attention is followed by a series of four rhetorical questions, fired off in quick succession, all worded to expect agreement. Amid these questions, an abrupt statement that accuses them of dishonoring the poor stands out. Because it is different from what comes before and after and because the plural pronoun "you" is emphatic, the sentence has additional rhetorical force.

Listen, my beloved brothers and sisters!
Q: *Has not God chosen the poor . . . to be rich in faith and heirs of the kingdom . . . ?*
<u>But you have dishonored the poor</u>!
Q: *Is it not the rich who oppress you?*
Q: *Is it not they who drag you into court?*
Q: *Is it not they who blaspheme the excellent name that was invoked over you?*

If these verses have their intended effect, readers and hearers will feel uncomfortable that by currying favor with the rich, they have sided against God and with the very people who oppress them!

Like the Old Testament prophets, James calls on his audience to *listen!* (Isa 7:13; Jer 6:19; Amos 8:4). With this attention-grabbing word and the familiar address, *My beloved brothers and sisters,* James alerts them to the gravity of what is coming next. When God's messengers call people to "listen," they are not merely asking them to attend to sounds entering their ears. Rather, in the Bible, to "listen" means to hear *and* to act accordingly.

2:5-6a The Actions of God toward the Poor

James begins with a theological reason for not showing favoritism. Although framed as a question, verse 5 is really making a claim: *God has chosen the poor in the world to be rich in faith and to be heirs of the kingdom* (AT paraphrase). The theme of God's choice or election is prominent in the Old Testament and central to Israel's identity as a people belonging to God (Deut 4:37-38; 7:7-8; 14:2). James 2:5 is talking about more than God's election in general, though. It is talking about God's choice of people who are economically poor and thus also socially marginalized and politically powerless. In the letter *the world* is that which is at enmity with God (4:4), and in the eyes of *the world* the poor are of little worth and dispensable. Yet the Old Testament consistently witnesses to a God who stands on the side of the poor and liberates the oppressed. Already in 1:9-11 James spoke of the upside-down actions of a God who raises up the lowly and casts down the rich.

Is God's election of the poor, then, not an example of the favoritism that James decries? On the contrary, it is representative of God's shalom justice throughout the Bible on behalf of those who cannot acquire justice on their own. Thus it is emblematic of God's unrelenting grace toward those who have nothing and indicative of God's upside-down choice of the unlikely. The Old Testament is adamant that the election of Israel is not based on its own merit (Deut 7:7). Rather, God delivers them on the basis of their need (Yoder 1987: 34, 44). Throughout the Bible, God acts in surprising and paradoxical ways, calling both individuals and nations to serve God's purposes despite their flaws and obvious lack of qualifications. God's choosing of the poor to be rich in the realm of faith is consistent with what Paul says in 1 Corinthians 1:27: "God chose what is foolish in the world to shame the wise; God chose what is weak in the world to shame the strong."

Does this text then idealize poverty? Does lack of wealth, status, and power necessarily make one *rich in faith*? First, the biblical tradition of the "pious poor" undoubtedly lies behind what James is saying. Being poor does not automatically make someone more godly or give someone deeper faith. At the same time, people who have deep needs often realize their dependence on God more easily than the self-sufficient, self-satisfied rich. Because they do not have the same access to resources and because social, economic, and political structures are often aligned against them, the poor must rely on God for deliverance. God's defense of the poor and powerless and the dependence of the poor on God's provisions led to the Old Testament tradition of the "pious poor" (*anawim* in Hebrew), found especially in the Psalms and wisdom literature (e.g., Pss 86:1-2; 69:32-33; Sir 10:22-24; 13:15-20). Thus, when James speaks of the poor as *rich in faith*, he is drawing on the robust biblical tradition that recognizes the poor as those who trust in God.

Second, to be *rich in faith* does not necessarily mean to have exceptionally strong faith. The Greek *en pistei* (in faith) is a dative of sphere (Hartin 2009a: 119; Maynard-Reid: 61). Even though they are materially poor in the eyes of the world, they are rich in the sphere of faith. They are rich because of what God is doing and will do for them: making them heirs of a kingdom. James echoes the good news that Jesus proclaimed: that the poor are blessed because they will inherit the reign of God (Matt 5:3//Luke 6:20). In the Beatitudes, Jesus did not declare his disciples blessed because their poverty had intrinsic merit but because of what God would do for them. James refers to this promise, which makes the materially poor to be rich in faith.

Although this is the only place where James uses the words "heir" and "kingdom," what he says is consistent with a rich vein of early Christian teaching and preaching about Christians being heirs of the promise (Rom 8:17; Gal 3:29; Titus 3:7; Heb 6:17). It would be wrong, though, to read this as saying that the poor should just be content with their lot since they will have their reward in the "sweet by and by." James consistently exhorts his readers to care for the vulnerable (1:27), resist discriminating against the poor (2:2-4), and feed the hungry and clothe the naked (2:15-16). The church is to participate in God's actions of making God's reign of shalom and justice a reality already in the present.

The last part of verse 5 confirms that those who inherit God's kingdom do so not only because they are materially poor but also because they love God. Jesus said that the two greatest commandments are to love God with all one's heart, soul, mind, and strength and to love one's neighbor as oneself (Mark 12:28-32 and parallels). James explicitly quotes the Scripture about loving the neighbor in 2:8. Perhaps his reference here to those who love God is a subtle acknowledgment of the first great commandment. The last phrase of verse 5, *that [God] promised to those who love him*, repeats verbatim what James said in 1:12 with regard to the crown of life. This repetition of language suggests that *crown of life* and *kingdom* are synonymous. To receive the crown of life is to inherit God's reign, which Jesus inaugurated and which will come in full on the last day.

The contrast between God's action and the actions of James's audience could not be starker. God honors the poor by promising them a share in God's reign, but James's readers and hearers have dishonored the poor (v. 6a). By showing favoritism to the rich, they have acted according to the values of the world instead of imitating God.

2:6b-7 The Actions of the Rich toward the Church

In verses 6b, 6c, and 7, James moves to an argument against favoritism on the basis of his readers' experience. He punches out three short rhetorical questions about the actions of the rich, with each charge more severe and specific than the previous. First, James explicitly identifies the oppressors as *the rich* (*plousioi*), a term that appears also in 1:9-11 and again in 5:1-6. The Greek word for *oppress* (*katadynasteuō*) is found only here in the New Testament and in Acts 10:38, where, interestingly, the devil is the subject of the verb. The word appears frequently in the Septuagint, where it connotes exploitation, domination, and often violent force. It is especially prominent in the prophets, who denounce the rich for exploiting the poor (e.g., Jer 7:6; Ezek 18:12; Amos 4:1; Zech 7:10). Throughout history, the rich have found ways to oppress the poor by appropriating their land, charging exorbitant taxes, not paying living wages, or denying them access to basic human rights, to name only a few examples of injustice. It was so in Jesus' day. It had not changed in James's time. It is no different today.

Second, James challenges them, *Is it not [the rich] who drag you into court?* One of the ways that the rich oppress the poor is by embroiling them in legal conflicts. In the ancient world (and even today) the justice system often favored the rich over the poor, who did not have the right connections or money to pay fees and penalties. This is why Paul urged the Corinthian church to resolve conflicts among themselves instead of taking them to the courts (1 Cor 6:1-8; Hays 1997: 93–94).

The third rhetorical question makes clear that the "rich" in these verses are not Christians, since they *blaspheme the excellent name that was invoked over you* (v. 7). Although the text does not specify that this honorable name is "Jesus," such an inference is reasonable since the unit begins by referring to *our glorious Lord Jesus Christ* (2:1 NRSV). The language of invoking or calling upon a name comes from the Old Testament and communicates belonging or relationship, especially with reference to God (Davids 1982: 113). "If one wants to say that the people of Israel belong to God, one says that the name of Yahweh was named over them (Deut 28:10; Jer 14:9; Isa 43:7; 2 Chron 7:14; 2 Macc 8:15)" (Dibelius: 140).

For the early Christians, the name of Jesus had the same function and was particularly associated with baptism, at which time the believer "took on" the name of Jesus. One can see the importance of the "name" of Jesus in Acts, for example, where healing, baptizing, forgiveness, and salvation are all associated with the "name" of Jesus (e.g., 2:38; 3:6; 4:7-12; 10:48; 19:5). The rich perpetrate economic injustice while also engaging in religious harassment. Although likely not victims of a formal or systematic religious persecution, these impoverished believers are experiencing trials on more fronts than the economic one.

With these three rhetorical questions (2:6b, 6c, 7), James highlights the irony and foolishness of believers giving preferential treatment to the rich. If they are being victimized by rich unbelievers and if God has chosen the poor to inherit God's reign, why in the world are they ingratiating themselves with the rich? Not only is their behavior blatantly illogical, it is also theologically misguided. By dishonoring the poor, they have sided with the rich oppressors instead of with a generous, gracious God. They have aligned themselves with those who blaspheme the very name that gives them identity. This is surely an example of the egregious double-mindedness and self-deception of which James is so critical (1:7, 16, 26). Most of all, it is inconsistent with their professed faith in the *glorious Lord Jesus Christ* (2:1, NRSV).

Biblical Rationale: The Law of Love 2:8-11

In this subunit, James appeals to Scripture—specifically the law—to argue that discrimination is incompatible with faith. He is not introducing a new topic or expounding on the law in an abstract, theoretical sense. In fact, the issue is not the law at all. Rather, faith must be expressed in practical deeds of mercy. As M. J. Evans says, "James's approach is practical and intuitive rather than theologically precise" (37). Because his focus is living with integrity and not the law itself, James does not define what he means by "the law" and assumes his readers will understand. Unfortunately, non-Jewish readers two thousand years later do not have access to such assumptions and must face some ambiguity.

When James refers to the law, he probably means the Jewish Torah, the law of Moses. This is evident from the fact that he specifically cites laws from the Decalogue and from the Holiness Code in Leviticus. Many or all of James's messianic Jewish readers would have held to the ongoing validity of the Torah and would have continued to adhere to the moral and likely also some ritual requirements of the law. The letter contains no hint of any conflict about whether Gentiles must be circumcised, as in Acts and Paul. At the same time, James's understanding of the law seems to be guided by his identity as a slave of the Lord Jesus Christ (1:1), which he shares with his readers (2:1). It is the Torah as interpreted by the life and teachings of Jesus, especially the law of love, that James has in view.

The subunit begins with two contrasting conditional sentences (vv. 8-9). The first envisions a situation that is commendable: *If you really fulfill the royal law . . . , you do well.* The second lays out the negative alternative: *But if you show partiality, you commit sin.* Although the unit focuses on transgression of the law, its purpose is not to scold but to encourage a more comprehensive obedience to the law of love.

In looking at James's argument from the law, it will be helpful to keep in mind some of the broader perspectives on the law in this letter (see also comments on 1:25). The topic surfaces three times: in 1:25; 2:8-13; and 4:11-12. In every case, James's perspective on the law is unwaveringly positive. Nowhere do we find anything resembling Paul's critique of the law or references to freedom from the law (Rom 7:1-13; Gal 3:10-19). Although it can be fruitful to compare James with Paul on topics that they both address, it is tempting for Christians today to read James only through the eyes of Paul and the lens of the Protestant Reformers. James needs to be heard on his own terms, however, and in his own context. That context is firmly rooted in the soil of messianic Judaism.

Most important is the fact that the law comes from God, the one Lawgiver and Judge (4:12). The commandments *You shall not commit adultery* and *You shall not murder* are God's words (*the one who said . . .*) (2:11). The law is complete or "perfect" (*teleios*, 1:25). As such, it is one of the good and perfect gifts that *come down from the Father of lights* (1:17). Second, when 2:8-13 speaks of "the law" (*nomos*), it mostly likely means the whole Torah, not individual commandments or law codes, such as the Ten Commandments. If the reference were to individual commandments, James would have used a different word (*entolē*). The law in its entirety was the expression of God's will for God's people, a gift from God to enable them to live in covenant relationship with God their Creator and Redeemer (Hartin 2009a: 135–37). Third, the letter focuses entirely on the ethical aspects of God's law. That is not to say that James is opposed to the ritual requirements of the law, such as circumcision, food laws, or Sabbath observance. He may well assume that his readers are adhering to them; he simply does not address them. These are not his concern, for this is not where the church needs guidance. These broader considerations are important background as we come to the specifics of 2:8-11.

The most difficult and widely disputed aspect of the verse is the meaning of *royal law* and its relationship to the phrase *according to the scripture* and to the quotation that follows, *You shall love your neighbor as yourself.* Does *royal law* refer to the whole Torah or only to the love command? In what sense is the law "royal"? Are the *royal law* (v. 8), *the whole law* (v. 10), and *the law of liberty* (v. 12) all referring to the same thing? Or is James making distinctions? Perhaps these questions would not have occurred to James, who was not writing a doctrinal treatise on the law. Nevertheless, they are questions that modern readers of the letter wonder about.

First, *the royal law* probably does not refer narrowly to the commandment *You shall love your neighbor as yourself* (Lev 19:18b) but to the Old Testament law more broadly. As already noted, James uses the word *nomos* here, not the word *entolē*, which would signify a particular commandment. So the law as a whole is royal, and James is talking about fulfilling this broader law by attending to a specific commandment: loving one's neighbor.

Second, the word "royal" (*basilikon*) could be translated "kingly," which would more clearly illuminate its connection to the word "kingdom"(*basileia*) in 2:5. The proximity of the two words suggests that the *royal/kingly law* (2:8) refers to the law of the kingdom of God (2:5), which the poor will inherit and which God has promised to those who love him. Jesus inaugurated God's royal rule by teaching about it in colorful parables, through his powerful acts of healing, and in his death and resurrection. When James refers to *fulfill[ing] the royal law*, then, he means the fulfillment of the Torah as it was interpreted by Jesus. He is talking about the law of God's reign, which Jesus inaugurated, God's will for people living under God's rule (Bauckham 1999: 143).

Third, *according to the scripture* introduces the quotation of Leviticus 19:18b that follows. "It specifies which part of this royal law James's listeners need to apply here" (Blomberg and Kamell: 117). Although not the typical way to introduce a specific quotation in James or the rest of the New Testament, this reading makes the most sense here. James is saying, "You do well if you fulfill the law of God's kingdom by obeying the Scripture that says, 'You shall love your neighbor as yourself.'"

The verse James quotes is from Leviticus 19:18 and is commonly called "the love command." Luke Timothy Johnson has argued persuasively that James had in mind all of Leviticus 19:12-18 when he cited the love command and that this text from the Septuagint influences the whole letter (Johnson 1982). In particular, Leviticus 19:15 explicates what loving one's neighbor means for James: "You shall not render an unjust judgment; you shall not be partial to the poor or defer to the great: with justice you shall judge your neighbor."

In addition to language of partiality (James 2:1, 9), Leviticus 19:12-18 includes admonitions about not swearing falsely (cf. James 5:12), not defrauding workers (cf. 5:1-6), and not slandering others (cf. 4:11). The "royal law," then, is "explicated concretely and specifically . . . by the immediate context of the Law of Love, the commands found in Lev 19:12-18" (Johnson 1982: 399. Discriminating against the poor and giving preferential treatment to the rich is, according to Leviticus, rendering "unjust judgments," making them *judges with evil thoughts* (2:4). It is *not* loving their neighbors as themselves, which epitomizes the law of God's kingdom.

James's citation of Leviticus 19:18b is significant not only because of its relationship to Leviticus 19:12-18, but also because of its connection to the ministry of Jesus. According to Jesus, the authoritative interpreter of the law of God's royal rule, the two greatest commandments are to love God with heart, soul, mind, and strength, and to "love your neighbor as yourself" (Mark 12:28-34// Matt 22:34-40). The former was part of the Shema (Deut 6:4-5), which begins "The LORD our God, the LORD alone" and was recited daily by Jews. James seems to allude to it in 2:19: *You believe that God is one*. Jesus places the commandment from Leviticus 19 to love the neighbor "on the same level as the most basic obligation of religion, the command to love God" (Garland: 229).

According to Jesus, "all the Law and the Prophets" depend on these two great commandments (Matt 22:40). Paul, too, understood the command to love one's neighbor as a summary of the entire law (Rom 13:9; Gal 5:14). As Patrick Hartin nicely summarizes, "The command to love one's neighbor operates as the embodiment of the Torah. It does not replace the Torah, but gives expression to the pulsating heart and direction of the Torah as God's will for God's people" (Hartin 1999: 84).

If indeed *the royal law* in James is the law of God's kingdom inaugurated by Jesus, and if this law is best encapsulated in the love command of Leviticus 19:18b, broadly understood, then to love one's neighbor means to love as Jesus loved and to take seriously what Jesus said about loving one's neighbor. The "neighbor" then includes not only the person living next door, who has similar lifestyles, beliefs, and socioeconomic background, and who is easy to love, but also the "other"—the foreigner, the despised, the despicable, and even the enemy (Matt 5:43-48; Luke 10:29-37). This is also consistent with Leviticus 19, which instructs Israel to love the foreigners and immigrants, who live among them, as themselves (vv. 33-34). To "love" the other does not necessarily mean "liking" the other or having warm emotional feelings toward them. Rather, to love people on Jesus' terms means to choose to act for the good of the other, whether one feels like it or not. It means to take concrete steps toward right relationships, to choose mercy and compassion over judgment and favoritism. Modern psychology tends to highlight the fact that we need to love ourselves first if we are going to *love [the] neighbor as [one]self*. This is, of course, true. The biblical injunction to love the neighbor, however, assumes that people tend to look after themselves first, as is surely most often the case. In short, if people really did love their neighbors as Jesus loved all people, they would be doing God's will, as it is reflected in the law that governs God's reign.

At first blush, it may sound like James is commending them, for he says, If you really love your neighbor, . . . *you do well*. The same clause, *You do well*, occurs in 2:19 (*You believe that God is one; you do well*), prompting a comparison between the two statements. Although "You do well" seems to be a genuine commendation in 2:8, yet more ironic in 2:19, the point of what follows each is corrective admonition. They are actually *not* doing so well!

James's readers may think they are following God's law, but if they are favoring the rich and dishonoring the poor, they are sinning. James does not mince words. The term "transgressor" (2:9, 11) is rare in the New Testament (elsewhere only in Rom 2:25, 27; Gal 2:18). It does not occur in most versions of the Septuagint and usually has a different meaning when used in secular Greek. In James (and Paul) it denotes someone who has overstepped or violated the law of God. With these words James not only draws attention to what his readers are doing (committing sin) but also to their character as *transgressors*.

James talked about sin earlier when he said that desire *engenders sin, and sin, when it is fully grown, gives birth to death* (1:15). If showing partiality is committing sin, what is the desire that "begets" *this* sin? Perhaps James's readers are simply conforming to common cultural practices of patronage and its value system in which people of lower status gave honor to the rich and powerful in return for benefits. If so, ancient readers were not so different from modern readers, who still long to enhance their own status by ingratiating themselves with the rich, powerful, and popular.

In 2:10-11, James expands on the biblical reasons why showing favoritism makes them transgressors. The principle that God's people are responsible for keeping the whole law and not picking and choosing certain parts of it was part of Jewish faith (cf. 4 Macc 5:17-21). It grows out of the conviction that the law in its entirety comes from God and is an expression of God's will. Since the law is an indivisible unity, keeping one part and ignoring another is simply not an option.

James turns to the Decalogue to make his point. The two commandments he selects as examples, murder and adultery, are the ones singled out in the Sermon on the Mount (Matt 5:21-26, 27-30) and cited first in other listings of God's commandments (Matt 19:18//Mark 10:19//Luke 18:20; Rom 13:9). In other words, these are serious commandments, not to be ignored. It might seem like a gross exaggeration to say that showing partiality is as bad as murder or adultery. But if the Torah is indivisible, as Jews believed, then minor commandments are as important as major ones. Transgression of laws with lesser significance can lead to transgression of major commands.

Is showing favoritism really as bad as murdering someone? Maybe not. But James is emphasizing the importance of the whole law and the unity of the law to make a point. Maybe some in his audience are not taking the lesser commandments seriously enough or are being too casual about some things like partiality (or slander, as in 4:11-12) because they are not as serious as murder. James claims that doing God's will is important no matter how small or large the commandment is. Loving one's neighbor means not only refraining from murder and adultery but, equally so, not showing favoritism to the rich and discriminating against the poor, which are more common than murder.

This emphasis on the unity of the law does still allow for God's laws to be reinterpreted for every age and for some laws to take priority over others. Honoring the law about the goring ox (Exod 21:28-32) will look different in twenty-first century North America than in ancient Israel, but it can still speak powerfully about our responsibility to ensure that what we own or invest in does not kill others (Janzen: 299–301, 321–22; see, for example, the article by Derek Suderman in the *Canadian Mennonite* for a creative application). Jesus himself prioritized some commands over others, focusing on mercy and justice rather than holiness and separation (Matt 23:23; Snodgrass: 369–71), and the church in Acts deemed some laws to be important for Gentiles even as other laws were not (Acts 15:19-21). The laws are not timeless truths but samples of how a people tried to live faithfully under God within a particular story. What is not acceptable, for James or for the church today, is dispensing with God's law simply because it is inconvenient.

It is crucial to remember the point of James's discussion in 2:8-11. The purpose is not to impress upon people that they must keep every single commandment or they will be hopeless sinners. Rather, the point is that they should not claim to be following God's law if they are showing favoritism to the rich and thus not loving their poor neighbors as themselves. James's readers probably did not view honoring potential wealthy patrons as a sin; it was simply conforming to cultural expectations. One could even argue that they were showing love to these rich neighbors. James compares their discriminatory behavior with murder and adultery to shock them into realizing that what they are doing *is* transgressing God's will.

In 3:2 James acknowledges that everyone "stumbles" (the same Greek word appears in 2:10). However, sin can be forgiven. In chapter 5 James speaks about confession and the healing power of forgiveness and restoration (5:15-16, 19-20). The goal in 2:8-11 is to remind readers that their discriminatory behavior is not God's desire so that they can confess their sin and live more consistently with their *faith in [their] glorious Lord Jesus Christ* (2:1, AT).

Concluding Reminder about Judgment and Mercy 2:12-13

The unit concludes with a summarizing admonition (v. 12) and a double-pronged, short saying (v. 13). With the admonition *So speak and so act*, James picks up earlier threads in the letter (1:19, 22-25, 26; 2:3) and prepares for further teaching on this recurring theme (2:14-26; 3:1-12; 4:13-17; 5:9, 12). The primary focus of these verses is the possibility of judgment (the idea appears three times). With the reminder of pending judgment, we return to a theme that surfaced at the beginning of the unit (2:4). Earlier James accused his readers of becoming *judges with evil thoughts* because of their discriminatory behavior. Now those same judges will be judged.

These verses are challenging because of the paradoxes they contain. Troy Watson's definition in a *Canadian Mennonite* column defines "paradox" simply and succinctly: "A paradox is when two or more incompatible truths are held together to reveal a deeper hidden truth" (12). James 2:12-13 requires readers to hold together ideas that may seem incongruous to people today: law and freedom, judgment and mercy. Many think of laws as restricting freedom, even if for good reason, because they prevent people from doing something they might otherwise want to do. We are accustomed to thinking of judgment as negative and mercy as positive, especially when they pertain to God's actions. For James, who is a master of pithy sayings and punchy teachings, these paradoxical ideas wrap up his exhortations on how not showing partiality fulfills God's royal law and introduce the diatribe that follows on lived faith.

In 2:12 James reminds the church that judgment on the basis of the *law of liberty* should guide how they speak and act. Presumably, this will discourage them from saying to the rich, "Here, take the best seat in the house," and from acting in a way that dishonors the poor. The law plays a role in convicting people of sin because it holds them accountable to what God desires (2:9). But how is this a *law of liberty?* James's association of the law with freedom seems to clash with Paul's words about Christ setting us free from the law (Rom 7:1-6; Gal 3:13, 23-26). James already used this phrase in 1:25 when he urged the church to gaze steadfastly into the mirror of the *perfect law, the law of liberty*, so that they might act on the implanted word of truth and not just hear it (1:18, 21).

It is helpful to think of the royal law as liberating when one considers its function in community. Adhering to laws can seem to limit freedom only when we think of ourselves primarily as individuals, as in modern Western societies. But the world of Jesus and James was much more communal than ours, and identity was determined in relationship to others. The function of the Torah was to shape the community and give it identity as the called-out people of God.

James's letter was written for the church, a community of believers created as God's first fruits. The royal law socializes them into the kingdom to which they belong and establishes the moral boundaries of the community, which make them distinct from the world around them (Hartin 1999: 79–83). The primary law of this community is love. This is what binds the community together. Because it is other-focused instead of self-focused, it is not restrictive but liberating. The law of God's kingdom is liberating because it sets people free from the desires that give birth to sin (1:15).

In individualistic North American culture, people often resent and resist laws that limit their freedom to do as they please. In the early 1980s mandatory seatbelt laws drew fierce opposition. In the pandemic of the early 2020s some strongly resisted mandatory masks, social distancing, and vaccination mandates. However, setting limits through laws or unwritten expectations also liberates people to say yes to other things, such as safety or health. To say no to adultery is to say yes to vulnerable, a trusting relationship with another person. Jesus' teaching not to store up treasures on earth sets limits on how much one can accumulate but frees one to share generously with others. In all these cases, not only individual freedom and desires are at stake, but also the well-being of others. The *law of liberty*, as James calls it, frees people to serve God with heart, soul, mind, and strength and to love their neighbors as themselves.

Verse 13 concludes the unit but is difficult to understand. The fact that it begins with the conjunction "for" (*gar*) suggests that the verse explains or gives the reason for the imperative in verse 12, but how it does that is opaque. The verse consists of two unconnected, proverb-like statements about the seeming paradox of judgment and mercy. In the first statement, "judgment" is dominant (*Judgment will be without mercy to anyone who has shown no mercy*). In the second, "mercy" prevails (*Mercy triumphs over judgment*). Contributing to the lack of clarity is the fact that it is not obvious whose mercy and whose judgment are in view: God's or people's?

The context of 2:8-11 demands that "judgment" in verses 12-13 refer to God's judgment or, more indirectly, the judgment of God's law, which convicts people of being transgressors. That God's *judgment will be without mercy to anyone who has shown no mercy* may trouble modern readers who prefer to emphasize God's compassion and grace over God's judgment. Jesus intertwined human and divine mercy in the parable of the unmerciful servant (Matt 18:23-35) and the fifth Beatitude (Matt 5:7). The point is surely not God's lack of mercy, since James himself insists that God is compassionate and merciful (5:11; cf. Exod 34:6-7; Ps 103:8-13). Rather, the point of James 2:13 is that those who claim to follow God's kingdom law must show mercy as God shows mercy, since the command to love one's neighbor is the epitome of that law. Those who do not show mercy to the poor demonstrate that *the implanted word* has not taken root (1:21) and that their religion is not *pure and . . . unstained* (1:27). The law of liberty will judge those who show no mercy because they are still enslaved to the world rather than free to serve God.

The second half of verse 13 sounds like an abrupt contradiction of the first half, but it actually restates it in positive terms. Since "mercy" at the end of verse 13a refers to mercy that humans do not show, it follows that "mercy" at the beginning of verse 13b also means human mercy, expressing God's mercy. What is assumed but not explicit in the second statement is that humans can and do show mercy to others. When they do, they experience God's mercy. This brings us back to the earlier comments about paradox. God judges people who do not show mercy *and* is lavishly merciful. Both are true. Yet mercy is more powerful than judgment. In fact, says James, it stands victorious over judgment. In the end, mercy both human and divine has the last word, not judgment.

THE TEXT IN BIBLICAL CONTEXT

Love Your Neighbor

James 2:8 quotes part of Leviticus 19:18 to explain what it means to fulfill the royal law: "*You shall love your neighbor as yourself.*" James is not the only New Testament writer to cite this Scripture. It is found in the synoptic gospels (Matt 5:43; 19:19; 22:39; Mark 12:31-33; Luke 10:27) and two of Paul's letters (Rom 13:9; Gal 5:14). Evidently, the verse was important for Jesus as well as for the early church. These texts shed light on who should be deemed a neighbor, what it means to love that neighbor, and how love for God and neighbor intertwine. We will look at each of these contexts in turn.

Leviticus

In Leviticus, the commandment is part of the Holiness Code (Lev 17–27). In his massive commentary on Leviticus, Jacob Milgrom calls 19:18b "'the culminating point' of [the Holiness Code] as well as the apex of Leviticus" (1656). At the beginning of Leviticus 19, God instructs Moses to tell the people of Israel, "You shall be holy, for I the LORD [Yahweh] your God am holy" (19:2). The words "I am the LORD" or "I am the LORD your God" are a recurring refrain throughout the chapter, including right after "You shall love your neighbor as yourself." As Samuel Balentine puts it, "When God says, 'I am,' what necessarily follows in the divine vocabulary are the words, 'You shall be'" (166). To love the neighbor is central to what it means to be the set-apart people of a holy God and has practical implications for their lives, ritually and morally.

The rest of chapter 19 gives glimpses into what it means to love one's neighbor and who the neighbor is. The Hebrew word for "neighbor" in verse 18b is better translated "fellow human," since it refers not only to the person living next door but anyone with whom one comes into contact (Yoder 2017: 198). Although it refers to a fellow Israelite in verse 18, this includes the poor and the foreigner (vv. 10, 15), the laborer (v. 13), and the deaf and blind (v. 14). Verses 33-34 say that love is to be extended also to the foreigner residing among them. According to Leviticus 19, then, the net encompassing those whom the people of God are to love is thrown wide. The immediate context of verse 18b also illumines what it means to love the neighbor: confronting a wrongdoer instead of harboring hatred, not nursing a grudge, and eschewing revenge. Evidently, loving one's fellow human being is not primarily about how one *feels* toward the neighbor but how one *acts*.

The Gospels

In the Gospels, the love command appears in two kinds of interactions with Jesus. It is quoted in response to someone asking about the greatest commandment (Mark 12:28-34//Matt 22:34-40) and in response to a question about gaining eternal life (Matt 19:16-22// Luke 10:25-37). Sometimes the context is hostile (Matt 22:34-40) and sometimes it is congenial (Mark 12:28-34). When asked which is the first or greatest commandment, Jesus first quotes Deuteronomy 6:5, to love God with all one's heart, soul, mind, and strength. But then he immediately adds a second, "You shall love your neighbor as yourself." The whole of Scripture hinges on the two commandments to love God and neighbor (Matt 22:40).

Scholars debate whether Jesus was the first to put these two commandments together in this way. Some argue that Jesus was an innovator (e.g., Furnish) while others maintain that Jewish writings had long put love of God and love of neighbor together as the heart of the law (e.g., Sanders; Kloppenborg 2008: 706). Certainly the two are inextricably intertwined and "assumed throughout Scripture" (Gardner: 330). For example, the first table of the Decalogue focuses on love for God (Exod 20:1-11) and the second on love for fellow humans (Exod 20:12-17). Although the Johannine literature never quotes Deuteronomy 6:5 or Leviticus 19:18b, the interrelatedness of love of God and neighbor is evident (1 John 4:7-21). Indeed, throughout the Bible, one shows love for God *by* loving the people whom God created in God's image.

"And who is my neighbor?" The legal expert's question in Luke 10:29 is asked by anyone who tries to make the love command manageable. Jesus flips the question away from defining "neighbor" to how to *be* a good neighbor. The scandal of the story about the compassionate Samaritan is not "Be nice even to despised outsiders" but "*Emulate* the despised outsider." Instead of fueling complacency about good deeds done to all one's neighbors, Jesus unsettles his listeners by urging them to be as indiscriminately compassionate as the neighbor they detest.

In Matthew 5:43-48//Luke 6:27-36 Jesus extends the command to love one's neighbor even to loving the enemy. As in Leviticus 19:18, love is not primarily an emotion but choosing to act in a certain way. Specifically, in Jesus' teaching, to love means to show compassion and mercy without expecting repayment, and to do good, bless, and pray for the enemy instead of retaliating with violence.

The Letters of Paul

The love command appears in the two letters of Paul that speak most to the place of the law in Christian life: Romans and Galatians. As in Leviticus and the teachings of Jesus, loving one's neighbor means, positively, serving others (Gal 5:13-14) and negatively, doing no wrong to the neighbor (Rom 13:9-10). The wider context in Romans suggests that to love means to bless those who persecute you, to refrain from taking revenge, and to overcome evil with good (Rom 12:14-21). In both Romans and Galatians, Paul says that the law is fulfilled in the command to love one's neighbor.

In summary, there is continuity across the biblical witness as to who is included in "neighbor" and what it means to "love" the neighbor. The neighbor is not only the person living nearby but any fellow human being, especially those who are in need, different from us, or even the enemy. Though not explicit in Scripture, the neighbor includes also the nonhuman creation for which God provides and which, like humans, awaits redemption (Ps 104; Rom 8:19-23). To love in the biblical sense is choosing to act for the well-being of the other and refraining from vengeance and harm against them. Thus one can love one's neighbors without necessarily liking them.

To be sure, 1 Corinthians 13:1-7 suggests that love is more than just words and actions; it is also a matter of the heart. But consistently, whenever the Law and the Prophets, Jesus, and Paul talk about loving one's neighbor, it is always more than just emotion. To love other people is inseparable from loving God. It fulfills God's will as revealed in the Law and the Prophets. This overarching message of love in the Bible should inform how the church reads those difficult texts that condone violence against the neighbor (e.g., Josh 8).

Justice for the Poor

James charges the church with *dishonoring the poor* (2:6). The reason is not merely that they have failed to feed and clothe the poor, though that may also have been a problem (2:15-16). Rather, they have discriminated against the poor on the basis of outward appearances and have treated them inequitably because of their social status. This is not only a failure of charity; it also is a matter of injustice.

Economic issues permeate the whole Bible, and central to these concerns is justice for the poor. The problem is not only that the poor do not have access to basic necessities of life, but also that they are powerless (Gowan: 344). The poor thus include the widow, orphan, and immigrant, who were "paradigms of the powerless" in the ancient world (Blomberg: 84). The death of the male head of the household threatened the survival of the extended family unit and made the widows and fatherless vulnerable. Sojourners and immigrants had no access to land or inheritance and were without social and safety networks. Together with the materially poor, these groups had a "precarious social status" that "made it possible for others to oppress them" (Gowan: 347; cf. Tamez 1982: 37–38).

The Bible consistently shows God to be on the side of the poor because God defends those who cannot defend themselves and liberates the oppressed. God "executes justice for the orphan and the widow, and . . . loves the strangers, providing them food and clothing" (Deut 10:18). The psalmist repeatedly beseeches and praises God, who "raises the poor from the dust and lifts the needy from the ash heap" (Ps 113:7), who "watches over the strangers [and] upholds the orphan and the widow" (Pss 146:9; cf. 9:18; 12:5; 35:19-20; 82:1-4; 107:4-9). This experience of God is grounded in the salvation event of the exodus. It was incarnated anew in Jesus, God's Messiah, who preached good news to the poor and liberation for the oppressed (Luke 4:18; 7:22-23).

Jesus pronounced the poor to be blessed, not because poverty is good nor because the poor are inherently righteous but because God will give them the kingdom and will fill the hungry with good things (Luke 6:20-21; cf. 1:52-53). This reversal of fortunes begins already with Jesus and the church that gathers in his name (Acts 4:32-35) but will be fully realized in the final coming of God's reign. James echoes Jesus' promise when he says, *Has not God chosen the poor in the world to be rich in faith and to be heirs of the kingdom that he has promised to those who love him?* (James 2:5).

God desires shalom for all people. The reality throughout the Bible and today, however, is that the poor and vulnerable continue to live in our midst. Despite the vision of equality and comprehensive blessing in Deuteronomy 15:4, this text immediately goes on to say, "If there is among you anyone in need . . ." (15:7), and gives instructions for sharing with the needy "since there will never cease to be some in need on the earth" (15:11; cf. John 12:8). Why is this the case? The reasons are diverse, of course. In ancient Israel and in first-century Palestine, most people lived at the subsistence level, but challenging circumstances could push them to or over the edge, such as drought and famine, accidents and disease, war, and death. The fact that "there will never cease to be some in need on the earth" is not because that is God's will or because the poor are culpable for their own misfortune or even primarily because of natural disasters. By far the greatest concern of biblical writers is poverty caused or exacerbated by the unjust and greedy behavior of the elite, the powerful, and the wealthy. As Donald Gowan states, the Old Testament "assumes throughout that there will always be some with relatively more possessions. . . . What is a scandal . . . is when those who do not have so much are deprived of what is rightfully theirs by those whose consciences do not bother them" (Gowan: 350).

Consequently, the Bible persistently critiques the predatory and extractive practices of the rich and powerful and advocates justice for the poor and vulnerable. In Walter Brueggemann's terms, the Bible offers an exposé of an "economy of extraction" and a testimony to an "economy of restoration" (xx; see TBC on 5:1-6 for more on the biblical critique of the rich). The Pentateuch contains various laws designed to curtail the exploitative practices of the rich. The Covenant Code (Exod 20–23), for example, prohibits extracting interest from poor Israelites or keeping a cloak overnight as security for a loan (22:25-27). Judgment is particularly harsh for those who abuse the widow, orphan, and immigrant (22:21-24). Similar laws about justice for the poor and vulnerable appear in Deuteronomy (16:19; 24:10-15, 17-18; 27:19) and Leviticus (19:13-16, 33).

Old Testament laws not only denounce injustice but also mandate positive institutional measures to care for the poor. Deuteronomy 15:7-11 urges God's people to open their hands to the needy and give ungrudgingly and liberally. Farmers are instructed to leave the edges of their fields unharvested so that the poor might glean (Lev 23:22; Deut 24:19-22). Every seventh year Israelites were to let the land rest and allow the poor to harvest whatever grew that year (Exod 23:10-11; cf. Lev 25:1-7). Every fiftieth year, the Jubilee laws mandated that God's people press the reset button and allow for a fresh start by forgiving debts, releasing slaves, and returning land (Lev 25:8-34).

The constant refrain is for Israel to remember that they were once slaves in Egypt and that God had delivered them. As a result, they must treat the vulnerable justly and mercifully. Although the degree to which these Old Testament laws were implemented is unknown, the fact that they were part of Israel's covenant obligations points to their importance in the people's relationship with God. The extent to which the community was living in faithful covenant relationship with God was manifested in their actions toward the most vulnerable.

The fact that the people of God were often *not* faithful in administering justice to the poor is evident in the historical writings, which depict kings oppressing the poor (e.g., 1 Kings 21), and in the writings of the prophets. The following is but a sample of the many prophetic calls for justice.

- "Is not this the fast that I choose: to loose the bonds of injustice, to undo the straps of the yoke, to let the oppressed go free, and to break every yoke? Is it not to share your bread with the hungry, and bring the homeless poor into your house; when you see the naked, to cover them, and not to hide yourself from your own kin?" (Isa 58:6-7)
- "Thus says the LORD: Act with justice and righteousness and deliver from the hand of the oppressor anyone who has been

> robbed. And do no wrong or violence to the alien, the orphan, and the widow, or shed innocent blood in this place." (Jer 22:3)

The Psalms and wisdom literature also urge justice for the poor. For example, "Give justice to the weak and the orphan; maintain the right of the lowly and the destitute. Rescue the weak and the needy; deliver them from the hand of the wicked" (Ps 82:3-4). "Speak out . . . for the rights of all the destitute. . . . Defend the rights of the poor and needy" (Prov 31:8-9).

Jesus came to fulfill the Law and the Prophets (Matt 5:17), not least in their persistent and vigorous demand for justice. Jesus inaugurated God's reign by setting people free from impoverishing disease, feeding the hungry, liberating the rich from the snares of wealth, and welcoming *all* people to sit at God's table. Jesus also called forth a recreated people to join him in implementing God's reign of shalom in their life together, not least in their economic practices. He told stories about forgiving debts (Matt 18:23-35) and about rich people ignoring the destitute on their doorstep (Luke 16:19-31). He taught his disciples to trust God rather than worry about material well-being, to hold loosely to their possessions, and to give generously to those in need (Luke 12:22-34; 16:1-13; 18:18-25). This was not a call for individual charity but a radical reorientation toward God's priorities of "enough for all."

Luke's summary statements in Acts signal the church's attempt to live out God's shalom justice in community (Acts 2:43-47; 4:32-37). Although Paul's writings speak less about justice for the poor than do the Gospels (Davids 2005), we catch glimpses of the church's concern for the vulnerable in Paul's collection for famine relief in Jerusalem (Rom 15:25-28; 2 Cor 8–9; Gal 2:10). The Letter of James stands solidly in the tradition of the Mosaic law, the prophets, and Jesus himself when it calls on the church to resist pandering to the rich and to act justly toward the poor.

THE TEXT IN THE LIFE OF THE CHURCH

Discrimination and the Church

It would not be surprising if Christians in an average North American congregation today would laugh nervously upon reading James 2:1-6. We like to think that all visitors would be welcomed equally warmly regardless of attire. Our discomfort arises from the deep-seated awareness that James's anecdote mirrors a truth we would rather not admit. Giving preferential treatment to some on the basis of wealth, status, ability, and appearance was an issue in James's churches two thousand years ago. It was present among the dinner guests to whom Jesus spoke about not inviting only those who could reciprocate (Luke 14:7-14). It was present in the Corinthian house churches, who were deeply divided over economic and status differences (1 Cor 6:1-8; 11:17-21; 12; 14:1-18). It has been present in the church throughout history and continues today.

Many Christian preachers have used James 2:1-6 to decry favoritism based on dress, to exhort parishioners to care for the poor, and to deplore the luxurious lifestyle of the rich (Gowler: 148–49). Around 1625 the Waterlander Mennonite Pieter Pietersz wrote a treatise titled *The Way to the City of Peace* (from the Dutch, *Wegh na Vreden-stadt*), in which he called the church to spiritual renewal and to a more faithful practice of social justice. He references James 2:5 when he says that good leaders and teachers "consider the poor as highly as the rich, they serve the least of them as much as the most, they do not flatter the rich, and are not judgmental or hard against the impoverished" (Dyck 1995: 250). The 1942 edition of *Doran's Ministers Manual* contains resources for a sermon on "The Harm of Showy Dress in Church" and concludes with the following quotation: "Full many people go to church, as everybody knows; some go to close their eyes, and some to eye their clothes" (quoted in Gowler: 89).

Unfortunately, in *practice* the church has often made distinctions on the basis of outward appearances, wealth, and status. One example is the practice of renting church pews in nineteenth-century mainline churches. Although the income supported the church's work, it meant that the wealthy could claim the best seats while the poor had to sit in the back (Moore-Keish: 91; Gowler: 150). Some church leaders lamented the practice even as they felt it necessary. The church no longer rents pews, but the influence of wealth and power is nevertheless persistent and corrosive. Whenever a Christian institution is unable to speak out about controversial justice issues for fear of losing financial support from wealthy constituents, the sin of partiality is alive. Whenever church committee members listen attentively to an economically secure, white, male businessman and ignore the voice of the young female student, the sin of partiality is alive. Money and status still speak loudly in the church and privilege some individuals over others.

Because the example James gives is about the privileged treatment of a richly dressed man, it might be tempting to limit our thinking about discrimination to issues of wealth or individual behavior. What James condemns is much broader and has wide-ranging implications. First, discrimination against some and preferential treatment of others in church and society today is based not only on economic status but also on the color of someone's skin, gender, age, sexuality, level of education, occupation, and so on. As Gay Byron writes, "Simple categories [such as rich and poor] do not reflect adequately the larger ethical and theological implications of this text or the subtle ways in which status and class are interlaced with other marks of distinction such as ethnicity, gender, age, ability, etc." (Byron: 465).

Second, the sin of discrimination not only characterizes individuals but is systemic and structural, deeply embedded in political, economic, social, and even religious institutions. It is persistent because it is often subtle and often overlooked by people of privilege who benefit from it. Followers of Jesus who heed James's admonition in 2:1-6 will take seriously the intersectional and systemic nature of discrimination in addition to the way it infects individuals.

Some Christian leaders have drawn on James 2:1-6 in their opposition to racial segregation in the United States and apartheid in South Africa. Benjamin Mays, born in 1894 to former slaves, eventually became a pastor, professor, and mentor to Martin Luther King Jr. In his 1954 address to the World Council of Churches, he argued that "since its inception, the Christian Church has held in its membership people of different nations, races, and even colors. Nowhere in the early church do we find distinctions drawn on the basis of country or race. James (2:1-6) condemns the separation of cultural or social groups in the local church" (quoted in Gowler: 153). D. J. Smit, a South African Reformed theologian and an outspoken opponent of apartheid, applies James's words on partiality to the church in South Africa:

> In many South African churches one will find the same kind of problem to which James refers in his example: . . . the church—in spite of the fact that they are poor, oppressed, powerless, "black" themselves—pay much more respect and honour to the rich and powerful, than to the poor, the women, the widows, the orphans, the children, among their own members. (66)

In North American society today, it is not hard to find examples of systemic social discrimination. Rich people receive preferential treatment at banks, benefit from better medical care, and have access to better schools (Brueggemann: 254). Stories of harassment and inequitable treatment on the basis of skin color are heart-breaking and ubiquitous. Evidence that the criminal justice system discriminates against black, Indigenous, and people of color is "overwhelming," according to some studies, and is reflected in the disproportionately high number of people from those populations in the prison system (see, e.g., the article by Radley Balko in *The Washington Post*, June 10, 2020). The rich and the famous who break the law get slapped on the wrist, while those without recourse to expensive lawyers or powerful connections receive lengthy prison sentences.

The problem is not limited to the broader society. The church also participates in systemic injustice, often ignorant of the way in which long-standing practices favor some and hurt others. Martin Luther King Jr. once said that 11:00 on Sunday morning is one of the most segregated hours in North America. Racial discrimination is still deeply embedded in the church today, to name only one example. Apathy, ignorance, and cowardice make the church complicit in the kind of favoritism James denounces. As D. J. Smit says, "The problem is that we can become so accustomed to this, that we may fully and enthusiastically agree with the rejection of 'partiality' and 'discrimination,' and still accept discriminatory practices and structures as natural, as the way things are and ought to be" (66–67).

This is not to deny that many churches and individuals are striving to become sanctuaries of justice and are working for change. But the road to justice for all is long, and we have "miles to go before we sleep." James would also chide the church today: *My dear brothers and sisters, how can you claim to have faith in our glorious Lord Jesus Christ if you favor some people over others?* (NLT)

James 2:14-26

Unity of Faith and Works

PREVIEW

Modern Christians disillusioned with the church criticize those who do not practice what they preach. They are turned off by the hypocrisy of Christians who act unlovingly while claiming to serve a God of love. This is also James's concern in 2:14-26. In the second half of the chapter, he virtually bludgeons his readers with a single message: faith is authentic only when accompanied by good deeds. This unit's "thesis" is reiterated in multiple ways: faith without works is dead (vv. 17, 26), barren (v. 20), useless (vv. 14, 16), and unable to save (v. 14). The second half of the unit makes the same point in positive terms: like Abraham and Rahab, people are in right relationship with God when their lives reflect their faith (vv. 21-24, 25).

Although the importance of lived faith is most concentrated and explicit in 2:14-26, the topic is a continuation of what James has already said. Privileging the rich and dishonoring the poor is inconsistent with faith in Jesus Christ. True faith is expressed in love of neighbor and deeds of mercy, fulfilling the law of God's kingdom (2:1-13). Integrity of faith and deeds means not only hearing God's word but also doing it (1:22-25). True faith guards the tongue, cares for orphans and widows (1:26-27), and endures trials and temptation (1:2-4, 12).

This section of the letter has also provoked the most controversy because of its apparent contradiction of Paul's theology of justification by faith alone. Although James and Paul use words such as "faith" and "works" in radically different ways and use common scriptural traditions (such as the Abraham story) for different ends, they both understand ethical living to be integral to faith in Jesus Christ. James's agenda in this unit is not a theoretical, theological debate with Paul; instead, it is urgent, practical instruction to Jewish messianic congregations in the Diaspora about the need for genuine faith to be evident in how they live.

OUTLINE

Faith without Works as Useless, Hypocritical, and Dead, 2:14-17
Objection and Rebuttal: True Faith and Works Are Inseparable, 2:18-20
Two Exemplars of Works Completing Faith: Abraham and Rahab, 2:20-26

These three subunits each end with the claim that *faith without works is dead* or barren (vv. 17, 20, 26). The first two argue *against* the separation of faith and works. The third argues *for* the necessity of both works and faith in salvation. Verse 20 is a transitional verse, both concluding verses 18-20 and introducing verses 20-26.

EXPLANATORY NOTES

Faith without Works as Useless, Hypocritical, and Dead 2:14-17

Unfortunately, English translations cannot fully capture how skillfully James uses language to mount an argument in 2:14-26. Rhetorical questions, repetition, imaginary interlocutors, chiasm, and scriptural allusions all become tools to hammer home one dominant conviction: genuine faith must be demonstrated in actions. The fact that this unit constitutes round two of an argument already made in 2:1-13 is evident in some structural parallels: (1) Both pericopes begin by addressing the relationship of faith and behavior (2:1, 14), followed by a long question envisioning a hypothetical encounter with a needy person in the church (2:2-4 and 2:15-16). (2) In the first half of the chapter, a quotation from Leviticus 19 is central to the argument (2:8). In the second half, two Old Testament exemplars play a key role.

James 2:14-17 consists of three rhetorical questions (vv. 14a, 14b, 15-16) bracketed by the words *What good is it?* and ends with the recurring thesis of the unit: *Faith . . . , if it has no works, is dead* (v. 17). The Greek phrasing of the questions is such that each anticipates a negative answer. The correct response to *What good is it . . . ?* (v. 14) is, "None at all!" and to *Such faith cannot save, can it?* (AT) is, "Of course not!" This is James's way of implying, "Surely you must agree with me!"

The NRSV translates verse 14 with the second person: *Can faith save you?* But the Greek actually uses third person: *If someone claims to have faith, . . . such faith is not able to save that one, is it?*" (AT; cf. NRSVue). As Holly Hearon points out, using third-person narration "creates room for the audience to stand back, observe, and consider whether or not they see their own speech actions reflected in the third-person characters, who are like them but who are not them" (Hearon: 355). Then in verse 16, readers are drawn closer with the more pointed second-person address: *One of you says . . .*

Taken out of context, the question *Faith cannot save, can it?* might confuse readers today. However, James is not referring to faith in general. In Greek the article before "faith" points back to the word "faith" in the previous sentence: "*What good is it, my brothers and sisters, if someone claims to have faith but does not have works?*" (Wallace: 219; Zerwick: 695). *Claiming* to have faith is not the same as having faith. What James is saying in verse 14c, then, is "*Such* a faith, which is professed but lacks deeds, cannot save someone."

This is not the first occurrence of the word "faith" (*pistis*) in the letter, but 2:14-26 contains a high concentration of such vocabulary: eleven of the sixteen uses of the noun (2:14 [2×], 17, 18 [3×], 20, 22 [2×], 24, 26) and the only three uses of the verb "to have faith/believe" (*pisteuō*; 2:19 [2×], 23). To be sure, sometimes "faith" in this unit is faith in name only, thus not really faith. If such word use sounds slippery to us, we should note that it is consistent with how James elsewhere uses words like "religion" and "wisdom." True religion is demonstrated by *care for orphans and widows*; *worthless religion*, betrayed by unbridled tongues, is not true religion (1:26-27). Wisdom characterized by *bitter envy and selfish ambition* is not really wisdom; true wisdom is *from above* and is demonstrated in fruits of *peace*, *gentle*ness, and *mercy* (3:13-18). Thus, true faith really does save, but faith that is not lived out is not true faith and thus cannot save. Claiming to have faith without corresponding deeds shows that one lacks integrity or is double-minded (1:8; 4:8).

So what then is true faith, according to James? The Greek noun *pistis* can be translated in various ways, including "belief, faith, fidelity, faithfulness, confidence" (BDAG). In James, true faith encompasses all these aspects. It is dynamic, holistic, and active. It involves head, heart, and hands. As Martha Moore-Keish says, it is propositional, personal, and practical (Moore-Keish, 38–39). Faith as *belief* includes assenting to the truth of something, such as believing *that God is one* (2:19), but it is much more than that. True faith is also relational. It is *trust* in God, who is infinitely good, gracious, generous (1:5, 17; 4:5-6), compassionate, and merciful (5:11). It is trust in Jesus as Lord and Messiah in the context of a faith family (2:1).

Faith is also *fidelity* to God, namely, "trust and commitment maintained, over time and through testing circumstances" (Bauckham 1999: 120). Although all these dimensions are present in James, the emphasis falls heavily on trust and faithfulness, not on belief. Because God is committed to the shalom of all people, fidelity to God finds expression in the context of community, in practical deeds of justice, mercy, and love for neighbor.

James claims that *faith without works* is useless because it *cannot save* (2:14). Modern readers hear the word "save" through twenty centuries of theological discourse and colored by contemporary religious expressions. But this letter is not a theological treatise: to understand what James means by the word, we need to be attentive to context. The immediate context suggests that to be saved is to be in right relationship with God, since the claim that *faith without works cannot save* is used in parallel fashion to *faith without works cannot justify* (cf. 2:24-25). Elsewhere in the letter, to be "saved" is deliverance from present adversity, such as physical sickness (5:15), and from eschatological judgment, as in 4:12 (God alone can *save* and *destroy*) and 5:20 (restoration of *a sinner* will *save the soul from death*).

Salvation is not only rescue from destruction, but also the bestowal of blessing. In 1:21 James says that when God's implanted word takes root, it has the power to *save your souls*, by which he means a person's whole self (see comments on 1:21). This implanted word is the same *word of truth* by which God births people into a new existence, making them the vanguard or first fruits of God's redeemed creation (1:18, 21). Those who are saved will receive *the crown of life* and are *heirs* of God's *kingdom* (1:12; 2:5). Salvation is thus a present reality and a future event, both deliverance from evil and bestowal of blessing.

What James means by "works" requires clarification. Luke Timothy Johnson suggests replacing the word with "deeds" to avoid the "faith and works" dichotomy of Protestant assumptions

(Johnson 1995: 237). For James, "works" constitute behavior consistent with the transformed life brought about by God's implanted word of truth. Works are actions that embody love for the neighbor, such as not showing partiality to the rich, caring for widows and orphans, and truthful speech. When James speaks about works as obedience to Torah, he is not referring to the ritual requirements of the law or distinctive Jewish identity markers such as circumcision or food laws, but of the practical outworking of faith in deeds of mercy and justice, summed up in the *royal law* of *love* (2:8). The issue James and Paul are addressing and the context into which they speak are thus quite different. (See further TBC below and the related essay *[James and Paul on Faith and Works, p. 348]*).

In this call to "practice" faith, James stands firmly in his Jewish heritage—in the line of prophets, for example, who repeatedly called on God's people to act with justice toward their neighbors and were critical of religious ritual devoid of ethical living (Isa 1:11-17; Amos 5:21-24). James is also consistent with the teachings of John the Baptist and Jesus (Luke 3:7-14; Matt 7:15-27) and, indeed, of Paul himself (Rom 2:6-8; 12:1-2; Gal 6:7-10; Phil 2:12-16), all of whom reiterate the importance of active, lived faith.

In verses 15-16 James presses his point by imagining a possible scenario. Although perhaps not an actual occurrence, the situation is fitting for a community in which disparities of wealth and poverty are not hypothetical. The picture James paints, with exaggerated effect, has just enough truth in it to prompt uneasy self-reflection: "Have *I* ever done something like this?" That the scenario takes place in the faith community and not elsewhere is evident by the fact that he speaks of a *brother or sister*, language used elsewhere for fellow believers, and says, *one of you*, not the generic *someone* of verse 14.

Interestingly, James explicitly includes *or sister* here. Throughout the letter he addresses his audience as "brothers," though this is often translated as "brothers and sisters" because the church then, as today, included women. Why does James suddenly now explicitly specify *a sister* (v. 15)? A possible reason is that women were among the most vulnerable in society (e.g., *widows* in 1:27), and so when he imagines someone in dire need, it is easy to imagine this being a woman.

The brother or sister in need *is naked and lacks daily food* (v. 15). We should not think of someone as literally nude here. Rather, James is using hyperbole to communicate the extreme vulnerability of a person who lacks adequate clothing (McKnight: 230). Interestingly, when James denounced his readers' biased conduct in 2:1-13, he also used clothing as an indicator of a person's socioeconomic status (vv. 2-4). The situation in verse 15 is even more perilous, for the person is nearly *naked*, not just clothed in rags, and goes day to day without knowing if there will be enough to eat.

The believer's caricaturized response sounds absurd: *Go in peace; keep warm and eat your fill.* Pious platitudes do not "warm and fill" someone who is "naked and hungry." Although wishing someone "peace" was a common greeting in ancient Middle Eastern society, the words mean more in Christian discourse. *Peace*, the equivalent of the Hebrew "shalom," connotes wholeness, well-being, and right relationships. It is closely tied to salvation. It is not just a state of mind or spiritual condition but embraces the whole body. In the Gospels, Jesus uses the words "Go in peace" or "Peace be with you" in the context of concrete acts of healing, forgiveness, and reconciliation (Luke 7:50; 8:48; 24:36). When Jesus grants people "peace," his words are performative speech. That is, they enact what they declare, proffering salvation by healing people's bodies, spirits, and minds. The hypothetical believer's words *Go in peace* thus present a striking contrast to Jesus' gift of shalom. They are devoid of meaning when not accompanied by actions that enact such peace, much like "thoughts and prayers" in response to gun violence are empty words without action to stem such violence. They are like the words of Israel's leaders, whom Jeremiah condemns for treating "the wound of my people carelessly" and proclaiming, "'Peace, peace,' when there is no peace" (Jer 6:14; 8:11). According to James, faith that offers such fake "peace" cannot be a saving faith (v. 14b). This is also a prime example of what James calls *worthless religion* in 1:26-27, for it exemplifies insensitive use of the tongue, self-deception, and failure to care for the vulnerable in their distress. The example ends with the same words that began verse 14: *What is the good of that?* (v. 16). By bracketing the material inside (vv. 14-16), these words emphasize the vacuousness of action-less faith.

The string of rhetorical questions concludes with the words, *So faith by itself, if it has no works, is dead.* This is the main point of the unit, and James hammers it home by repeating it two more times (vv. 20, 26). The language is stark and uncompromising: Faith that is not evident in deeds is not just a weak or sick faith, but a corpse. It is no faith at all!

Objection and Rebuttal: True Faith and Works Are Inseparable 2:18-20

James's critique of faith that does not go beyond religious clichés could provoke a comeback from people who think they have faith but *deceive their hearts* (1:26). In this subunit, James voices such an objection from an imaginary conversation partner (*But someone will say . . .* ; 2:18a) and gives a two-part rebuttal (vv. 18b-c, 19). The subunit concludes with the recurring thesis of the passage, phrased as a rhetorical question (v. 20). The practice of engaging an imaginary interlocutor in dialogue in order to argue a point was a Greek literary convention and effective teaching method called a diatribe. It is used elsewhere in Scripture and early Christian writings (e.g., Rom 9:19; 11:19; 1 Cor 15:35; Barnabas 9.6).

Many commentators have described James 2:18 as one of the most difficult verses in the letter. Although the overall sense of it is clear enough in context, the wording is confusing. The opening words of verse 18 make it sound as if James's sparring partner (*someone*) claims to have works, but that is precisely what the someone (*you*) in verse 14 does *not* have. James's response in verse 18bc (*Show me your faith . . .*) would make more sense if his opponent had said, "I have faith and you have works"; but instead he says, *You have faith and I have works* (v. 18a). This confusion raises several questions: Is the imaginary conversation partner in verse 18 an opponent of James or an ally of James? To whom do the pronouns *you* and *I* refer? And does the referent change in the middle of the verse? How far does the speech of the conversation partner extend, and where does James's rejoinder begin?

There are five main options for making sense of this difficult text:

First, something was dropped or changed in the transmission of the text so that the current wording is not what the letter originally said. However, since no manuscript evidence supports such a hypothesis, it is unconvincing.

Second, perhaps the "someone" in verse 18 is an ally of James rather than an opponent, and this ally says to the works-less person in verses 14-17, "You say you have faith and I have works. Fine. Show me this faith without doing any works. It's not possible, is it? On the other hand, I can you show you my faith by the works I do." However, the most natural way to take the first words of verse 18 are as an objection to what precedes, not a confirmation. The *but* (*alla*) that introduces verse 18 would have to be translated "indeed," which is not impossible but unlikely. Also, that James would introduce and quote a hypothetical "someone" on his side so abruptly is unconvincing.

Third, perhaps the speaker changes at the first "and." That is, an opponent challenges James with a question, "Do you really have faith?" (The Greek can be read either as a question or as a statement.) To this James replies, "[Yes!] *And I* have works! Show me your faith without works." Again, this is unconvincing because of how the Greek "and I" (*kagō*) would normally function, namely, to tie two clauses together, not to introduce a different speaker. Besides, the problem is not whether James has faith, but whether the opponent has works.

Fourth, another proposal takes the words in verse 18a as indirect discourse, so that James is recounting what a third party might say: "But someone will say that you (interlocutor) have faith and that I (James) have works." This interpretation is appealing because it is consistent with verse 14 in representing the "you" as someone with "faith" and the "I" as James, who has works. Unfortunately, this solution is grammatically untenable because it does not conform to how Greek signals indirect speech.

Fifth, a proposal that many scholars consider most viable understands the pronouns "I" and "you" as not specific but referring to two different kinds of people, that is, "some people have faith and other people have works" (e.g., Ropes, McKnight, Johnson 1995, McCartney 2009, Hartin 2009a). In verses 18bc-19, James reacts strongly against the idea that faith and works can be separate and distinct, like different spiritual gifts. The flaw with this proposal is that it is hard to understand why James would use Greek emphatic personal pronouns ("*You* have faith, and *I* have works") when he simply meant "one person" and "another," for which Greek had perfectly acceptable alternatives. Moreover, in verse 18bc the pronouns really do seem to mean "you" and "I," requiring a sudden switch. As Peter Davids concedes, "If this is what James means, he has expressed it very awkwardly" (1982: 123–24).

There is no problem-free solution to 2:18, and we may need to be content with not fully understanding what James meant. Yet the following explanation, most closely aligned with the fifth option, seems the most compelling. In verses 14-17 James provides an example of someone who claims to have faith but does not demonstrate it in deeds, thereby exposing it as pseudofaith. In verse 18a he imagines a critical rejoinder: *But someone will say, "<u>You</u> have faith and <u>I</u> have works."* This new hypothetical "someone" thinks that faith and works can be separated and not everyone needs to have both.

The emphatic personal pronouns accentuate the contrast between the imagined speaker, who does a lot of good deeds, and his fellow Christian, who has strong beliefs. In good diatribe style, James responds to this hypothetical situation by showing how outlandish it is. His comeback is "Okay then, show me how it is even possible for faith to exist without works." Implicit, of course, is the reality that such is not possible. Faith cannot be "shown" apart from tangible actions. James follows by stating what he, in contrast, *can* do: I will you show you what faith is by my actions (2:18).

The point is not the merit of James's own actions but rather the fact that faith is visible only when embodied in corresponding deeds. Despite the ambiguity of the wording in verse 18, the main point of James's argument is nevertheless clear: far from being an optional add-on, deeds cannot be separated from genuine faith any more than heat can be separated from fire or breath from a living being (McCartney 2009: 156). The First Nations Version captures this sense well: *But someone will say, "Faith is what is needed," while another says, "Good deeds are what is needed." I say that both are needed.*

Part 2 of James's rebuttal begins with another rhetorical question: *Do you believe that God is one?* (v. 19, AT). The word "believe" (*pisteuō*) is the verb form of the noun "faith, trust, fidelity" (*pistis*) in verses 14-18. In verse 19 it has the sense of "to believe something to be true, to give intellectual assent to," whereas elsewhere in James the sense is more "to rely on, be loyal to" (as in 1:6; 2:23), without necessarily excluding the former (believing something is true).

James's question, "Do you believe that God is one?" zeroes in on one of the fundamental convictions of Jewish and Christian faith: the belief that there is only one God. Most commentators see in this verse an allusion to the Shema, the ancient Hebrew credo that begins, "Hear, O Israel: The LORD is our God, the LORD alone" (or "the LORD is one"; Deut 6:4-5). James's primarily Jewish audience likely recited this regularly in worship, and to them he says, "Good for you!" His commendation, however, is laced with irony, for in the next breath he reminds his reader: *Even the demons believe—and shudder*. Of course, the Shema itself assumes more than a mere profession of belief, for it continues, "You shall love the LORD your God with all your heart and with all your soul and with all your might" (Deut 6:4-5). In other words, love with a whole-person commitment to the one true God. For the purpose of his argument, however, James assumes verbal profession of monotheistic belief is possible without it affecting the whole of life (Bauckham 1999: 121).

In the synoptic gospels, Jesus heals people by casting out "demons" or "unclean spirits," which represent the realm of Satan (e.g., Matt 9:34; Mark 1:34; Luke 8:27-39). These demons "believe" that Jesus has come from God and acts with divine authority, but they do not "trust" Jesus or submit to him out of loyalty. Their "faith" is only intellectual assent to something, and Jesus' word elicits a response of terror. This is a far cry from the trusting response of the poor who love God and will inherit God's kingdom (James 2:5). James is not accusing people who do not do good works of being demonic. As elsewhere in the letter, he uses dramatic language to make his point: A faith that is not incarnated in concrete deeds of justice and mercy is no better than the gutless, fearful acknowledgment of demons.

The subunit ends with yet another reiteration of the main point of the chapter: *Do you want to be shown, you senseless person, that faith apart from works is worthless?* (v. 20). Literally, James says, *You empty person!* ostensibly "empty" of good sense or wisdom since they don't "know" and "need to be shown." Given James's warnings elsewhere about uncharitable speech (1:26; 3:2-12; 4:11; 5:9), we may object to James addressing his listener as *you senseless person.* However, he is not calling people nasty names, speaking to an actual individual, or even asking a question that expects an answer. He is using conventional debate rhetoric. The word that NRSVue translates as *worthless* is a play on words in the Greek. The word for "works" is *erga* and for "worthless" is *argē (a+erga).* A literal equivalent in English would be, "Faith without actions is inactive" or "Faith without works doesn't work." Faith that does not result in deeds is but a hollow shell—useless, unproductive, matching the "emptiness" of the person who claims such a faith.

Two Exemplars of Works Completing Faith: Abraham and Rahab 2:20-26

In the two preceding subunits, James emphasized the shallowness of claiming to have faith without corresponding deeds (vv. 14-17) and the impossibility of separating true faith and works (vv. 18-20). Now he puts forth a *positive* rationale for why faith must be accompanied by action, doing so by turning to the testimony of Scripture. The argument is enclosed in the now-familiar insistence that faith without works is useless or dead (vv. 20, 26).

Verse 20, a transitional verse, both concludes the previous subunit and introduces the next one. Verses 20-26 are structured as a chiasm, a literary device in which words, phrases, or ideas in the second half of a unit parallel those in the first half, but in reverse order, in an *A B C B′ A′* pattern. Organizing ideas in this manner highlights what lands in the center, in this case a quotation from the Torah and an assertion about *our ancestor Abraham*. The shape of the unit is as follows:

- ***A*** *Faith without works is worthless* (v. 20 AT)
  - ***B*** Rhetorical question expecting a "yes" answer and holding up a model from Scripture: *Abraham [was] justified by works* (v. 21)
    - ***C*** *You* (sg.) *see*; faith and works are *both* necessary and work together (v. 22)
      - ***D*** [Scripture was fulfilled in one who was a *friend of God* (v. 23)]
    - ***C′*** *You* [pl.] *see*; faith and works are *both* necessary and work together (v. 24)
  - ***B′*** Rhetorical question expecting a "yes" answer and holding up a model from Scripture: Rahab was *justified by works* (v. 25)
- ***A′*** *Faith without works is . . . dead* (v. 26)

The parallels between *A* and *A′* plus *B* and *B′* are obvious in Greek, where phrases are word-for-word the same. Leading into the center (vv. 20-22), James uses singular verbs, and the focus is on Abraham. When James turns from the center (vv. 24-25), the scope broadens (pl. *you* and generalized: *a person is justified*), and the complementary example of Rahab is briefer. In verse 26 the main point of the chapter is restated one final time.

The unit begins in verse 20 with a rhetorical question posed to the same imaginary interlocutor of previous verses who is challenging the necessity of "works." The question is more of a statement, though, since it is really a platform from which James will launch his case. James's first statement about Abraham is also framed as a question that expects an affirmative answer (v. 21). He wants his listeners to agree with him, to see things from his perspective, like modern speakers who end their sentences with "right?"

James establishes kinship with his readers by calling Abraham *our ancestor* (lit., *our father*). The idea that Abraham was the father of the Jewish people is present elsewhere in biblical and noncanonical literature (e.g., Isa 51:2; Sir 44:22; 4 Macc 17:6; Matt 3:9; John 8:39; Acts 7:2; Rom 4:1). Although the designation *our father* points to the Jewishness of James and his readers, the phrase does not exclude Gentile believers, who became part of the people of

God and descendants of Abraham through faith. The fact that Rahab is the other example suggests that non-Jews drawn to faith in Israel's God—specifically, through the Messiah Jesus—are also included in the community of faith.

James uses Abraham and Rahab to make the point that people are justified not by faith alone (which would not be true faith in any case, according to James) but by faith *and* deeds working together. The most difficult word in verse 21 is the Greek verb translated "justified" in the NRSVue. The verb (*dikaioō*) is related to the noun "righteousness" or "justice" (*dikaiosynē*; 1:20; 2:23; 3:18), and the adjective "righteous" or "just" (*dikaios*; 5:6, 16). Unfortunately, there is no cognate verb for "righteousness" and "righteous" in English. We cannot say someone was "righteous-ified." So it is not evident that "justify" in verses 21-25 is simply the verb form of "righteousness" in 2:23. If one translates the noun and adjective as "justice" and "just," the connection to "justify" is more evident. E. P. Sanders coined the verb "righteoused" as an alternative to "justified" to make verbal connections in the "righteousness" word group more transparent (Shillington: 89, n. 49).

What does "justify" mean in these verses? The answer to this question often gets tangled up in Paul's understanding of "justification" in Romans and Galatians, but for now we will limit our comments to the Letter of James *[James and Paul on Faith and Works, p. 348]*. Although the word "justify" (*dikaioō*) appears with several possible meanings in biblical literature, two are most relevant for James: (1) the juridical sense of "to *declare* someone to be righteous or just," to acquit of wrongdoing; or (2) "to *prove* or demonstrate that someone is righteous or in the right" (BDAG 249; McCartney 2009: 162). The former is most common in the Bible, but James 2:14-26 encompasses both.

In verse 21, James says that Abraham was *justified by works when [or because] he offered his son Isaac on the altar*. Here the second sense of the word "justify" applies, for Abraham was proven to be righteous when he was willing even to give up the son of promise. The near-sacrifice of Isaac in Genesis 22, often referred to as the *Aqedah* (Hebrew: "binding") demonstrated Abraham's complete commitment to God. Many ancient Jewish writings speak of this event as the climax of ten tests that Abraham endured and connect Abraham's righteousness to his faithfulness to God through times of trial. For example, 1 Maccabees 2:52 says, "Was not Abraham found faithful when tested, and it was reckoned to him as righteousness?" (also Sir 44:20: "When [Abraham] was tested he proved faithful"; and Jubilees 17–18). Readers of James may recall 1:3-4, where James says, *The testing of your faith produces endurance. And let endurance complete its work, so that you may be complete and whole*; enduring trials successfully results in God's gift of the *crown of life* (1:12). These words certainly apply to Abraham, who proved faithful when he was tested, most severely when the fulfillment of God's promise of descendants seemed impossible.

James knows that God's vindication or declaration of Abraham as righteous (first definition) occurred even before this occasion of testing. God justified Abraham not only on the basis of his works but because his faith and actions were "coworkers." Abraham's deeds completed or perfected a faith that already existed and on the basis of which God deemed him righteous (vv. 22-23). Because Abraham trusted God fully and was committed to God, he obeyed God's command to leave homeland and family.

In Genesis 15, God promised Abraham and Sarah an heir and as many descendants as the stars in the sky. Despite there being no sign of this happening and no reasonable way it could come about, Abraham believed that God could make the impossible possible. As a result, God deemed him righteous (*It was reckoned to him as righteousness*; James 2:23, quoting Gen 15:6). Abraham's willingness to give up Isaac, the child of promise, in obedience to what God seemed to be asking, "fulfilled" Genesis 15:6 because it confirmed what was already true, that God reckoned Abraham as righteous. In Genesis 22:12 the angel of the Lord says, "For now I know that you fear God, since you have not withheld your son, your only son, from me." Thus, Abraham was considered righteous because he demonstrated his trust in God through concrete actions of obedience to what he understood God to be commanding, even when they seemed to jeopardize God's promises.

Although "faith" and "works" are not the same, for James they cannot be separated in a righteous person. To argue about whether Abraham was justified because of his faith or because of his deeds misses James's point, for the two cooperate equally in a person whom God declares to be in right relationship with God. James does not, here or anywhere in the letter, explicitly say it is faith in Jesus Christ that cooperates with works to justify. However, in 2:1 he questions how his audience can show favoritism while also having faith in *our Lord Jesus Christ*, suggesting that Jesus is the implicit object of faith in James.

The quotation from Genesis 15:6 lies at the center of the chiasm in 2:20-26 and is the focal point toward which the text moves because it is vital that James's argument for the integrity of faith and deeds is firmly grounded in the church's Scriptures. The center of the chiasm includes another element, however: that Abraham *was called the friend of God* (v. 23d). The Septuagint does not use the Greek word "friend" (*philos*) anywhere for Abraham but it does refer to Abraham as "beloved" (a form of *agapaō*) of God in 2 Chronicles 20:7 and Isaiah 41:8 (translated "friend" in NRSVue). In Genesis 18:17 the relationship between God and Abraham is so intimate that God cannot hide from Abraham the thing God is about to do. When Philo cites Genesis 18:17, he does use the phrase "friend of God" (Allison 2013: 495). The closest the Old Testament comes to calling someone a "friend" of God is in Exodus 33:11: "Thus the LORD used to speak to Moses face to face, as one speaks to a friend." Nonetheless, the tradition that Abraham was a friend of God runs deep and wide in Jewish and Christian literature before and after James. The book of Jubilees, which highlights Abraham's lifelong faithfulness, is one such writing: "He was found faithful, and was recorded on the heavenly tablets as the friend of God" (19.9-10; see also Philo, *On Abraham* 273 and *On Sobriety* 55; Damascus Document 3.2; 1 Clement 10.1).

What does it mean for Abraham to be called *the friend of God*? Why is this claim at the heart of James's argument about faith and works? Among Greek writers, friendship was one of the most highly esteemed relationships and the subject of much philosophical and ethical discourse. "It was regarded as a particularly intense and inclusive kind of intimacy, not only at the physical level but, above all, at the spiritual" (Johnson 1985: 173). Greek writings emphasize equality as an essential characteristic of friendship. Friends were "one soul" or "another self" and shared a common outlook (Johnson 1995: 243–44). If one considers that God is the giver of *every good and perfect gift*, including *the kingdom* and *the crown of life* (NIV: 1:12, 17; 2:5) and that God is the *one lawgiver and judge who is able to save and destroy* (4:12), it is evident that Abraham and God are not equals.

We find a clue to what James means by calling Abraham the friend of God in 4:4, where he says that to be *a friend of the world* is to be *an enemy of God*. His comments about friendship belong within the ancient Jewish conception of "the two ways," contrasting the way of death and the way of life (see below, on 4:1-6). It is a dualistic frame of reference in which the world, worthless religion, and wisdom from below constitute the wrong path; and God, pure religion, and *wisdom from above* are the right path. The *world* operates with wisdom from below, which is characterized by *selfishness*, *envy*, and *wickedness* (3:14-16), whereas wisdom from above is *gentle*, *peaceable*, and *merciful* (3:13, 17-18). True religion is *unstained by the world* because it cares for the vulnerable; worthless religion is characterized by loose lips and a deceived heart (1:27).

According to Jewish wisdom and to James, one cannot walk both roads at the same time. To try to do so is to be double-minded (1:8; 4:8), to lack integrity, to not be whole or complete (1:4). It is in this context that we must think of Abraham as a friend of God, not a friend of the world. Although not equal with God, Abraham, like a true friend, had his attitudes, values, perceptions, and commitments aligned with God's. His faith was not *worthless religion* or *barren* or *dead* because it was expressed in faithful obedience. Abraham was a friend of God because his trust and actions had a unity or integrity impossible in the double-minded person. As Luke Timothy Johnson says, for James, faith made Abraham the friend of God because he "accepted God's way of seeing the situation and acted on it" (1985: 174). In the Wisdom of Solomon, a Jewish writing that dates from within a century of the Letter of James, wisdom is said to enter "into holy souls and make them friends of God" (7:27). As a friend of God, Abraham had this kind of wisdom. To trust in God, as Abraham did, and to demonstrate such faith in the *fruit of righteousness* (3:18) and in *works* of right living (3:13) is, according to James, the wisdom that makes one a friend of God.

From the center of the chiasm in verse 23, James begins to move outward again, reinforcing what has been said so far. In verse 24 he rephrases verse 22, extrapolating from Abraham to "a person" in general: *You* [pl.] *see that a person is justified by works and not by faith alone.* Note that James never says a person is justified *only* by works, but it also cannot be only by faith since that is not true faith.

James then calls up another witness from Scripture, again using a rhetorical question that anticipates agreement (v. 25). A more different example from Abraham could hardly be found. Abraham is *our ancestor*, a respected patriarch of the Hebrew people. Rahab is a woman, an innkeeper/prostitute, a foreigner in Israel. Perhaps James uses these two characters as examples because they represent opposite ends of the spectrum with regard to gender, social status, ethnicity, and religious heritage. If what he is saying about faith and works can be exemplified by two such dissimilar models, then surely it is applicable to everyone in between.

Rahab's story is found in Joshua 2. As with Abraham, James's point is that her *works* of hospitality and protection to the Hebrew messengers "justify her" and demonstrate her righteousness. Rahab's words to the spies may be considered an expression of faith in the God of Israel: "I know that the LORD has given you the land. . . . For we have heard how the LORD dried up the water of the Red Sea before you. . . . The LORD your God is indeed God in heaven above and on earth below" (Josh 2:8-11). This acknowledgment of God's sovereignty and God's powerful acts of deliverance on Israel's behalf prompts her to act with courage and wisdom to save her own family. Her "works" demonstrate what can be considered "faith." James is not interested in the fact that a Canaanite expresses such confidence in Israel's God, however, nor is he concerned to stress Rahab's actions to preserve life. His focus is entirely on what she does for the Israelite "spies/messengers" (see further TBC below).

Some commentators think James mentions Rahab's acts of hospitality because he knows of Abraham's hospitality to strangers in Genesis 18. However, nothing in the text suggests this. More likely, James uses Rahab as an example because of the *lack* of hospitality in the churches to which he writes (2:1-4, 14-16). Rahab showed hospitality to the stranger, even the enemy, and by these works of mercy was proven righteous. If his readers truly have faith in their *glorious Lord Jesus Christ* (NRSV), the church should also show hospitality to the poor and needy among them. Both Abraham and Rahab appear in Hebrews in the litany of heroes of faith, and the author also mentions their actions as the outcome of faith (Heb 11:8-12, 17-19, 31).

Verse 26 concludes the unit by hammering home the thesis yet one more time: *Faith without works is dead* (cf. 2:14, 17, 20). This time James compares faith without deeds to a body without a spirit—in other words, to a corpse. One could also use the analogy of a dead tree. The trunk and branches of a dead tree are still visible, but if it never grows leaves or fruit, the tree is not alive. So also faith without accompanying actions is not alive. With this insistence on the absolute necessity of faith being evident in deeds, James stands in line with both John the Baptist and Jesus: "Every tree that does not bear good fruit will be cut down and thrown into the fire" (Matt 3:10; 7:19).

In this unit James pulls out all the stops to convince his readers of how it is absolutely essential that their faith in Jesus Christ be demonstrated in how they live. He uses literary techniques like rhetorical questions, diatribe, and chiasm. James narrates a hypothetical situation that he hopes will strike them as outlandish as it sounds (2:15-16). He repeats the main point over and over again:

Faith without works is dead. He reinforces his point by quoting and alluding to Scripture texts that lie at the heart of Israel's story (Gen 15:6; Deut 6:4). He lifts up two different heroes of faith as models to emulate—Abraham and Rahab—even commending Abraham as the *friend of God.* The message is clear. As true for so much in this letter, the problem is not understanding what he says. The challenge is to live it.

THE TEXT IN BIBLICAL CONTEXT

Abraham and Rahab

The two Old Testament characters James holds up as models of justification by deeds *and* faith could not be more different. Abraham was a respected patriarch and father of the Jewish people. Rahab was female, an innkeeper/prostitute, and Canaanite. Abraham's name appears over three hundred times in the Bible, Rahab's only eight. Abraham was ready to kill his son. Rahab saved the lives of strangers.

Abraham

Abraham is an important character in the story of God's people. Three of the major world religions (Judaism, Christianity, and Islam) view Abraham as their ancestor. His story is told in Genesis 11:27–25:11. The New Testament mentions Abraham more often than any other Old Testament figure (seventy-two times) besides Moses. To be a descendant of Abraham was a mark of identity for the Jews. In the Old Testament, Israel is called "the people of the God of Abraham" (Ps 47:9), and Abraham is their "father" (Isa 51:2). Psalms of Solomon, a Jewish writing from the first century BCE, says "You are God and we are the people whom you have loved. . . . For you chose the descendants of Abraham above all the nations, and you put your name upon us, Lord, and it will not cease forever" (9.8-9).

This sense of identity is evident also in the New Testament, where characters appeal to "our father Abraham" or speak of being sons and daughters of Abraham (Luke 13:16; 16:24; John 8:33-40; Acts 7:2; 13:26; Rom 11:2; 2 Cor 11:22). Of course, physical descent from Abraham alone is not sufficient. John the Baptist rails against those who claim Abraham as their father but do not "bear fruit worthy of repentance" (Matt 3:8//Luke 3:8). Paul too differentiates between "children of the flesh" and true descendants of Abraham (Rom 9:6-8).

In Jewish and Christian literature, Abraham is important as (a) a testament to God's faithfulness, (b) a model of someone who trusted God fully, and (c) a paradigm of faithful obedience. First, in response to humanity's sinfulness in Genesis 3–11, God begins a new salvation strategy and chooses Abraham to be a conduit of blessing for all the families of the earth. God makes a covenant with Abraham, promising him land, descendants, and blessing (Gen 15:7-21; 17:1-8). And God proves faithful, not only to Abraham and Sarah and their descendants but also to outsiders like Hagar and Ishmael (Gen 16–17, 21). This refrain of God's faithfulness to Abraham extends throughout the Bible. When God hears the groaning of the Israelites in Egypt, God remembers God's covenant with Abraham and acts powerfully to deliver them (Exod 2:23-25). Both Mary and Zechariah praise God for remembering God's promises to Abraham and for God's covenant faithfulness (Luke 1:54-55, 72-76).

Second, Abraham's trust and obedience are a response to God's faithfulness. God's covenant with Abraham requires both nothing and everything from him. When God makes a covenant with Abraham in Genesis 17, God's promises of descendants, land, and blessing are not conditional on Abraham doing anything. Yet Abraham must trust God to fulfill God's promises despite all evidence to the contrary. The need for such radical trust is most evident in the promise that he will have more descendants than stars in the sky, for Sarah is barren and well past menopause. Despite the seeming impossibility of it, Abraham believes God and "the LORD reckoned it to him as righteousness" (Gen 15:1-6). Abraham can only know that he will receive land because God says so. He will not experience it in his lifetime, for his descendants will be oppressed in a foreign land for four hundred years (Gen 15:7-21). It is not that Abraham's faith is perfect or passive. Abraham argues with God, questions God, and makes egregious mistakes, such as lying about Sarah being his wife or sleeping with Hagar and then casting her out. Despite his fallible humanness, Abraham is a "hero of faith" in the Bible and Christian tradition.

For the apostle Paul, God's declaration of Abraham as righteous based on this radical faith is primary. Paul emphasizes that Abraham was not justified on the basis of circumcision, which was given later as a sign of the covenant, nor on the basis of obedience to the law of Moses, which the people received centuries later at Sinai. God declared Abraham righteous solely because he trusted God. This is essential for Paul's argument in Romans and Galatians because he is making the case that the Gentiles do not enter into right relationship with God by following the Mosaic law but simply as a gift, received through the same kind of faith that Abraham had. Thus, Gentiles too are children of Abraham, through faith (Rom 4; Gal 3:6-9).

Third, as important as Abraham's faith was, he is even more notable for his obedience to God in the Bible and Jewish tradition. His deeds cannot be separated from his faith. Abraham has a prominent place in the "cloud of witnesses" of Hebrews, but the examples given show faith in action: relocating to a foreign land and offering up Isaac, the son of promise (Heb 11:8, 17-19). God extends the covenant promises to Isaac "because Abraham obeyed my voice and kept my charge, my commandments, my statutes, and my laws," even before the law was given (Gen 26:5). Bernard Anderson describes this faith of Abraham well:

> Belief in God is not assent to doctrines or reflection on ethical values. Rather, belief is a response to the call of God which, as in the case of Abram, upsets one's accustomed way of life and gives new motivation and direction. It is trust demonstrated in a walking, a going, a journeying, even when the way is not clear and the horizon of God's promise is overcast. (Anderson: 359)

Intertestamental Jewish writings also support this understanding of Abraham as righteous because of his faithfulness. According to tradition, Abraham had to undergo ten trials, the climax of which was the near-sacrifice of Isaac (Jubilees 17.15-18.16; cf. Philo, *On Abraham* 167: That obedience was "of more importance than all the actions of piety and religion put together"). In all this testing, Abraham proved faithful and thus was deemed righteous before God (e.g., 1 Macc 2:52; Sir 44:19-21; Jubilees 23.10). Although some modern interpreters understand Abraham's readiness to sacrifice his child as him failing the test of faith, Jewish and Christian Scripture views Abraham's actions positively. Jewish writers credit Abraham with fulfilling the law of Moses even before that law was given. His "faith" (Gen 15:6) was inextricably tied to "works" of circumcision, covenant keeping, and obedience (Gen 17:4-14; 22:1-9). Abraham's faith was reckoned to him as "righteousness" because of his whole life, and James's portrayal of Abraham as justified by faith *and* works is thoroughly Jewish.

Rahab

Rahab receives much less attention in the Bible than Abraham, and it is curious that James chose her as a second example. Other than

Josephus (who refers to her as an innkeeper rather than a prostitute), Jewish writings before James do not mention her, nor is she ever associated with Abraham in early rabbinic sources (Allison 2013: 500–1). Her story is told in Joshua 2 and 6:15-25, and she appears in the New Testament in Matthew 1:5; Hebrews 11:31; and James 2:25. Matthew's genealogy of Jesus includes five unconventional women, one of whom is Rahab the mother of Boaz. She appears last in the cloud of witnesses in Hebrews 11 (Abraham is the first) and is the only woman. Both James and Hebrews identify her as a prostitute, and both highlight her protection of the spies as the reason she was kept safe or justified.

The story of Rahab and the spies in Joshua 2 is colorful, narratively rich, and theologically intriguing. Her identification as a common prostitute living on the margins of the city wall immediately marks her as someone with a low social status and moral stigma. And yet, her identity is not as straightforward as it seems. Rahab has a family—mother, father, siblings—for whose safety she feels responsible (Josh 2:13). Perhaps economic hardship or family debt forced her into doing one of the few things a woman could do to provide for her family in crisis. The fact that she has a house implies some degree of independence. Perhaps she also made clothing, since she had flax on her roof and a crimson "cord of thread" ready at hand (Creach: 39). If her occupation is morally suspect, the behavior of the Israelite spies is no less. Sent out to "view the land," they immediately enter her house and spend the night (lit., "lie down").

Despite the negative connotations of being a Canaanite, a woman, and a prostitute, Rahab proves to be an assertive, courageous, and admirable character. Hebrews interprets her story as paradigmatic of great "faith," and James focuses on the exemplary nature of her "works." In the context of Joshua, she does exhibit both, though not as unambiguously as later Jewish and Christian tradition portray.

Both Jewish and Christian commentators have interpreted Rahab's speech in Joshua 2:9-11 favorably, as indicative of her adopting the Israelite God as her own and abandoning her Canaanite tradition. Later rabbinic tradition has Rahab marrying Joshua, with seven kings and eight prophets descending from her (Creach: 36). Postcolonial critics, however, evaluate her actions negatively since she appears to be coopted by the colonizers' agenda and a traitor to her own people. There is nothing explicit in the story to indicate that Rahab "converted" to the Israelite faith (she says "your God" in 2:11), and her "confessional" speech of verses 9-11 could merely be the shrewd words of someone desperate to save her family. Nevertheless, in the broader context the reader is intended to recognize her as a Canaanite who acknowledged the sovereignty of Israel's God and who acted wisely and courageously to preserve life.

After the king's men leave and before the spies go to sleep, Rahab approaches them. In language reminiscent of Deuteronomic theology, she begins by claiming that God has "given [them] the land," implying that the land belongs to God (Josh 2:9; cf. Deut 1:21; Josh 1:2-3, 6, 11, 15; Creach: 36). Her reference to the defeat of Sihon and Og recalls Moses' first speech in Deuteronomy (1:4). She and her people have heard about God's powerful acts in bringing God's people out of Egypt (Josh 2:10). She says, "All the inhabitants of the land melt in fear before you" (2:9). Prior to 2:9, 24, the word "melt" is used only in Exodus 15:15, in the Song of Moses (Matties: 72). In contrast to others who hear reports of Israel's conquests (Josh 5:1; 9:1-2; 10:1-2), Rahab does not respond with fear or counterviolence. Instead, she acknowledges God's cosmic sovereignty: "The LORD your God is indeed God in heaven above and on earth below" (2:11). These are words that are "used elsewhere only by Moses (Deut 4:39) and Solomon (1 Kings 8:23)" (Matties: 73). Whatever her motivations are, "in recounting the great mercy and judgment of God in Israel's experience, Rahab speaks as one who knows and owns Israel's story as articulated in Deuteronomy" (Matties: 77).

James is not interested in Rahab's confessional speech but only in her subsequent actions. By showing hospitality to the spies and lying to the king's men, she puts herself at risk. She then asks for *ḥesed* (mercy) in return for showing *ḥesed* to the spies (2:12). This theologically loaded Hebrew word is often translated "covenant faithfulness" or "loving-kindness" and is regularly used to describe God's faithfulness to God's people (e.g., Exod 34:6-7; Deut 7:9, 12; 1 Kings 8:23; Isa 54:10). Here Rahab uses it to characterize her own relationship with the Israelite spies. Whether or not Rahab has adopted their God as her own, the narrator communicates that she is acting in the character of that God to save the spies. She is also acting as a moral agent, given the circumstances. As Sarah Melcher argues, Rahab "puts her primary relationships first—that is, her close relationships with family members. Viewing Israelite victory as inevitable, she makes the best choice available to protect her family from harm, even when it means abandoning the town where she plied her trade" (168). She acts assertively, making them swear an oath that her family will be saved.

The significance of Rahab's actions lies not only in the salvation she accomplishes for herself and her family. Within the broader context of the Deuteronomistic History, this story also problematizes who is "in" the people of God and who is "out." By her works, this Canaanite outsider proves more faithful than some Israelite insiders (e.g., Achan in Josh 7). Although Deuteronomy commands Israel to obliterate the Canaanite people, the reality is more complex, for some Canaanites remain in the land and are not as reprehensible as Deuteronomy suggests (Creach: 42; Matties: 29, 84, 453). As Ellen Davis says, "In the story of Rahab, the stock notion of Canaanite wickedness is ironized and radically relativized, if not demolished altogether" (Davis: 742).

James's citation of Rahab as an example of someone justified by works is so brief that we cannot know how much of her story he had in mind. He does not refer to her acknowledgment of the sovereignty of Israel's God (her "faith," as in Heb 11:31), nor does he hint at the canonical and theological significance of her "works" in the Deuteronomistic story, as later interpreters do. She does stand side by side with the patriarch Abraham as a model of someone whose courageous actions proved her to be righteous in God's eyes.

Faith and Works

Many texts in the New Testament echo the conviction that words and beliefs must be accompanied by corresponding right action. People who profess to love God must also love neighbor in concrete, practical ways. To do anything less is hypocritical and will incur judgment on the last day. Jesus said, "Not everyone who says to me, 'Lord, Lord,' will enter the kingdom of heaven, but only the one who does the will of my Father in heaven" (Matt 7:21). The writer of 1 John says, "Little children, let us love not [just] in word or speech, but in truth and action" (3:18), and Paul's letter to Titus criticizes those who "profess to know God, but deny him by their actions" (1:16). Paul's letters all emphasize that faith in Christ must be expressed in righteous living and must bear good fruit (Rom 2:13; Gal 6:9-10; Eph 2:10; Col 1:10). James's teaching on faith and works in 2:14-26 fit snugly into this broader New Testament emphasis.

At the same time, his words have also stirred up controversy and confusion far beyond what might be expected, given this broad biblical insistence on faith that "works." The reason is that they *seem* to conflict with what Paul says in Romans and Galatians about faith and works. Paul's theology has been enormously influential in the history of the church, especially in Western Protestantism. Paul insists that "a person is justified by faith apart from works" (Rom 3:28; cf. Gal 2:16), whereas James is adamant that *a person is justified by works and not by faith alone* (2:24). Both use the example of Abraham to support their claims, and both quote Genesis 15:6, though for different ends. The fact that the words and phrases they use are virtually the same and found only in these letters in the New Testament (Allison 2013: 445–50) makes it hard to avoid comparison and the inference that they are arguing with each other.

A closer study of James and Paul reveals, however, that they are not as far apart as they seem. They use the same vocabulary (faith, works, justified, law) but in different ways, and they speak into entirely different contexts, confronting distinct problems *[James and Paul on Faith and Works, p. 348]*.

In Galatians and Romans, Paul is addressing the question of how Gentiles can become part of God's covenant people and, more broadly, how sinful people can be put into right relationship with God. He argues that people are "justified" (that is, declared "just" or "righteous" by God) solely by God's grace, because of the death and resurrection of Jesus the Messiah. That gift of salvation is appropriated by faith (that is, trust in God's saving work in Christ) and is not earned by anything people can do (Rom 3:28; Gal 2:15-16; Eph 2:8-9). Specifically, justification is not achieved by doing "works of the law," by which he means the laws of Moses.

To belong to the justified and redeemed people of God, then, Gentiles do not need to adhere to Jewish ritual laws, such as circumcision, Sabbath observance, and purity laws—the boundary markers setting Jews apart from non-Jews (Toews: 413–14). Paul uses Abraham as an example of someone whom God counted as righteous because of his faith and not because of his works. He quotes Genesis 15:6 as proof of this (Rom 4:3; Gal 3:6) and concludes that Gentiles too can be descendants of Abraham through faith (3:7). The "work" of circumcision *followed* God's declaration of Abraham as righteous, demonstrating that circumcision is a sign of justification, not a requirement (Rom 4:11). To be sure, Paul also believes that those who are "in Christ" will no longer let sin reign in their lives but will "walk in newness of life" (6:3-4) and will be obedient to God, but they are not justified because of what they do.

The Letter of James speaks into a completely different context and uses the same vocabulary in service of a different argument.

The questions about how Gentiles can be incorporated into the covenant people of God or how God can declare sinners righteous is not even on the horizon in this letter. Rather, James's concern is that people who profess to follow Jesus as Lord and Messiah should live consistent with that identity and demonstrate their faith in their actions. Put differently, his sparring partners are not Jewish Christians who think Gentiles must be circumcised in order to be justified, but Jewish Christians who do not exhibit any evidence that they *are* justified.

Like Paul, James also believes in God's transforming work of grace, since God, the giver of *every good and perfect gift* (NIV), has given the church birth by the word of truth and made us into the first fruits of God's creatures (James 1:17-18). His question is not how that birth happens, but how one lives as a result. When he says that Abraham was *justified by works* (James 2:21), he uses the verb in a slightly different sense than Paul to mean "proven to be righteous" rather than "declared to be righteous" (see comments on 2:21). Abraham's willingness to give up the son whom God promised him demonstrated his total trust in God and proved him righteous.

When he says faith needs "works" to complete it, James does not mean the ritual requirements of the Mosaic law, such as circumcision, but good deeds of mercy, compassion, and justice (1:27; 2:1-6, 15-16; 3:17-18). James would never speak of the Torah as something that enslaves or that could be a curse (Rom 7:6; Gal 3:13). Rather, it is a royal law of freedom, epitomized by the command *Love your neighbor as yourself* (James 1:25; 2:8, 12). For James, faith and works, trust in Jesus Messiah, and good deeds are indivisible and inseparable. Paul would agree if he were speaking into James's situation, but his concern is something else entirely.

THE TEXT IN THE LIFE OF THE CHURCH

Lived Faith

It is hard to imagine any individual Christian or church denying the importance of concrete deeds of compassion in a life of faith. James 2:14-26 is so well-known and so beloved because the truth it professes seems obvious: faith must be lived out. The disagreement arises over how central such "works" are for salvation, largely because of how James compares with Paul. Despite the controversy over the centuries, in every Christian tradition one finds abundant evidence that good works are important.

In History

From the time of the early church, biblical interpreters noticed the apparent differences between James and Paul on the question of faith and works, but they invariably concluded that the two do not contradict each other and that both faith *and* works are essential in the Christian life. Augustine (354–430) exemplifies one approach to James and Paul: "Therefore the opinions of the two apostles, Paul and James, are not opposed to each other when the one says that man is justified by faith without works, and the other says that faith without works is useless: because the former (Paul) speaks about works that precede faith, while the latter (James) speaks about those that follow faith; as even Paul shows in many places" (*De diversis quaestionibus LXXXIII* 1.75 *[MPL 50:89];* quoted in Hartin 2009a: 167).

In the centuries between Augustine and the Reformation, James received relatively little attention (George: 370). This changed during the Reformation when the letter became a source of controversy, largely because of this question about the relationship of works and faith. Martin Luther is well known for dubbing James an "epistle of straw," and he once quipped that he almost felt like "throwing Jimmy into the stove" (LW 34:317). Central to Luther's critique of James was the letter's apparent contradiction of the Pauline doctrine of justification by grace through faith alone (cf. James 2:24; Rom 3:28 in Luther Bible, adding "alone"). According to Luther, God imputes righteousness to sinful humanity solely as a gift because of the atoning sacrifice of Christ on the cross. Human beings are sinful and can do nothing of their own accord to be saved. On this doctrine "the church either stands or falls," said Luther (quoted in George: 373). Luther was not opposed to good works, however, and insisted that they were vital, even if they had no role in justification. In his preface to Romans, his words sound remarkably compatible with James:

> What a living, creative, active powerful thing is faith! It is impossible that faith ever stop doing good. Faith doesn't ask whether good works are to be done, but, before it is asked, it has done them. It is always active. Whoever doesn't do such works is without faith; he gropes and searches about him for faith and good works but doesn't know what faith or good works are. Even so, he chatters on with a great many words about faith and good works. (http://www.ccel.org/l/luther/romans/pref_romans.html)

Other Reformers, like Zwingli and Calvin, were much more favorable toward James than Luther and did not see the same contradiction with Paul. They too believed that justification occurs solely by the grace of God but insisted on the necessity of good works. They reconciled James and Paul by saying that they were speaking to different audiences in different contexts. In his influential commentary on James in 1550, Calvin argued that although righteousness is imputed and received by faith, true faith must be demonstrated by the fruit of good works. If the latter were missing, it casts doubt on whether someone was justified (George: 378). Calvin was writing at a time when many persecuted Protestant refugees were fleeing France for Geneva, and his sermons on James emphasized that Christians must care for the poor (George: 376).

Among the Anabaptists, this emphasis on lived faith was stronger. To be sure, there was diversity in what Anabaptists believed in different places and times. Yet overall, Anabaptists vehemently rejected the severance of works from faith and "agreed that 'faith without works is dead' (James 2:17). The absence of works or fruits of faith (obedience) was their primary criticism of the larger groups in the Reformation" (Dyck 1995: 52–53). Countless examples of this can be found in early Anabaptist writings, which often cite James 2. Most explicit is Menno Simons:

> The Lutherans teach and believe that faith alone saves, without any assistance by works. They emphasize this doctrine so as to make it appear as though works were not even necessary; yes, that faith is of such a nature that it cannot tolerate any works alongside it. And therefore the important and earnest epistle of James (because he reproves such frivolous, vain doctrine and faith) is esteemed and treated as a "strawy" epistle. (*CWMS*: 333)

In 1526, Balthasar Hubmaier wrote,

> Faith alone and by itself is not sufficient for salvation. . . . [It] is like a green fig tree without fruit, like a cistern without water, like a cloud without rain. . . . Oh, we wish to be good evangelical Christians; we boast about our great faith, but have never touched the works of the gospel and faith with the smallest finger. Therefore we are, as stated above, nothing but mouth Christians, ear Christians, and paper Christians, but not action Christians. About these St. James severely admonishes us in his Christian and useful epistle when he writes [2:14-19]. (Klaassen 1981: 43–44)

Although their opponents accused them of "works righteousness," Anabaptists believed in salvation as a free gift of God received through faith and in Jesus' atoning death. Unlike the

Reformers, however, they thought human response plays a role in salvation. Works are not just fruit that grows after the work of justification, as an add-on, but are integral to salvation. Luther believed that God "imputes" righteousness, objectively declares sinners to be righteous; Anabaptists believed that God subjectively changes people through new birth (James 1:18) and enables them by the indwelling power of the Holy Spirit to live differently. Through repentance and regeneration, the will is set free to choose the good. To use theological terms, sanctification does not *follow* justification but *is inseparable* from it.

For Anabaptists, lived faith was not primarily about obeying rules or doing good deeds, however, but about following Jesus: discipleship in life and death. Jesus' teachings, especially the Sermon on the Mount, provided essential guidance for such discipleship. Following Jesus in daily life and having faith that was not dead included sharing material goods, loving the enemy, serving others, and not swearing oaths. Such expressions of faith applied not only to individuals but also to the church. Anabaptist ecclesiology emphasized that the church was the visible body of Christ, comprised of baptized believers who were committed to lived faith in community.

In Today's World

Debate about the relationship between faith and works has cooled considerably since the Reformation. Although some Christian denominations continue to emphasize that justification by grace is primary, few if any would say that good works are irrelevant for faith. One would be hard pressed to find a church body that does not have some branch of service ministry. Anabaptist-related groups continue to underscore discipleship and service as essential to faith. This is evident in the hymns they sing, in written confessions of faith, and in participation in service organizations. The Letter of James continues to be a favorite for many Christians of all stripes because of its practical teachings on how to live.

As in the sixteenth century, so today there lies the potential danger of an overemphasis on either faith or works. On one end of the spectrum are those who are so concerned about correct articulation of a specific atonement theology or focused so narrowly on the individual's experience of salvation that a commitment to right living becomes almost irrelevant. They may profess that lived faith is important, but sometimes their actions belie their words. Paul rightly anticipated that some people might say, "Then let us sin all the more that grace may abound" (cf. Rom 6:1): in modern language, "It doesn't really matter what I do in life because I'm saved by God's grace."

On the other end of the spectrum are those whose focus on discipleship and good works slides into legalism and perfectionism. The temptation for them is to forget that serving others, fighting against injustice, living simply, and working for peace are not ends in themselves but are part of being followers of Jesus Christ, by whose life, death, and resurrection they receive new life and are reconciled to God and to others. Such people might profess that salvation (their own or the world's) is not achieved by what they do, but they sometimes talk and act as if it is.

The Letter of James speaks an important message to the spectrum of Christian experience. It insists that faith must be lived. It must be demonstrated in concrete acts of compassion for the "widow and the orphan," in feeding the hungry, working for justice, and caring for creation. As Menno Simons said, "True evangelical faith . . . cannot lie dormant" (*CWMS*: 307). To identify as a Christian but not live as a follower of Jesus in daily life is to not have true faith. At the same time, works of justice and service are inseparable from an abiding trust in God and the Lord Jesus Christ. Followers of Jesus do good works not because they have been told they should nor only because they want to change the world, but because they have been given *birth . . . by the word of truth* (James 1:18), because the church is the first fruits of God's new creation (1:18), and because they love God. In the life of the church today, as in James's day, faith and works are inextricably intertwined. New birth means new living.

James 3:1-12

Faithfulness in Speech

PREVIEW

"Sticks and stones may break my bones, but names will never hurt me." This childhood retort is simply not true, as anyone who has been wounded by words knows. Words *do* things. Like an arrow shot from a bow, they cannot be stuffed back into the mouth once released. The power of words to harm and to heal is found everywhere in commonplace wisdom: "Good words are like a string of pearls." "The tongue is but three inches long, yet it can kill a man six feet high."

Speech ethics was frequently addressed among ancient Greco-Roman moral philosophers and in Jewish wisdom literature. In his discourse on the tongue in 3:1-12, James adds his voice to these ancient writings. In fact, this is a major concern in the letter, for the subject comes up repeatedly. It is already present in the first chapter, in a kind of overview of the whole letter (1:19, 26), and again in 2:2-4, 12, 15-16; 4:11-12; 5:9, 12, 13-18. Out of a total of 108 verses, at least 36 of them have something to do with speaking.

James could have made his point quite plainly and concisely: Be careful how you speak, since your words can do untold damage. Instead, he uses memorable metaphors and provocative language to impress upon his readers how powerful speech is. Appropriate for his subject, James embodies how the tongue effectively collaborates in cleverness by drawing attention to itself with the sounds it makes and words it forms. By using puns, alliteration, metonymy, onomatopoeia, hyperbole, parallelism, and rhetorical questions, he captures readers' imagination. Paul employed lists of vices to warn against the sins of speech (e.g., Rom 1:29-31). James's approach is more like Jesus', who also used evocative images, rhetorical questions, and hyperbole to persuade his listeners (e.g., Matt 6:25-34). James uses Greek words that are rare or nonexistent elsewhere in the New Testament, over a dozen in these twelve verses alone—for example, "guide" (3:3-4), "forest" (v. 5), "cycle" (v. 6), "sea creature" (v. 7), and "brackish" (v. 11). Prosaic language would not accomplish what the author set out to do, to move his audience to act, and so we must pay attention not only to *what* James says, but also to *how* he says it.

Although James seems to be starting a new topic with 3:1, it is not unrelated to the immediately preceding argument about faith and works. Speech is a kind of "deed" that reveals faith. This is evident in 1:26-27, where James contrasts failure to control the tongue (worthless religion) with the action of caring for orphans and widows (pure religion). Throughout the letter, James is concerned about integrity. Speaking (2:12, 15-16), hearing (1:22-25), and believing (2:14-26) must be consistent with living. *Not* to have integrity in word and deed is to be double-minded. It is failure to live out one's identity as the first fruits of God's creatures, given birth by the word of truth (1:18). The discourse on speech in 3:1-12 leads into a broader reflection on wisdom (3:13-18), for only through the wisdom granted to all who ask for it (1:5) can believers manage their unruly tongues.

OUTLINE

Warning about Becoming Teachers, 3:1-2a

The Power of the Tongue, 3:2b-8

- 3:2b-5a The Immense Influence of Relatively Small Things
- 3:5b-8 The Tongue as Destructive and Dangerous

Inconsistency in Speech: This Ought Not to Be! 3:9-12

EXPLANATORY NOTES

Warning about Becoming Teachers 3:1-2a

The unit begins with a warning: *Not many of you should become teachers, my brothers and sisters.* The double irony is that James is himself a teacher, and he is about to warn them—using words—about the risky business of speaking! Some interpreters have seen a disconnect between 3:1-2a and the rest of the chapter. However, James launches his discourse on the tongue by singling out teachers because speaking is so integral to the work they do.

Teachers had an important ministry role in the early church, along with apostles, prophets, healers, and others (Acts 13:1; 1 Cor 12:28-29; Eph 4:11; 1 Tim 2:7; 2 Tim 1:11). Although the unique distinctions and functions of this calling would not have been as well-developed in the first decades of the church as later, it was a position of responsibility and influence. Since James counts himself among the teachers (in James 3:1, he says, *We who teach*), perhaps this letter is a good example of what teaching in the early church entailed. As with Jewish rabbis who interpreted and applied the Torah, so teachers in the church passed on the traditions about Jesus, expounded on and applied his teachings, interpreted the Law and the Prophets as fulfilled in Jesus, and provided ongoing ethical instruction. In a society where literacy levels were low, teachers were essential transmitters of the faith.

Because they were knowledge-keepers, teachers also had authority, and with such power comes responsibility. James warns the church that the responsibility of teaching is not to be taken lightly and that not many should take it on. We can only speculate about why James thought this warning was necessary for his community. Did some in the community want to become teachers because of the status or influence it gave them? Were some overly confident in putting themselves forward? Did the community give greater honor to teachers, as they did to the wealthy (cf. 2:1-13)? We cannot know the situation, only that James cautions against taking on this role too quickly.

The reason he gives for such caution is that although everyone makes many mistakes in life, teachers will be judged more strictly—presumably because they have more responsibility and influence. The judgment in view here is God's end-time judgment, not the evaluation of fellow humans, since elsewhere in the letter James refers to God as the only Judge and decries people judging each other (4:11-12). James is giving sensible advice about the responsibility of teachers but is also speaking out of religious conviction. The clause *will receive a greater judgment* (3:1 AT) can mean either that punishment will be harsher or that they will be held to a higher standard, though the latter is probably intended in this case. These words are reminiscent of Jesus' words in Luke 12:48: "From everyone to whom much has been given, much will be required; and from the one to whom much has been entrusted, even more will be demanded." James's concern here is not false doctrine of teachers who lead people astray, as in the pastoral epistles (e.g., 1 Tim 1:3-7; 2 Tim 4:3-4; Titus 1:10-11), but *how* teachers speak.

It is evident that James counts himself among those who teach, since he uses "we" and "us" in 3:1b-2a. He too will be judged with greater strictness, and he too must be careful about what he says and how he speaks, for he is among those who *make many mistakes.* One wonders whether his language might have been harsher than it already is (e.g., 4:1; 5:1-6) if he had not prefaced his criticisms by warnings about the acerbic power of the tongue.

Some commentators maintain that all of 3:1-12 and even 3:13-18 (on wisdom) is directed specifically to teachers and not intended for a general audience (e.g., McKnight: 274–75). Although advice about care-filled speech is especially relevant for teachers, such a narrow audience seems unlikely, for several reasons. The unit begins with *my brothers and sisters*, which is how James addresses his readers throughout the letter. Moreover, when he says, *Not many of you should become teachers*, he is obviously addressing some people who are *not yet* teachers; otherwise the warning would be irrelevant. Finally, the universal applicability of his teaching on the tongue is evident in the generalized language in verse 2: *We <u>all</u> stumble in many ways* and *if <u>someone</u> does not stumble in word, this is a perfect person* (AT). Finally, the topic of right speech surfaces repeatedly in the letter, suggesting that this is a concern James has for the whole faith community, not just a subgroup of teachers.

James acknowledges that *we all stumble in many ways* (AT) or *all of us make many mistakes* (NRSVue) before narrowing his focus to the tongue. This is proverbial wisdom, found in many ancient writings:

- "Surely there is no one on earth so righteous as to do good without ever sinning." (Eccl 7:20)
- "A person may make a slip without intending it. Who has not sinned with his tongue?" (Sir 19:16)
- "We have all sinned—some in serious [things], others in trivial things; some from deliberate intention, some by chance impulse." (Seneca, *De clementia* 1.6.3)

The word "stumble" also appears in 2:10, where it refers to transgressing the law: *Whoever keeps the whole law but stumbles in one thing has become accountable for all of it* (AT). James is both pessimistic and realistic about human nature; all people sin at some point. This is especially true with regard to speech.

The Power of the Tongue 3:2b-8

3:2b-5a The Immense Influence of Relatively Small Things

James now moves from the general to the specific. Not only is it impossible not to stumble; it is apparently impossible not to err in one's speech, since *no one can tame the tongue* (v. 8). With this James begins one of the most memorable and challenging parts of the letter. The topic of speech, both its risks and potential, was popular among ancient Greco-Roman writers. Rhetoricians taught the fine art of crafting words for persuasive effect. According to Luke Timothy Johnson, Greek moralists valued taciturnity and brevity as signs of self-control, wisdom, and strength (2004d). Brevity required greater skill than long-windedness and was associated with youth and power, whereas "garrulousness [was] a sign of age and weakness" (2004d: 159).

Teachings about speech also appear in Hellenistic Jewish writings, such as those of Philo of Alexandria, a first-century Jewish philosopher. The following excerpt is only one example: "Nor, because you have been made endowed with a mouth and a tongue and the organs of speech, ought you to say everything and to reveal what ought not to be spoken, for there are times when to hold one's peace is useful" (*The Worse Attacks the Better* 27.102). We have noted how James incorporates many themes and stylistic features of Jewish wisdom literature, which probably influenced him more than Greco-Roman philosophy.

The following represent only a small sample of the many wisdom proverbs about speech:

- "When words are many, transgression is not lacking, but the prudent are restrained in speech." (Prov 10:19)
- "The tongue of the wise adorns knowledge, but the mouths of fools pour out folly." (Prov 15:2)
- "When a sieve is shaken, the refuse appears; so does a person's waste when he speaks." (Sir 27:4)
- "The blow of a whip raises a welt, but a blow of the tongue crushes the bones. Many have fallen by the edge of the sword, but not as many as have fallen because of the tongue." (Sir 28:17-18)

Not only does James stand firmly in the tradition of Greek philosophy and Jewish wisdom, but more importantly, his teachings on integrity of speech also align with those of Jesus the Messiah. Like other Jewish sages, Jesus taught his disciples that how they speak to others is an important aspect of godly living (Matt

5:21-22; 7:21-23). To the religious leaders he said, "How can you speak good things, when you are evil? For out of the abundance of the heart the mouth speaks. . . . I tell you on the day of judgment you will have to give an account for every careless word you utter; for by your words you will be justified, and by your words you will be condemned" (Matt 12:34-37). Clearly, what James says about speech fits into what others in his day were saying. His task is to provoke the imagination of readers so that they are compelled to reflect in their living what they already know to be true.

In verse 2b James says, *Anyone who makes no mistakes in speaking is mature/perfect*. The Greek word for *mature/perfect* (*teleios*) was already used to describe the *perfect* gifts God generously gives (1:17) and the *perfect* law of freedom (1:25). In 1:4 James urged his readers to let endurance do its *perfect work* in them so that they might be *perfect and whole, lacking nothing* (AT). The same word appears in Matthew 5:48, "Be perfect, . . . as your heavenly Father is perfect"; and 19:21, "If you wish to be perfect, go, sell your possessions, and give the money to the poor, and you will have treasure in heaven." These texts are not about perfection*ism*, but about being mature, complete, and whole—undivided in one's loyalty. People who do not sin with their speech have integrity and are not double-minded. Their words align with their beliefs and actions.

When James talks about "making no mistakes" in speech, he is not referring to speaking without stumbling or not making factual mistakes. The rest of the letter shows that making mistakes in speaking has to do with anger (1:19-20), cursing others (3:9), maligning and judging others (4:11), and grumbling (5:9). But if *all of us make many mistakes* and *no one can tame the tongue* (3:2, 8), what is the point of encouraging readers to be whole or perfect in their speech? James's warnings about the evils of the tongue in 3:1-12 are so dire that integrity seems an unreachable goal. In short, 3:2 presents a paradox: James expects followers of Jesus to strive for wholeness and maturity (1:4), including not sinning in their speech (3:2b), *and* he is realistic enough to know that *all of us make many mistakes* (3:2a). Both are true.

James refers to *the whole body* three times in 3:2b-8 (vv. 2b, 3, 6). This phrase can be understood in two different possible ways:

1. *The whole body* could refer to the church, with horse and ship being metaphors for this corporate body (Martin: 110; McKnight: 276). Competent teachers, represented by the "tongue," are able to direct and control the community (v. 2b).

2. *The whole body* could refer to a person's physical body (McCartney 2009: 181-83; Allison 2013: 525). The "tongue" is then a metonymy for a speech, and the point of verse 2b is that self-control in speaking affects one's whole life. The horse and ship are simply illustrations, not metaphors for the church.

The first interpretation assumes that James is addressing teachers in all of chapter 3 and that "speaking" refers to their "teaching." It also implies that the letter is meant to shape an ecclesial community and is more than moral advice for individual Christians. The analogy of the tongue and the illustrations in verses 3-5 work slightly better in this interpretation, for the tongue does not literally direct the physical body as a bit guides a horse or a rudder the ship. The wise speech of teachers, on the other hand, is indeed able to guide the communal body.

Several factors make the second interpretation more convincing. First, nothing in the letter suggests that James thinks of the church as the body of Christ, as Paul does in 1 Corinthians 12–14 (see also discussion of James 4:1). Second, James's previous uses of the word "body" (2:16, 26) also seem to refer to the human physical body, and in 3:3 *the whole body* can only refer to a horse's physical body. Finally, if the "body" is the church and the "tongue" represents teachers, the language in verses 6-8 is incomprehensibly harsh on teachers (McCartney 2009: 182). It is hard to imagine James speaking of teachers, himself included, as a *restless evil full of deadly poison* (v. 8). It makes more sense, then, to understand 3:1-12 as a warning meant for the church as a whole about the powerful effect speech can have on others, rather than narrowly about the ability of teachers to direct the community. Even so, James's words about speech have everything to do with how the community of faith lives together wisely and faithfully.

James uses three striking illustrations in 3:2b-8 to argue that seemingly small and insignificant things can have an enormous impact: a bit guiding a horse, a rudder steering a ship, and a spark setting a forest on fire. These images, alone or in combination, are ubiquitous in ancient literature. Here are only two examples:

- "I must, every time, rein in my discourse like a horse, and not let it run away with me as though it had no bridle in its mouth." (Plato, *Laws* 701C; quoted in Allison 2013: 526)
- "It is both character and speech [that persuade], or character by means of speech, just as a horseman uses a bridle, or a

> helmsman uses a rudder, since virtue has no instrument so human or so akin to itself as speech." (Plutarch, *Moralia* 33F; quoted in Hartin 2009a: 174)

The following quotation from Philo of Alexandria is a remarkable parallel in that it combines the images of horse, ship, and fire.

> When the charioteer is in command and guides the horses with the reins, the chariot goes the way he wishes, but if the horses have become unruly and got the upper hand, it has often happened that the charioteer has been dragged down. . . . A ship, again, keeps to her straight course, when the helmsman grasping the tiller steers accordingly, but capsizes when a contrary wind has sprung up over the sea, and the surge has settled in it. Just so, when Mind, the charioteer or helmsman of the soul, rules the whole living being as a governor does a city, the life holds a straight course, but when irrational sense gains the chief place, a terrible confusion overtakes it, . . . for then, in very deed, the mind is set on fire and is all ablaze, and that fire is kindled by the objects of sense. (*Allegorical Interpretation* 1.79.223–24)

Horses and ships were the most common forms of transportation, apart from walking; in using these common images, James was probably not working from written sources but simply drawing on what was "in the air," culturally and literarily (McCartney 2009: 183).

In many ancient Greek writings, the bit and rudder (or charioteer and helmsman) represent the mind's control over the emotions, senses, or speech, and fire is often a metaphor for passion and desire (Dibelius: 192). In James 3:2b-5a, the images are applied instead to the tongue and its ability (or lack thereof) to direct action. The metaphor of the ship has greater detail and illumines the disproportional impact of something small on a larger, more powerful force. As Luke Timothy Johnson remarks, "James makes all three components explicit: the guiding desire (the steersman), the means of control (the rudder), and that which is controlled (the ship), corresponding in turn to human desire, the tongue, and the body" (1995: 258).

Just as ancient Greek writers used these metaphors positively to argue that reason should control the will, so also James 3:3-5a points to the positive potential of the tongue. Bits and bridles *can* guide horses when used well, and rudders *do* direct ships to where the pilot wishes to go. The main point of comparison in these verses, though, seems to be the "contrast . . . between the smallness of the instrument and the greatness of its effect" (Dibelius: 186). Verse 5a makes this explicit and also begins to bend the image toward the tongue's harmful capabilities with its use of the word "boast." Although this Greek word appears only here in the New Testament, the verse recalls other texts, especially Psalm 12:2-4, with which it has strong parallels (Allison 2013: 531–32). Given the emphasis on the tongue's destructive power in what follows and the negative evaluation of boasting elsewhere in this letter (3:14; 4:16), the reader should not look favorably on the tongue's boasting here. The text then takes a dramatic turn toward warning in 3:5b-6, when James switches the metaphor to fire and its destructive effects. Yes, the potential for the tongue to speak wisely and constructively is present in verses 3-4, but this is not where James is going.

3:5b-8 The Tongue as Destructive and Dangerous

Up until verse 5b, James has encouraged readers to think about the immense, and potentially positive, impact little things can have, such as bits in horses' mouths and ships' rudders, and has only hinted at the tongue's capacity for wrongdoing (boasting). He now turns to a different metaphor: fire. James would resonate with the 1970s camp song that begins, "It only takes a spark to get a fire going." He is not interested in fire as a metaphor for God's love, as in the song, but only in its destructive capacity: it can set a huge forest ablaze! And then comes the punchline: *And the tongue is a fire* (3:6). For modern-day repeat readers who know where James is going, the image does not startle. Early Christians listening to the letter for the first time, however, may have felt the rug being pulled out from under them at this sudden dire turn.

This is not to say that the metaphor of the tongue as fire was unconventional. As with other images in James, it appears in the literature of Greek philosophers, as well as the Bible and other Jewish writings. James and his readers were likely influenced by the latter more than the former. The following are only a few examples:

- "Scoundrels concoct evil, and their speech is like a scorching fire." (Prov 16:27)
- "His lips are full of indignation, and his tongue is like a devouring fire." (Isa 30:27)
- "It [the tongue] has no power over the godly; they will not be burned in its flame." (Sir 28:22)

With this image James transitions to a more pessimistic view of human speech than his Greek contemporaries had. Like the bit and rudder, fire has enormous power. Fires provide welcome warmth on cool camping nights, but a mere spark can also wreak havoc in tinder-dry forests. Recent devastating forest fires in North America, as global temperatures rise, have made James's imagery especially potent. The tongue does not only guide a horse and steer a ship; the tongue also destroys, and its fury is relentless. *No one can tame the tongue—a restless evil full of deadly poison[!]* (v. 8).

James 3:6 is grammatically and syntactically difficult, as reflected in the great variety of English translations. Although some suggest that the original Greek must be corrupt, no textual evidence supports such a solution. One problem is that the sentence consists of a string of nouns (or equivalents) with only one main verb, "is placed," and how the various pieces relate to each other is opaque. One of these grammatically unconnected phrases is *world of iniquity*, which could be taken either (1) in apposition to the previous clause: *And the tongue is a fire, the very world of unrighteousness; the tongue is set among our body's parts* (NASB); or (2) as part of the predicate of what follows: *And the tongue is a fire. The tongue is placed among our members as a world of iniquity* (NRSVue). Regardless of syntactical ambiguity, James's purpose is clear: to heap up disparaging descriptors of the tongue.

The meaning of the phrase *world of iniquity* also gives interpreters pause. The second noun "iniquity" or "unrighteousness, wrongdoing, wickedness" (*adikia*) is the opposite of the word "righteousness" (*dikaiosynē*) and should be understood adjectively, describing *the world.* The tongue is *an unrighteous world* (AT), an evil world, among the members of our body (cf. "unrighteous mammon" in Luke 16:9, 11 AT, RSV, and "unrighteous steward" in Luke 16:8 ASV, AT).

So what does James mean by calling the tongue *an unrighteous world?* James 1:26-27 has interesting verbal connections to chapter 3. The words "bridle" and "tongue" appear only in 1:26 and in 3:2-8 in the letter. The word "stain" in 3:6 has the same root as the word "unstained" in 1:27. As James said earlier, keeping oneself *unstained by the world* means bridling the tongue and caring for the vulnerable (1:26-27), but in 3:6 he says it more negatively: The unrighteous world (or *world of iniquity*) enters and stains the whole body (individual and corporate) through the unbridled tongue. When the tongue is not *slow to speak and slow to anger,* it does not further *God's righteousness* (1:19-20) but is itself an entire world of "unrighteousness."

The two other difficult phrases or words in 3:6 that require some comment are *cycle of life* and *hell*. The tongue sets the *cycle of life* on fire and is set on fire by *hell*, says James. The phrase that the NRSVue translates *cycle of life* is odd; it could also be translated "wheel of nature" or "course of existence." Many commentators mention the occurrence of this phrase in Orphic mystery religions, where it refers to the soul continuing in an unending cycle of life, death, and new life. It seems unlikely that James would be drawing from this tradition directly, however. Rather, he is voicing an idea as common in Jewish literature as it is in Greco-Roman, namely, that life "rolls along" or that the "course of our existence" progresses. Specifically here, the imprudent tongue can have an impact on the whole course of life as it unfolds from beginning to end. Like a forest fire, the damage of spoken words spreads far and wide.

The word "hell" is literally *Gehenna* (Gk.), which refers to the Valley of Hinnom (Hebrew, *ge-hinnom*), south of Jerusalem (e.g., Josh 15:8). In that valley in Old Testament times, people sacrificed children to the pagan gods Moloch and Baal, a practice that the Hebrew prophets roundly condemned (2 Chron 28:3; Jer 7:31-32; 32:35). By the New Testament era, it was a garbage dump where fires burned constantly, and it had become a symbol of judgment on the wicked. The word occurs only twelve times in the New Testament and elsewhere always in the synoptic gospels in a context of future punishment (Matt 5:22, 29-30; 10:28; 18:9; 23:15, 33; Mark 9:43-47; Luke 12:5).

There are two ways to understand what James might have meant by the tongue being *set on fire by Gehenna/hell*. The first is to understand Gehenna, that place of judgment and symbol of iniquity, as kindling the tongue's destructive flames. Gehenna or hell is then a metonym for the devil or evil (McCartney 2009: 190–91) and is the source of wickedness (cf. Matt 23:15). This is how most commentators take the verse. However, according to Dale Allison, "No first-century text depicts Gehenna as a source of evil on earth or as a home for the devil" (Allison 2013: 541). Many Jewish texts do, however, refer to judgment coming on evil tongues, and this is how Allison interprets *set on fire by Gehenna*. Just as the tongue sets things on fire, so God will punish the fiery tongue on the day of judgment. One finds a parallel to this in Matthew 5:22: "If you say, 'You fool,' you will be liable to the hell [Gk., Gehenna] of fire." Whichever interpretation one takes, this verse once again confirms that James's teaching strategy is not to lecture his readers with prosaic rules or rational arguments. Rather, he paints graphic pictures that stir the imagination and prod his readers' moral will.

In verses 7-8 the metaphor shifts again, from fire to wild beasts. James lists the four categories of creatures found in other biblical lists: beasts, birds, reptiles, and sea creatures (Gen 1:24-26; 9:2; Deut 4:17-18; 1 Kings 4:33). The word for "tame" is used elsewhere only in Mark 5:4 in the New Testament, where Jesus "subdues" a demonized man. In James it also does not mean "to domesticate" but rather "to bring under control" or "govern" in the sense that God gives humans the mandate to "steward" the created order in Genesis 1:26, 28.

It is not that humans can control every species of animal; James is again using hyperbole here. His point is that the human species cannot even control their own bodies, despite being able to tame other creatures God made. The tongue is a *restless evil, full of deadly poison* (v. 8). Earlier James used the same word "restless, unstable" for the double-minded person, whose doubts toss them to and fro (1:8). In the context of references to reptiles and beasts, James's readers may also think of snakes whose "tongues" are "restless" and can inflict poisonous wounds (see also Pss 58:4; 140:3-8; Rom 3:13). All in all, this passage about the tongue gets increasingly more dire and dramatic as it progresses.

Inconsistency in Speech: This Ought Not to Be! 3:9-12

In the last part of this unit, James shifts his tactics. Instead of a blistering critique of the tongue's potential for harm, he focuses on the inconsistency of both good and evil coming from the same source. Instead of metaphors, he uses straightforward speech. The point of the subunit is the same though: followers of Jesus who live with integrity must not tear others apart with their words.

James 3:9-10 contains some repeated words and parallel phrases, such as "bless" and "curse." As a result, the phrases that are *not* repeated stand out more clearly: *People* [are] *made in the likeness of God* and *My brothers and sisters, this ought not to be so!*" The word for "likeness" appears only here in the New Testament (though cognates are plentiful). Genesis 1:26 is one of the few places it occurs in the Septuagint: "God said, 'Let us make humans in our image, according to our *likeness*.'" Perhaps James used it instead of the more common word "image" to allude to the Genesis creation story. In these verses James is doing what is typical of wisdom literature: drawing on creational images and making commonsense observations about daily life to impress on his listeners how absurd it is to bless God and simultaneously vilify someone whom God created in God's own likeness. When framed like this, the listener should be prompted to think, "Of course! That makes no sense!" The problem is practicing what one knows to be true.

Just after James calls God *the Lord and Father*, he addresses his audience as *brothers and sisters*, reminding them that God is their common Parent. Such familial language reinforces the irony of what he is saying. How can they curse a brother or sister while at the same time blessing their Father? The inconsistency recalls 2:1-13: How can they show favoritism to the rich, who oppress them, and discriminate against the poor, whom God has chosen to be heirs of the kingdom? This is not in keeping with their faith in their Lord Jesus Christ. *This ought not to be so* (3:10). It is being double-minded.

In 3:11-12 James reinforces his point with two rhetorical questions and a concluding statement. Both questions pose something preposterous and assume "no" for an answer. A spring does *not* give both fresh and unpotable water at the same time. A fig tree *cannot* yield olives, nor can a grapevine produce figs. As elsewhere in the letter, James draws on familiar images from the natural world. Figs, olives, and grapes would have been common agricultural products in first-century Palestine. Springs of water were vital for life in an arid climate. Normally a spring of water gushing from a crack in a rock would be fresh and clean at its source. However, in some areas of Palestine, as in the Great Rift Valley along the Jordan, the water could have so many minerals in it as to make it undrinkable (McCartney 2009: 193). But a spring cannot produce both *fresh and brackish water* at the same time. Creation can teach humans lessons about consistency and integrity.

James's point about consistency between tree and fruit is not unique to him but found in many ancient writings, as in the following examples:

- Plutarch, *Tranquility of Mind* 13 [472E]: "But as it is, we do not expect the vine to bear figs nor the olive [bear] grapes."
- Seneca, *Epistle* 87.25: "Therefore, good is not born from evil nor evil from good, any more than figs come from olive trees."

Perhaps most familiar and most relevant are the words of Jesus, whose teachings James is passing on: "You will know them by their fruits. Are grapes gathered from thorns or figs from thistles? In the same way, every good tree bears good fruit, but the bad tree bears bad fruit. A good tree cannot bear bad fruit, nor can a bad tree bear good fruit" (Matt 7:16-18). As he often does, James uses vivid, familiar images to impress upon his audience the importance of his message and to motivate their behavior.

What James is pushing for in 3:9-12 is consistent with a theme that pervades the whole letter. Followers of the Messiah Jesus must exhibit integrity and wholeness (perfection) in their lives as individuals and as a community of believers. They must not be double-minded, divided in their allegiance. To try to walk two different paths at the same time is impossible. To say one thing and do another is to be a living contradiction. Just as a person cannot be both friends of God and friends with a world opposed to God, just as one cannot care for the needy while also pandering to the rich, just as one cannot love both God and mammon (wealth), so also one cannot, or should not, use the same tongue to bless God and speak evil of people created in the likeness of God. Of course, modern readers will realize that they often do exactly what James decries, as first-century readers surely did also. But this is why James writes the way he does. He wants his readers to feel the prick of discomfort about behavior that is inconsistent with the faith they profess.

Earlier we noted that ancient Greek philosophers and Hellenistic wisdom traditions often addressed the ethics of speech. However, in comparison to other ancient writers, James is much more pessimistic. Where Greek moralists emphasized the difficulty of restraining the tongue, James says it is impossible (3:8) and intensifies the capacity of the tongue for evil (Johnson 2004d: 164). For James, in addition, one's speech is also integrally related to faith and to one's relationship with God. It is not just a matter of having good sense or being an effective communicator. As Johnson so nicely puts it, James has a "covenantal perspective, in which the speech and actions of humans are fundamentally qualified by the speech and action of the God who chooses to be involved with humans" (Johnson 2004d: 165). This is particularly evident in 1:18-21.

In 1:18, 21, James reminds his readers that they have been given birth by a *word*, the *word of truth*. They have become first fruits of God's creatures, and the *implanted word* has the power to save them. In the middle of these identity-framing statements stands the counsel about being *quick to listen, slow to speak, and slow to anger* (1:19). The implication is that being shaped by the true and redeeming word of God must have some impact on the words that God's redeemed creatures speak. The interconnectedness of one's speech and one's covenantal relationship with God is evident elsewhere. Cursing a brother or sister made in the likeness of God is inconsistent with blessing God the Parent. Those who stumble in their speech are not only fools, as in wisdom literature, but make themselves liable to God's judgment (3:1; cf. 4:11-12; 5:9). Inability to control the tongue renders one's piety *worthless* (1:26). Controlling one's speech, then, is not just a matter of common sense but has eternal consequences; it is essential for loving one's neighbor (2:8) and being friends with God (4:4).

Yet people in James's churches and today invariably sin in their speech. Is there no hope, since the tongue is doomed to cause stumbling? Despite James's pessimistic rhetoric, the whole point of his speech is not to condemn hearers but to encourage them. Language about the impossibility of controlling the tongue (3:8) stands side by side with language implying that "bridling the tongue" is, in fact, possible (3:2; 1:26). In the next section (3:13–4:10), James contrasts *wisdom from above* with wisdom from below (3:17), and friendship with God with *friendship with the world* (4:4). People who use their tongues for boasting and lying (3:14) lack the wisdom from above, a wisdom that infuses speech with peace, gentleness, and mercy (3:17).

Earlier James reassured readers that any who lack such wisdom need only ask for it because God, the generous Giver of every perfect gift, will grant it (1:5, 17). Believers who struggle to control their tongues should know that God's gift of wisdom can and will help moderate the tongue's destructive power. Although in 3:1-12 James dwells more on the tongue's harmful potential, other parts of the letter reveal that he also knows about the power of the tongue for good. In 5:13-20 we will hear about how the tongue can be used to pray, to bless, to heal, and to forgive.

THE TEXT IN BIBLICAL CONTEXT

Human Speech in the Bible

The Bible begins with God speaking the world into being (Gen 1). God's voice takes on clarity and color when God's Word becomes flesh in Jesus of Nazareth (John 1:1-14). God also gives speech to humans, allowing the first human to participate in God's world-making words by naming the fellow creatures (Gen 2:19). The word of the Lord comes to the prophets, who announce that word to God's people (Jer 1:4-8; Mic 1:1). Jesus sends his disciples out to proclaim the advent of God's reign (Luke 9:2) and to teach (Matt

28:20), and he promises to give them words when they are called to testify in his name (Luke 21:13-15).

God's people do not always speak graciously, however. From the beginning, human words blame (Gen 3:12-13), boast (4:23-24), deceive (27:19-24), and complain (Exod 16:2-3). Speech not only unites people; it also separates them (Gen 11:1-9). This seems to have also happened in the early church, where people sometimes engaged in dishonest, exclusionary, and hurtful speech (Acts 5:1-11; 1 Cor 1:11-12). Sins of speech are, it seems, endemic to human nature.

Recognizing this, the biblical writings contain many teachings about human speech. To be sure, we also learn about what kind of speech is and is not pleasing to God by paying attention to the narratives. Here, however, we focus on what the Bible explicitly says *about* speech, as in James.

The laws in the Pentateuch include prohibitions against slander (Lev 19:16), swearing falsely (19:12), and lying (19:11). Time and again the people of God failed to abide by the commandments. Among the many sins of Israel and Judah that the prophets condemned were sins of speech. "They do not speak honestly," says Jeremiah (8:6), and the false prophets proclaim, "'Peace, peace,' when there is no peace" (5:12-13; 6:14; 8:11). Neighbors slander and lie to each other (Isa 59:3, 13; Jer 9:4-5). Concern about right speech is especially prominent in wisdom literature and in the Psalms.

John W. Miller counts around fifty sayings about right and wrong speech in the main collection of Proverbs (chaps. 10–22; J. Miller: 144). In many of these sayings, the tongue, mouth, or lips are a metonymy for speech. "Death and life are in the power of the tongue," says Proverbs 18:21. Evil words can destroy a neighbor; they are like a sharp sword (12:18), a scorching fire (16:27), or a serpent's tongue (Ps 140:3). Proverbs especially highlights the sins of lying, slander, and gossip (11:13; 16:28). In the Psalms, betrayal by a neighbor often takes the form of speech in gossip, slander, and malicious taunting (Jacobson and Jacobson: 23). Such is the speech of the wicked (Pss 15:2-3; 41:6-7; 50:19-20). People who talk indiscriminately and too much are foolish (Prov 10:19; 15:2). They also invite calamity (Prov 13:3; 17:20) and are liable to judgment (Ps 101:5). Words spoken in anger are particularly dangerous (Prov 19:11; Eccl 7:9).

Many writings of the New Testament address the dangers of the tongue. In the Sermon on the Mount, Jesus teaches his disciples not to express their anger in harsh insults (Matt 5:22), for in such speech lie the seeds of murder (5:21-22). He urges them to be truthful in all speech and not just in oaths (5:33-37). Speech is a window into a person's character or heart, and a good heart will produce good fruit (Luke 6:45; cf. James 3:9-10). Speech appears in the catalogs of vices and virtues in Paul's letters. The sins of speech listed there are similar to those found elsewhere in the Bible: lying, slander, gossip, evil talk, abusive and obscene language, quarreling, and boasting (Rom 1:29-30; 2 Cor 12:20; Eph 4:25, 29-31; 5:4; Col 3:8-9; 2 Tim 3:2-4). "Slander is the most commonly named speech sin in the NT, occurring at least eighteen times, appearing on most of the sin lists" (Baker 2011: 735).

Wrongful speech receives considerable attention in Ephesians and Colossians. In Ephesians, attentiveness to how one speaks is part of what it means to "learn Christ." Putting off the old self and clothing oneself with the new self, created according to the likeness of God, means discarding lies and speaking the truth in love (Eph 4:14, 25; cf. Col 3:9-10). Christians should speak truthfully not only to members of the body of Christ but also to one's "neighbors," presumably any person one meets. The reason is that "we are members of one another" (Eph 4:25), we are all connected in the human family. Human community cannot thrive without a foundation of trust and transparency, built on truthful speech. Because truthful speech is sometimes unkind, Paul goes on to say that "evil talk" must be stripped away and Christians should speak "only what is good for building up, as there is need, so that your words may give grace to those who hear" (4:29; cf. Col 3:8). Paul's concern is always that which builds up the church, the body of Christ. In 1 Corinthians 14 he elevates prophecy over speaking in tongues because prophecy can "build up" the church (v. 4). When someone speaks in tongues, there should be an interpreter so that the church is "built up" (v. 5). Slander, gossip, insults, and foul language do not "give grace to those who hear" and are not "good for building up" (Eph 4:29).

All these exhortations about not using destructive speech might give the attentive Bible reader pause. Do not the writers of Scripture themselves sometimes use harsh language? Although prophets speaking for God, and Jesus speaking as God's Messiah, might be excused for their harsh rebukes, texts like Ezekiel 16 and John 8:44-47 still trouble readers. The psalmist voices the rage and despair of the exiles in Babylon: "Happy shall they be who take your little ones and dash them against the rock!" (137:9). Paul vents his frustration by wishing that the men who are unsettling the faith of Galatian believers "would castrate themselves!" (Gal 5:12). Even some of James's language sounds abrasive to modern ears.

Likely such speech employed contemporary rhetorical and cultural conventions and perhaps ancient ears would have heard them somewhat differently than we do. Perhaps because it is written and deliberate, it should not count as "speech." Still, biblical writers were human and also faced the challenge of "controlling the tongue." In fact, harsh defamatory speech has characterized many Christian leaders throughout history. For example, Martin Luther and Menno Simons are two Reformation preachers who used their fiery tongues against their opponents.

The Bible does not only instruct and scold on matters of speech, of course. Many of the psalms express praise in beautiful, poetic language. The Song of Songs uses speech to express appreciation for the human body and human love. Prophets like Second Isaiah (Isa 40–55) offer words of hope to exiles that still comfort and sustain today. Just as James recognizes that the tongue can be used to bless, to pray, to confess, and to sing (3:9; 5:13-20), so also Paul speaks of the positive potential of human speech. In Colossians, he encourages the hearers to put on virtues consistent with their new life in Christ, including the following speech habits:

> Let the word of Christ dwell in you richly; teach and admonish one another in all wisdom; and with gratitude in your hearts sing psalms, hymns, and spiritual songs to God. And whatever you do, in word or deed, do everything in the name of the Lord Jesus, giving thanks to God the Father through him. (Col 3:16-17)

The voice is essential for bearing witness to what God in Christ has done and is doing for the world. At Pentecost the Holy Spirit enables the apostles to speak in many tongues "about God's deeds of power" (Acts 2:6-11). Although the authorities try to stifle their testimony, the Holy Spirit gives them power to speak with boldness and courage (4:18-20). Prophecy, interpretation, teaching, and preaching are among the gifts that the Holy Spirit gives to the church for mutual upbuilding (1 Cor 12; Eph 4:11-13). So the tongue is not only a destructive fire. Like the bit in the horse's mouth or the rudder of a ship, it also has power to guide, influence, and mold the church for good.

THE TEXT IN THE LIFE OF THE CHURCH

Discipleship of the Tongue

James's mini-essay on the tongue has timeless relevance. Everyone at some point has regretted words spoken or written too hastily or has had to bite their tongue when tempted to lash out. James makes this common human experience a religious matter, not just a matter of good sense. Gossip, lying, slander, and boasting characterize religion that is *worthless* (James 1:26), not faith in Jesus Christ (2:1).

It is obvious how James's admonitions about speech apply to interpersonal relationships in church, whether casual conversations in the foyer, disagreements in congregational meetings, or sensitive pastoral-care issues. They apply equally to loving our neighbors at work, in the grocery-store lineup, and at the dinner table.

Such concerns have always been part of Christian teaching. The Spanish Reformer Juan de Valdéz (d. 1541) referred to James's teaching on the tongue in writing about loving God and neighbor in *The Christian Alphabet* (Italian: *Alfabeto Christiano*, ca. 1538; Williams and Mergal: 390). Dietrich Bonhoeffer in *Life Together* forbade community members from speaking about others behind their backs, even under the guise of being helpful (1954: 92). In *The Way of the Heart*, Henri Nouwen drew on James when encouraging silence as a spiritual discipline (44, 50). As with many of James's teachings, the difficulty lies in practicing them.

Although James does not provide a list of "10 Easy Steps for Controlling Speech," he does offer practical guidance throughout the letter. First, he says we should be *quick to listen, slow to speak* (1:19). Listening well is hard work. In an argument it is much easier to be preoccupied with formulating a clever repartee than to give the other person one's full attention. Being quick to listen and slow to speak means not jumping in with unsolicited advice, no matter how well-meaning. It means listening to body language, unspoken words, and emotions beneath the words. It means not letting the mind wander to undone chores or to the more interesting conversation across the room.

Second, James counsels us to ask God for wisdom (1:5). The wisdom from above is, among other things, peaceable, considerate, willing to yield, gentle, sincere (3:17). Wise speech is all of these things. It is kind. It is not deliberately inflammatory. It does not insist on being right. It is gentle but truthful.

Third, loving our neighbors as ourselves (2:8) goes a long way toward controlling the tongue. Loving a neighbor does not mean liking that neighbor, but choosing to act for the well-being of the other even when one does not feel like it. Loving one's conversation partner means speaking in a way that enhances (or at least maintains) their well-being regardless of topic or difference of opinions; it also calls for hearing as one would like to be heard.

To limit these teachings about the tongue only to the spoken word or to interpersonal communication does not do justice to their relevance for the church today. James was writing at a time when communication was primarily oral. Letters to churches would have been read aloud. Today, however, the written word and the electronic word are powerful and ubiquitous. Christians also need to bridle their tongues in text messages, emails, and on social media, not only in face-to-face speech.

James's words about speech pertain also to the church as a corporate body, not only to individuals. What language does the church use to speak good news to the world? In its history, that good news has sometimes been stifled by actions that oppress and dehumanize. The church's peace witness has sometimes been diluted by violent speech. When the church speaks truth to power, how can its language confront and challenge without becoming vitriolic? Conversely, sometimes the church bridles its tongue too much and fails to speak out against racial injustice and sexual violence. How might the church's voice help to turn around the huge ship of resource extraction, colonialism, and capitalism? If the church is a spring from which the water of life can pour, it must not at the same time offer people brackish water.

Another way to think about the tongue is the capacity of language not only to reflect reality but also to create reality. Communication theorists talk about communication not only as the transmission of information from sender to receiver but also as a "symbolic process whereby reality is produced, maintained, repaired, and transformed" (Carey: 23). New Testament scholar Luke Timothy Johnson says, "The real peril of the tongue is not found in the passing angry word or the incidental oath or the petty bit of slander. It is found in the creation of distorted worlds of meaning within which the word of truth is suppressed" (1998: 205). He reflects on how the seductive use of half-truths in advertising and the lying and slandering that characterize political campaigns distort the way we perceive reality.

The church would do well to reflect regularly on the kind of world it is shaping by the language it uses. How does its language intentionally or unintentionally create a reality that excludes some people? How does language empower some people at the expense of others? Does our language reify the world? Or is it supple enough that the breath or Spirit of God can blow through our words to enliven the church? In every age the church must be attentive to how its speech, in any form, can participate in God's work of speaking the new creation into being.

A Cautionary Word to Teachers

One of the spiritual gifts in the body of Christ is the ministry of teaching (Rom 12:7; 1 Cor 12:28-29; Eph 4:11-12). In addition to James, several books in the New Testament express concern about teachers. The early church had to contend with false teachers (Titus 1:10-11; 2 Pet 2:1-3; Jude 3-4), and Jesus warned his disciples about religious teachers who did not live with integrity and craved honor (Matt 23:1-12). Although James recognizes the importance of the teaching ministry in the church and is himself a teacher, he counsels not many to become teachers (3:1).

Throughout history, people have used this verse in James to buttress their views about who should or should not be teaching. Martin Luther appealed "to James 3:1 in arguing against papal authority, because humans need to listen to God," not human commandments (Moore-Keish: 126; cf. Gowler: 210). Some Reformers, such as Zwingli, used James 3:1 to denounce the early Anabaptists, who, for the most part, were not scholars and formal teachers and yet taught and preached the Word of God (see, e.g., Zwingli's 1525 tract "Concerning the Office of Preaching" in Harder: 408). The Anabaptists emphasized the priesthood of all believers and interpreted the Bible in the context of the church community; thus the teaching office was not restricted to recognized leaders as some thought it should be (Murray: 157).

James 3:1 does not give any guidelines about *who* is allowed to teach in the church and thus cannot legitimately be used to disqualify certain people from teaching. The main impact of his words is to make any who *are* teachers reflect on the weightiness of their vocation. Teachers have immense influence on others both for good and ill. Because they have considerable power, accountability is essential.

In chapter 3, James is concerned about the way teachers wield power through their *words*. As the rest of the letter makes clear, however, James would be equally concerned about how the *actions* and *character* of teachers influence their students. In the ancient world, imitation was an important form of teaching, which is why Paul often calls the church to imitate him (1 Cor 4:16; 11:1; Phil 3:17; 1 Thess 1:6). Like Jesus in Matthew 23, James insists that what people do should be consistent with what they say. This is especially relevant for teachers. Anyone who has taught young children knows that they imitate behavior as much or more than they are guided by words. Just as apprentices learn by watching an experienced teacher, so disciples are made when they observe and are mentored by wise and mature Christians. James is thus a teacher for whom character is as important as speech when it comes to influencing others.

James 3:1 is sobering for any teachers in the church today. It is not that people called to teach should refuse, for teaching is an important ministry in the body of Christ. James does remind us that teachers have power, and such power can be abused. Therefore, discernment and vigilance are necessary if one is going to be a teacher. High-profile, effective teachers sometimes become intoxicated with success, influence, and status. We need only look to prominent church leaders who have used their words and influence to groom and sexually abuse women to realize how such power can be egregiously misused.

On a smaller scale, a teacher's careless words that a student will "never amount to anything" can have a lifelong effect on a sensitive young person whose confidence is already low. At the same time, like a small rudder on a large ship, a teacher can pilot a student toward greater faithfulness, maturity, and service. It is not surprising, then, that James urges those who would be teachers to pause and consider their responsibility lest they metaphorically burn down a whole forest.

James's counsel to those called to a teaching vocation today would be similar to what he gave his readers two thousand years ago. Teachers need wisdom from above—wisdom that is *pure, . . . peaceable, gentle, willing to yield, full of mercy and good fruits, without a trace of partiality or hypocrisy* (3:17). This is a wisdom that God will generously give them when they ask for it (1:5). Because of their positions of influence, teachers must take to heart James's call to humility (4:10), to submit to God and draw near to God (4:7-8) if they want the "devil" of disordered desire and distorted power to flee. Above all, teachers should *love* their *neighbor*s (in this case, their students) as themselves (2:8). This love will always look out for the well-being of the other and will—in word, deed, and character—be a channel of Christ's love for all people.

James 3:13–4:10

The Two Ways of Wisdom and Friendship

PREVIEW

Robert Frost's poem "The Road Not Taken" begins with the words "Two roads diverged in a yellow wood." James also envisions two distinct paths for followers of Jesus. Although the idea of two ways permeates the whole letter, it becomes most explicit in 3:13–4:10. In this unit James contrasts true wisdom, given by God, with a pseudowisdom in opposition to God. These two ways correspond to the two ways of *[friendship] with God* compared to *friendship with the world* (4:4). The latter is the way of disordered desire that gives birth to sin and death (1:14-15). The other is the way of the word that gives birth to salvation (1:18, 21). To try to walk two paths at once is to be *double-minded* (1:8; 4:8) and not "whole" or "perfect" (1:4).

Although such dualistic language may not appeal to contemporary readers, James is drawing on a long-standing Jewish tradition of two ways: the way of life or death, and the way of blessing or curse. His task is like Joshua's, who called Israel to "choose this day whom you will serve": Yahweh or the gods of the nations (Josh 24:15). James's purpose for setting forth these stark alternatives is to call his readers back to the way of *our glorious Lord Jesus Christ* (2:1 NRSV) and away from their destructive behavior and attitudes—that is, to repent and live with integrity.

James's tone is uncompromising and at times harsh. In almost every other unit of the letter, James addresses the church as *[beloved] brothers and sisters*, including three times in 3:1-12 (vv. 1, 10, 12) and once immediately after this unit (4:11). Not so in this unit. Instead of familial terms of address, we find vocatives such as *adulterers, sinners,* and *double-minded.* The purpose of such strong rhetoric is not to condemn but to persuade and transform. The unit ends with urgent calls to *submit . . . to God, draw near to God,* and *humble yourselves before the Lord*; it holds out the promises that God *gives grace to the humble* and *will draw near to you.*

This unit has similarities to both Jewish wisdom literature and the prophets. Like the former, James explicitly characterizes wisdom (3:13-18), and he quotes the book of Proverbs (James 4:6). Like the prophets, he bluntly chastises the church for its sins against the neighbor. He accuses them of committing adultery in their relationship with God (4:4) and calls for repentance. Various scholars have argued that James employs strategies of argumentation outlined in ancient Greek rhetorical handbooks (Hartin 2009a: 206–16; Batten 2017b: 149–69). According to Luke Timothy Johnson, 3:13–4:10 is a coherent literary unit that treats the conventional topic of envy in Hellenistic literature in a standardized manner, calling his audience to conversion (Johnson 2004b).

Whether persuaded by effective Greek rhetoric or drawn to the text's resonance with Jewish wisdom and prophetic literature, James's original readers would have found this central portion of the letter impactful. Contemporary Christian audiences may also find James's call to turn away from envy and strife and toward God's wisdom and peace compelling.

OUTLINE

True and False Wisdom, 3:13-18
Friendship with the World and Enmity with God, 4:1-6
Submission and Repentance, 4:7-10

EXPLANATORY NOTES

True and False Wisdom 3:13-18

The subject of 3:13-18 is wisdom, a topic that James introduced in 1:5, where he urged any who lack wisdom to ask God for it. James begins this subunit by contrasting the true wisdom of God with the false spirit festering among them. His words are especially appropriate for teachers or aspiring teachers (3:1-2), who had the reputation of being *wise and knowledgeable*. Given the deep-seated *conflicts and disputes* troubling the church (4:1-4), however, his words are relevant for all who lack wisdom.

The first sentence in the subunit (3:13a), though a question, is not asking for information but posing a rhetorical challenge: *So you think you are wise and understanding? Prove it by how you live!* (paraphrased). It thus functions more as the "if" part of a conditional sentence, with the command in verse 13b as the implied "then" (as in the NLT). In verse 14 the condition and subsequent command are explicit, paralleling verse 13 in function if not in form. This is followed by a characterization of the "wisdom" inherent in each condition, but in reverse order, in this *A B B′ A′* pattern:

- ***A*** If someone is wise and understanding, they should show that by their life. (v. 13)
  - ***B*** If you have bitter envy and selfish ambition, do not boast and be false. (v. 14)
  - ***B′*** Envy and selfish ambition are not wisdom from above but result in . . . turmoil and evil. (vv. 15-16)
- ***A′*** Wisdom from above is characterized by . . . and results in righteousness and peace. (vv. 17-18)

The word "wisdom" (*sophia*) appears frequently in the New Testament, but the Greek word for "knowledgeable" or "understanding" (*epistēmōn*) is found only here. In combining these two qualities, James is perhaps influenced by the Septuagint and other Jewish literature, where "wisdom" and "understanding" appear together (e.g., Exod 31:3; 36:1-2; Deut 1:13, 15; Job 12:2; Isa 33:6; Dan 2:21). The rest of this unit shows that "wisdom and understanding" refer not only to intellectual knowledge, cognitive ability, or cleverness, but also encompass the heart and hands as well as the head.

Richard Bauckham defines wisdom as "the God-given ability of the transformed heart to discern and to practise God's will" (1999: 152). The wisdom of James is relational in that it has to do with how people in a community treat each other. Second, it is active in that it is integrally tied to behavior. Like faith (2:14-26), it must be evident in the fruit of good works. The Greek word for *good life* refers to an overall pattern of conduct that is not only morally upright, but also attractive, praiseworthy, and noble. The works of a wise and understanding person will be part of such a wider pattern of living. Third, the wisdom that James describes is characterized by gentleness or humility. It is not full of itself and its own desires but is conscious of its origins in and dependence on God.

In 3:14-16 James addresses the contentious spirit that lurks in their communities, a spirit contrary to the wisdom he commends. The fact that *envy* and *selfish ambition* appear twice in these verses (14, 16) emphasizes James's conviction that these vices are the root of the problem. The Greek word *zēlos* (envy) has a range of meanings in the Septuagint and New Testament. Positively, it can denote zeal or enthusiastic devotion (e.g., Num 25:13; 2 Sam 21:2; Acts 22:3; Gal 1:14). It can also mean "jealousy," an "intense concern for protecting one's possessions from the encroachments of perceived rivals" (Elliott 2007: 346; e.g., Exod 20:5; Num 5:14-15; Prov 6:34; 2 Cor 11:2). Finally, it can refer to "envy," a resentment that someone has something of value that one lacks and a hunger to have it for oneself, even at the expense of the other's life. Envy arises out of a perception that what we have and even who we are is not enough.

While all three senses express intense emotion, zeal and jealousy may have a positive connotation, whereas envy is always a vice (Elliott 2007: 346). "Since envy entails malice and destructive intent toward others, it is obviously inimical to social harmony and group cohesion and often is condemned together with the vices of strife and dissension" (Elliott 2007: 347). In James 3:14 the word has the third sense and is characterized as *bitter*. This perpetual dissatisfaction is closely tied to the cravings that James talks about elsewhere in the letter (1:14-15; 4:1-2) and to the *selfish ambition* (3:14) that pushes one to acquire more and be more.

In the first-century Mediterranean world, honor and shame were strong cultural values motivating behavior. It is not unthinkable that people in James's churches too sometimes vied for influence, status, and honor and envied others. James has already warned his readers about the evils of the tongue (1:19, 26; 2:15-16; 3:1-12). Now he criticizes the arrogant, untruthful speech of people who harbor envy and selfish ambition (3:14). Their self-promoting words and self-interested behavior expose their wisdom as a lie, since true wisdom is humble and not boastful. A good life, marked by deeds done in modesty and with quiet wisdom, will speak for itself.

The pseudowisdom spouted by those who harbor envy and selfish ambition is not wisdom *from above*, that is, not from God (note that in 1:17 *from above* is synonymous with *Father of lights*). Like the Jewish wisdom tradition, James knows that wisdom is a divine gift bestowed generously on all who ask God for it (1:5). Wisdom of Solomon 8:21 says, "I perceived that I would not possess wisdom unless God gave her to me" (cf. Prov 2:6-7; Sir 1:1). Solomon is the quintessential example of someone who requested and received wisdom from God (1 Kings 3:5-12, 28).

A dualistic worldview governs James's perspective in this unit. He lays out the two ways of false wisdom from below (3:15-16) and true wisdom from above (3:17-18). In 4:4 he will talk about the two ways in terms of friendship with the world or with God. As Scot McKnight notes, "There is an obvious moral dualism here: the above versus the below, the heavenly versus the earthly, the spiritual versus the unspiritual, and the divine versus the devilish. Such moral dualism make [*sic*] moral injunctions more forceful" (306). The adjectives describing false wisdom as *earthly, unspiritual, devilish* (v. 15) belong to the negative pole of this oppositional binary. In history this triad has sometimes been summed up as "the world, the flesh, and the devil," as in the 1549 Anglican Book of Common Prayer and stemming from even earlier church writings (Moore-Keish: 133). It has entered into English usage in widely different contexts since then, ranging from a 1950s science-fiction film to writings on spiritual warfare.

James's characterization of counterfeit "wisdom" as *earthly, unspiritual, devilish* requires some interpretation for contemporary readers, since these adjectives can be (and have been) taken as a denigration of physical human bodies and the created world (Moore-Keish: 133). This would be a misunderstanding of James, who knows the beauty of flowers (1:11), cares about the bodily needs of the naked and hungry (2:15-16), and identifies with farmers who await rain for their *precious crop* (5:7). James does not hope for a disembodied soul's escape from its fleshly existence but for the coming of the Lord (5:7). To be *earthly* is to be oriented to and aligned with the unjust, disordered desires of human society instead of with God's will.

In the New Testament the Greek word *psychikos* (unspiritual) is sometimes contrasted with *pneumatikos* (spiritual). The *psyche* is the self or one's life on earth, whereas that which is "spiritual" comes from the *pneuma*, or "Spirit." Perhaps a better translation than "unspiritual" in verse 15 would be "self-ish," meaning "focused on the advancement of one's own earthly personal welfare" (McCartney 2009: 201).

To say that false wisdom is *devilish* means that its origin lies in a power opposed to God (Moore-Keish: 132). The ancient world's belief in the existence of malevolent spiritual beings is reflected in James (2:19; 4:7). Although Western Christians today might not think of demons in the same way, an awareness of intangible evil forces still exists. Just as demons' "belief" in God is not true faith (2:19), so also "wisdom" that is demonic is not true wisdom. The pseudowisdom James talks about in verse 15 refers to the dominant value system of empire, which is concerned more about self-promotion than about the other. It is the antithesis of who God is and of what God gives.

When a community is infected by *envy and selfish ambition*, there will be *disorder and wickedness of every kind* (v. 16). The noun *disorder* is related to the adjective translated "unstable" in 1:8 and *restless* in 3:8. That is, James is not just talking about untidy clutter or rowdy behavior but about a fundamental volatility that breeds chaos in a community and is the opposite of the *peaceable* wisdom from above. The phrase *wickedness of every kind* (3:16) could also be translated "every evil deed" (cf. John 3:20; 2 Cor 5:10). When people seek honor and strive for power, envying those who have something they want, they cause fractured relationships and community pain. Like anger (1:20), envy and self-aggrandizement do not further God's justice.

James next lists seven attributes of wisdom that come from God (v. 17). He again uses language for rhetorical effect by stringing together words with similar sounds. Four words in sequence begin with the Greek letter *epsilon* (*e* in English) and have similar internal sounds (*pei/pā* sound in Greek). The last two adjectives in the series also begin and end with the same sounds. Reading this aloud, as most letters would have been in the ancient world, would create a euphonious sound and rhythmic flow. Like any good communicator, James knew that desirable virtues must be couched in equally pleasing language: form must match content. In contrast, the Greek words for *earthly, unspiritual, and devilish* (v. 15) all have different sounds, creating a bumpy, unharmonious effect (Witherington 2007: 503). James knew that effective rhetoric has the power to persuade and shape community.

Wisdom that comes from God is first of all pure. Why *first pure*? This quality of wisdom is primary because it undergirds the others. To be pure is to be untarnished by sin and unclouded by muddy motives—like pure orange juice unspoiled by additives. Using a synonym for "pure," James earlier said that "pure religion" is one that is not stained by the values of a world that neglects widows and orphans (1:27). Readers might recall that Jesus pronounced a blessing on the pure in heart because they would see God (Matt 5:8).

Wisdom that comes from God is *peaceable, gentle,* and *willing to yield* (James 3:17). Wisdom and peace are also linked in Jewish wisdom literature in such texts as Proverbs 3:17: "All [wisdom's] paths are peace." Although these three adjectives have different nuances, they all have to do with treating others with respect and forbearance and being conciliatory. The Greek word for "gentle" is a synonym of the word "gentleness" in verse 13, which could also be translated "humility." People who embody this *gentle* wisdom are not quarrelsome, rude, or pushy. They do not insist on their own way but are *willing to yield* (a word used only here in the New Testament). They are not so hardened in their thinking and being that they cannot be flexible and capacious in their ability to embrace ideas or people who are different than they are.

Some might infer, then, that Christians must be spineless or wishy-washy, passive avoiders of conflict. This is not what James is saying. "Peace" here should be understood in the broader biblical sense of shalom, that robust, iridescent word for well-being, wholeness, and right relationships among God, humans, and all creation. *Peaceable* people actively foster shalom by the way they live. This is the opposite of the envious person, who creates *disorder* (v. 16). That James considers being peaceable an active trait is evident in the next verse, where he refers to *making peace* that bears fruit in justice. Being *gentle* and *willing to yield* often demands more courage, self-control, and strength than stubborn, unbending insistence on being right or rude impulsiveness. Since this kind of wisdom comes from God, it can never be wisdom that yields to injustice or hatred but always bends toward love. This is evident in the next phrase describing wisdom.

Wisdom that comes from God is *full of mercy and good fruits.* To be merciful is to be compassionate. This is not just an attitude but an action. Mercy bears fruit in deeds of kindness and compassion, such as caring for the poor and vulnerable (1:27; cf. 2:15-16). Like true faith, true wisdom must be demonstrated in life. In characterizing wisdom as full of *good fruits,* James echoes Jesus, who said, "You will know them by their fruits" (Matt 7:16, 20). Like the previous qualities, the fact that wisdom is *full of mercy and good fruits* suggests that wisdom is relational, expressed in and essential for faithful Christian community.

Wisdom that comes from God is *impartial and sincere* (James 3:17 NIV). The Greek word for *impartial* occurs only here in the New Testament and is sometimes translated "showing no favoritism" (NLT), "unwavering" (NASB), or "fair" (CEB). It is the opposite of *making distinctions* (2:4) on the basis of fine clothing (2:3). Like envy and selfish ambition, making unfair judgments that discriminate against some and favor others destabilizes community. Likewise, wisdom that is sincere and *without . . . hypocrisy* leads to transparency, honesty, and unpretentiousness in relationships. Such wisdom builds up community.

The last verse of this subunit (v. 18) has a proverb-like quality that has led some scholars to view it as a free-floating aphorism that James just tacked on. However, it is a fitting conclusion to the comparison of true and false wisdom in verses 13-17 and closely connected to it. The word *fruit* ties this verse to the preceding one, which says wisdom from God is *full of . . . good fruits.* One of those good fruits is *righteousness,* which could also be translated "justice" (3:17 CEB; cf. 1:20). When peacemakers sow seeds of peace, the fruit they harvest is righteousness or justice. This confluence of terms appears also in Old Testament visions of shalom. See, for example, Psalm 85:10, "Righteousness and peace will kiss each other"; and Isaiah 32:17, "The effect of righteousness will be peace, and the result of righteousness, quietness and trust forever." In the latter, peace is the fruit of justice or righteousness, but James turns this around: justice results when people pursue peace in a peaceful manner (Swartley: 262). God's justice is established when God's shalom reigns; God's shalom is possible only when there is also justice. The implication is that peace must not only be the desired outcome of work for justice, but it must also be the path toward that justice.

Having wisdom that comes from God means not merely "keeping peace" but also "making (or doing) peace." The difference is significant. James 3:18 and Matthew 5:9, "Blessed are the peacemakers," are the only two New Testament texts that use the Greek words "make" and "peace" to refer to our calling to be peacemakers (Batten 2017b: 154), although the idea of divine and human peacemaking appears elsewhere (cf. Luke 19:42; Rom 14:19; Eph 2:14-15; Col 1:20). Actively working toward God's shalom is much more difficult than "keeping the peace," for it requires confronting injustice and working through conflict. Those who mouth platitudes like *Go in peace; keep warm and eat your fill* (James 2:16) but do nothing to enact a just shalom proclaim a false peace, which the prophets also condemned (Jer 6:13-14; Ezek 13:8-10). African American antiracism activist Frederick Douglass used James 3:17-18 to challenge oppression and the false peace that does not grow the sweet fruit of justice (Aymer; Moore-Keish: 136).

Some scholars have noticed that the characteristics of wisdom in James 3:17 resemble the fruits of the Spirit in Galatians 5:22-23 and have suggested that "wisdom in James functions as the Spirit does in Paul" (Davids 1982: 56; cf. Kirk). Supporting this connection is the fact that wisdom and spirit are closely connected in some Jewish Scriptures (Deut 34:9; Isa 11:2; Wisd of Sol 1:4-7). In the New Testament, Stephen is filled with the Holy Spirit and wisdom (Acts 6:3, 5, 10). God gives both the Holy Spirit (Luke 11:13) and wisdom (James 1:5) to any who ask.

However, saying that James has a wisdom pneumatology overstates the case (Baker 2008). He never refers explicitly to the Holy Spirit, and 3:17 shares little vocabulary with Galatians 5:22-23. Despite similarities, wisdom and Spirit are not interchangeable elsewhere in Scripture. For example, although an agent of God at creation, wisdom is created by God, whereas the Holy Spirit is not. Wisdom is one of many gifts God bestows on those who lack it, whereas the Holy Spirit dwells in people in a unique and ongoing way.

Despite a lack of overlap in vocabulary, the characteristics of wisdom in James also recall the Beatitudes and the qualities of those whom Jesus blesses (Matt 5:3-12): pure, gentle or meek, merciful, peacemaking. It remains unclear if James was consciously paraphrasing Jesus' teaching for a new context, whether here or in other parts of the letter that resonate with the Sermon on the Mount. It may be that James was so soaked in the thought of Jesus, his teacher and brother, that they unconsciously seeped out in his correspondence with churches *[James and the Jesus Tradition, p. 353]*.

Although the Letter of James is sometimes characterized as "the wisdom book of the New Testament" *[The Wisdom Tradition and James, p. 376]*, the wisdom he commends cannot simply be characterized as commonsense observation and practical teaching about the good life. The qualities of wisdom in James are relational and behavioral. Like the Beatitudes, they are countercultural and upside-down, not only in James's day but also today. Humility, not judging others, yielding to others instead of insisting on one's own way, mercy, and gentleness are not qualities that make for personal advancement nor offer grounds for boasting. True wisdom from above is embodied most fully in Jesus Christ, the upside-down Wisdom of God (1 Cor 1:30). Whether in the first century or the twenty-first, faith communities would do well to act with this kind of wisdom when they meet to make decisions or gather to be the church together.

Friendship with the World and Enmity with God 4:1-6

James 4:1-6 belongs with 3:13-18 since both passages begin with a rhetorical question ending in *among you* and both speak about two poles of a dualism. The words *among you* indicate that 4:1-6 is not about the origins of violence in general but about toxic conflict *within* the church. Its origins are *earthly, unspiritual, devilish,* the antithesis of *wisdom . . . from above* (3:13-18); this dissension belongs to *friendship with the world,* not with God (4:4). James 4:7-10 follows this reprimand with a *therefore* that calls hearers to repentance.

The subunit begins with two rhetorical questions, the second of which is really a "yes" to the first: The *conflicts and disputes <u>do</u>* come from *cravings . . . at war within* us! The NRSVue translation is actually milder than the original Greek, for James uses dramatic, repetitive language of *war, conflicts*/fighting, and *murder* in verses 1-2. This "combination of terms suggests acute and chronic hostilities" (Vlachos: 129), not mere "dispute."

Before we consider what these words mean in the context of a Christian community, we must attend to a thorny grammatical issue in verse 2 that results in diverse translations. The punctuation adopted by the editors of the Greek New Testament and some English translations (e.g., NKJV) results in something like the following:

> *You desire and you do not have.*
> *You murder and envy (or covet) and cannot obtain.*
> *You fight and make war.*

The phrasing in the NRSVue and many other English versions (e.g., NIV, NLT, ESV) is more like this:

> *You desire and do not have,*
>   *[so] you kill;*
> *and you envy and cannot obtain,*
>   *[so] you fight and wage war.* (AT)

Since the verse contains few conjunctions and many verbs, the relationship between clauses is ambiguous in Greek. Perhaps James intentionally heaped up several terse clauses so that the language itself communicates the heightened tension of his subject matter. Although the word "so" is not in the original, the second translation is preferable because it illumines the relationship between clauses and makes clear that murder is the result of selfish desire and that fighting results from envy. James is emphatic that evil deeds are the outcome of sinful attitudes and that self-centered desire and greed bear fruit in violence.

Is it possible that the Christian recipients of the letter were actually killing each other? A few interpreters take James's words literally and thus have suggested that some may have been part of the violent Zealot movement (Martin: 144; Townsend). There is little to support this, however, and more plausible solutions are available. Erasmus (ca. 1466–1536) and some later commentators have surmised that the Greek word for "you murder" (*phoneuete*) is a corruption of an original "you envy" (*phthoneite*). This is a creative and appealing solution, since the letter elsewhere talks about envy, but no manuscript evidence supports such a textual change.

Luke Timothy Johnson argues persuasively that the language of violence and war is part of the ancient Hellenistic *topos* on envy (2004b: 190–93). According to Abraham Malherbe, *topoi* (pl.) are "traditional, fairly systematic treatments of moral subjects which make use of common clichés, maxims, short definitions, and so forth, without thereby sacrificing an individual viewpoint" (quoted in Hartin 2009a: 204). In other words, James was likely drawing on traditional imagery and vocabulary associated with envy, not speaking about literal murder among his readers. He used severe metaphorical language for its shock value to impress upon the church the seriousness of their dissension. In this, he stands in the tradition of Jesus, who also used hyperbole and associated anger with murder (Matt 5:21-22). Perhaps their envy and selfish ambition, their boasting and angry speech were figuratively killing the church.

The idea that jealousy, envy, and coveting lead to murder and war is a common notion in ancient Hellenistic literature, both secular and sacred. One finds it in Greco-Roman thinkers such as Plato (e.g., *Laws* 9.869E), Epictetus, and Cicero, to name a few, as well as in Jewish writings (e.g., Wisd of Sol 2:24; Testament of Simeon 2–4). Although the Old Testament does not explicitly name envy as a motive for Cain's murder of Abel, the author of 1 Clement does: "You see, brothers, jealousy and envy brought about a brother's murder" (4.7, with more examples in 4.8–6.4). Other biblical examples include Rachel's envy of Leah, the story of Joseph and his brothers, Ahab's murder of Naboth to acquire his vineyard, and Joshua's envy of Eldad and Medad. The Didache, an early Christian document of moral instruction, says, "Do not be jealous or quarrelsome or hot-tempered, for all these things breed murders" (3.2). Surely James drew on the wisdom of his scriptural tradition when teaching the church about godly living.

James uses several different terms in verses 1-3 to talk about what lies at the root of destructive deeds. The word "cravings" is always used negatively in the New Testament (Luke 8:14; Titus 3:3; 2 Pet 2:13) and is the origin of the English word "hedonism." Although most versions opt for the translation *within you* (James 4:1), the Greek literally says, *among your* [pl.] *members*. Some commentators interpret "members" to refer to members of the church; if so, verses 1-2 are about conflict in a community, not within individuals (McCartney 2009: 207; Martin: 140).

However, since the term *members* was used in 3:5, 6 to refer to parts of an individual's body, and since James seems to be talking about personal vices such as envy in chapter 4, he is likely referring to a person's internal, not interpersonal, conflict (Allison 2013: 600; Davids 1982: 157; Hartin 2009a: 196). These cravings for pleasure create a struggle *within* believers when they vie for dominance over Christ-centered virtues that come from godly wisdom (cf. Rom 7:21-23; 1 Pet 2:11). This struggle is related to being *double-minded* (1:8; 4:8) and not whole, a dominant concern in the letter. At the same time, these inner battles have a devastating effect on the communal body: they result in *wars and fighting* (4:1 AT) James is concerned about the personal struggle between good and evil precisely because of how it affects the well-being and faithfulness of the whole community.

Cravings (4:1) lead people to *want* or *desire* what they do not have and to act aggressively to acquire it (v. 2). Although desire in the Bible can be positive (someone can desire God's commandments or desire to be with Christ), in James it refers to self-centered, self-gratifying yearning for something. To desire something another person has amounts to coveting that thing (the same word appears in the prohibition against coveting in LXX of Exod 20:17; Deut 5:21). This word appears as a noun in James 1:14-15: *But one is tempted by one's own desire, being lured and enticed by it; then, when that desire has conceived, it engenders sin, and sin, when it is fully grown, gives birth to death* (NRSV).

In 4:1-3, then, James spells out how this unfolds: covetous, disordered desire triggers selfish, sinful grasping, which leads to enmity and even some kinds of death. He charges them with envying in verse 2 (NRSVue: *you covet*). Envy is an intensification of desiring or coveting what another person has. In 3:14-16 James says *envy and selfish ambition* are *earthly, unspiritual, devilish,* leading to *disorder and wickedness of every kind*. Fighting, violence, murder, and war surely fall into the category of such disorder and wickedness.

James is not condemning desire as such nor saying that pleasure is sinful. Rather, he is critical of envious desire for what others have and the compulsion to possess at the expense of others' well-being. As John Painter says, "Desire is unquenchable, inexhaustible. Desire does not recognize 'enough.' Desire has created the consumer society. Desire flourishes because it seems that there is always more, and more is never enough" (Painter and deSilva: 138). Such compulsive desire is toxic to Christian community. Even though people may not be literally killing each other, such selfishness and greed will prove fatal for a community that claims to follow Jesus as Lord.

In 4:2c-3 James addresses the problem of desire from another angle. Earlier he told his readers that if they lack wisdom, they should ask God, who *gives to all generously and ungrudgingly* (1:5). James confirms what his readers might now be thinking: *You do not have, because you do not ask* (4:2). Lest they assume that God should and will give them everything they want, James immediately qualifies his words by saying, *You ask and do not receive because you ask wrongly* (4:3).

The translation *wrongly* does not communicate well here what James intends. It is not that people who pray need to ask a certain way, with eloquent words or formulas or even with unshakable belief. There is not one right way to pray. A better translation would be *because you ask wickedly* (*kakōs*). Their petitions are evil because they are self-centered, indulgent desires for pleasure. The gifts God so generously gives are gifts, like wisdom, that bear the good fruit of mercy and peace, not conflict.

In practice, James's guidance becomes more ambiguous. When is a prayer too "selfish" to be prayed? If prayer is defined as genuine and open communication with God, should we not bring *all* our requests and concerns to God (cf. Phil 4:6)? We must remember that James's admonition here is not first of all instruction on *how* to pray, but a reminder that the insatiable desire to consume and possess will destroy community and is not of God. These words remind Christians to align their desires with God's desires: to cultivate friendship with God, not the world.

In verse 4 James literally addresses his readers as *adulteresses,* although most translations render it in gender-inclusive terms such as "adulterous people." A far cry from the typical, congenial *brothers and sisters*, this vocative alerts readers to the seriousness of what follows. Textual variants that read "adulterers and adulteresses" assume that the sin is sexual and are early scribal attempts to accuse both men and women (Johnson 1995: 278). James is not, however, accusing anyone of literally committing adultery. Rather, his use of the feminine form stems from the prophetic tradition that posed an adulterous wife as a metaphor for Israel's covenant unfaithfulness (Hosea; Isa 1:21; 57:3; Jer 3:1-12; Ezek 16:15-43; 23). "This image implies a male-gendered God bound in marriage to a female-gendered people who wander away from their covenant commitments" (Moore-Keish: 142). John J. Schmitt argues that James had Proverbs 30:20 (LXX) in mind: "Such is the way of an adulterous woman who, when she has performed the act, will wash herself and say that she has done nothing improper." Like this woman, James's readers lack a moral compass and seem indifferent to how they wrong their neighbors (Schmitt: 336–37). Jesus used similar imagery when he spoke of his generation as "adulterous" (Matt 12:39; 16:4).

Readers today might find this language troubling and need to be cautious about perpetuating sexist and patriarchal assumptions about female infidelity in their interpretation of the text. Since the point of the address is the *audience's* unfaithfulness rather than a supposed female proclivity to sin, modern interpreters and preachers will want to find language that communicates this in culturally appropriate terms.

James does not continue with the infidelity imagery but shifts to thinking about faith commitments in terms of friendship. The first clause in verse 4 is another rhetorical question anticipating the answer "yes," and the second repeats and reinforces it:

> *You know that friendship with the world is enmity with God, right? Therefore, whoever intends to be a friend of the world is established as an enemy of God.* (AT)

Since the rhetorical question implies that they should already know this, it functions as a critique of their present behavior. The ethical dualism in 4:4 is a foundational conviction for James and a theological umbrella over many of the letter's dominant motifs. Some scholars have seen it as the thematic center of James's whole argument (Hartin 1999: 106; Johnson 1995: 84–85). Before addressing why that is so, we need to look briefly at the meaning of two key terms, "friend/friendship" and "world."

Discussions about the subject of friendship appear in many Greek and Roman writers of antiquity, including Pythagoras, Plato, Aristotle, and Cicero (see also comments on Abraham as *friend of God* in 2:23). Although equality was an important characteristic of friendship, people who were not equal could also be friends. Benefactors, for example, might be considered "friends" even though they had a higher social-economic status than their beneficiaries. Aristotle, Cicero, and Plutarch spoke of friends being "one soul/mind" or "another self" (Batten 2017b: 42–44). Friends shared perspectives and values, as this quote from Cicero exemplifies: "We shared the one element indispensable to friendship, a complete agreement in aims, ambitions, and attitudes" (*De amicitia* [On Friendship] 4.15, quoted in Hartin 2009a: 198). Friends were loyal to each other, trustworthy, humble, and open to instruction. Many writers talk about friends "sharing all things in common" (cf. Acts 2:44). Friendship also figures prominently in Jewish wisdom writings, such as Proverbs, Ecclesiasticus (Sirach), and Wisdom of Solomon. In fact, the word "friendship" (*philia*), found only in James 4:4 in the New Testament (though cognates abound), appears in the Septuagint only in these three wisdom writings and Maccabees (the word "friend," *philos*, is more common). Sirach warns against fair-weather friends (6:7-13) and says faithful friends are rare, "a sturdy shelter . . . , a treasure . . . , beyond price . . . , [and] life-saving medicine" (6:14-16). (For a full study of friendship in James, see Batten 2017b.)

What does it mean to be a friend of God? In antiquity the idea of divine-human friendship was not as common as friendship between humans, but it is still present (Batten 2017b: 48–54). Those who receive the gift of wisdom become friends with God (Wisd of Sol 7:14, 27). Moses was like a friend of God because God spoke to him face-to-face, as a friend (Exod 33:11). James considered Abraham a friend of God because he trusted God absolutely and demonstrated his fidelity in obedient action (2:21-23). Someone deemed a friend of God would not be God's equal, however. Although Jesus called his disciples "friends," he was also their teacher, not their equal, and he gave them commandments that he expected them to obey (John 15:12-17).

In 4:4, James accuses his readers of wanting to be friends of the world. In the Hellenistic understanding of friendship, to be a friend of the world means to share the perspectives and values of the world and to be loyal to the world. It means holding to the same deep commitments as the world and demonstrating them in action, just as Abraham showed he was a friend of God by living out his faith. The Greek word for *wishes* in verse 4b connotes intentionality or purposeful behavior (as in 1:18, describing God's will). One *chooses to be a friend of the world* (NIV). As is true for friendship with

God, being a friend of the world does not make one *equal* to the world. In fact, because the world can become a jealous taskmaster and demand things its subjects do not wish to give, one might question whether *friendship* is really a good descriptor for one's relationship with the world.

Our understanding of *world* is further informed by the fact that James sets friendship with it in opposition to friendship with God. The *world* does not refer to the physical world created by God nor to the realm of human interaction. Rather, like the Gospel of John, James uses *world* to name the dimension of reality that is actively opposed to God or indifferent to God. This was already evident in 1:27, where James says religion that is pure and pleasing to God is that which responds to the needs of the vulnerable and is *unstained by the world* (see comments on 1:27). God has chosen people who are poor by the world's standards to inherit the riches of God's kingdom (2:5), for what the world values is not what God values. A similar perspective is found in 1 John 2:15-17, which contrasts love of the world with love of God.

The words of James 4:4 sound so uncompromising that contemporary readers might struggle with them. Is such a severe ethical dualism really necessary or practical? Can we not live with "both-and" instead of "either-or"?

It is helpful to understand James's dualistic framework from the perspective of the Jewish "two ways" tradition. The two ways represent two contrasting ways of life: a life of virtue and of vice, a life of following God and of not following God. The following texts exemplify this tradition:

- "See, I am setting before you today a blessing and a curse: the blessing, if you obey the commandments of the Lord your God that I am commanding you today; and the curse, if you do not obey the commandments of the Lord your God but turn from the way that I am commanding you today, to follow other gods that you have not known." (Deut 11:26-28; cf. Ps 1)
- "To this people you shall say: 'Thus says the LORD: See, I am setting before you the way of life and the way of death.' " (Jer 21:8)
- "God has given two ways to the sons of humans, and two inclinations, and two kinds of action. . . . For there are two ways of good and evil, and with these are the two inclinations in our breasts discriminating them." (Testament of Asher 1.3-5)

The Didache, an early Christian writing of moral instruction, continues this Jewish perspective: "There are two ways, one of life and one of death, but a great difference between the two ways" (1.1). Jesus, too, talked about the two ways in Matthew 7:13-14, urging disciples to take the narrow gate and hard road that lead to life. Perhaps the teaching of Jesus closest to James 4:4 in laying out two stark alternatives is Matthew 6:24: "No one can serve two masters, for a slave will either hate the one and love the other or be devoted to the one and despise the other. You cannot serve God and wealth."

Clearly James stands firmly in the tradition of Jewish Scripture and of Jesus when he says that *friendship with the world is enmity with God*. Each day one must choose whom to serve. The call for undivided allegiance to God is consistent with the rest of the letter. Trying to walk two paths at the same time is being divided or *double-minded* (1:8; 4:8). Instead, James calls Christians to be *whole* or *perfect* (1:4). Living with wholeness or integrity means loving God with heart, soul, mind, and strength and being consistent in faith and action (2:19-26): not only *hearing* but also *doing* the word (1:22-25); not only *knowing* but also *doing* the right thing (4:17); not only *speaking* but also *acting* with integrity (2:15-16; 3:9-12). If one adheres to the false wisdom of the world, which is envious, selfish, and leads to disunity, one cannot at the same time be friends with God, who gives wisdom from above. God's claim on the lives of God's people is total, and friendship with God is incompatible with friendship with a world fundamentally opposed to God.

To be a friend of God does *not* mean separation from culture, society, or politics, or from *people* who are "friends of the world." It does mean that all aspects of life take second place to the claims of God. Such an uncompromising demand may seem unrealistic to people today who prefer "both/and." Who is not inconsistent at times? Who does not falter in allegiance?

James does not expect the impossible: he recognizes that people are not perfect (3:2) and need forgiveness (5:15). Still, if a road divides and leads in two opposite directions, one cannot walk down both ways at the same time without splitting oneself in two. James uses dramatic rhetoric to urge his readers to choose the right direction. Of course, his readers are not standing on neutral ground while trying to decide where to go. They are already followers of *our glorious Lord Jesus Christ* (2:1 NRSV). But they are experiencing trials, and their faith is being tested (1:2-3). James calls them to resist the disordered desires of the world, which lead to violence, and return to the road of friendship with God when they stray from the path.

In 4:5-6 James supports his claims by citing Scripture, as he does elsewhere in the letter (2:8, 11, 23; 4:6). The problem is that 4:5 is one of the thorniest verses in the letter: there is no consensus among scholars ancient or modern about how to translate it or what it means. Fortunately, no great doctrine of the Christian faith is at stake here.

The NRSVue and the NRSV (similarly NIV, ESV, NASB) differ in how they translate 4:5. The NRSVue says, *Or do you suppose that the scripture speaks to no purpose? Does the spirit that God caused to dwell in us desire envy?* The NRSV has, *Or do you suppose that it is for nothing that the scripture says, "God yearns jealously for the spirit that he has made to dwell in us"?* More variations can be found in other versions. One problem is that the second half of the verse (which NRSV puts in quotations marks), does not resemble anything in Hebrew or Greek Scripture. Is James quoting a lost ancient writing, such as Eldad and Modad, a pseudepigraphon (extant only in fragmentary references; Allison 2013: 617–21)? Or could he be referring to the Scripture in general without intending a specific text? If either of these were so, he would likely not have written *The scripture* speaks or says, since the two other times James uses the term *scripture* he quotes a specific verse from the canonical writings (2:8, 23). Also, elsewhere in the New Testament the phrase always "introduces a direct scriptural reference or allusion" (Martin: 149).

Perhaps James was writing from memory and garbled the verse. Perhaps he used an unknown Greek version of the Old Testament. Perhaps he intended to introduce the quotation in 4:6 by first paraphrasing it. All these proposals are possible but have enough problems to make none of them compelling. In the end, all we can say is that, in verse 5, James refers to something in Scripture that is no longer available to us or awkwardly inserts a comment before getting to the actual quotation in verse 6.

Another problem with James 4:5 is the lexical and grammatical ambiguity of the second half of the verse. Since it is not possible to identify the Scripture reference, we cannot compare what James wrote with the original, leaving us with some key critical issues:

1. Are the words *But God gives all the more grace* (v. 6a) part of the quotation? Or does it end with verse 5?
2. Does *spirit* refer to the Holy Spirit or the human spirit?

3. Is *spirit* the subject or object of desire/*yearns*? (Both *The spirit he [God] made to dwell in us yearns* and *He [God] yearns for the spirit he made to dwell in us* are possible in Greek.)
4. Does yearning *with jealousy/envy* have a negative or positive connotation?

The following translation seems the most plausible. The subsequent responses to the above questions offer a rationale. [5]*Or do you suppose that in vain the Scripture says, "The spirit which he [God] made to dwell in us yearns enviously,* [6]*but he gives a greater grace"? Therefore it says, "God opposes the arrogant, but to the humble he gives grace"* (AT).

1. In most English translations, the Scripture quotation (if it is a quotation) ends at the end of verse 5. More likely, it extends to include the first clause of verse 6, *but he gives a greater grace* (AT). This is where modern Greek editions put the question mark. The end of the first quotation is thus parallel to the end of the second quotation in verse 6b and 6c, since both Greek clauses conclude with exactly the same words: *He gives grace.*

2. *The spirit that he [God] has made to dwell in us* is likely a reference to the life-giving breath God gave human beings, not to the Holy Spirit. Nowhere else in the letter does James mention the Holy Spirit, and the only other mention of the "spirit" (*pneuma*) in James (2:26) seems clearly to refer to the human spirit.

3 and 4. The question of whether God or the human spirit is the subject of the verb *yearns* is tied to the question of what "with jealousy/envy" means and whether "to yearn" (or "strongly desire") has positive or negative connotations. In brief, is the text saying (a) that God yearns jealously for God's people (as in Exod 20:5, which says, Yahweh is "a jealous God"); or (b) that the human spirit is filled with envious desire, a negative quality? Since God is not explicitly named in this verse, the subject of the verbs must be inferred from the context. In favor of the first option (a) is that God is clearly the implied subject of *made to dwell* and *gives*, so it would make sense to understand God as the subject of *yearns* also. Since the verb "yearn, strongly desire" has a positive connotation in the eight other occurrences in the New Testament (Rom 1:11; 2 Cor 5:2; 9:14; Phil 1:8; 2:26; 1 Thess 3:6; 2 Tim 1:4; 1 Pet 2:2), it is feasible that God is the one "yearning" in verse 5.

On the other hand, the word *yearn* does appear in other Greek writings with the more negative connotation of "crave" or "wrong desire" (e.g., Ps 62:10 [61:11 LXX]; Wisd of Sol 15:19; Sir 25:21). A serious obstacle to understanding God as the subject of the verb is that the Greek noun modifying it (*phthonos*, often translated *jealousy* but more accurately *envy*) is *always* a vice in both the Septuagint and the New Testament and always used for humans, never for God (e.g., 1 Macc 8:16; 3 Macc 6:7; Wisd of Sol 2:24; 6:23; Matt 27:18; Rom 1:29; Gal 5:21; 1 Tim 6:4).

When the Old Testament speaks of God being a jealous God, which it does many times, a different word is used (*zēlos, zēlotēs*; e.g., Exod 20:5). If envy in antiquity was "a malice directed against perceived rivals and their success and well-being supposedly gained at the envier's expense," it is impossible for God to envy (Elliott 2007: 360). Illogically, it would attribute envy to God for something (the spirit) that God conferred (Elliott 2007: 360). Despite James's frequent use of synonyms and provocative language, it is unlikely that he would attribute something to God that is always evil or sinful elsewhere, and thus the translation of James 4:5b as *God yearns enviously . . .* seems impossible.

The context helps to illumine further the meaning of 4:5b. The opening words of verse 5, *or do you suppose*, imply that the verse follows logically on what preceded it. James has just twice reiterated that friendship with the world is enmity with God. Prior to this he talked about how cravings, selfish desire, and envy lead to fighting among them. Immediately after the puzzling reference to Scripture in 4:5b-6a, James quotes another Scripture text, this time from Proverbs 3:34 (LXX): *Therefore it says, "God opposes the proud, but gives grace to the humble."* Because James prefaces the quotation with *therefore*, it must explicate the preceding one. The fact that both Scripture references end with the same words, *he gives grace* (4:6a, 6c), suggests that the second known one is reinforcing what the first unknown one says.

In light of these grammatical and contextual considerations, the least problematic translation of 4:5-6a is the one proposed above. James's argument is this: Selfish desire and envy lead to fighting and violence within the community. Such behavior is indicative of friendship with the world and not with God. An unknown Scripture passage rightly recognizes that the human spirit, given by God, is filled with such envious desire. However, God's grace is even greater. A second, known Scripture quotation confirms this: God opposes the arrogant and other vices that characterize friendship with the world. Once again, there is good news, for God gives grace to the humble. James has laid out two opposing ways for his readers in 3:13–4:6. Friendship with the world is characterized by pseudowisdom from below, selfish desire, envy, and bitter conflict. Friendship with God is characterized by wisdom from above, humility, gentleness, and peace. Although the human spirit is often inclined to the former, God's grace is greater than human sin.

The content of 4:1-6 is thus consistent with the rest of the letter. In 1:14-15 James writes about *desire* breeding sin and death, which sounds remarkably like 4:1-2. James 1:9-11 refers to God lifting up the lowly or *humble* (the same word as in 4:6c) and the rich withering away. This echoes the quotation from Proverbs in 4:6. Elsewhere the letter clarifies that for God to give grace to the lowly means that God gives *the crown of life* to those who endure testing (1:12) and promises *the kingdom* to the poor who *love* God (2:5).

Submission and Repentance 4:7-10

The previous subunit ends with the assurance that God *gives grace to the humble* (v. 6). If that is the case, how ought readers to respond to the sharp criticisms in 4:1-4? This is the point of 4:7-10, which begins with the word "therefore." Even though they covet and fight with each other because of their selfish desires, God remains gracious to the humble. *Therefore*, they should *submit* to God (v. 7) and *humble [themselves] before the Lord* (v. 10). The verb *humble yourselves* (*tapeinōthēte*) in verse 10 explicitly connects this subunit to the previous one, which ends with the noun *humble ones* (*tapeinois*, v. 6).

Verse 7 brings a dramatic shift in tone. The previous six verses consisted of rhetorical questions and statements but did not contain a single imperative. In verses 7-10, however, there are no less than ten imperative verbs: *submit, resist, draw near, cleanse, purify, lament, mourn, weep, let laughter . . . be turned*, and *humble yourselves*. This rapid-fire battery of commands in a series of short clauses has a forceful rhetorical effect on the reader. The tone shifts from accusation to urgent appeal. If the recipients of this letter were feeling remorseful or chagrined because of all the wrongdoing in their midst (*you desire, you murder, you covet, you ask wrongly*, and so on), verses 7-10 immediately provide them with an appropriate response. The antidote for their sinful and destructive habits is to seek God and repent.

Attending to the following structure of this subunit will help us to see the literary artistry of the text as well as to understand better the force of the message James is communicating (Vlachos: 142):

7Submit yourselves therefore to God.
Resist the devil, and he will flee from you.
8Draw near to God, and he will draw near to you.
Cleanse your hands, you sinners,
and purify your hearts, you double-minded.
9Lament and mourn and weep.
Let your laughter be turned into mourning and your joy into dejection.
10Humble yourselves before the Lord, and he will exalt you.

The text is framed by verses urging submission to God and humility (vv. 7, 10). These two ideas are not synonymous, but they are closely related, for the former necessitates the latter. Within this *inclusio* lie three pairs of exhortations that expand on what being subject to God entails. The first pair (vv. 7b-8a) consists of two opposing actions, resisting the devil and drawing near to God: *resist* contrasts with *draw near*; *the devil* contrasts with *God*; *will flee* contrasts with *will draw near*. The second pair (v. 8b-c) urges synonymous actions, the cleansing and purifying of hands and hearts, which represent different facets of the human experience. Each line in this pair ends with a vocative that characterizes the readers as wrongdoers (*you sinners, you double-minded*). The third pair (v. 9) consists of two synonymous lines that heap up words of lament in order to drive home a call for repentance. We will now look at each of these lines in more detail.

John Painter says, "To submit to God is to acknowledge God as God and to recognize that humans are the work of God's hands" (Painter and deSilva: 143). In other words, submitting to God is living as though God really is God and we are not. It involves acknowledging that we do not exist apart from the life and breath that God gives us. We recognize that ultimately God is in control and we are not. We bend our wills, our minds, and our bodies to the greater will and wisdom of God, as far as we are able to discern it.

Painter also states, "Unbridled desire is an expression of practical atheism" (Painter and deSilva: 147). Allowing our cravings and our covetousness to destroy a brother or sister in Christ is acting as though God does not exist. It amounts to assuming that we must take matters into our own hands instead of relying on a generous, gift-giving God to provide (1:5, 17). That is the opposite of submitting to God since it implies that our own desires and wishes have priority over others *made in the likeness of God* (3:9). Submitting to God is the first step to correcting the divisive and damaging behavior James criticizes in 4:1-4.

The command *Resist the devil* assumes that people are under attack by the devil. Such language may sound foreign to moderns who are disinclined to think of evil as a personified devil. *Diabolos* (*devil*) is the Greek word that the Septuagint uses to translate the Hebrew noun *satan* in the Old Testament. The word *satan* simply means "accuser" or "adversary" (*NIDB* 5:112). Only in the intertestamental period did the idea of the "satan" or "devil" as a nonhuman, evil power in opposition to God develop (Stokes). This is the understanding reflected in James 4:7.

James does not absolve humans of responsibility for sin by blaming the devil, for in 1:14-15 he says people are tempted by their own desires, which drag them into sin and death. At the same time, the fact that *Resist the devil* appears in the context of 4:1-4 implies that selfish desire, envy, coveting, fighting, violence, and so on belong to the realm of the devil. People whose loyalty and love lie with the "world" and the seductions it offers are vulnerable to attack from powerful forces diametrically opposed to God, referred to here as *the devil*. But the devil can be resisted. This belief is also present in Jewish writings of this era, especially in the Testaments of the Twelve Patriarchs (T. Sim. 3.5; T. Iss. 7.7; T. Dan 5.1; T. Naph. 8.4).

There is an implicit relationship between the first and second half of the sentence in verse 7b: *when* or *if* they resist the devil, *then* the devil will flee. Such an action brings with it an equal and opposite action: when they draw near to God, God will also draw near to them. There is a promise and reassurance inherent in this: God is stronger than the devil and will draw near to those who seek God. Here James does not specify *how* the devil can be resisted nor *how* his audience should draw near to God, but the letter as a whole gives clues. They can ask God for wisdom (1:5). They can guard their tongues, especially when angry (1:19-20, 26). They can love their neighbors, even the neighbors without status and money (2:1-9). They can resist envying and coveting what others have (4:1-3). Of course, the God who has given them birth *by the word of truth* and made them the *first fruits of his creatures* (1:18) will enable them to resist and to draw near.

The second and third pairs of commands in 4:8b-9 offer further guidance on how to resist the devil and draw near to God. Both have to do with repentance. The command to *cleanse your hands* and *purify your hearts* calls to mind Psalm 24:3-4, which is also about drawing near to God, even though the wording in the Septuagint is slightly different from James: "Who shall ascend the hill of the LORD? And who shall stand in his holy place? Those who have clean hands and pure hearts, who do not lift up their souls to what is false, and do not swear deceitfully."

Language of washing and purification is often associated with ritual purity in the Bible. But here the words should be understood metaphorically to refer to ethical cleanliness in the tradition of the prophets, who urged Israel to cleanse itself from sins of injustice, oppression, idolatry, and wickedness (Ps 51:2; Isa 1:16-17; Jer 4:14). They are to cleanse both their outward actions (the hands) and their inward motivations (the heart; Lockett 2007: 67).

James addresses his readers as *sinners* and *double-minded*, strong accusatory language intended to provoke a reaction, similar to the way *Adulterers!* (4:4) would have. The two words are not synonymous, but using them together here suggests that they inform each other. They are sinners not only because they are envious, selfish, and contentious (4:1-3), but also because they show favoritism (2:9) and because they are not acting on what they know to be right (4:17). Moreover, to be a sinner is to be *double-minded*, a word James used once before in 1:8.

Although the meaning is straightforward enough, *double-minded* (*dipsychos*) occurs nowhere else in Greek writings before James, leading some scholars to speculate that James coined the word. To be *double-minded* is to try to walk two paths at the same time. It is to want to be friends with the world *and* friends with God at the same time, something not possible in James's view (see notes on 1:8 and 4:4). Whoever is double-minded is not single-minded in loyalty to God and to *the glorious Lord Jesus Christ* (2:1 NRSV). Thus they must repent and be washed clean. This is at least part of what it means to submit to God, resist the devil, and draw near to God.

The language of verse 9, the third pair of exhortations in this subunit, is also language of repentance. The words *mourn* and *weep* appear together frequently in the Bible, but this verse also demonstrates James's penchant for unique vocabulary, since four of the words in verse 9 appear only here in the entire New Testament: *lament* (*talaipōreō*), *laughter* (*gelōs*), *be turned* (*metatrepō*), and *dejection* (*katēpheia*).

When we read this verse in the context of the larger unit, we can recognize what it is saying and is not saying. Extracted from its context, verse 9 might be confusing and even dangerous for people who struggle to find joy in life. James exhorts his readers, *Lament and mourn [penthēsate] and weep [klausate]. Let your laughter [gelōs] be turned into mourning [penthos] and your joy into dejection.* Does God really intend for people to be gloomy and unhappy as they go through life? What about Paul's instruction "Rejoice in the Lord always" (Phil 4:4; 1 Thess 5:16)? Or the psalmist's prayer, "Restore to me the joy of your salvation" (Ps 51:12)? James's words in verse 9 are not encouraging depression or a pessimistic outlook on life or perpetual sadness. They are about repentance and lament for the harm that sin causes. Hovering in the background are Jesus' woes in the Gospel of Luke (6:25): "Woe to you who are laughing [*gelōntes*, the cognate verb of "laughter" in 4:9] now, for you will mourn [*penthēsete*] and weep [*klausete*]." In 5:1 James tells the rich, "Weep [*klausate*] and wail at [your] miseries."

James wants his readers to understand that submitting to God, resisting the devil, and drawing near to God—all part of choosing friendship with God instead of friendship with the world—require a drastic turning around from the destructive behavior so vividly described in 4:1-3. This is no request for a perfunctory "I'm sorry" but a demand for deep and sincere remorse that is evident in changed behavior (Painter and deSilva: 145).

This language also recognizes that God will reverse the fortunes of the oppressed and needy and raise up the lowly (cf. 1:9). The poor are blessed because God will give them the kingdom (2:5), and the persecuted are blessed because they will receive the crown of life (1:12). Conversely, the rich oppressors, those who are too comfortable and self-sufficient to know their need for God, must lament and mourn and change their behavior. Lament is a concrete sign of repentance. Laughter is inappropriate when sin is the topic under discussion. These may be uncomfortable words in a culture where the pursuit of pleasure and personal happiness have become obsessions, where people are quick to cast blame on someone else rather than take personal responsibility. James reminds the church that there is a place for genuine lament, for real mourning, for deep grief over the sin and brokenness of the world and of ourselves. Perhaps James recognizes that only when we recognize the depth of the wrong can we truly turn around and change.

Verse 10 reinforces the opening command of this subunit: to submit to God (v. 7), believers must humble themselves. That is what drawing near to God and repenting of sin entails. These words are not about self-abasement or humility for its own sake, nor about groveling in the dust like a worm. James is urging his readers to submit to God and humble themselves before God so that God can work in their lives. He is simply telling his readers to acknowledge what is already true: before God they are poor and needy. When they do that, God will lift them up.

Although this is eschatological language about what God will do for them ultimately in the future, they can experience it already now in part in the church. The promise in verse 10 echoes the reversal language of Jesus in the Gospels: "All who exalt themselves will be humbled, and all who humble themselves will be exalted" (Matt 23:12; Luke 14:11; 18:14). With this verse, James draws the entire unit to a fitting conclusion. Humility before God is the appropriate corrective to envy, selfish ambition, arrogance, and boasting, the attitudes and behaviors that James censures in 3:13-18 and 4:1-6.

THE TEXT IN BIBLICAL CONTEXT

Who Is Wise?

The word "wisdom" is often used adjectivally to describe a tradition, a genre of writing, a general perspective on life, or a kind of theology (e.g., "wisdom literature" or "wisdom theology"). The Letter of James is part of this "wisdom tradition" in the Bible both because of the literary forms it includes and because of the topics it addresses. This aspect of the letter is discussed in the essays *[The Wisdom Tradition and James, p. 376]*. In James 3:13-18 the words "wise" and "wisdom" are used more narrowly than this. Here we will focus on the specific question James asks: *Who is wise?* (and what does it mean to have wisdom?), in terms of how other parts of the Bible might answer that question.

Wisdom is hard to define because of the wide range of meaning it has in the Bible. It can have both a positive connotation and a negative one. Wisdom can be described in anthropocentric terms as well as theological. It encompasses both practical skills and abstract virtues. The Greek word for "wisdom" is *sophia,* and the Hebrew word is *ḥokmah*, although sometimes wisdom ideas are present even when the vocabulary is not.

To be wise can mean to have practical skills and knowledge. In the book of Exodus, people who had the artistic and technical ability to design and construct the tabernacle and all its furnishings are called "wise" (NRSVue: "skillful"; Exod 35:10, 25; 36:1, 8). Those who have the ability to interpret dreams are considered wise (Gen 41:8; Dan 2). Wise people are able to discern a situation and give counsel about prudent or just action (2 Sam 20:16-22; 1 Kings 3:16-28). Joseph is recognized as wise for his ability to assess the situation and give shrewd counsel to Pharaoh (Gen 41:39; Acts 7:10).

The book of Proverbs contains many terse sayings about how a wise person thinks and acts. For example, wise people don't speak rashly but are judicious and persuasive in what they say (12:18; 16:23). Wise people hold back anger (29:11) and are impartial in their judgments (24:23). Because wise people accept teaching and learn from rebuke, they grow in knowledge (9:8-9; 15:2, 7; 18:15; 21:11). Strong community leaders should be chosen for their wisdom (Deut 1:13, 15). Wisdom is gained by observing and drawing lessons from the natural world and human experience.

All these qualities described so far can characterize any wise person, whether religious or not. In the Bible, however, truly wise people understand that wisdom comes from and begins with God (1 Kings 4:29-30; Job 28:12-28; Ps 51:6; Prov 2:6; 9:10). God created the world through wisdom, and God's wisdom surpasses human understanding (Ps 104:24 [LXX 103:24]; Prov 3:19; Jer 10:12; Rom 11:33). The wise obey God's laws. Whoever ignores God's ways does so at their own peril (Deut 4:6; Prov 10:8; Jer 8:9). In the New Testament, wisdom characterizes people like Stephen, who are filled with the Holy Spirit (Acts 6:3, 10), and the disciples, who are empowered to stand up to governors and kings with incontrovertible wisdom (Luke 21:15). Although James is full of practical wisdom, consistent with the wisdom sayings in Proverbs, the letter also begins with the acknowledgment that wisdom is a gift from God (1:5), that true wisdom comes from above (3:17).

That wisdom originates in God and that God's wisdom ultimately transcends human understanding means that the Bible also contains a robust thread of critique and even judgment on human wisdom. What seems wise to human creatures does not always conform to what is wise in the eyes of God. This is especially true when human wisdom is conventional wisdom that conforms to the values of the surrounding culture. Such critique is evident already in the Old Testament but sharpens in the New Testament with God's revelation in Jesus Christ. The wise men of Egypt and Babylon are unable to interpret the times or give sound counsel to the Pharaoh or kings they serve (Genesis, Daniel). Their wisdom is insufficient to interpret the will of God. Through the prophet Isaiah, God tells a recalcitrant people, "The wisdom of their wise shall perish, and the discernment of the discerning shall be hidden" (29:14), because they do not truly serve God with their hearts. Sometimes the Bible denounces human wisdom because it is not truly wisdom. Instead, it is self-inflated and false perception that panders to human desires, status, and power. This is the case in Jeremiah 8:8-11:

> How can you say, "We are wise, and the law of the LORD is with us," when, in fact, the false pen of the scribes has made it into a lie? The wise shall be put to shame; they shall be dismayed and taken; since they have rejected the word of the LORD, what wisdom is in them?

In the New Testament, 1 Corinthians contains twenty-eight of the thirty-four occurrences of *sophia* (wisdom) and *sophos* (wise) in the undisputed letters of Paul. As Richard Hays notes, "The Corinthians, with their prized speech-gifts, make a show of possessing wisdom and honouring God with their lips, but their fractious behaviour shows that in fact their hearts are far from God" (Hays 1999: 115). Paul, in fact, quotes Isaiah 29:14 in 1 Corinthians 1:19. Wisdom that is really no wisdom at all is what James decries in 3:14-16 as well.

There is yet another dimension of the wisdom critique in the Bible. God's wisdom, the wisdom revealed in Jesus Christ, stands over against not only the pseudowisdom that Isaiah, Paul, and James warn against. In many respects it also runs counter to prevailing conventional wisdom, which, from a human point of view, *would* actually be considered wisdom. This alternative wisdom, sometimes called subversive wisdom, is exemplified by and embodied in Jesus' life and ministry. Luke's comments that Jesus was "filled with wisdom" (2:40) and "increased in wisdom" (2:52) frame the story of Jesus as a boy as he confounds the teachers in the temple, the purveyors of conventional religious wisdom. Jesus dines with the outcasts and befriends sinners, surely unwise behavior in the eyes of proper religious folk, yet "wisdom is vindicated by her deeds" (Matt 11:19; cf. Luke 7:34-35).

The wisdom of Jesus promises eschatological blessing to the poor, the poor in spirit, the meek, the mourners, the persecuted—qualities scorned by the conventionally wise (Matt 5:3-12). Filled with the Spirit, Jesus thanks God for hiding the upside-down message of God's reign from the wise and intelligent and revealing it to infants (Matt 11:25-27//Luke 10:21-22), that is, to the "little ones" without power.

The most vigorous challenge to conventional wisdom comes in the death and resurrection of Jesus, as Paul so beautifully captures in 1 Corinthians 1–3. To Jews and to Greeks, thus to everyone, the cross is foolishness. This is especially true for the Corinthians who value knowledge, eloquent rhetoric, and social standing, but it is also true for others. What kind of Messiah, what kind of "Savior of the world" willingly submits to a shameful and tortured death on the most abhorrent symbol of imperial power (John 4:42; 1 John 4:14)? Yet, Paul insists, "God's foolishness is wiser than human wisdom, and God's weakness is stronger than human strength" (1 Cor 1:25). The subversive wisdom of the gospel is that "God has chosen to save the world through the cross, through the shameful and powerless death of the crucified Messiah" (Hays 1999: 113).

Moreover, contrary to all human understanding, God raised Jesus from the dead, thereby definitively conquering evil, sin, and death. As the body of Christ, the church is called to live out this unconventional, even subversive wisdom of God. Richard Hays articulates what this meant for the Corinthian church, a group of people of mixed socioeconomic status and education:

> In Paul's view, the relatively low status of most of the Corinthian Christians is a sign of what God did in the cross and therefore is doing in the world: overturning expectations. God is creating the new eschatological community out of unimpressive material precisely in order to exemplify the power of his own unmerited grace. Thus, the social composition of the church is an outward and visible sign of God's paradoxical wisdom. (Hays 1999: 116–17)

The Letter of James reflects a spectrum of biblical wisdom. It contains the commonsense wisdom gained from human observation and experience. For example, since a spring does not pour out both brackish and fresh water, neither should a mouth both bless and curse a fellow human being (3:10-11). Telling someone who is naked and hungry, *Keep warm and eat your fill*, is not only useless but unwise (2:15-16). Even though the seemingly foolish wisdom of the cross is absent from the letter, the idea that the church is a community of people embodying a different wisdom than the surrounding world is evident. Rather than privileging the rich and giving greater honor to those with status, they are to love their poor neighbor as themselves, for the poor are inheritors of the kingdom (James 2:1-9). They are to trust God completely and resist friendship with the world (2:23; 4:4). They are to show that they are wise by being humble, gentle, peaceable, willing to yield, and merciful—qualities that the crucified One also showed in his life on earth (3:17-18). God is the source of all true wisdom and will give generously to all who need help in discerning what wisdom is needed in a specific time and place.

Resisting the Devil

The worldview of James and his churches encompassed not only faith in God, the Giver of all good, but also belief in malevolent beings, chief of which was the devil. The conviction that powerful superhuman beings exist to seduce people away from God or to influence them to do evil was not always part of the biblical worldview. Belief in the devil or Satan developed in the Second Temple period and is virtually absent from the Hebrew Bible. Furthermore, most modern conceptions about the devil are shaped more by Christian theological and literary traditions *after* the time of the New Testament than by the Bible itself.

In the Septuagint the Greek word *diabolos* (devil) almost always translates the word *satan* in Hebrew. *Satan* is not a proper name in the Old Testament but simply means "accuser" or "adversary." It is used sometimes to refer to a human adversary (1 Sam 29:4; 1 Kings 11:14; Ps 109:6 [108:6 LXX]), and in Numbers 22:22 the angel of the Lord rises up to accuse (or oppose; the LXX uses the infinitive verb *endiaballein*) Balaam on behalf of God. The only places in the Old Testament where "devil" (*diabolos* in the LXX) is clearly a nonhuman heavenly being are Job 1–2 and Zechariah 3. (The reference in 1 Chron 21:1 is ambiguous.) In both of these, the devil has an adversarial role, accusing or testing a human on God's behalf. However, in both there is also some critique of the devil's actions, suggesting that God is not wholly in favor of the devil's adversarial actions (Job 2:3; Zech 3:2). In the Writings part of the Hebrew Bible, the accuser/devil, demons, evil spirits, and fallen angels are all distinct entities and operate independently of each other (Stokes: 148–49). In general, however, "in the OT God's power is without rival. Notions of Satan as the personification of evil opposing God's rule as his adversary or enemy are ideas about Satan's identity not found in the OT" (Conrad: 113).

In the two to three centuries before James was written, the Jewish understanding of the devil and other such harmful beings developed and changed considerably. In Second Temple Jewish writings—such as 1 Enoch, Jubilees, and the Dead Sea Scrolls—demons, evil spirits, fallen angels, and the devil came to be associated with each other (Stokes: 148–50). Other names for the devil in later Jewish and New Testament literature include Belial, Mastema, Beelzebul, Tempter, and Prince of Demons. Demons oppress and harm humans and thus served the devil. By the time of the New Testament, the devil or Satan was understood to be a nonhuman being that actively opposes God and has the power to tempt humans and lead them into sin.

In the Gospels the devil is the one who tests Jesus in the wilderness (Mark 1:12-13; Matt 4:1-11; Luke 4:1-13). New Testament writers speak of the devil as the ruler of this world (John 12:31; 16:11; Eph 6:11-12), who oppresses people (Acts 10:38) and tries to ensnare them in sin (Eph 6:11; 1 Tim 3:7; 2 Tim 2:26; 1 Pet 5:8). Those who commit sin are said to be children of the devil (John 8:44; Acts 13:10; 1 John 3:8). Jesus came to destroy the works of the devil, including the power of sin and death (Heb 2:14; 1 John 3:8). In his ministry Jesus liberates people oppressed by Satan and by demons (Mark 5:1-20; Luke 11:14-22; 13:16; Acts 10:38); through the ministry of healing and proclamation that the disciples carry out in his name, Jesus sees Satan fall (Luke 10:17-18). By his death and resurrection, Jesus conquered the devil, and on the last day Jesus' final victory over evil will be consummated (Matt 25:41; 1 Cor 15:24-25; Rev 20:10). In the meantime, humans must continue to resist the devil, the enemy of God and God's people.

In addition to references to "the devil" or "demons," the New Testament letters contain a variety of other terms for powers that oppose God. Examples include "the ruler of the power of the air" (Eph 2:2), "the rulers of this age" (1 Cor 2:6, 8), "rulers and authorities" (or KJV: "principalities and powers," Eph 3:10; Col 2:15), "cosmic powers of this present darkness," and "spiritual forces of evil in the heavenly places" (Eph 6:12). Contemporary understandings of these powers vary, from seeing them as personal beings to be cast out through exorcism and spiritual warfare to seeing them as impersonal spiritualities of institutions and systemic sociopolitical and economic forces to be resisted through public activism. (Discussion of these "powers" is complex and vast; see, e.g., Wink 1984, 1998; Yoder Neufeld 2002: 353–58; Swartley 1988.)

The Letter of James assumes the broader New Testament understanding of the devil and mentions the devil or demonic forces three times (2:19; 3:15; 4:7). The demons believe that God exists but do not act on the basis of that belief, which causes them to *shudder*, perhaps with fear of the coming judgment (2:19). As Ryan Stokes rightly argues, "James depicts the superhuman realm as one that is active in the moral corruption of human beings. The devil and demons are behind human sin" (Stokes: 156). At the same time, humans are not absolved from responsibility for sin, for they are *lured and enticed* by their own disordered desires (1:14-15). Even though the devil may lead humans astray, people have the ability with God's help to *resist the devil*, causing the devil to *flee* (4:7).

The idea of resisting the devil may strike some readers as being at odds with Jesus' command in the Sermon on the Mount to "not resist evil/an evildoer/the evil one" (Matt 5:39 AT). The word for "resist" here is the same as in James 4:7 (*anthistēmi*), but the word *ponēros* can be variously translated as "evil" or "evil one" or perhaps "one who does evil." If it is taken as "evil one" or even "the Evil One," then James seems to be contradicting Jesus. Even if the verse in Matthew is translated as "Do not resist evil" or "Do not resist the person who does evil," it can be interpreted to mean that followers of Jesus should be passive in the face of violence and injustice.

The historical Anabaptist/Mennonite stance of nonresistance derives from such a reading of the text but has rightly been challenged in the last century. Since Jesus himself defies the Evil One and resists evil by banishing demons and rebuking injustice, it seems unlikely that Jesus would not also call his followers to do the same. Some interpretations of Matthew 5:38-42 suggest he does just that. As Walter Wink and various other scholars have argued, there are compelling reasons to understand Jesus' words in Matthew 5:39 as meaning "Do not resist by evil means" or perhaps "Do not violently resist the evil one" (Wink 1992: 184–86; Yoder Neufeld 2011: 22). This is consistent with what Paul says in Romans 12:17, 21: "Do not repay anyone evil for evil. . . . Do not be overcome by evil, but overcome evil with good."

What James exhorts his readers to do in 4:7, *Resist the devil*, is thus not at all inconsistent with Jesus' teaching in the Sermon on the Mount. Jesus too fought against the devil and evil, but "waged war" in a completely upside-down manner by giving his life instead of taking life. Jesus' followers are also to resist the forces of evil and sin. Ephesians 6:10-17 urges Christians, "Put on the whole armor of God . . . to stand against the wiles of the devil"; and 1 Peter 5:8-9 exhorts readers also to "resist" the devil, who "prowls around, looking for someone to devour." Followers of Jesus are not powerless in the face of evil. With God's help they can actively resist forces of evil that threaten to undermine or destroy life, however those powers might be recognized today. At the same time, Christians must resist the devil without becoming the very evil they are opposing. They are to live by *wisdom from above*, which is peaceable, humble, and merciful, and they will sow *a harvest of righteousness* by making peace (3:17-18 NRSV).

THE TEXT IN THE LIFE OF THE CHURCH

Yielding to God

Like the Old Testament prophets before him (e.g., Ezek 18:30-32; Joel 2:12-13), James calls his listeners to repentance (4:7-10) after indicting them for their failings (4:1-6). The pericope begins with the exhortation *Submit . . . to God* and ends with *Humble yourselves before the Lord*. Such a posture of humble submission is premised on the biblical assurance that *God gives grace to the humble* (4:6). This is how the devil can be resisted and how believers can draw near to God. It is expressed in mourning for sin and purification of heart and hands (4:7b-9).

Although this text from James does not appear to have been utilized much in Anabaptist writings on the subject, the theme of humble submission to God was central to Anabaptist spirituality. What James describes in these verses epitomizes what early Anabaptists meant by *Gelassenheit*. This German word is variously translated as "yieldedness, surrender; submission; resignation; abandonment" (Kraybill 2010: 93). Sixteenth-century Anabaptists believed that the first step on the Christian journey was abandoning oneself to God and yielding fully to the will of God. This required repenting from sin and choosing to become obedient to God, exactly what James talks about in 4:7-10. "What must be done, the Anabaptist insisted, is to 'give up' and 'stop striving' for one's own desires, accepting instead what God wishes to accomplish through one's life" (Snyder 2004: 41). Thus, although Anabaptists firmly believed that salvation was by the grace of God, human participation in bending the fallen will toward God was essential (Snyder 2004: 51–59). Such participation was thus not so much doing as letting go. Yielding to God opened the door to new birth, to God's work of transformation and regeneration in one's life.

The concept of *Gelassenheit* was not invented by Anabaptists. It finds its roots in late medieval mysticism. Similar ideas appear in the spiritual writings of Johann Tauler (14th c.), Thomas à Kempis's *The Imitation of Christ* (early 15th c.), and the anonymous *Theologia Germanica* (late 14th c.). Anabaptists were influenced by these writings, whether directly or through the teachings and writings of people like Andreas Carlstadt and Thomas Müntzer (Klaassen 1991: 27; Snyder 2004: 163). One finds the emphasis on yielding to God particularly in the writings of Hans Denck, "the most mystic of the Anabaptists" (Klaassen 1991: 27), but also in Hans Hut, Leonhard Schiemer, Pilgram Marpeck, and in the *Martyrs Mirror*. In 1526 Hans Denck wrote the following, which, while not quoting James 4:7-10, resonates with James's exhortation, *Submit yourselves therefore to God . . . . Draw near to God, and he will draw near to you . . . . Humble yourselves before the Lord, and he will exalt you.*

> Anyone who offers himself to the Lord in the depth of his soul and in truth, in such a way as to surrender his will and seek the will of God, must look to the work of God. Then the merciful Father will receive him and take him back with great joy, regardless of how he conducted himself earlier. (Furcha: 210)

Gelassenheit has both an inner and an outer component. A deep personal, inner yielding to God was expressed in adult baptism and in an outward yielding to the community, the body of Christ (Snyder 2004: 43). *Gelassenheit* among Anabaptists thus had a strong ethical component, with implications for daily discipleship, church discipline, and economics. If you were really submitting fully to God, yielding your will to God's, you would also be obedient to Jesus' teachings and follow him in daily life. Saying "no" to the world and individualistic desires was a way of saying "yes" to God. Among the Hutterites, a crucial aspect of yielding all desires to God was giving up private possessions and the communal sharing of property, as was practiced in the early church (Acts 2:44-45; 4:32-35). The inseparability of *Gelassenheit* and sharing of goods is evident in Hutterite writings of the sixteenth century, such as the Five Articles of Faith (ca. 1547).

The ultimate expression of submission to God was martyrdom. As Snyder nicely summarizes, "The baptism of blood was the ultimate test of personal *Gelassenheit*: the readiness to yield one's life for Christ's sake was as convincing a piece of evidence as one could present, that one's own will had been set aside" (2004: 164). Countless writings in the *Martyrs Mirror* reflect this willingness to yield to God even in death. For example, while in prison in 1527, Michael Sattler wrote, "In this peril I completely surrendered myself unto the will of the Lord, and . . . prepared myself even for death for His testimony" (*MM*: 419). The following excerpt from a hymn, written by Hutterite missionary Hans Mändl in 1548 before he was martyred, also epitomizes the attitude of *Gelassenheit*:

> For to you only, O my Father,
> I have totally yielded myself. . . .
> For God desires a pure heart,
> Which has totally submitted itself
> To Him and to the holy church

With his whole life.
For we must strive for the church
And yieldedness [Gelassenheit] here
If we wish to inherit the kingdom
With God and his saints. (Snyder 2004: 165–66)

Virtually all these concerns that appear in Anabaptist writings about *Gelassenheit* show up in the Letter of James in some form or another. James, too, urges readers to keep *unstained by the world* (1:27), to show their faith in deeds of mercy for the brother or sister in need (2:14-17), to be patient in suffering (5:7-11), to surrender plans for the future to the greater will of God (4:13-15), and to act with wisdom that is humble, gentle, and willing to yield (3:13, 17). All this is part of the new life that is born out of submitting to God, drawing near to God, purifying one's heart and hands, and humbling oneself before God (4:7-10).

In his 1955 article on "*Gelassenheit*," Robert Friedmann concludes, "Present-day Mennonitism has lost the idea of Gelassenheit nearly completely; yet with the recovery of the ideal of discipleship also Gelassenheit may be revived." Among some groups descended from the first Anabaptists, yielding fully to God and to the body of Christ is no doubt still part of the grammar of faith and ingrained in daily living.

For many contemporary North American Christians, including those with Anabaptist roots, however, the virtue of *Gelassenheit* and the commands in James 4:7-10 will not be attractive. With the possible exception of *Resist the devil* and *Draw near to God*, James's exhortations go counter to prevailing cultural values; Christians are not immune to the influence of such values. People today do not want to submit to authority or humble themselves. They want to craft their own futures and be in charge of their own lives. They want to be self-sufficient, proud of themselves, and in control. Verses 7 and 10 grate harshly against prevailing sentiments claiming, "No one has the right to tell me what to do." Commands to "sinners" to purify and cleanse themselves sound puritanical and restrictive. Commands to lament, mourn, weep, and transform joy into gloom sound downright harmful to one's mental health. The goal in life is to be happy, and people spend a great deal of money entertaining themselves so that they might not need to mourn.

But James is not speaking to society in general. He is addressing *brothers and sisters* who are followers of *our glorious Lord Jesus Christ* (2:1 NRSV) and a church whose edges are fraying and whose seams are coming apart under stress. He is speaking prophetically and vigorously in an effort to remind them of who they are, what they believe, and how they should therefore live. This is speech intended to persuade and transform. It is not ivory-tower academia but wisdom borne out of the real tensions and experiences of living as Christ-followers in a world that often undermines and challenges Christian faith and practice. Preachers of James need to reenvision in each age and context how to make the words of this letter both as hard-hitting as the writer wanted them to be and as renewing as they have the potential to be. Perhaps like the medieval mystics and the sixteenth-century Anabaptists, modern Christians will find James's exhortation the right place to start: *Submit . . . to God*, who *gives grace to the humble* (4:6-7).

Making Peace and Harvesting Righteousness

According to James, pursuing peace and being *peaceable* are important for living by the wisdom of God. James emphasizes peace in these verses; a form of the word *eirēnē* (peace) occurs three times in 3:17-18. Nevertheless, this text does not figure prominently in the writings of early Anabaptists nor in contemporary peace-church traditions nor in peace documents of the wider church (Loewen; Gwyn, et al.). More often, teachings about peace in the Christian life are based on the Sermon on the Mount (Matt 5:9, 38-48), the life of Jesus, and the words of Paul (e.g., Rom 12:9-21). Yet, as pointed out in the notes, James is closest to the cadence of Jesus in Matthew 5:9, "Blessed are the peacemakers," when he commends *those who make peace* (James 3:18).

Many Christians, including but not limited to those in the historic peace churches (Mennonites, Brethren, Quakers), understand peace to be at the heart of what God is about in the Bible. This peacemaking work is triple-pronged:

1. In Jesus Christ, God made peace between humanity and God (Rom 5:1-11), reconciling us to God and setting us free from sin.
2. In Jesus Christ, God also made peace between alienated peoples, breaking down hostility and creating one new humanity (Eph 2:11-21).
3. Finally, God's peacemaking project encompasses all of creation, which now still groans but will one day be renewed and restored to full shalom (Isa 65:17-25; Rom 8:19-23; Rev 21:1-5).

Moreover, God entrusts this peacemaking, reconciling work to all who are made new in Christ and live by the Holy Spirit's power

(2 Cor 5:17-19). Just as Jesus sent out his disciples to proclaim peace and the reign of God to others (Luke 10:5-9), so followers of Jesus in all times and places are called to participate in God's peacemaking activity.

Christians have not always agreed on what it means to be a peacemaker or how best to make peace, especially in the public and political arena. For some, serving in the government's armed forces is not incompatible with making peace, for ultimately their goal is ending violent conflict and injustice. For followers of Jesus in the historic peace church tradition, to be involved in God's peacemaking activity has meant not using violence, not resisting enemies, and not going to war. For many of the early Anabaptists (though not all), not retaliating against those who persecuted them was absolutely central to following Jesus in daily life. *Martyrs Mirror* contains innumerable accounts of Anabaptists who refused to retaliate against their oppressors and resisted participation in state-sponsored violence (Braght). Nonresistance is one of the seven articles of the Schleitheim Confession, authored by Michael Sattler in 1527 and summarizing certain tenets of Anabaptists in the Swiss and South German area. Nonresistance and conscientious objection to military service dominated the way many peace churches expressed their commitment to following Jesus' way of peace for centuries and continues to characterize the peace witness of many, including conservative or traditional Anabaptist churches.

For many Christians, however, Jesus' call to love one's enemies and to participate in God's peacemaking activity requires something less passive than nonresistance. It demands active engagement in a wide range of contexts, including the social, economic, and political arena. James's naming of the work born of divine wisdom as *making peace* (cf. James 3:18), instead of just "keeping the peace" or only being "peaceable," provides solid ground for this perspective. Peacemaking or peacebuilding work encompasses not only interpersonal conflict and inner self-conflict but also institutional, systemic, and international conflict. Because true peace or shalom is inextricably tied to justice, many participate in the work of *making peace* by working against injustice and advocating for the marginalized. Christian peacemaking encompasses a wide range of activity: providing relief to people suffering from war and natural disasters, caring for God's creation, conflict mediation and victim-offender reconciliation programs, combating domestic and sexual violence, antiracism training, civil disobedience, and so on.

Although people involved in the daily work of God's peacemaking activity may not appeal to James 3:17-18 nor even be cognizant of the way this text undergirds their work, they are nevertheless involved in sowing the *harvest of righteousness* that James commends to his readers (3:18 NRSV).

James 3:17-18 suggests that the manner in which Christians engage in the active work of making peace must be consistent with the end goals. That is, peacemakers sow the fruit of justice or righteousness *peaceabl[y]* and by means of or *in peace*. According to this text in James, being peacemakers precludes the use of violent force, coercion, or unjust means. Yet the work of peacemaking may sometimes be confrontative, since standing up to violent and unjust powers often stirs up conflict before it makes peace. Difficult and even painful measures sometimes are needed to lance the wounds of injustice. At the same time, peacemakers who sow peace and then reap a *harvest of righteousness* will be empowered by *wisdom from above*, which is *pure, peaceable, gentle, willing to yield, full of mercy and good fruits, without a trace of partiality or hypocrisy* (cf. 3:17-18). They will do their sowing of righteousness by strategies, methods, actions, and behaviors that ultimately are oriented to shalom.

James 4:11-12

On Judgment—God's and Ours

PREVIEW

Hate speech, polarizing language, and judgmentalism are ubiquitous in our world. In this context, James 4:11-12 has a simple but forceful message for the church: Those who revile and judge others are putting themselves above the law and in the place of God, who alone has the authority to judge. If one pays attention to the repetitive language, the point is impossible to miss. The word "judge" occurs no less than six times in only two verses. Other repeated words are "law" (4×), "to malign" (3×), and "brother(s)" (3×). Sandwiched between two longer memorable passages, this compact unit might be easy to glide over. But that would be a loss, for the problem it addresses is as toxic for communities today as it was for James's church.

In this unit James returns to the topics of speech, neighborliness, law, and judgment found elsewhere in the letter (1:19, 26; 2:8-13; 3:1-12; 5:9). As in 3:9, the problem is not only interpersonal and practical but also theological: acting as if one were God by judging a neighbor is as inconsistent and double-minded as cursing people made in the image of God. Slandering a brother or sister (4:11) is not motivated by divine wisdom (3:13-18). Like envy and selfish ambition, it will destroy community (4:1-6).

EXPLANATORY NOTES

Because this unit consists of only two verses, most commentaries link 4:11-12 to the passage before or after. The connections are tenuous, however, and these verses are best taken as a discrete unit.

Several elements indicate a shift in tone and content from the preceding verses. First, whereas in 4:1-10 James addresses his readers as *adulterers, sinners,* and *double-minded,* now he reverts to the more personal and personable *brothers [and sisters].* This familial vocative frequently signals a shift in tone or content elsewhere in the letter (e.g., 2:1, 14; 3:1; 5:7). Second, the preceding verses consisted of positive commands (*submit, draw near, cleanse, lament*); here 4:11 prohibits wrong behavior (*Do not malign,* AT). Finally, the notable repetition of vocabulary (*law, judge, malign*) not used elsewhere in the immediate context binds verses 11 and 12 together and sets these verses off from the preceding unit.

James 4:11-12 is also distinct from what follows (4:13–5:6). The topic changes after 4:12, from derogatory and judgmental speech within the community to the arrogant and oppressive practices of merchants and rich landowners. James 4:13-17 also belongs with 5:1-6 structurally, since both begin with the words *come now.* The brevity and distinct character of 4:11-12 draw attention to it and highlight its importance.

The message of this short unit is clear: do not malign another person and do not judge each other. The word "malign" or "speak evil" is literally "to speak against" and is sometimes translated "to slander," to make false and defamatory statements about someone. Slander is certainly included in what James is talking about, but the scope is broader than that. To *speak evil against* someone encompasses any kind of speech that is disparaging of and hurtful to others, whether spoken directly to them or indirectly about them, whether falsely or truthfully. With these words James recalls his earlier warnings against the damage a fiery tongue can do (3:1-12).

James associates defamatory speech with the problem of judging others. Here he is thinking specifically about relationships within the church, evident from the address *brothers [and sisters].* Though obscured in some translations, this familial imagery is repeated twice more in verse 11: *The one who speaks against a brother or sister or judges a brother or sister speaks against the law and judges the law* (AT; cf. Exod 20:16). He is emphatic that they are family! But the problems of insulting and judging others pertain not only to behavior within the church, for verse 12 speaks more broadly about judging *the neighbor*, which could be anyone. Keeping unstained from the world (1:27) and not being friends with the world (4:4) might prompt some in the community to think of themselves as above their neighbors and thus to judge them negatively (Ellul: 187).

The word "judge" dominates this short pericope; it is important to understand what James is and is not saying. He is surely not prohibiting moral discernment, critical thinking, or mutual accountability. James himself criticizes his readers for their behavior throughout the letter, and in 5:19-20 he speaks about community practices of confronting and restoring a believer who sins, which requires making judgments about wrongdoing. The fact that James links "judging" with "speaking against" is a clue to what he means. To speak negatively about someone is to assume the stance of a judge (Johnson 1995: 293). James is addressing the all-too-human tendency to make a negative decision about someone's character or actions without knowing the circumstances or motivation, without accurate information, without mercy and kindness. When such condemnation is combined with disparaging speech, the results are toxic to community and as destructive as envy and selfish desire (4:1-3).

James uses the word "neighbor" one place other than in 4:12: *You shall love your neighbor as yourself* (2:8; Lev 19:18). The kind of judging James has in mind is antithetical to loving one's neighbor. The opposite of judging others is showing grace and giving others the benefit of the doubt. Acting in this manner is acting in the character of God, *who gives to all generously and ungrudgingly* (1:5) and *gives grace to the humble* (4:6). In warning his audience against speaking evil and judging others, James echoes the teaching of Jesus, who also commanded his disciples, "Do not judge, and you will not be judged; do not condemn, and you will not be condemned" (Luke 6:37//Matt 7:1).

James equates maligning or judging someone with maligning or judging the law. What is the relationship between the two? What does James mean by "the law"? In James 2:8-13, which has the most concentrated references to the law, the word refers to the Torah, which God gave Israel and which continues to guide God's people. The law is also *royal*, that is, the law of God's *kingdom*, which was most fully revealed and interpreted by Jesus. It is the *law of freedom* because it is characterized by and gives freedom.

Living by God's law is being conformed to God's will and word, planted within people (1:21). The royal law is summed up in the words of Leviticus 19:18: *You shall love your neighbor as yourself* (2:8). When one looks at the context of the love command in Leviticus 19, the relationship between slander, judging others, and the law becomes clearer. In the Septuagint the first part of Leviticus 19:16 reads, "You shall not walk deceitfully among your people." But the Hebrew text says, "You shall not go around as a slanderer among your people." According to the Torah, then, speaking evil against someone is a violation of the law of loving one's neighbor.

Earlier James said that showing favoritism to the rich neighbor makes one a transgressor of the law as much as committing adultery or murder (2:9-11). The same could be said for maligning a brother or sister or judging a neighbor. It is not that all transgressions have equally serious ramifications (e.g., taking a life is not the same as insulting someone). Nor is James addressing the changing applicability of laws in new contexts (e.g., circumcision was not required for Gentiles; Acts 15). Rather, he is making the point that deliberately flouting God's will as revealed in Jesus Christ and in Torah is setting oneself above the law, as though one were beyond its reach. To assume that one is above the law of God is supreme arrogance, whether it is a minor infraction or an egregious evil. Slandering or judging someone is contrary to the kingdom law of loving one's neighbor. It flagrantly defies the law that Jesus identified as the second greatest commandment and is therefore equivalent to maligning the law.

James says, *If you judge the law, you are not a doer of the law but a judge* (4:11). In Greek, the word "you" is singular (not pl.), which makes the statement more pointed and personal. He is prodding individual listeners to reflect on their own behavior in the context of the community. The phrase *doer of the law* is parallel to two phrases that appeared earlier: *doers of the word* (1:22) and *doer of work* (1:25 AT). The "word" is the "word of truth" that gave them birth and is implanted in them to give salvation (1:18, 21). It too is a word that must be acted on and not only heard (1:22-23). Like the "word," God's royal law (2:8) must be lived out, not only heard and then ignored. It must take on flesh and bones in loving actions toward neighbors. Followers of Jesus must be doers of the word, not hearers only, and they must be *doers of the law* not *judges* of it, who decide when and whether to obey it.

In 4:12 James gives the theological rationale for not judging others. If they malign and judge others, they are not obeying the law of love and therefore are setting themselves above the law. In effect, they become their own arbiters of what is right and true and good. People who do this put themselves in the place of God, who alone is *Lawgiver and Judge* (v. 12). In Greek this sentence begins with and highlights the word "one," as does 2:19, *You believe that God is one*. The parallelism is obvious: The *one* true God is the *one* Lawgiver and Judge. The word "lawgiver" occurs only here in the New Testament, although the idea of God as the giver of the law appears elsewhere (Ps 9:20 NRSVue, "Put them in fear, O LORD," is translated in 9:21 LXX as "Set a lawgiver over them, O Lord"; Ps 84:6, "The early rain also covers it with pools," is in 83:7 LXX as "The Lawgiver will give blessings"; cf. 2 Esd 7:89, "Lawgiver"). Some Jewish and Christian writings speak of Moses as the giver of the law (e.g., John 1:17; 7:19), but ultimately the law comes from God through servants like Moses. God gave the law, and God will be the one to judge God's people on the last day.

The Old Testament knows God as "the Judge of all the earth" (Gen 18:25; Pss 67:4; 94:2; Isa 33:22). In the New Testament, Jesus acts on behalf of God in judging humankind (John 5:22, 26-30; Acts 10:42). In 5:9 James speaks of *the Judge . . . standing at the doors*, reminding his audience that this time of judgment is imminent and that Jesus ("the Lord"; cf. 1:1; 2:1) will be God's agent in judging God's people. James says that, as Judge, God is the one uniquely able *to save and to destroy*. This is a good reminder that God's role as judge is not only about condemnation but also about making decisions, which include vindication, exoneration, saving, and making things right. The idea that God has control of life and death and is able to save and to destroy is a conviction found throughout the Bible (e.g., Deut 32:39; 2 Sam 2:6). By basing his argument on the monotheistic faith in the one true God of Israel, who alone can save life and take life and who alone is Judge of all the earth, James exposes the implicit hubris of those who pretend to "play God" by standing in judgment on their neighbors.

Accusatory, harsh, and slanderous speech is never Christian behavior, regardless of its target. But it is particularly painful when it happens within the community of believers, as was apparently happening in James's churches. The fact that he addresses them as *brothers and sisters* and commands them to stop speaking destructively to *each other* highlights this fact. This is not the kind of speech that should characterize people who have been given birth *by the word of truth* and are now the *first fruits of [God's] creatures* (1:18). The religion of those who cannot hold their tongues in check is worthless (1:26). Such demeaning speech is not only detrimental to the community; it also is theologically dangerous, for it implies that the speaker is above the law and not accountable to the Giver of the law. The arrogance of this is expressed in the final rhetorical question, "Who do you think you are, that you can judge your neighbor?!"

THE TEXT IN BIBLICAL CONTEXT

Making Judgments

The verb "to judge" can mean to make a decision about something or someone after careful deliberation, as when a judge makes a decision in court. It can also have a more negative connotation, as in the exclamation, "Don't judge me!" In this case "to judge" means to criticize or condemn. Both usages occur in the Bible, but it is the latter that James addresses in 4:11-12.

The Bible's starting point on the subject of judging is also James's: God alone is the just Judge over the whole world (Gen 18:25; Ps 9:7-8). The prophets pronounce God's judgment on the wicked, whether Israel or the nations (Isa 3:13-14; Ezek 30:13-19; Mal 3:5), and look forward to the day when God will judge the nations with equity, when God's justice will prevail (Isa 2:4; 33:22). The psalmist expresses hope in God, who will judge enemies with righteousness (Pss 58:10-11; 82; 96:10-13). Jesus and the New Testament writers all look to the future day when God will judge the world (Matt 25:31-46; 2 Tim 4:1; 1 Pet 4:5). As God's agent, Jesus has been granted authority to make judgments on behalf of God, both during his earthly ministry and in the future (John 5:22, 30; Acts 10:42). This is the context in which all human judgments must take place.

Humans make judgments, and they need to do so (deciding: the first definition above). A prime example of the need for moral discernment and accountability in the church is 1 Corinthians 5:9-12, where Paul explicitly counsels the Corinthians to judge and discipline believers who sin. Judgment of those outside is to be left to God, says Paul (5:13). Matthew 18:15-20, while not using the language of "judging," outlines a process by which disciples should make judgments about sin in their midst. The purpose of such discipline must always be restoration of an erring brother or sister. It must be carried out with compassion and humility and must have forgiveness as its goal (Matt 18). Judgment must not be based on appearances but be done "with right judgment" (John 7:24). The writer of 1 John counsels the church to "test the spirits to see whether they are from God" (4:1). In short, some judgments are expected and appropriate in the ecclesial community.

At the same time, James, Jesus, and Paul all tell their listeners in no uncertain terms: Stop judging each other! The Bible offers various reasons for this prohibition in addition to those given by James. First, they should remember that they are no better than the person they are judging and just as prone to sin. It is hypocritical to condemn others for what we ourselves do. The prophet Nathan confronted David with this message when he told the parable of the rich man who took the poor man's only pet lamb (2 Sam 12:1-15). David's judgment of the rich man bounces back at him when Nathan pronounces, "You are the man!"

Jesus also teaches his disciples not to judge, using a hyperbolic analogy "designed to stick in the imagination" (Tannehill: 122): How can they hope to take a speck out of someone's eye when they have a log in their own (Matt 7:1-5; Luke 6:37, 41-42)? His purpose for saying they must remove their log before trying to take out the neighbor's speck is not to give instructions about how to confront a wrongdoer but to attend to one's own faults so that one might not harm a neighbor (Gibbs 2006: 370). Perhaps the neighbor's speck will have disappeared after one has cleared the log from one's own vision. Paul provides a similar reason for not judging: "In passing judgment on another you condemn yourself, because you, the judge, are doing the very same things" (Rom 2:1). Condemning evil in others does not prove one to be a moral person if one continues to do evil oneself (Achtemeier: 44–47).

Second, God's people should not judge others because of who God is. On the one hand, the fact that God is a judge and will hold people accountable functions as a warning. "Do not judge, so that you may not be judged" (Matt 7:1//Luke 6:37) could be understood as "If you do not judge others, *they* will not judge you"; but more likely this is the divine passive and means that *God* will not judge you. Paul makes the same point more explicitly in Romans 2:3. On the other hand, the character of God can also function positively as motivation for forgiving rather than judging. This is most clear in Luke 6:37-38:

> Do not judge, and you will not be judged; do not condemn, and you will not be condemned.
> Forgive, and you will be forgiven; give, and it will be given to you.
> A good measure, pressed down, shaken together, running over, will be put into your lap.

As Robert Tannehill has pointed out, this is carefully crafted language in which two negative commands in line 1 are contrasted with two positive commands in line 2 (120). Followers of Jesus are to act in the character of God, who is "kind to the ungrateful and the wicked" (Luke 6:35) and does not give according to human measures of strict reciprocity but with extravagant generosity and grace (in line 3).

A third reason for not judging others is the importance of love and mutual upbuilding in the body of Christ. In Romans 14 Paul addresses the issue of "the strong" passing judgment on "the weak." It is not clear who the strong and the weak were, but evidently there were differences of opinion about practices such as eating meat, observing special days, and avoiding what was unclean. Each party practiced what they believed to be faithful, what they thought would honor God (14:6). Paul does not take sides on who is correct but has the same advice for both groups: "Respect the convictions of the other group" (Achtemeier: 216). Paul counsels them to "no longer pass judgment on one another, but resolve . . . never to put a stumbling block or hindrance in the way of [another believer]" (14:13).

The motivation is poignantly articulated in Romans 14:15: "If your brother or sister is distressed by what you eat, you are no longer walking in love. Do not let what you eat cause the ruin of one for whom Christ died." There will always be differences within the church about what is faithful practice. Rather than judging those who believe differently, the strong in faith should emulate Christ by practicing forbearance and showing grace, rather than pleasing themselves (15:1-3). Judging others does not build up the body of Christ.

Although followers of Jesus must discern what is good and have the responsibility to hold each other accountable, they must be cautious in doing so. A greater danger than moral laxity is the arrogance of assuming that one knows enough to judge another person. It is far too easy to put oneself in the place of God, who alone is able to save and destroy. The parable of the wheat and the weeds in Matthew 13:24-30, 36-43, while not explicitly about judging, reminds Christians that it is not their job to pull out the weeds from the field but to leave that to God.

THE TEXT IN THE LIFE OF THE CHURCH

"Who Are You to Judge Your Neighbor?"

Although there is a difference between moral discernment and the kind of judging the Bible condemns, it can sometimes be tricky to differentiate the two in practice. Most of the divisions in church history, including the various Anabaptist groups, are the result of one group making judgments about another group. Is this the kind of judging that James condemns? Or is this holding firm to one's convictions?

The tension between appropriate and inappropriate "judging" is evident in two contrasting impulses in contemporary society that also affect the church. On the one hand, personal criticism is quickly met with the rejoinder, "Don't judge me!" In our strongly individualistic society, most people feel that their personal lifestyles, spending habits, use of resources, colorful language, entertainment choices, and much more are no one's business but their own. Even good friends hesitate to confront each other for fear of sounding judgmental. This is no less true in the church. Harsh and exclusionary practices of church discipline have rightly been abandoned by the Mennonite church, but often at the cost of appropriate mutual accountability.

On the other hand, many people are extremely judgmental and quick to condemn others for behavior that does not conform to their own standards. This is true in the church as well, where people judge each other on everything from clothing choices to worship styles, from how they spend their money to how they raise their children. Even those who pride themselves on being open-minded and tolerant can be intolerant of people on the other end of the political or theological spectrum. The vitriol seems to become more acerbic the more polarized our society becomes. We may be guilty of othering people and become "righteously indignant" when their beliefs and behaviors don't agree with our own. In other words, we judge them.

How should the church navigate this tension? When is it "judging"? When is it appropriate Christian admonition? No set of rules can be universally applied. Following Jesus' advice to "judge with right judgment" (John 7:24) takes practice, discernment, and wisdom. It also requires loving one's neighbor as oneself (James 2:8). The kinds of things James "judges" are examples of how the church is *not* loving their neighbors: showing favoritism to the rich (2:1-6), apathy toward the vulnerable (1:27; 2:16), envy and selfish ambition (3:14-16; 4:1-2), anger (1:19), lack of integrity in word and deed (2:14-16), intemperate and unkind speech (1:26; 3:2-12; 4:11; 5:9). These are also the kinds of things Jesus criticized. Christians have a responsibility to hold each other accountable for such things. But even such mutual discerning must be done without "judging" and tearing others down.

The fact that James pairs *judging* with *speaking evil against* someone (4:11) is instructive for what not judging others means. Maligning the character of others and verbal attacks are never loving one's neighbor as oneself. This is true whether one is confronting sin or simply has a different opinion. Heeding James's admonitions elsewhere about what it means to live faithfully will help to mitigate habits of wrongly judging others and to promote love of neighbor. In the passage immediately prior to 4:11-12, James urges the church to repent, purify their hearts, lament, and humble themselves. Taking the logs out of our own eyes first and having enough humility to receive correction from others will check our tendency to judge others. Asking God for wisdom will also temper the impulse to judge quickly and harshly, since this wisdom from above is peaceable, gentle, willing to yield, merciful, sincere, and not envious or selfish (3:13-18).

The admonition not to judge others is only one of many prohibitions in James, giving some the impression that the letter does not contain a lot of grace. It is instructive to formulate James's warning against judgment in positive terms. To refrain from criticizing or condemning others for something one disapproves of means to show them grace. When we are generous with others and frame their actions or words in the best possible way, we are choosing not to judge them. Glimpses of such a nonjudgmental, gracious posture are evident elsewhere in James's letter. In 3:2 he says, *All of us make many mistakes*, and in 5:15-16 he reminds hearers that there is forgiveness for those who sin. In 2:13 he concludes, *Mercy triumphs over judgment*. Being attentive and receptive to the grace that God shows us helps us to be more gracious with others and less judgmental.

James 4:13–5:6

Warnings about Arrogance and Wealth

PREVIEW

"James is hard on the rich!" said someone in a youth Sunday school class I was teaching on James. Another commented, "James reminds me of the Old Testament prophets." Such impressions derive largely from James 4:13–5:6, especially the last six verses.

The section consists of two subunits, each beginning with the arresting words, "Come now!" In the first pericope James castigates traveling merchants for their economic practices. In the second he tackles wealthy landowners for their exploitative, excessive lifestyles. The critique of the merchants focuses on their flagrant disregard of God; the critique of the rich centers on their extravagant lifestyle and their unjust treatment of the poor.

James's message in this unit is consistent with earlier comments about material wealth and treatment of the poor (1:9-11; 2:1-7), but this rebuke is by far the hardest-hitting section in the letter. God will overturn unjust structures and lift up the lowly. Followers of Jesus must live accordingly. The rhetoric in 5:1-6 is particularly blistering and should make wealthy Christians squirm even today, though it was undoubtedly intended to comfort James's original readers, who were undergoing trials and testing of various kinds (1:2-3).

Although the issues James raises are uncomfortable for many Christians in North America, they are questions that the church ignores at its own peril. For churches in the southern hemisphere who have been impoverished by unjust and oppressive policies of powerful nations, James's clarion call for social and economic justice is a welcome message.

OUTLINE

Admonition to Arrogant Merchants, 4:13-17
Condemnation of Rich and Unjust Landowners, 5:1-6

EXPLANATORY NOTES

Admonition to Arrogant Merchants 4:13-17

This subunit contrasts the speech of merchants, who confidently and independently make business plans (v. 13), with the speech of those who consider the will of God (v. 15). James charges his audience with doing the former when they should be doing the latter. These admonitions about what they should and should not say alternate with reasons why the merchants' attitude is reprehensible: Their life is fleeting (v. 14), and their boasting is evil (v. 16). A final aphorism drives home the point (v. 17).

The opening words, *Come now*, command attention and pair this unit with 5:1-6, which begins the same way. What follows is a diatribe (as in 2:14-26) in which the speaker addresses an absent conversation partner. By quoting his imagined interlocutors (v. 13), James characterizes them in a certain way. A string of four future verbs portrays the merchants as decisive and confident in planning for the future: *We will go, . . . we will spend a year, . . . we will do business, . . . we will make a profit* (AT). The staccato-like sequence of the verbs and the fact that the phrases become progressively shorter is more evident in Greek than in English translations. These merchants are "movers and shakers" who have a strategy for where and when they will travel, what they will do, and what the outcome will be.

At this point, it is not obvious that their ambitions are problematic, though the last two verbs in verse 13 might give a hint. The Greek words for *doing business* and *making money* do not have negative connotations elsewhere in the New Testament or Greco-Roman literature (although in 2 Pet 2:3 the former means "to exploit"). However, in the context of this letter's critique of economic disparity (2:1-7), selfish ambition (3:14, 16), and violent acquisition to satisfy desire (4:1-3), those last two verbs of 4:13 become suspect.

The text raises questions about the identity of the merchants: What was their socioeconomic status? Were they part of the churches to whom James wrote? Some interpreters argue that only the very wealthy would have had resources to travel for extended periods of time and do business (e.g., Hartin 2009a: 232–33). Alternatively, some studies of first-century economies note that merchants could belong to a "middling group" that included small traders and people "on the way up," not only rich large-scale entrepreneurs (Painter and deSilva: 151; Downs: 158–62; Davids 2005: 378). Although James does not provide enough information to know specifics about the situation, it seems clear that the people addressed in 4:13 had sufficient assets that they were not living at a subsistence level. They had the time and resources to make a profit on business trips.

Were the merchants themselves believers in *our glorious Lord Jesus Christ* (2:1 NRSV)? Or rich outsiders who *oppress* the poor and *blaspheme the excellent name . . . invoked over [the hearers]* (2:6-7)? If the former, James, as a leader in the church and a "brother," is holding them accountable for their arrogant behavior. If the latter, the text serves a different function. The most cogent argument for understanding the merchants as *not* believers is the text's close relationship to 5:1-6. Because both subunits begin with *Come now*, and both deal with economic matters (business ventures in far-away lands and agricultural practices at home), the people addressed probably fall into the same category. Since the accused "rich" in 5:1-6 are likely not part of the church (see below), and since James does not explicitly call the addressees in 4:13-17 "brothers" (as in 4:11-12 and 5:7, 9-10), it is conceivable that the merchants are not Messiah followers. However, the argument that they *were* part of the church is stronger.

Most compelling is that James assumes they should care about doing God's will (v. 15) and about what is evil and sinful (vv. 16, 17). It does not make sense to urge people to consider what *the Lord wishes* (v. 15) if they do not strive to obey the Lord. As Elsa Tamez states, "I believe that they are members of the Christian community since James reproaches them for not consulting the Lord about their plans and for not sharing what they earn with the poor" (2002: 25). Additionally, Ben Witherington argues for different audiences in 4:13-17 and 5:1-6 based on the different styles of the two pericopes: "The former paragraph manifests the diatribal style, while the latter is more like a woe oracle. What this suggests, rhetorically, is that the former group are those whom James thinks he has and can still have a dialogue with, while the latter are not" (2007: 523). That James does not specifically identity the merchants in verses 13-17 as "brothers" when criticizing them cannot imply that they are outside the church, since language for fellow believers is equally accusatory in 4:1-10 (*adulterers, double-minded, murder[ers],* and *enem[ies] of God*).

Although James does not give enough information to know for certain, it is unlikely that the merchants were part of the wealthy elite class of 5:1-6, who owned massive landholdings, defrauded their workers, and were not part of the churches whom James was addressing. Rather, in 4:13-17 we see followers of Jesus Messiah who were not the most oppressed and poverty-stricken in the church but had sufficient resources to travel and make money. If so, that might make it more difficult for comfortable capitalist North Americans Christians to distance themselves from the target of James's critique.

James slams his readers' inflated strategic planning with a terse message: "You really know nothing about the future. You don't even know whether you will be alive!" (paraphrased). Bible versions differ on how to translate the first half of verse 14, in part because of textual variants in the Greek manuscripts, in part because of uncertainty about how to punctuate the Greek, and in part because of the syntax. The clause that NRSVue and NIV choose to render as a question, *What is your life?* is better taken as appositional to the first clause, specifying what is unknown about tomorrow: *You do not know about tomorrow, what your life will be* (AT). In any case the point is clear: regardless of how much planning we do, we cannot know or control what the future will hold.

Not only can we not be certain about the future; life itself is tenuous. In verse 14 James uses one of the memorable, vivid metaphors for which he is so well-known. *You are a mist that for a little while appears and then disappears* (AT). The word *mist* could also mean "smoke," "vapor," or "breath." The sentiment of this verse is commonplace, found in both Jewish writings (esp. wisdom literature) and in Greco-Roman literature. Proverbs 27:1 says, "Do not boast about tomorrow, for you do not know what a day may bring"; Job 7:7 states, "Remember that my life is a breath." In Wisdom of Solomon 2:4, the sage announces, "Our life will pass away like the traces of a cloud and be scattered like mist that is chased by the rays of the sun and overcome by its heat." In the first century, the Roman Stoic philosopher Lucius Seneca (Seneca the Younger) lamented the transience of life in a discourse *On the Shortness of Life*.

James draws on this common storehouse of wisdom to rebuke the presumptuousness of people who make grand business plans without considering that their life is not their own, that they are not ultimately in control of the future. Readers may hear echoes of Matthew 6:30-34, where Jesus urges disciples not to worry about tomorrow and invites them to consider "the grass of the field, which is alive today and tomorrow is thrown into the oven."

Syntactically verse 15 is a continuation of verse 13, with verse 14 being a grammatically complex interruption. Instead of saying, "We will do this and that" (v. 13), they should begin by placing themselves and their plans within the larger purposes of God (v. 15). The phrase *If the Lord wishes* or "God willing" (Latin *Deus volente*) is sometimes called the "Jacobean condition." For James, this is not just a catchphrase to tag onto the end of a sentence, though that is sometimes how it is used today. It is not merely paying lip service to God's approval for whatever one has already decided to do. Rather, James is calling his readers to the humble submission to God that he wrote about in 4:7, 10. The words *If the Lord wishes, we will live* (v. 15) pick up on the uncertainty about life in verse 14 by acknowledging that life itself is a gift from God. Saying *If the Lord wishes, we will . . . do this or that* does not mean that God has a predetermined plan, which one needs to figure out and fit into. Rather, it is discerning God's ethical will and conforming one's activities and work to what God always desires of God's people (McCartney 2009: 227–28).

Although James does not explicate here how one should discern God's righteous will, there are plenty of clues throughout the letter, not least of which is the *royal law* expressed so succinctly in *You shall love your neighbor as yourself* (2:8; Lev 19:18). James is not telling his self-assured merchant audience that they should not make plans but that, when they do, they must remember that they are ultimately not in control of the future; that their security lies in God, not in material possessions; and that their priority must be God's business, not their own. Jesus said it this way: "But seek first the kingdom of God and his righteousness, and all these things will be given to you as well" (Matt 6:33).

The idea of submitting to the will of the gods (or the phrase "the gods willing") appears also in ancient non-Christian Greco-Roman literature. For example, in the last line of Plato's dialogue *Laches*, Socrates says, "I will not fail, Lysimachus, to come to you tomorrow, God willing" (201.c). The play *Peace* by the ancient Greek writer Aristophanes contains the line, "How everything succeeds to our wish, when the gods are willing and Fortune favors us! How opportunely everything falls out" (939–40).

Although even worshipers of Greek gods appreciated the need to defer to the gods when making decisions, James's admonition is directed to the church. The "Lord" to whose will they must submit is named thirteen other times in the letter, referring either to Jesus (1:1; 2:1; 5:7-8) or to the God of Israel (1:7; 3:9; 4:10; 5:4, 10-11). In 1:18 James also references God's will, using a different verb (*God gave us birth by the word of truth* because he "willed" it [paraphrased]). For James, the one God governs history: it is the will of this God whom he urges his Christian brothers and sisters to consider as they strive for financial gain and overconfidently make plans for economic opportunities. In this, James accords with other New Testament writers, who also use expressions like "the Lord willing" (Acts 18:21; 1 Cor 4:19; Heb 6:3); and with Jesus, who taught his disciples to pray, "Your will be done" (Matt 6:10; cf. Mark 14:36).

In 4:16 James reveals a third reason for his disapproval of their behavior, and here he ramps up the rhetoric. It is not *only* that their planning for profit ignores the uncertainty and transitory nature of life. It is not *only* that their behavior leaves God out of the picture. They are also *boasting in [their] arrogance*, which James bluntly denounces as *evil* (4:16). Every occurrence of this Greek word for *arrogance* and its cognates in the New Testament (1 John 2:16; Rom 1:3; 2 Tim 3:2) has a negative connotation. It is ambiguous whether they are boasting arrogantly or, more likely, whether their schemes are arrogant. Either way, such behavior is not right for followers of Jesus.

This is not the first time James has talked about boasting in the letter, although previously the context was different. In 1:9-11 James urged lowly believers to boast in their exalted status and the rich in their debasement. Why would James encourage "boasting" in one case and denounce it in another? In 1:9-11 God is the one raising up the lowly and casting down the rich. This is part of God's justice-making activity, so those who trust in God to set things right can and should glory in God's action on their behalf. Conversely, the merchants in 4:13-17 are glorying in their own activity, following schemes to make themselves wealthier (in a world that perceived all good as limited) and to set themselves above others. Such behavior is diametrically opposed to God's desires and God's action of raising up the lowly and putting down the rich.

It is no wonder that James condemns their boasting as *evil*, the same adjective he used in 2:4 to characterize the thoughts and motives of those who give special honor to the well-dressed person in their assembly and demean the poorly clad one. In both cases the behavior of the believer is *evil* because it reflects a desire to be a *friend of the world* (4:4) instead of a friend of God, who *opposes the proud but gives grace to the humble* (4:4, 6). Such boasting grows out of *bitter envy and selfish ambition, . . .* not *wisdom . . . from above* (3:14-15).

A pithy aphorism brings this subunit to a close. The relationship of verse 17 to the preceding verses has puzzled interpreters for a long time: although the sentence begins with *then/therefore*, it is unclear how it is a consequence of what came before. Some have concluded that there is no logical relationship. Rather, in what is characteristic of James's choppy style throughout the letter, James simply chose to end the subunit with a wise saying, as he did in 2:13 and 3:18. Unless we assume that James was a careless writer, however, the word "then/therefore" suggests that we push harder to understand the connection. Since he names this as *sin*, Christian readers then and now ought to pay attention to the serious warning.

What is the *good* or *right* thing a Jesus-follower should know to do? The immediate context gives us a clue. In verse 15 the "right" thing to do is discern the will of God and submit to God's will when planning for the future. The fact that the merchants are *not* doing that (v. 13) implies that they are sinning, as does their boasting, which is evil. Instead, they are tempted by their desire for profit, and that desire has conceived and given birth to sin (1:14-15).

If we look to the wider context of the letter, we receive further illumination on God's will and the "right" thing to do, particularly when it comes to economics. The "right" thing to do is to tame one's tongue (and therefore not boast) and care for the most vulnerable in society (rather than just heap up profits; 1:26-27). The "right" thing to do is to love one's neighbor even when and especially when that neighbor is poor. To give preferential treatment to the wealthy, on the other hand, is sin (2:1-9). The "right" thing to do is give food and clothing to the brother or sister in need rather than speak empty platitudes (2:15-16).

By concluding the subunit with the aphorism in verse 17, James is returning to the theme of integrity, which pervades the letter. Hearing must result in doing (1:22-25), seeing must result in doing (2:15-16), and believing must result in doing (2:14-26). Now in 4:17, knowing must result in doing. When one's actions are not consistent with what one knows, hears, sees, and believes, one is double-minded. Whoever does not show faith in action has a dead faith, sins, and lives as though God does not exist.

Verse 17 is then, after all, an apt conclusion to the pericope. Its general, aphoristic nature encourages wide application and prods readers to consider situations in which they have known the right thing to do but have not done it. To be sure, sometimes we are unable to act on what we know is right, and sometimes we do not know what is right. But for James, it is *knowing* what is right and deliberately turning one's back that falls short of the integrity God desires. James names this as sin. Of course, as James says in 3:2, *All of us make many mistakes*, and everyone sins. Although he does not provide a solution to this problem here, he does come back to it in 5:13-20. In the church there is confession and forgiveness of sins (5:16).

Condemnation of Rich and Unjust Landowners 5:1-6

In this section James continues his tirade against those whose chief concern is their own success and prosperity rather than submission to the will of God. As in 4:13-17, James begins with the words *Come now,* suggesting that this unit should be read together with the previous one. In 5:1-6, however, he explicitly addresses "the rich" (*plousioi*), a term that is used elsewhere in the letter for people who are not Messiah followers (2:6-7). But what is the point of writing something that rich nonbelievers will not hear?

James is likely using a rhetorical figure called an apostrophe here, that is, "direct and explicit address either to an absent person or to an abstract or nonhuman entity" that creates "a sudden emotional impetus" (Abrams: 182). If so, he would be speaking in the manner of some of the Old Testament prophets, who denounced the surrounding nations even though their message was for Israel (e.g., Ezek 25–32; Amos 1–2). In the Gospel of Luke, Jesus likewise uses this kind of speech when he speaks "woes" against the rich even though he is teaching his disciples, who are not rich (Luke 6:20-26).

If the recipients of the letter are not the primary target of James's scathing critique of the rich here, what purpose does it serve? It seems unlikely that James would write to gloat over their catastrophic downfall. Nor does he explicitly call the rich to repentance, the purpose of which would be questionable if they are indifferent to God's will.

The biting critique of the wealthy and powerful who are *not* listening is for the benefit of the powerless poor who *are* listening.

Its purpose is to reassure, comfort, and give hope to those in James's churches who are suffering (Hartin 2009a: 238; McCartney 2009: 231; Maynard-Reid: 97). As the next pericope (5:7-12) will show, James does not advocate that the poor engage in violent rebellion to obtain justice. Rather, his strong social-justice stance is rooted in the theological conviction that God hears the cries of the poor and oppressed and will act on their behalf. In turn, the people of God must participate with God in establishing this justice. They must act on behalf of the most vulnerable and not passively wait (1:27; 2:15-16). A secondary purpose for the harsh prophetic rhetoric in 5:1-6 is to warn or admonish those in the church who might covet the wealth of others and be seduced by its allure. Those who have material resources might be tempted to pander to the rich (as in 2:1-6) or become so consumed with acquiring more that they forget God and boast in their own achievements (as in 4:13-17). This unit warns followers of Jesus about the ephemeral nature of riches and of the dangers associated with unjust wealth.

This unit contains some of the harshest language in the letter, and its tone is relentlessly accusatory. John Painter says it well: "This multiplication of language of despair and disaster communicates an overwhelming sense of distress and anguish" (Painter and deSilva: 153). This pericope has earned James the moniker "the Amos of the New Testament." Virtually every clause contains the words "you" or "your," evoking an image of a finger jabbing at the listener. Only one clause is not in the second person: *The cries of the harvesters have reached the ears of the Lord of hosts* (5:4b). This sudden pause in the unrelenting string of accusations brings the reader up short and deepens the seriousness of the offense: God the Warrior has heard the cries of the oppressed. We will return to this ominous warning below.

James begins by offering the wealthy a glimpse into the disaster that awaits them: *Weep and wail for the miseries that are coming to you.* Although the letter has many features of Jewish wisdom literature, in this pericope the language most resembles the abrasive, accusatory rhetoric of the Old Testament prophets. The onomatopoeic Greek word for "wail" (*ololyzontes*) is found only here in the New Testament but appears twenty-one times in the Septuagint, all in the prophets and primarily in declarations of judgment (e.g., Isa 13:6; Zech 11:2). The words "weep" (e.g., Jer 22:10; Joel 1:5; in Isa 15:2 together with "wail") and "misery" (e.g., Isa 47:11; Jer 4:20; 20:8; Joel 1:15) also feature in prophetic oracles of doom. This similarity to the prophets continues in phrases like *Lord of hosts*, *day of slaughter*, and *last days* (James 4:3-5).

The structure of 5:1-6 reveals that James's condemnation of the rich boils down to two key things:

1. They have amassed wealth, spending it selfishly and profligately (vv. 1-3, 5-6a).
2. They have defrauded and oppressed the innocent (vv. 4, 6b; Maynard-Reid: 82–83; Hartin 2009a: 236–37).

James alternates between these two charges with the effect that the sins of acquisition and oppression become inextricably intertwined. Because of their behavior, the rich are ripe for judgment. Like the prophets, James thinks and writes eschatologically; twice in this unit he alludes to *the day(s)* when God will call them to account for their unjust living (vv. 3, 5). The implication is that the "day" does not lie in the distant future: James wants them to feel its hot breath on their necks.

In verses 2-3 a series of five short clauses tells the rich why they should weep and wail: their wealth is wasting away and will ultimately destroy them. Although the perfect tense of the first three verbs sounds like the destruction has already happened, James is using a standard rhetorical convention common to the prophets before him: the anticipation of what is to come is so real and so vivid that he speaks about it as if it had already happened (Allison 2013: 672; cf. Isa 45:20-21; Ezek 29:3-7; Amos 1:2–2:3). The two future verbs in verse 3 envision the devastating results when riches will inevitably decay.

The images of moth-eaten clothes and rusted treasures would not have been unfamiliar to ancient readers, just as they are not new for us. One finds this proverbial language, for example, in Isaiah 51:8, "The moth will eat them up like a garment"; Proverbs 25:20, "Like a moth in clothing, . . . sorrow gnaws at the human heart"; and Sirach 29:10, "Do not let [your silver] rust under a stone and be lost." It may seem odd that James speaks of gold and silver as rusting, since in reality such metals are precious precisely because they do *not* rust. Whether he is using hyperbolic language or is simply not concerned about accuracy, his point is clear: earthly treasures like gold and silver do not and cannot last. Moreover, clothing that is worn does not get moth-eaten, nor do possessions get rusty when regularly used. The wealthy in this text have so much that they cannot use it all and are hoarding it, making their opulence even more deplorable (Painter and deSilva: 154).

Riches are not only impermanent; they are also destructive. The word for "rust" in verse 3b (*ios*) is the same word translated "poison" in the description of the tongue (3:8). Both wealth and speech, two prominent themes in James's letter, are thus characterized as potentially toxic. James personifies rust by suggesting that it will be a witness against the wealthy person. In his commentary, Dan McCartney uses the following apt analogy: "When one sees the telltale flaky reddish brown on a used car being considered for purchase, the rust 'testifies' against the vehicle by revealing its corroded and crumbling condition" (2009: 233). James uses graphic imagery to warn against the looming judgment: *It will eat your flesh like fire* (v. 3c). *Flesh* here is a synecdoche for the whole person, and *fire* is commonly associated with punishment in the biblical tradition (Isa 9:18-19; Jer 5:14; Amos 1:4, 7, 10, 14; and many more). Just as fire ravages everything in its path, so also great wealth can consume people and indict them at the judgment.

The words *You have laid up treasure during the last days* (5:3d) have an ironic double meaning. On the one hand, the rich are making actual financial investments for the future—their last days, so to speak. On the other hand, the phrase "last days" in the New Testament almost always has an eschatological significance, which gives these words a more ominous connotation. Ironically, the "treasure" that they are amassing is their future judgment. The word "during" or "in" implies that they are already in the "last days." Although God's final judgment lies in the future, it is beginning even now in how they steward their wealth. In the next pericope, James says, *The coming of the Lord is near* (5:8), and *The Judge is standing at the doors!* (5:9). By accumulating and hoarding material possessions today, they are storing up judgment for the imminent future.

For a modern reader familiar with the Gospels and an ancient reader steeped in the teachings of Jesus, James's words sound familiar. Although verbal correspondence is not exact, the text has a strong thematic resonance with Matthew 6:19-21//Luke 12:33-34. James accuses the rich of doing precisely what Jesus warned his disciples not to do, namely, "store up . . . treasures on earth, where moth and rust consume" (Matt 6:19). The parable of the rich fool in Luke 12:13-21 also vividly depicts the impermanence of earthly wealth and the poverty of storing up treasures for oneself. James thus not only stands in the tradition of the prophets in castigating the rich but is also firmly anchored in the teachings of Jesus.

In 5:4 we find a shift in rhetoric marked by the dramatic word *Listen!* (or *Behold!*) James now turns to the second main reason for his condemnation of the rich: their oppression of the powerless. The focus of attention switches from the wealthy to their agricultural laborers. Two different words for "cry" lie at the center of the two main clauses in this verse:

> *The wages of the laborers . . . cry out [krazei],*
> *and the cries [boai] of the harvesters have reached the ears . . .*

The verb *cry out* comes at the end of a string of modifiers as if the writer wanted to build up tension before getting to the point. The synonymous noun "cries" directly follows. Literarily, this centers the readers' attention on the plight of the workers.

The socioeconomic context of 5:4 is typical of first-century rural Palestine and is also reflected in the Gospel parables. Wealthy landowners expanded their holdings by expropriating land from subsistence farmers unable to pay their taxes, repay loans, or grow enough food in years of drought. These same impoverished farmers would become tenant farmers, sharecroppers, or day laborers, sometimes working the very land they had lost. Without status or power, they were easily subject to exploitation and lived a precarious existence. At the same time, more and more land was concentrated in the hands of an elite few, who were usually absent from the actual running of the estates.

Such were the conditions of agricultural laborers, not only in Palestine where power was concentrated in the hands of aristocratic Jews on good terms with Rome, but also throughout the Roman Empire, where imperial policy benefited those who already had status and wealth and further marginalized the poor. Such impoverished peasant farmers were likely among James's readers.

Old Testament law spoke directly against withholding wages from workers, as did the prophets. James's readers, steeped in the Jewish Scriptures, would readily have called to mind such texts as these:

- "You shall not defraud your neighbor; you shall not steal; and you shall not keep for yourself the wages of a laborer until morning." (Lev 19:13)
- "You shall not withhold the wages of poor and needy laborers.

. . . You shall pay them their wages daily before sunset, because they are poor and their livelihood depends on them; otherwise they might cry to the LORD against you, and you would incur guilt." (Deut 24:14-15)

- "Woe to him who builds his house by unrighteousness and his upper rooms by injustice; who makes his neighbors work for nothing, and does not give them their wages." (Jer 22:13)

According to the Law and the Prophets, James's relentless critique of the rich is certainly warranted. Texts such as these also provide the basis for the defrauded workers to appeal to *the Lord of hosts* (5:4). Their cries of suffering contrast with the weeping and wailing of the rich, who face disaster. Throughout the biblical tradition, the poor and oppressed cry out to God, and the God of justice and compassion hears their cry (Gen 4:10; Exod 2:23-24; Ps 18:6 [17:7 LXX]). James echoes Isaiah 5:9 (LXX), "For these things were heard in the ears of the Lord Sabaoth."

The rare phrase *Lord of hosts [sabaōth]* in 5:4 requires some comment. It is only one of two occurrences in the New Testament, and its presence here is noteworthy. (The other is in Romans 9:29, where Paul quotes Isaiah 1:9). *Lord of hosts* is how the NRSVue translates the Greek *kyriou sabaōth* (in the NT), which is *YHWH* ṣəbā'ôt in Hebrew. The typical Septuagintal translation of the Hebrew is *pantokratōr* (Almighty/All-Powerful) (2 Cor 6:18; Rev 1:8; 11:17), but the simple transliteration *sabaōth* also appears 64 times. English Bible translations vary in rendering *kyriou sabaōth* in James 5:4: *Lord of hosts* (ESV, NRSV), *Lord of Heaven's Armies* (NET, NLT), *Lord Almighty* (GNT, NIV), *Lord (of) Sabaoth* (ASV, NASB 1995, NKJV), *Lord of Armies* (GW, NASB), *heavenly forces* (CEB), and *Master Avenger* (MSG).

"LORD Sabaoth" appears as a divine name in the Hebrew Bible approximately 260 times. It is an ancient name for God that reflects Israel's understanding of God as Warrior, leading the faithful into battle (e.g., 1 Sam 4:4; 17:45) or commanding the hosts of heaven (e.g., Ps 103:19-21). The name "Lord Sabaoth" thus connotes both military and royal power. In Isaiah, where most of the occurrences of transliterated *Sabaoth* in the Septuagint occur (over 50 times), this name for God is primarily associated with impending judgment on the wicked. One cannot help but think James was deliberate in choosing the loaded title "Lord Sabaoth" in a text that castigates wealthy landowners for their unjust treatment of workers.

Modern readers from peace-church traditions may feel uneasy about such militaristic language for God, especially because of how it can be coopted to support human aggrandizement. However, as Martha Moore-Keish notes, "James slyly employs a military metaphor not to support human imperial power, but to subvert it" (Moore-Keish: 175).

The clause *the cries of the harvesters have reached the ears of the Lord of hosts* is also the *only* clause in the subunit (5:1-6) that is entirely in the third person, not containing the words "you" or "your." Far from being "almost parenthetical and rhetorically function[ing] as sidebar revelation" (McKnight: 383), this clause boldly jumps out as the central theological claim of the unit. God hears the cry of the oppressed and is going to wage war against unjust and rich oppressors!

Verses 5 and 6 reiterate the two main charges of verses 2-4, that the rich are guilty of luxurious, self-indulgent living and violent injustice against the innocent. In a chain of five staccato-like accusations, James heaps up words like the rich heap up luxury goods:

> *You lived for pleasure on the earth*
> *And you lived luxuriously;*
> *You fattened your hearts in a day of slaughter.*
> *You condemned,*
> *You murdered the righteous one.* (AT)

The third clause evokes images of killing a fatted calf for a celebration, but in this case *day of slaughter* parallels *the last days* in verse 3, a time of judgment and doom rather than celebration. Although the phrase "day of slaughter" occurs only here in the New Testament, it echoes judgment oracles in the prophets (e.g., Jer 12:3; 25:34; cf. Isa 30:25; 34:2-8).

Two strong verbs in quick succession accuse the rich of acting unjustly (5:6). The word "condemn" does not simply mean to criticize or judge, but refers to finding someone guilty in court, possibly condemning them to death (Allison 2013: 684; McCartney 2009: 235). One can imagine wealthy landowners taking poor farmers to court for their inability to pay their debts and forcing them into penury by expropriating their land. The accusation that the rich have *murdered the righteous (or innocent) one* is the third occurrence of the word *murder* in the letter. In 2:11 James quoted the commandment "You shall not murder," and in 4:2 he accuses his listeners of killing each other to satisfy their covetous desires. That is a lot of speech about murder in a short letter!

The identity of *the righteous one* and the meaning of *does not resist you* have puzzled many interpreters. First, some understand Jesus to be this *righteous one* since he suffered unjustly at the hands of wicked people. He is named the Righteous One in Acts 3:14; 7:52; and 22:14 and described as righteous in many other texts (Matt 27:19; Luke 23:47; 1 Pet 3:18; 1 John 2:1). Several reasons make this association unlikely, however. Nowhere else does the letter say anything about the life, death, or resurrection of Jesus, nor was the wealth of his killers the issue. Still, since Jesus always stood with the oppressed, the wealthy landowners' unscrupulous treatment of the poor can be viewed as participating in the murder of God's unique Righteous One.

Second, perhaps James the brother of Jesus is *the righteous one* since early church tradition speaks of him as "the Just" or "the Righteous" (e.g., Eusebius, *Ecclesiastical History* 2.23; citing Hegesippus). This option assumes that James did not pen the letter himself. Again, this is unlikely since James was a church leader killed by powerful political forces, not a marginalized person oppressed by the rich.

Third, it is grammatically possible to translate the final clause as a question expecting an affirmative response: "Does he not resist you?" The referent of "he" could be God, implying that God does indeed oppose the rich (Johnson 1995: 305). This would be consistent with the use of the same verb *(antitassetai)* in 4:6: *God resists the arrogant* (AT). By oppressing the poor and living self-indulgently, the rich are acting arrogantly. However, it is more natural to understand the antecedent of "he" as being the immediately preceding victim of violent injustice than finding a more distant reference to God. Taking the laborers' cries to the Lord of hosts as a form of resistance against the rich is also unconvincing (so McKnight: 399–400).

The most logical (and most common) way to understand the last clause of verse 6 is simply as a statement, *He does not resist you.* The righteous individual who does not resist is representative of an entire class of people who are suffering injustice at the hands of the rich. Perhaps these oppressed ones feel unable to resist because they are dependent on the landowner for their livelihood. More likely, they are righteous because they have chosen not to resist with violence and are patiently enduring suffering, as 5:9-11 counsels. The word *righteous* in verse 6 could also be translated *just* or *innocent*. Such a person has done nothing to deserve abuse but remains committed to furthering God's justice (1:20). In using this language, James is probably drawing on the Old Testament topos of "the oppressed poor person who trusts in God for deliverance, as in several psalms (e.g., Ps. 34:15-22; 37:12-40) and prophetic writings (Lam 4:13; Amos 2:6)" (McCartney 2009: 236–37) The idea that the righteous do not engage in violent resistance resonates also with Jesus' teaching (Matt 5:38-42).

Could James be speaking hyperbolically in 5:6, as he likely was in 4:2? Or are the rich actually killing the righteous? Even if the language were metaphorical, the accusation highlights the seriousness of the unjust practices of the wealthy landowners. Certainly cheating tenant-farm laborers out of their wages could lead to poverty and death, as this text from Sirach recognizes: "The bread of the needy is the life of the poor; whoever deprives them of it is a murderer. To take away a neighbor's living is to commit murder; to deprive an employee of wages is to shed blood" (34:25-27 [LXX 34:21-22]). Many other Old Testament texts similarly accuse the wicked of killing the righteous (e.g., Ps 37:32; Prov 17:15; Hab 1:4, 13). According to James, withholding wages necessary to sustain life is on par with murder.

Similar to 5:4, the final clause in verse 6 abruptly concludes a sequence of five accusatory verbs in 5:5-6 with a statement in the third person: *You lived for pleasure, you lived luxuriously, you fattened your hearts, you condemned, you murdered the righteous one. He does not resist you* (paraphrased). The terse declarative statements at the end of verse 4 and verse 6 turn the listeners' attention away from the flagrant behavior of the rich to the actions of the oppressed righteous one, whom God will surely hear. It is such behavior that James wants them to notice and emulate.

To conclude, the literary apostrophe in 5:1-6 echoes the style of Old Testament prophets like Amos and Jeremiah, who castigate the wealthy for extravagant living and oppressive practices. This would have had a twofold effect on James's first-century church. First, assurance of God's judgment upon the unjust rich would comfort and encourage poor believers who were suffering. The God of justice will overturn unjust systems. The Lord of hosts hears the cries of the poor! Second, this text reminds James's church that those who do have resources must love their neighbors by sharing what they have, caring for the marginalized, acting for justice, and not succumbing to selfish desires, envy, greed, and literal or metaphorical murder (James 1:14-15, 27; 2:8, 14-26; 3:14-16; 4:1-4). This text can and will function in these ways for the twenty-first-century church also, in addition to delivering a sobering warning to the affluent.

THE TEXT IN BIBLICAL CONTEXT

First-Century Sociocultural Perspectives on Wealth

It is unclear whether the recipients of the Letter of James were city dwellers (see Batten 2014) or peasant farmers. If the letter was addressed to several Christian assemblies *in the dispersion* (1:1), perhaps they included both. Evidently issues of wealth and poverty were directly impacting them, causing suffering, testing of faith, and strain in community relationships. Likely some were poor, some were well off enough to help the poor, and some envied the rich or felt compelled to honor them. Understanding something of the economic and social world of the first century assists readers today to grasp more fully the import of James's strong critique of the rich. Issues of wealth and poverty were never only about economics but were also closely tied to social, political, and religious dimensions of life.

The first-century Mediterranean economy was preindustrial and primarily agrarian. Urban centers depended on surrounding villages and farms for food, despite also importing goods from a distance. The little surplus producers acquired was siphoned off to the urban elites through taxes, tribute, and rents. By far the majority of the population in the Roman Empire (perhaps 90 percent) were peasants and artisans living at a subsistence level, with most of the wealth concentrated in the hands of a small elite at the top of the socioeconomic pyramid (Powell: 41). Although there was no middle class comparable to today, society included a small retainer class that served the interests of the elites and included merchants (Batten 2019: 179). Strong class hierarchies governed relationships between the powerful haves and the have-nots. Land was often owned by wealthy absentee landlords and farmed by tenant farmers, day laborers, and a huge slave population. Subsistence farmers lived a precarious existence since their livelihood depended on the weather and was subject to droughts and famine.

Crucial to understanding perceptions of wealth in ancient societies is the cultural notion of "limited good." This is hard for modern industrialized people to understand, since our economies are based on the belief that unlimited growth is possible and desirable. Ancient peoples believed that all goods in life, whether material or immaterial, were finite and usually in short supply. These included land, money, food, water, honor, power, friendship, and security (Batten 2019: 179; Malina 1993: 95). If someone acquired more of something, that meant another person would get less, upsetting the equilibrium, the status quo. The notion of limited good might lead to competition for scarce resources and envy of those who had more, but it also prompted a defensive stance in which people tried to maintain the status quo.

The fundamental social values of honor and shame also impacted perceptions of wealth. "Honor is a claim to worth along with the social acknowledgment of worth," particularly in the intersection of power, gender status, and religion (Malina 1993: 31). Honor could be "ascribed" by virtue of one's birth or "acquired." Although "shame" could have the positive connotation of concern for one's reputation, it also denoted loss of honor in one's social group. Because society was communally oriented and not individualistic, as it is today, people always perceived themselves in relation to others. Wealth could contribute to a person's power, but far more important was the status and honor one held in the community.

Because all goods were limited and because one person's gain was another's loss, the accumulation of wealth for its own sake was viewed as greedy, dishonorable, and even evil (Malina 1993: 104; Batten 2019: 181). Instead, "honor lay in using wealth to benefit one's society and particularly to acquire clients to whom one was patron" (Jobling: 826). A benefactor with power and wealth would thus give goods and protection to people at a lower social level in exchange for their public recognition, gratitude, and service.

The dishonorable rich acquired wealth by trading, tax collecting, and moneylending, all of which forced people to relinquish their share of the limited good (Malina 1993: 104). The merchants in James 4:13-16 are making a profit by buying from some and selling it to others at a higher price. They are benefiting from others' losses, which is dishonorable. Not only are the landowners in 5:1-6 not using their wealth to benefit the poor, they also are making a profit by withholding their workers' fair wages. Instead of gaining honor through benefaction, they are acting in dishonorable ways: stockpiling goods, allowing them to rust and rot, and leading self-indulgent lives.

In this context, the message of Jesus and James becomes even more radical. Jesus invited everyone into the reign of God, regardless of wealth or honor. The wealthy were expected to give to the poor, but they would have regarded as outlandish the idea that they should not expect to increase their status and honor through their benefaction (Luke 6:27-36) or that people should not extend special honor to a rich person to gain their patronage (James 2:1-13).

The Perils of Wealth

James's critique of the rich is consistent with much of the biblical witness. Although the Bible offers alternative voices and nuanced understandings of material possessions, its overall message is that wealth is fraught with problems and is even dangerous for the people of God.

The starting point for a biblical understanding of material possessions is that everything is created by God and belongs to God (Lev 25:23; Ps 24:1). Humans are given what they have in trust to tend and use for the flourishing of all people and creation. The Bible is not against materiality nor does it idealize poverty. In the Old Testament, material blessings of land, livestock, and prosperity are signs of God's favor (Gen 24:35; Deut 8:17-18; 1 Kings 3:13). The hope of return from exile includes the promise of abundance (Isa 54:11-13; 60:5-7, 11; 61:5-7). Proverbs speaks positively about wealth as a reward for hard work and righteous living (e.g., Prov 8:18; 10:4, 15, 22).

The wisdom literature of the Old Testament is emblematic of the diversity of voices in the Bible. Juxtaposed with proverbs that extol the benefits of wealth are sayings that claim the opposite. "Riches do not profit in the day of wrath, but righteousness delivers from death" (Prov 11:4), and "Those who trust in their riches will wither" (11:28). Job and Ecclesiastes even more strongly refute conventional wisdom's association of piety with security, long life, and prosperity: the hardworking righteous do not always prosper (Job), and wealth leads to worry, insecurity, and greed (Eccl 5:10-17).

The prophetic literature contains the most strident critiques of wealth. Although some oracles are directed against rich foreign nations (e.g., Ezek 27), Israel and Judah are often the targets. James's two-pronged condemnation of self-indulgent living and oppression of the vulnerable appears also in the prophets. Amos lampoons the opulent lifestyles of the rich in Israel (6:4-6). Jeremiah denounces the luxurious homes of the rich and associates a lifestyle of excess with unjust practices (22:13-15). Storing up wealth for one's own pleasure means *not* using it to help the needy (e.g. Isa 1:23; Ezek 16:49). The rich profit at the expense of the poor since their prosperity feeds on the cheap labor of others. Numerous texts illustrate these prophetic critiques (e.g., Isa 10:1-4; Jer 5:26-28; Mic 2:1-2; 6:11-12; Mal 3:5), but Amos again stands out (2:6-8; 4:1; 5:11-12; 8:4-6). In addition to critiquing luxurious living and injustice toward the powerless, the prophets also associated wealth with idolatry. With their silver and gold the people made idols, emulating the surrounding nations (Ezek 7:19b-20a; Isa 2:7-8; 46:6-7; Hos 2:8; Blomberg: 71–72; Witherington 2010: 24).

The prophets warn that God's judgment will come upon God's people and their wealth will be taken from them (Jer 20:5; Ezek 7:11). If the rich wish to avoid God's judgment, they must turn from their exploitative economic practices. They must seek justice for the oppressed and give generously to the poor and needy (Isa 58:6-7; Amos 5:21-24). Walter Brueggemann notes how Christian theology has highlighted Habakkuk 2:4 ("The righteous live by their faithfulness") but ignored the following verses that castigate the wealthy and envision their demise (Hab 2:5-19; Brueggemann: 151–52).

The Old Testament notion of wealth as a sign of God's blessing and a reward for faithfulness does not, for the most part, extend into the New Testament (Blomberg: 83–85, 242). To be sure, the early church included people of means: Barnabas sold a field and brought the proceeds to the church (Acts 4:36-37); the church in Antioch included Manaen, a member of Herod's court (Acts 13:1); and Timothy's church included rich people (1 Tim 6:17). Joseph of Arimathea was a rich disciple who laid the body of Jesus in his own tomb (Matt 27:57-60). References to wealth as either neutral or positive are rare, however, and the New Testament primarily speaks critically about wealth.

The Gospel of Luke contains the most teachings about wealth, possessions, and poverty, including many parables and stories found only here (e.g., 12:13-21; 16:1-9, 19-31; 19:1-10). Jesus' stance toward the rich is summed up by his words "Woe to you who are rich" (6:24). But what is it about wealth that evokes such censure? Are material possessions inherently evil? Foundational to the gospel message is God's desire that *all* people have enough; in God's reign there will be no hunger, poverty, or suffering. The problem with wealth is that some have too much and others not enough. Jesus' message of "good news to the poor" (4:18) and his feeding of the crowds in the wilderness signal this divine purpose (9:12-17). The powerful will be brought down and the rich sent away empty in order that the lowly can be lifted up and the hungry filled with good things (1:52-53 summarized). Such leveling is the point of the reversals in the Gospels (e.g., 6:20-26).

The target of Jesus' critique is similar to James's: it is greed and self-indulgent luxury that ignores the plight of the poor and perpetuates injustice. Wealth is dangerous because of its power to seduce people into thinking and acting as though life does indeed "consist in the abundance of possessions" (Luke 12:13-31). The rich have a difficult time entering the reign of God because they foolishly believe they are self-sufficient and do not need God. Their hearts are invested in their treasures rather than in God's kingdom. As a result, they forfeit the invitation to God's great banquet (12:32-34; 14:15-24). Their riches become the master, preventing the word of God from bearing fruit while blinding them to the need of others (8:14; 12:13-21; 16:19-31). Both God and wealth demand exclusive loyalty, says Jesus (16:13).

What then should followers of Jesus do with their money and possessions? The message in the Gospels (and the whole New Testament) is clear: share generously with others. If the goal of God's reign is that *all* have enough, then the responsibility of Jesus' followers who "have" is to give to those who "do not have" (Luke 3:10-14; 8:1-3; 16:1-9, 19-31). Jesus' urging his hearers, "Sell your possessions," is followed by "and give . . . to the poor" (Luke 12:33; 18:22). The point of divestment is investment in the well-being of others. Although it is hard for the rich to enter the reign of God, it is not impossible, as demonstrated by Zacchaeus, a rich tax collector, who gives half his possessions to the poor and receives assurance of salvation (19:1-10).

That wealth is intended to be used for the sake of others is evident throughout the New Testament, not only in the Gospels. The writer of 1 Timothy urges the rich not to trust in wealth, but to be generous (6:17-19). He warns those who desire wealth that the love of money is dangerous (6:9). Hebrews likewise counsels, "Keep your lives free from the love of money, and be content with what you have" (13:5). A notable theme in the Pauline correspondence is the collection for the poor in Jerusalem (Rom 15:25-27; 1 Cor 16:1-12), and in 2 Corinthians Paul urges a fair balance between abundance and need (8:1-15). Acts portrays Christians sharing their possessions so that "there was not a needy person among them" (2:44-45; 4:32-37).

Finally, Revelation issues a damning indictment of corporate and systemic greed and oppression on par with the most strident Old Testament prophets. To be sure, its target is not the church but

Rome, which syphoned off shippable produce and wealth from its subjugated people to feed its insatiable appetite. Merchants, sailors, and anyone profiting from Rome's extractive economic policies are also subject to judgment (Rev 17–18). John's word to the church is, "Come out of her, my people, so that you do not take part in her sins" (18:4). He calls the church of Laodicea to repent from its material prosperity and spiritual bankruptcy (3:14-22). Economic hardship was the consequence for Christians who resisted participation in guilds influenced by the idolatrous emperor cult. The final book in the New Testament thus confirms its overall critical perspective on wealth.

THE TEXT IN THE LIFE OF THE CHURCH

Rich and Christian

James 5:1-6 offers hope for the poor: God hears their cries and will overturn systems of injustice. This is the message that interpreters from the global South hear and amplify in this text (Maynard-Reid; Tamez 1982). Wealthy Christians, on the other hand, may find James's harsh condemnation profoundly unsettling. Although the temptation for preachers will be to soften the blow, there is value in sitting with discomfort. James's words can provoke change so that the rich too may be liberated from the stranglehold of their possessions.

One of the greatest threats to Christian faith in the North American church is its wealth. Despite the good that money can do, its dangers are even greater. This is true on the personal, individual level as well as on the institutional, structural level. Dom Helder Camara, a Brazilian archbishop who devoted his life to the poor, says this:

> I used to think, when I was a child, that Christ might have been exaggerating when he warned about the dangers of wealth. Today I know better. I know how very hard it is to be rich and still keep the milk of human kindness. Money has a dangerous way of putting scales on one's eyes, a dangerous way of freezing people's hands, eyes, lips, and hearts. (quoted in Sider: 97)

The seductive allure of material possessions and prosperity is not a new danger. Since the time of Ananias and Sapphira (Acts 5:1-11) the church has struggled with the issue of wealth.

For early Anabaptists, true Christianity "involved the avoidance of riches, and had to include the care of those who had need"

(Snyder 2004: 141). Jan Wouterss wrote to his wife from prison in 1572, cautioning her not to let the business grow too large, "lest your heart become surcharged" (*MM*: 911). Over time, Anabaptist Christians also faced the threat that prosperity brings. Dutch Mennonites became increasingly well-off in the seventeenth century, which concerned some ministers. In *Mirror of Greed* (from the Dutch, *Spiegel der Gierigheydt*, 1638), Pieter Pietersz of the Waterlander Mennonites quoted James 5:1-3 to criticize employers who paid low wages but lived in luxury:

> When the wage is negotiated with a day laborer they [the greedy] make it as low as possible, knowing well that the laborer cannot live on what is offered, and if they hesitate they are told sharply: if you won't do it for this price[,] I can easily get someone else; and the poor laborers think they had better take the work at half-wages lest they not find other work at all. (quoted in Dyck 1995: 132)

Menno Simons used James 5:1-6 to condemn rich Christians for their greedy, luxurious living and neglect of the poor (*CWMS*: 367). Although he allowed for the possibility of God-fearing merchants, he thought they were liable to become greedy.

Five hundred years later, descendants of these Anabaptists struggle with the same temptations of wealth as their forebears. Statistics about the growing disparity between the obscenely rich and the impoverished majority of the world's population are not difficult to find. Books like *Rich Christians in an Age of Hunger*, by Ronald Sider, have been a voice of conscience for the church for decades, reminding Christians in the West of their enormous affluence, responsibility, and complicity in the suffering of the world. And yet, staggering inequities continue, and the prosperity gospel still has appeal. A 2018 survey revealed that a full 32 percent of American adults agreed or strongly agreed with the statement "God will reward the faithful with health and wealth" (Lewis and Timmons).

Most Christians do not manage multinational corporations that underpay workers to maximize profits, and many do not live in mansions or drive expensive cars. Even so, all are inevitably enmeshed in structures, systems, and institutions that perpetuate inequity. The earth itself groans under the weight of the extractive, exploitative materialism of the rich.

What is the church to do? Is it possible to be rich and Christian? The words of James 5:1-6 offer only relentless judgment. As Jesus' disciples asked, If it is so hard for the rich to get into the kingdom of God, "Then who can be saved?" (Mark 10:25-26). Yet, Jesus replied, "For God all things are possible" (10:27). In the Gospel of Luke these words are followed by the story of a rich person who *is* saved when he relinquishes his wealth (19:1-10). But it is also very difficult—as difficult as getting a camel through the eye of a needle.

The calling of the church is to be a sign of God's reign of "enough for all." This begins in the body of Christ itself, as people take care of each other and break down dividing walls of inequity. But it cannot end there. The wealthy church in North America should not be content until *all* God's children have enough. If the church would spend itself and its money until that were the case, there would be fewer rich Christians.

There is much that the church and individual Christians can and should do in light of James's critique of the rich. Individuals can donate to organizations that provide microloans to people in poverty. They can choose not to purchase new vehicles, designer clothes, and luxury-vacation packages. They can look carefully at their investments and choose ethical options. Churches can choose to invest in people rather than in bigger and better buildings. They can draft budgets in which the proportion designated for helping others is greater than the amount allocated for their own needs. They can sponsor refugees and invest in green energy. Even so, the church in North America will still be much richer than most of the world's population. And James's words will continue to trouble.

"The Lord Willing"

When asked about weekend plans, a former colleague would invariably end his response with "LW" (Lord willing). Although spoken lightheartedly, these words reflected his serious desire to live life mindful that it belonged to God. Arabic speakers frequently use the phrase "*In sha' Allah*," which similarly means "If God wills." Some people are familiar with the Latin version of the phrase, "*Deo volente*," or simply D.V. The sentiment behind this "Jacobean condition" (James 4:15) is not unique to the letter. Jesus taught his disciples to pray "Your will be done" (Matt 6:10) and modeled it himself (26:42). Paul, too, submitted his planning to God's will (1 Cor 4:19; 16:7).

The expression "the Lord willing" was common in Christian speech in previous eras. In the sixteenth century, the reformer John Calvin recommended saying, "God willing" when making "any promise for future time," but acknowledged that he does "not want to make a fetish of this, as though the omission should be an offence" (quoted in Allison 2013: 643). James 4:15 is cited in the *Martyrs' Mirror* with the admonition not to think "we can do anything of ourselves," but to seek God's will in everything (*MM*: 745). For the most part, though, this expression has fallen away in modern speech and is often seen as a pious cliché.

James 4:13-17 speaks not about general usage but is addressed to merchants making business plans. Despite vast differences separating this text from today, the parallels are not hard to envision. Whether a multinational corporation or a nonprofit organization making a ten-year business plan or an individual seeking advice from a "wealth management" adviser, James's words prick the Christian conscience.

Many scholars are quick to state that James is not discouraging responsible budgeting or denouncing commercial activity. What many fail to note is that people who can barely pay their monthly bills do not have the luxury of such long-term planning. "Financial planning for the future" assumes a degree of economic stability and control of what might happen. The situation is reminiscent of Jesus' parable of the rich fool (Luke 12:13-21), in which a farmer whose harvest is abundant plans what to do with his wealth. He will invest in the business and take a well-deserved vacation. His plans are all for naught, though, since his life is *a mist that appears for a little while and then vanishes* (James 4:14; cf. Eccl 6:12; 11:10).

James is critical of Christians who are arrogant enough to think they are "masters of their own destiny." In 1937 Napoleon Hill wrote in *Think and Grow Rich*: "You are the master of your destiny. You can influence, direct[,] and control your own environment. You can make your life what you want it to be." Whether in business dealings or in daily life, James urges his readers to consider first whether their actions are consistent with what God desires. Faith in God and economic activities are not separate realms but part of an undivided or "perfect" life.

Although most Christians would likely say that their lives are in God's hands, that ultimately they are not in control, many act more like the rich fool in Jesus' parable, who is oblivious to God's will in his past, present, or future. As several commentators have said, they are "functional" atheists (e.g., Hartin 2009a: 233; Wall: 217). It often takes a crisis, such as a natural disaster, a pandemic, or a health challenge to make them realize that they are not the "masters of their destiny." James reminds the church to humbly seek God's will at all times, not only in a crisis.

Becoming more attuned to the will of God is not a matter of sprinkling D.V. or "Lord willing" into sentences, nor is it a resigned stoicism that says, "Whatever will be, will be." Rather, it is a lifelong discipline of considering God's will in whatever one does. For James this was especially true in business dealings. Today it applies not only to individual followers of Jesus but also to the church as a community as it prepares budgets, plans church renovations, or engages in community outreach.

James 5:7-12

Living Patiently and Speaking Faithfully

PREVIEW

When people are under stress or suffering, they sometimes become impatient with others and say things they later regret. This is true not only for individuals but also for church bodies. In this unit James circles back to themes that have appeared before: the need for endurance in times of trial (1:2-4, 12) and speaking rightly (1:26; 3:1-12; 4:11-12). Beginning and ending the letter with the topic of endurance forms an *inclusio*. These bookends suggest that everything in the middle should be read in light of the situation of James's readers, who are struggling with injustice and socioeconomic disparity. James's focus in 5:7-12 shifts from scolding rich landowners (5:1-6) to encouraging these suffering *brothers and sisters* in Christ.

Underpinning James's exhortations is a vibrant eschatological vision, which has been evident throughout the letter (1:12; 2:5; 3:1; 4:12) but is expressed most explicitly here. His message is clear: the church's hope is in the Lord, who will return as Savior and Judge. While they wait, they must endure suffering with active patience. James offers three models of patience: a farmer waiting for his crop, the prophets, and Job. The theme of patient endurance (vv. 7-8, 10-11) alternates with that of faithful speech (vv. 9, 12), implying that the two are intimately related. How they endure suffering impacts how they speak to each other and the world, and both are animated by a robust hope in the return of Christ.

OUTLINE

Living Patiently Until the Lord Returns, 5:7-8
Speaking Faithfully without Complaining about Others, 5:9
Living Patiently While Enduring Suffering, 5:10-11
Speaking Faithfully and Truthfully without Oaths, 5:12

EXPLANATORY NOTES

This text consists of four brief subunits in an *A B A′ B′* pattern (5:7-8; 9; 10-11; 12). Most commentators recognize the internal coherence of 5:7-11, but no consensus exists about the relationship of verse 12 to its immediate context. Some link it with the previous verses, but many others attach it to verses 13-20 or, more commonly, treat it as an isolated saying. For the following reasons, it makes sense to treat verse 12 as the fourth subunit in this *A B A′ B′* structure.

First, each of the subunits begins with the vocative, *brothers [and sisters]* (*adelphoi*). This word is used frequently in the letter, but four of the fifteen vocatives are concentrated in these six verses. Second, each subunit is governed by a main imperative verb. The verbs are grammatically alike in the first (vv. 7-8) and third (vv. 10-11) subunits, with aorist imperative commands; the second (v. 9) and fourth (v. 12) subunits use present imperative prohibitions. Third, in terms of subject matter, the first and third subunits are about patient endurance and hold up models for James's readers to emulate. They also each include references to *the Lord*. The second and fourth subunits warn readers against a certain kind of speech (either grumbling or swearing oaths), and both refer to judgment or the judge. This structure communicates that living patiently and speaking faithfully are intertwined.

James 5:7-12 is related to the preceding unit in a parallel but contrasting manner. It begins with *therefore*, indicating that what James says here to his readers follows logically from his previous words. That a new section begins here, however, is evident from the contrasts that exist between 5:1-6 and 5:7-12. The former addresses rich, unbelieving oppressors; the latter encourages suffering Christian brothers and sisters. Except for the initial admonition to *weep and wail*, the verbs in verses 1-6 are all in the indicative mood, whereas verses 7-12 consist primarily of imperatives. The tone therefore changes from one of indictment for wrongdoings to exhortation and encouragement. Both units look ahead to God's action in the future.

Living Patiently Until the Lord Returns 5:7-8

This unit once again begins with a reminder that the church consists of *brothers and sisters.* James writes as a pastor and brother, not a top-down expert.

The verb "to be patient" appears three times in verses 7-8 and again as a noun (patience) in verse 10. A similar word, "to endure/endurance" appears twice in verse 11. This repetition of vocabulary makes the main focus of this unit abundantly clear! It is less clear whether James is making a distinction in meaning between these two Greek words (*makrothymein* and *hypomenein* and cognates) or whether they are virtually synonymous (see further the comments on v. 11). In the Septuagint, God is frequently characterized as "patient" (often translated "slow to anger"; Exod 34:6; Num 14:18; Ps 86:15; Joel 2:13; Jonah 4:2; Sir 18:11; Wisd of Sol 15:1). God is merciful, withholding judgment and endlessly forbearing, giving second and third and a hundred chances. The patience of God is not slowness or indifference, but a persistent, dynamic waiting that yearns for the salvation of all (Hos 11:8-9; 2 Pet 3:9, 15). This divine patience provides space for humans to bend toward God's purposes and offer grace to each other. Recipients of the extravagant patience of God must themselves be patient with fellow human beings (Matt 18:23-35). Thus, in many New Testament texts, patience is a virtue Christians are urged to embody (Gal 5:22; Col 3:12; 2 Tim 4:2; see TBC below). So here in 5:7-8 James urges the church to be patient.

But what are they supposed to be patient about? And why? Here the word "therefore" is important. Just prior to this, James warned the wealthy and unjust landowners that God has heard the cries of the poor and that the fortunes of both are about to turn (5:1-6). The word "therefore" indicates how they are to live in light of this reality. Precisely *because* God will deliver the poor, the church must wait patiently and live faithfully, even though the temptation might be to despair or to act inconsistently with what they believe (that is, be double minded). Some commentators see in this an implicit exhortation to Christians not to take vengeance but to wait for God to act (Blomberg and Kamell: 218; Davids 1982: 182; Martin: 187).

The fact that James urges them to *strengthen [their] hearts*, confirms that some might be growing faint of heart in this context of oppression. Elsewhere James refers to the *heart* negatively: it can be deceived (1:26), is full of selfish ambition (3:14), needs purifying (4:8), and is fattened by rich living (5:5). Now, the heart also needs encouragement. Although in Jewish literature the expression "strengthen the heart" can refer to taking physical nourishment, here it has to do with persevering in courage and faithfulness and not giving in to doubt or despair in time of crisis (cf. Ps 112:8 [LXX 111:8]; Sir 22:16; 1 Thess 3:13; 2 Thess 2:17). One way to strengthen their hearts is to ask God for wisdom from above, as James has encouraged them to do elsewhere (1:5; 3:17-18). In 5:7-8 the motivation for strengthening the heart and being patient is eschatological.

James admonishes the church to *be patient . . . until the coming of the Lord* (v. 7) and to *strengthen* their *hearts, for the coming of the Lord is near* (v. 8). James could be referring either to the Old Testament "day of the LORD," when God would come to judge and save; or to the return of Christ, since in the letter he has used "Lord" for both God (1:8; 5:4) and Jesus (1:1; 2:1). The coming of God as judge is a common theme in Jewish literature. In the Testaments of the Twelve Patriarchs, for example, "the coming of the Lord" is used three times to refer to God (Wall: 251; e.g., T. Sim. 6.5; T. Naph. 8.3).

In this case, however, James likely means the coming (*parousia*) of Christ in glory at the end of the age. The term *parousia* literally means "presence." It is used in Hellenistic literature to refer to the arrival of an important person, like a king, but it is not a term that the Septuagint uses for the coming of the Messiah or God. The overwhelming majority of references to the *parousia* in the New Testament are to the coming of Christ at the end of time, and the word became virtually a technical term for Christ's return in early Christian usage.

This then is the hope toward which James directs his readers in verses 7-8. Interestingly, the return of the Lord is not what they are supposed to wait for patiently, as one might expect, but the *motivation* for how they live meanwhile. They are to live, speak, and act with patience in the face of trials and sufferings *until* (v. 7) and *because* (v. 8 NIV) Jesus' coming is *near*. It is both temporally near in that it could happen at any time, like the *rains* (v. 7), and spatially near, like someone *standing at the doors* (v. 9). It is like the reign of God, which the synoptic gospels also repeatedly say is "near" or "at hand" (using the same Greek word, *ēngiken*; Matt 3:2; 4:17; Mark 1:15; Luke 10:9-10).

As an example, James holds up the farmer who waits patiently for the earth to produce its *precious crop*. The word *precious* typically describes jewels and crowns, not ordinary crops (1 Cor 3:12; Rev 17:4). But for the small-scale subsistence farmer whose family's livelihood and well-being depend on what the earth produces each year, this fruit is indeed precious. In Palestine the much-needed rain fell in mid-October to November and then in again in March and April (Blomberg and Kamell: 227). This familiar feature of eastern Mediterranean geography and the image of the farmer eagerly awaiting the rains would have resonated with James's readers. Although the use of this example suggests to some interpreters that James was writing in or for a rural Palestinian context, the power of the imagery does not depend on this. James may have drawn the phrase "early and late rains" from Scripture (Deut 11:14; Jer 5:24; Hos 6:3; Joel 2:23; Zech 10:1), which highlights God as the one who gives rain and calls to mind God's faithfulness.

The example is an apt one for James's readers, whose faith is being tested both by external pressures and internal conflicts. The patience they must nurture while they wait for the coming of their Lord as they anticipate receiving *the crown of life* (1:12) and inheriting *the kingdom* (2:5) is not a passive waiting but an active "urgent patience," as Paul Doerksen calls it in an essay. Farmers cannot control when the rains come nor can they force the grain to grow or the olive trees to bear fruit. What they can and must do is create the best conditions for growth, tending to the soil and the seed as best they can (Tamez 2002: 45).

Like these farmers, James's readers must live faithfully, hopefully, and with patience, not giving in to despair or apathy, envy or violence, but trusting that one day God will use their labors to bring the world back to what God has always intended it to be. Unlike the rains, which may sometimes fail, the coming of the Lord is a reliable basis for trust and patience.

Speaking Faithfully without Complaining about Others 5:9

Before returning explicitly to the theme of patience in verses 10-11, James admonishes his readers to stop grumbling against each other. At first blush, this subunit seems unrelated to the material that frames it (see Dibelius: 244). Although James does often hop from one topic to another, the charge of incoherence here is unwarranted. In verse 9 James returns to subjects that he has already raised repeatedly: right speech (1:26; 2:12; 3:1-12; 4:11-12; 5:12) and judgment (2:4, 12-13; 4:11-12; 5:12). In wording, sentence structure, and content, this verse most closely resembles 4:11; both warn believers not to speak negatively about each other:

> *Do not speak against each other, brothers and sisters.* (4:11 AT)
> *Do not grumble against each other, brothers and sisters.* (5:9 AT)

But does 5:9 have any connection to the immediately preceding verses? After chastising the rich landowners and urging his readers to stand firm until the Lord returns, James here spells out a concrete implication of what such active patience means: not grumbling against each other. In the Septuagint this verb is used frequently in contexts of groaning or complaining to God in painful, oppressive circumstances (Exod 2:23-24; Job 30:25; Isa 59:10-11; Lam 1:22; 1 Macc 1:26).

In this case, James says to refrain from grumbling *against each other*, not against the rich oppressors or against God. His admonition recognizes that under duress even believers may become short with each other, blame each other, or get angry. To malign another unjustly is to pass judgment in a manner unworthy of followers of Christ. James has warned them earlier about the dangers of judging others (2:4; 4:11-12). Practicing active patience and strengthening their hearts, therefore, has concrete implications for their life together. The object of their patience is not primarily the intangible future return of Christ but the very real brother or sister in their midst, someone who in times of stress might try their patience sorely. To practice forbearance while waiting means not to blame or grumble against such fellow believers. It is yet one more example of faithful and right speech.

Verse 9 is also linked with verses 7-8 by its eschatological outlook. In verses 7-8 the coming of the Lord was positive motivation for steadfast patience; now in verse 9 the impending judgment acts as a deterrent against disparaging speech. The two attitudes, with their accompanying behaviors, are mirror opposites. It is unclear whether the judge standing at the door is God or Jesus. Since the context references the *parousia* (coming, vv. 7-8), it is reasonable to consider Jesus as the judge (so Davids 1982: 185; Martin: 192; McCartney 2009: 242). However, the close association of 5:9 with 4:12 (*There is one lawgiver and judge*) could mean that *Judge* in 5:9 refers to God (see Laws: 213; Hartin 2009a: 242).

Perhaps James does not closely distinguish between God or Jesus as judge since elsewhere in the New Testament, Jesus is the agent through whom God will judge the world at the end of the age (cf. John 5:22, 27; 8:16; Acts 10:42; 17:31; Rom 2:16). More significant is the fact that the Judge is standing *at the doors!* This imagery (also in Mark 13:29) is not primarily about Jesus being spatially near to believers (see Witherington 2007: 537) but refers to the fact that the Lord could return at any time. In that sense, the final clause of verse 9 is parallel to the final clause in verse 8: *The coming of the Lord is near//the Judge is standing at the doors!* Eschatology has implications for ethics: they are to be patient and not tear others down with negative speech, since Jesus will return soon to judge and to save.

Living Patiently While Enduring Suffering 5:10-11

In this subunit James again addresses his readers as *brothers and sisters* and returns to the topic of patience. In verse 11 the word he uses is *endurance* (*hypomonē*) or *to endure*. Although close in meaning to *patience* (*makrothymia*, vv. 7-10), these words have a slightly different nuance in Scripture. In the Septuagint *hypomenō* is often used in contexts of human response to adversity. Those who are oppressed "wait for the LORD" (Ps 25:3 [24:3 LXX]; Isa 40:31) and "hope" in God (e.g., Ps 39:7 [38:8 LXX]; Jer 14:8). In the book of Job, especially, it refers to enduring suffering (e.g., Job 6:11; 14:14, 19). This is the connotation in many New Testament texts as well (Matt 10:22; Mark 13:13; Rom 12:12; 2 Tim 2:12; Heb 12:2-3; 1 Pet 2:20) and is how James uses the word. Whereas *makrothymia* refers to forbearance in contexts of complaint or judgment, *hypomonē* is about being steadfast and persevering through hardship. Elsa Tamez argues that the latter "is a militant patience that arises from the roots of oppression" (Tamez 2002: 44).

In verses 7-8 James used an ordinary Palestinian farmer as an example of patience. Now he draws on Scripture for models he wants the church to emulate. One of them is general (*the prophets*, v. 10), the other specific (*Job*, v. 11), but both are examples of people who faced crises in their walk with God. The words *suffering and patience* (v. 10) are a hendiadys: the second word is really a modifier of the first. Thus the call is not to emulate suffering but to have patience in suffering. James reminds his readers that the prophets *spoke in the name of the Lord* and thereby draws on a rich theological heritage of people who endured suffering because of their faithfulness to God. Like the farmer with active patience, the prophets did not merely grit their teeth while passively waiting for God to act but persisted in confronting injustice and idolatry. Jeremiah continued to speak God's word despite persecution. Daniel remained faithful under pressure to conform, and the Maccabean martyrs refused to compromise (cf. 4 Macc 9:8; 17:23, where the vocabulary resembles James 5:10).

Ordinarily, people who endure suffering are not deemed fortunate, at least not by those who treasure *friendship with the world* (4:4). James, however, claims that those who endure are *blessed*, reiterating his earlier reassurance that any who endure testing or temptation are "blessed" (1:12; 5:11). Such blessing does not necessarily equate with happiness or good fortune but refers to being deeply favored by God. They are blessed because they will receive the crown of life that the Lord has promised to those who love him. The idea that suffering is the mark of a true prophet and that endurance brings divine blessing is not unique to James in the New Testament (Matt 5:12; 23:34-37; Luke 6:22-23; 11:49-52; 13:33; 24:25-26; Acts 7:52; Phil 3:10; Col 1:24; Heb 11:32-38). In these verses James invites his readers to place themselves within a theological tradition and face their own trials and hardships with patience and endurance, as their forebears did.

The second example of patient endurance is Job (James 5:11). This is the only reference to Job in the New Testament, although 1 Corinthians 3:19 quotes Job 5:13 and Romans 11:34-35 likely alludes to Job 35:7. The "patience of Job" has become a proverbial expression, but careful readers might remember that, in the Old Testament, Job is portrayed as anything but patient. Job challenges God and complains bitterly about his undeserved sufferings (7:11-16; 10:18; 23:2; 30:20-23). The idea of Job as a model of patient endurance may derive loosely from noncanonical traditions about Job. In the intertestamental Testament of Job, Job's wife complains vigorously (chaps. 7 and 9), but Job himself is a model of steadfastness, worthy of God's praise. Yet even the canonical Job never lets go of God, despite crying out to God and even challenging God. Rather, "he kept clinging tightly and unyieldingly to God as the context of his life, which is the very reason he felt such a cognitive dissonance" (McCartney 2009: 243).

James calls his readers to hear and to see (v. 11) as they consider that God blesses those who endure. The clauses *You have heard of the endurance of Job* and *You have seen the purpose [telos] of the Lord* (AT) are parallel, but the exact meaning of the second clause is ambiguous, as the diversity of translations and interpretations reveals. "The Lord" could refer either to Jesus (as in 5:7) or to God (as in 5:10). The word *telos* can mean the end of a process, the purpose of something, or the outcome (BDAG: 998). The clause *telos of the Lord* could thus refer to

a. the end of Jesus' life;
b. the return of Christ at the end;
c. God's purpose in allowing Job to suffer; or
d. the outcome of Job's story: his restoration by God.

The first two options are unlikely because "Lord" probably refers to God here (as in v. 10) and a sudden reference to Jesus' death would be unexpected. Options (c) and (d) are both possible and equally favored by interpreters. For example, Davids says, "The sense of the phrase is not that of teleological end, i.e., God's purpose, . . . but the result God brought about as known from the story of Job, i.e., blessing" (1982: 188). The NRSVue favors *the outcome that the Lord brought about*, as does Dan McCartney, who believes the reference to God's mercy and compassion seems to point to the end of Job's story (2009: 244). Alternatively, Martin (195) and Blomberg and Kamell (230) favor the interpretation that God had a reason for allowing Job to suffer, which would encourage Christians facing adversity.

Perhaps such a distinction is unnecessary since the difference between purpose and outcome is less significant when one considers the actions and intentions of God (to the extent that they are discernible). God's purpose is to bless and give life, and what God purposes, God also brings to fruition. This is so because God is faithful, abundantly *compassionate, and merciful* (v. 11d). Blessing is the purpose and outcome of God's actions toward those who endure; that is true not only for Job but also for James's readers. When we recall James's words in 1:12, the logic of 5:11 becomes apparent: Those who endure are *blessed* (5:11a) because they will receive *the crown of life* promised them by God (1:12). Since Job endured, Job is blessed (5:11b) and will receive *the crown of life.* In Job, therefore, the purposes of the *compassionate and merciful Lord* are made manifest.

Job was not blessed because he suffered, as if suffering is inherently redemptive. Job remained stubbornly faithful throughout his time of testing and was blessed because God is extravagantly *compassionate and merciful* and because God's purposes for life and love, truth and goodness, will ultimately prevail. This is James's message for his church. The patient endurance to which he summons his readers is grounded in the compassion and mercy of God. The church that experiences trials and hardships can look to Job and the prophets for encouragement and as models for their own practice of patience, confident that endurance will result in blessing and that God's purposes will ultimately be realized.

Speaking Faithfully and Truthfully without Oaths 5:12

The relationship of 5:12 to what comes before and after is ambiguous enough that commentators tend to either take it as an isolated admonition, a "stray logion" (Dibelius: 248), or as a bridge between 5:7-11 and 5:13-20 (e.g., McCartney 2009: 245; Moore-Keish: 182). To be sure, the verse does function as a suitable segue into the final section of the letter. Verses 13-20 are about using speech positively in the context of community worship (prayer, confession, admonition), and verse 12 leads into that with an admonition about speaking truthfully. However, as argued above, there are good reasons for taking verse 12 as the fourth part of an *A B A′ B′* pattern in 5:7-12, where James addresses the readers as brothers and sisters (as also in 5:7, 9, 10), and the form and content are similar to verse 9.

Part of what makes the relationship of verse 12 to its context unclear is the puzzling introductory phrase *above all*. In relation to what is this prohibition of oaths *above all*? Is it the most important of the admonitions in verses 7-12? The climax of all the teachings in the letter? If so, why is it preeminent? Or is it meant to direct our gaze ahead? In other Hellenistic literature *pro pantōn* (above all) can function as an "epistolary convention to signal a final series of remarks" (Johnson 1995: 325–26).

In this vein, some interpreters have understood it not as "most important of all" but as a structural marker "that the letter is drawing to a close" (Hartin 2009a: 246; cf. Davids 1982: 189). This would be similar to Paul's use of "finally" at the end of a letter (Vlachos: 178). However, in 1 Peter 4:8 the phrase "above all" does not signal the end of the letter and arguably *does* introduce something important above all else: love.

It is unlikely that James thinks swearing oaths is worse than complaining about fellow believers (v. 9) or any other sin he has addressed. "It is better to see *above all* simply as drawing particular attention to this exhortation (cf. 1 Pet. 4:8)" (Moo: 219). The teaching about oaths is one final admonition in a letter full of exhortations about how to speak with integrity, honesty, and kindness. It is also possible to see this prohibition as closely related to the subject of verses 7-11, but before exploring that connection, we must consider James's concern in verse 12.

The first half of the verse says what the audience should *not* do (swear oaths), and the second half what each believer *should* do (mean what you say). Here James is not talking about profanity but about swearing oaths to buttress the truthfulness of a statement or promise. In the ancient world, people invoked the name of God or substitutes (such as heaven or earth) as a guarantor that their words were true (e.g., Gen 24:2-3; cf. Heb 6:16). Failure to fulfill the oath would result in divine sanctions, it was believed.

The Old Testament is concerned about how oaths are sworn and especially that oaths be kept (e.g., Exod 22:10-11; Num 30:2-3), but it does not prohibit them absolutely. Even God is said to swear oaths (Exod 13:5; Deut 7:8; Isa 45:23). Leviticus 19:12 warns against swearing falsely and thereby profaning the name of God, one of several connections between James and Leviticus 19 (Johnson 1982: 397–98). The prophets also warn against false swearing of oaths (e.g., Jer 5:2; 7:9; Zech 5:3-4; Mal 3:5).

Numerous other texts in both Jewish and non-Jewish literature strongly discourage oath-taking, although they do not seem to forbid that entirely (Allison 2013: 731–33). Thus Ben Sirach advises, "Do not accustom your mouth to oaths" in a longer passage about sins of speech (23:9-11). Philo says, "To swear not at all is the best course and most profitable to life" (*On the Decalogue* 84). And Epictetus advises, "Avoid taking oaths, if possible, altogether" (*Enchiridion* 33.5; cited in Allison 2013: 732). In the New Testament, Paul calls on God as his witness, demonstrating that oaths continued to be used (e.g., Rom 1:9; 2 Cor 1:23; Gal 1:20).

Strikingly, James makes a categorical prohibition of oaths, much like Jesus' teaching in the Sermon on the Mount (Matt 5:34-37). Although Matthew's version is longer, in their repetition of *No, no* and *Yes, yes*, the two versions are virtually identical. Of all the material in James that echoes Jesus' teachings, this is the closest. Likely James had access to a pre-Matthean version of Jesus' words or perhaps received them through oral tradition *[James and the Jesus Tradition, p. 353]*.

Many interpreters argue that both Jesus and James were prohibiting only casual use of oaths in everyday speech, not the use of oaths in juridical contexts or legal transactions (McCartney 2009: 248; Blomberg and Kamell: 236). They say that oaths were part of James's Jewish heritage, and his concern is only "the trivialization of the oath" (Hartin 2009a: 262). This seems to miss the point of the prohibition, however. The second half of the verse suggests that James, like Jesus, is urging believers, in every circumstance, to be truthful, to say what they mean and mean what they say. The use of an oath seems to imply that all other speech is not necessarily truthful or that one is only committed to truth when swearing the oath.

Nothing in verse 12 or its context suggests that avoiding oaths applies in some situations but not others, that in formal legal contexts it is necessary to invoke God as guarantor of one's speech, but in casual contexts truthfulness should be assumed. Perhaps interpreters' attempts to qualify the plain sense of the text stems from a desire to harmonize it with others in which oaths are exhibited or permitted. James's (and Jesus') approach to truth telling is truly countercultural and "reminds us that oath-taking is for those with a credibility gap that no Christian should have" (Witherington 2007: 541).

Verse 12 also has a closer connection to the previous verses than is sometimes thought. In 5:7-11 James urges his readers to be steadfast and patient with each other as they endure affliction and wait for the coming of the Lord. Oaths can imply impatience and lack of trust, a desire to take control and hurry things along when life is uncertain or difficult. McCartney suggests that James could have used the negative example of Jephthah to make his point (Judg 11). When Israel was oppressed by the Ammonites, Jephthah "did not wait patiently for the Lord to deliver them, . . . but instead he rashly swore an oath as a bargaining chip with God (and paid dearly for it)" (2009: 247).

James's emphasis on truth telling resonates with his call elsewhere not to be *double-minded* (1:8; 4:8) and to embody divine wisdom that does not *lie about the truth* (3:14). Perhaps James says *above all* because truthful speech must surely be the basis for all interaction in the church, including mutual admonition, encouragement, and confession (5:13-20). Being *slow to speak* and *slow to anger* (1:19), *bridl[ing]* the *tongue* (1:26; 3:2-12), not *boasting* (3:14 NRSV; 4:16), and not *speaking evil* or *grumbling* against others (paraphrased: 4:11; 5:9) are all related to speaking truthfully with one another. In short, "people of faith have no need of oaths, either to give their words weight or to prompt a solution to suffering; they wait patiently and prayerfully for the Lord and always keep their promises, cognizant that God always keeps his" (McCartney 2009: 247).

THE TEXT IN BIBLICAL CONTEXT

Patient Endurance

The idea that enduring hardship is part of living faithfully as God's people is present throughout the Bible. Prophets like Elijah and Jeremiah suffered immensely for proclaiming unpopular messages from the Lord but did not give up (1 Kings 19:1-18; Jer 11:18-23; 20:7-18). The theme of steadfastness through undeserved suffering is strong in Second Temple Judaism. In 4 Maccabees the Jewish martyrs are models of righteous piety that perseveres even to death. Despite his complaints, Job exemplifies the righteous sufferer who remains faithful to the end. It is not surprising that James cites both the prophets and Job as examples of endurance.

Patient endurance in the biblical tradition is not the capacity to refrain from complaint, but rather the commitment to remain in relationship with God while voicing complaints. Job's faith is celebrated partly because of his complaints or his laments. Jeremiah, the lament psalmists, Habakkuk, Moses, and the believers in Revelation 6:10 all demonstrated their faith through their complaints and laments.

In the New Testament, followers of Jesus must cultivate virtues of endurance and patience in an often-hostile world. Jesus teaches his disciples that they will encounter rejection and even persecution as they carry on his mission (Matt 10:16-33; Luke 10:1-16; John 17:14-18). Yet Jesus blesses the persecuted, promising them the kingdom (Matt 5:12; Luke 6:23), and says that "one who endures to the end will be saved" (Matt 10:22//Mark 13:13; cf. Luke 21:18-19). In Acts, believers like Paul "stand before governors and kings" to bear "testimony" (Mark 13:9; Acts 23:11). Even when imprisoned and persecuted, the Holy Spirit protects and empowers them (e.g., Acts 1:8; 12:1-5; 16:19-24).

The letters of Paul include endurance and patience in lists of Christian virtues (2 Cor 6:4-6; Col 3:12; 1 Thess 5:14; 1 Tim 6:11). Like James, Paul recognizes that suffering can produce endurance, which in turn strengthens character (Rom 5:3-4). Paul himself endured great hardship for the sake of Christ (2 Cor 1:6; 6:4) and encourages his readers to remain steadfast in affliction (Rom 12:12; 2 Thess 1:4). For suffering Christians, such as the recipients of 1 Peter and Hebrews, Jesus Christ becomes a model to emulate, since he too remained faithful while suffering unjustly (Heb 12:2-3; 1 Pet 2:19-21; 4:12-16). Finally, the theme of faithfulness and patient endurance through suffering pervades Revelation, whose first readers experienced the brunt of the Roman Empire's economic, religious, and political power when these believers refused to compromise their allegiance to Christ as Lord (2:2-3, 19; 3:10; 13:10; 14:12).

In the New Testament, the Christian's endurance of suffering is not merely a product of personal inner strength. Rather, patient endurance comes from God (Rom 15:5) and rests in an unwavering hope that God will ultimately deliver the one who trusts in the Lord and remains faithful. At the same time, such endurance is not passive but also works actively to resist injustice, even loving the enemy. Just as believers are to persevere in the face of trials, so also they are to be patient with each other. God is long-suffering, merciful, and patient, giving all the opportunity to repent (Exod 34:6; Ps 86:15; Neh 9:17; Joel 2:13; Rom 2:4; 9:22; 2 Pet 3:14-15). Because they have been the beneficiaries of God's extravagant patience, Christians also are called to embody forbearance with others (Matt 18:23-35). Patience is a fruit of the Spirit (Gal 5:22) and a mark of Christian love (1 Cor 13:4).

In a society where fast food, instant messages, and "quick fixes" simply add fuel to the fire of our impatience, and in a society where people go to great lengths to avoid suffering, the New Testament's exhortations to patience and endurance even in the face of adversity sound radical. For Christians, however, patience is a way of being in the world, which is ultimately grounded in the mercy and patience that God has shown them in Christ.

Awaiting the Return of Christ

Although James says nothing about Jesus' life, death, or resurrection, he does have a robust expectation in the future return of Christ (5:7-9). This eschatology undergirds the letter's ethical teachings and encouragement of those who suffer. It is expressed both as promises of future blessing (1:12; 2:5) and as warnings about judgment (2:12; 3:1; 5:1-3).

This thoroughgoing hope for the future aligns James with the rest of the New Testament. Although they do not speak with a uniform voice, virtually every book anticipates the future consummation of God's redemptive work. Because the New Testament writings are contingent, written in varied contexts for different purposes and needs, they speak about eschatology in diverse ways. In 1 Thessalonians, Paul addresses the church's worry about believers who die before Christ returns. In 1 Corinthians 15, he emphasizes the bodily resurrection to counter the heightened "spirituality" of some believers. Other writings reassure persecuted readers of the certainty of God's final victory (1 Peter; Revelation). Despite their varied contexts and emphases, the New Testament writings all look forward to the full realization of God's purposes.

To be sure, the salvation of God can already be experienced in the present, at least in part. In word and deed, Jesus proclaimed that the reign of God was already breaking in (Matt 4:17; Luke 11:20; 17:20-21). In the Gospel of John, eternal life begins now, for anyone who believes in the Son has already "passed from death to life" (5:24). Paul speaks of "the ends of the ages" meeting in Jesus Christ (1 Cor 10:11), such that the "new creation" is already a present reality (2 Cor 5:17). Empowered by the Holy Spirit, those who are "in Christ" can already walk in newness of life (Rom 6:4; 8:1, 9-11; 2 Cor 5:17; Eph 4:15-16; Col 3:1-4). Then in its life together, the church can be a sign of what it means to live in God's reign.

Yet the New Testament also acknowledges the sober reality that all is not as it should be; God's reign is not yet here in full. Jesus taught his disciples to pray, "Your kingdom come" (Matt 6:10). Paul says that the whole creation groans in labor pains, "wait[ing] with eager longing" for its redemption (Rom 8:19-23). The writer of 2 Peter assures his discouraged readers that the Lord is "not slow" but "patient" with all and that "in accordance with his promise, we wait for new heavens and a new earth where righteousness is at home" (3:9, 13). That future time when God will make all things new is spoken of in various ways, such as the kingdom of God (Matt 25:34; Luke 21:31; 1 Cor 15:50), "the end of the age(s)" (Matt 13:39-40, 49; 24:3), "the last day(s)" (John 11:24; 12:48), and "the day of the Lord/Christ" (1 Cor 1:8; 2 Cor 1:14; Phil 1:10).

What will happen on that final day? Again, the New Testament writings highlight different aspects, depending on the context, and often use picture language for what can never be fully known. We can only note a few facets of New Testament eschatology here.

First, the future hope rests on the return of Christ, that is, the *parousia* (1 Thess 3:13; 4:15; 2 Thess 2:1; James 5:7-8; 2 Pet 1:16). In the eschatological discourses of the synoptic gospels, Jesus looks ahead to the destruction of Jerusalem, yet also beyond that to the coming of the Son of Man on the last day (Matt 24:27, 36-44; Mark 13:24-27; Luke 21:15-28). Some of the epistles speak of Christ's return as the "reveal[ing]" (1 Cor 1:7) or "manifestation" of Christ (Col 3:4; 1 Tim 6:14). Whatever the language, the culmination of God's promises will begin with the return of Jesus Christ in glory at the end of this age.

Second, the future will bring judgment on those who insist on loving the darkness more than the light, those who refuse the invitation to the Lord's banquet. Revelation is most strident in its claims that God will ultimately be victorious, destroying evil and bringing all oppressive, anti-God forces to justice. Some of Jesus' kingdom parables in the Gospels paint pictures of this day of "sorting" the righteous from the unrighteous (Matt 13; 25:31-46; Luke 13:22-30). Paul also speaks about God's future judgment on evildoers (Rom 2:5-6; 2 Cor 5:10; 2 Thess 1:5-10).

Third, the return of Christ in glory will be accompanied by the resurrection of the dead. Because Christ was raised from the dead, all who are "in Christ" will also be raised to eternal life (John 6:39-54; 1 Cor 15:12-28; 2 Cor 4:14). This is not merely an escape of the soul from this earthly "vale of tears" into a disembodied heavenly existence, but involves "the redemption of our bodies" (Rom 8:23). Christ is the first fruits of all those who will be raised to life with a new kind of body (1 Cor 15:35-56). This vibrant hope in the future resurrection motivates and sustains Paul when he is in prison (Phil 3:10-11); it is the source of hope for the readers of 1 Peter in their suffering for Christ (1:3-7). On that day, not only human bodies but also the earth's body will be restored (Rom 8:18-21).

In this future reign of God, people will gather from east and west and north and south to feast at God's rich banquet table (Luke 13:29). The New Testament ends with a glorious vision of a new heaven and a new earth in which the new Jerusalem descends to earth and God comes to dwell among mortals. In this new creation will be no death nor mourning, and no sun or moon will be needed since the glory of God and the Lamb will be its light (paraphrase of Rev 21:1-4, 22).

Fourth, while the New Testament does sometimes speak about signs of the end, it consistently says we cannot know exactly when that end will come (e.g., Matt 24:36//Mark 13:32). Some of its writers expect Christ to return soon (Rom 13:12; 1 Cor 7:29; 1 Pet 4:7; Heb 10:37; Rev 22:20). Others contend with the reality that Christ may not return for some time yet. Even so, they maintain a fervent expectation that Christ *will* return someday to bring God's good work to completion (Luke 19:11-27; 2 Pet 3:3-10).

Finally, much more important than the question of timing is how to live in the meantime. Many of Jesus' parables urge disciples to remain alert and faithful while they await the coming of the Son of Man (Matt 24:42-51; 25:1-30; Luke 18:1-8; 21:9-19, 34-36). In the Gospel of John, Jesus prepares his disciples for his absence not only by reassuring them of his return (14:3), but even more by urging them to love each other, keep his commandments, and witness to a world that will hate them (chaps. 14–17).

Although many of Paul's letters have a robust eschatological hope, nowhere does he expect Christians simply to sit and wait. Rather, they are to "walk in newness of life" (Rom 6:4), "live by the

Spirit" (Gal 5:16-26) "in a manner worthy of the gospel of Christ" (Phil 1:27), and "do everything in the name of the Lord Jesus" (Col 3:17). Even in 1 Thessalonians, which envisions Christ's return as imminent, Paul urges believers to "keep awake and be sober" and live as "children of light" (5:4-22). First Peter not only encourages persecuted Christians to remember their inheritance in heaven (1:3-4) but also to remain steadfast in suffering, do good, and give an account for their hope (2:12; 3:14-17; 4:1-11). The writer of Hebrews urges his readers to "run with perseverance the race . . . set before [them]" (12:1) even as they await their "Sabbath rest" (4:9-10).

In every New Testament writing, eschatology and ethics walk hand in hand. Having a vibrant hope in the return of Christ, the resurrection of the dead, and the final renewal of all creation energizes living already now as redeemed and recreated followers of Jesus, loving and serving each other, showing mercy and hospitality, bearing witness, and exhibiting the fruits of a Spirit-driven life.

THE TEXT IN THE LIFE OF THE CHURCH

Swearing Oaths and Speaking Truthfully

An oath is a declaration that one's words are trustworthy, with the invocation of God or a sacred object as guarantor. Failure to keep the oath invites judgment upon the speaker. Although oaths have been sworn throughout history, the prohibition of oaths in Matthew 5:33-36 and James 5:12 has resulted in differing interpretations about the appropriateness of Christians taking oaths.

Early church fathers such as Origen, Tertullian, and Chrysostom unequivocally rejected swearing oaths for the simple reason that Jesus prohibited it. Because they refused to swear allegiance to the state, Christians were persecuted. This all changed when Christianity became the official religion of the empire. As a servant of the state, the church willingly complied with the state's demand for oaths. Augustine provided theological support for oaths, and numerous councils and popes after him understood the swearing of oaths to be divine law. Although some medieval sects (e.g., Waldensians and Hussites) rejected the use of oaths, the sixteenth-century Reformers generally continued to support the practice. Luther's Large Catechism (1529) and the Heidelberg Catechism (1563), a Reformed statement, both view oaths positively as upholding truth, peace, and the well-being of the neighbor.

Against this dominant Christian consensus, the Anabaptists struck a discordant note in their adamant refusal to take oaths.

This is articulated clearly in the Schleitheim Confession of 1527, which states: "Christ, who teaches the perfection of the law, forbids his [followers] all swearing." The Confession counters possible objections to this position and gives a rationale. To be sure, the Anabaptists were not uniform in their opposition to oaths. Balthasar Hubmaier, for example, did not oppose the oath because it belonged to the realm of governing authorities ordained by God. Hans Hut supported oaths as long as they did not make demands against God. And Pilgram Marpeck seems to have sworn civic oaths at times while at other times he refused. But for many Anabaptists, Jesus' command was clear: anything more than "yes" or "no" was from the evil one.

Even Anabaptists who agreed that Christians should not swear oaths articulated the rationale differently. For example, Hans Denck was more concerned about the spirit of Scripture and took a less literalistic approach than the Schleitheim Confession. Some writings differentiate between calling on God as witness and swearing an oath that promises something for the future. Denck allowed the former but not the latter. Menno Simons did not address the matter of oaths until late in his career. His rationale is thoroughly Christocentric: Although the Jewish law permitted swearing of oaths, Jesus supersedes the law. Because Jesus commanded his followers not to swear oaths but to speak truthfully, a Christian's affirmation should be as binding as an oath (*CWMS*: 517–21, 922–27). The prohibition of oaths remained a consistent part of all Mennonite confessions of faith in the centuries to follow (e.g., the Dordrecht Confession of 1632 and the Cornelis Ris Confession of 1766) and continues in the present (e.g., *Confession of Faith in a Mennonite Perspective*, 1995).

Although the motivation for refusing to swear oaths was mostly a literalistic reading of Jesus' command and a dogged commitment to obedience, other factors also came into play. In the sixteenth-century political context, the refusal to swear oaths had dire socio-political implications. Oaths were an instrument of powerful governments and wealthy overlords, who demanded ultimate allegiance from their subjects.

> For early modern Europeans, oaths defined and legitimated the relationships between governing authorities and their constituents or subjects, . . . and served as the glue that held both urban and rural socio-political structures in place. The existence of a community without an oath was unthinkable. Thus the refusal of the oath seemed like a repudiation of society. (Pries, as quoted in Snyder 1995: 267)

Thus, Anabaptists who steadfastly refused to swear oaths were considered rebellious and came into conflict with the government. They were expelled, denied civil and voting rights, and generally persecuted for their religious convictions.

Over the next few centuries, Anabaptists in Europe gradually acquired the privilege of substituting a simple affirmation for the oath. In the United States and Canada, Mennonite immigrants were allowed to "affirm" instead of "swear," on grounds of conscience (Neff, Bender, and Klassen: 5). The modern climate of religious tolerance in the West makes it relatively simple for not only Mennonites but also anyone to choose to "affirm" rather than to "swear" an oath in court.

The freedom not to swear oaths does not satisfactorily address the relevance of Matthew 5:33-36 and James 5:12 for Christians today, however. In modern secular society, calling on God as witness or swearing on the Bible has essentially become irrelevant and does not ensure that the swearer tells the truth. The oath is only a legal mechanism to allow for punishing perjury. Moreover, scrupulous refusal to swear oaths in a courtroom is meaningless if one fails to keep one's word elsewhere. The point of James's words is to speak truthfully and show integrity in word and deed, not only to refuse oaths.

Inflated words and empty promises are common in today's society. Because "talk is cheap," people want action, not words. Voters are cynical about politicians who liberally promise tax breaks and new programs before an election. Couples break their marriage vows, and friends equivocate instead of telling the truth. Advertisers make outlandish promises about a new product, and consumers remind themselves to "read the fine print," even as they open their wallets. James's exhortation urges believers today, as in the first century, to let their "yes" be a true "yes" and their "no" a sincere "no." Their speech should be simple, direct, and trustworthy. It should stand in radical contrast to the empty or inflated speech of much of North American society. The word of a Christian should be so trustworthy that it needs no oath to give it extra weight, whether in court or in day-to-day life.

Present-day Christians who stand in continuity with the Anabaptists would do well to reflect on the sociopolitical ramifications of not swearing oaths. In the sixteenth and seventeenth centuries, Anabaptists refused to swear oaths at least in part because they did not want to swear allegiance to any lord but Christ. Political parties, fraternities, clubs, and street gangs are only some examples of present-day groups that expect their members to swear allegiance, either explicitly or implicitly. Particularly in times of war, a nation will exert considerable pressure on its armed forces and citizens to profess loyalty to the state. Sometimes political leaders go so far as to elevate loyalty to themselves above doing what is right. History provides many examples of political leaders who attempted to elevate themselves by demanding political loyalty. Christians today might want to consider whether, through oaths or actions, their loyalty to earthly rulers, movements, or ideologies compromises their allegiance to Christ as Lord of all.

James 5:13-20

The Church as a Healing, Confessing, and Forgiving Community

PREVIEW

Beware the evils of speech, says James! Can any good come from the tongue? In this final unit we hear that, yes, speech has the positive potential to heal and restore. That the focus of this unit is prayer is evident from the number of times prayer is mentioned (three different words used, eight times altogether). Interwoven with this emphasis are themes of healing and confession of sin. All of this takes place within the *ekklēsia* (5:14), the community of faith.

Although much of the letter's teaching has individual application, here the emphasis is firmly on life in community. When one member is sick, the whole church prays. When an individual sins, the whole body needs healing. Prayer, healing, and confession are practices of the church that are grounded in mutuality and loving care for one another.

None of this is new subject matter in the letter. Although the word "prayer" does not appear before 5:13, James has mentioned asking God for things in 1:5-8 and 4:2-3. And James 5:4 assumes that God hears the cries of the oppressed. Enduring trials and suffering (1:2-4, 12; 5:10-11) surely encompasses sickness. The problem of sin is explicit in 1:14-16; 2:9-11; and 4:17 and implicit throughout the letter, although this is the first time James mentions mutual confession.

Prayer, healing, and confession of sin also relate to James's emphasis on integrity and wholeness. Healing restores a sick individual not only to physical wholeness but also to the community. Confession and forgiveness heal rifts in the community created by judging, complaining, and favoritism. James 5:13-20 also has obvious connections to 5:7-11 in its language of suffering and responding to hardship. Both also refer to speaking *in the name of the Lord* (5:10, 14), and both hold up an Old Testament character as a model to emulate (5:11, 17-18).

Verses 19-20 conclude not only this unit but also the entire letter. It is perhaps fitting that a letter so full of chastisement and rigorous admonition closes with words about restoration.

OUTLINE

Responding to the Ups and Downs of Life, 5:13-14
Communal Prayer and Confession, 5:15-16
Elijah, the Prayer Warrior, 5:17-18
Restoring a Believer Who Has Strayed, 5:19-20

EXPLANATORY NOTES

Responding to the Ups and Downs of Life 5:13-14

James 5:13-14 envisions a situation that could characterize any gathering of believers, whether in the first century or the twenty-first: some are burdened with life's difficulties, and some are upbeat. These verses consist of three parallel pairs of clauses. The first of each pair is often translated as a question: *Are any among you suffering?* (NRSVue, NIV, NLT, ESV), but could equally be a statement with an implied condition: *If any of you are suffering* (CEB). Rendering them as questions captures more vividly their rhetorical force and is consistent with the diatribe style James frequently uses. The second half of each pair specifies what the person must do in that situation: *pray*, *praise*, and *call for the elders* to *pray*. No matter what life brings, engaging the Divine is crucial.

James asks whether anyone is suffering in the churches to whom he writes. Given what the letter says elsewhere, some are experiencing oppression at the hands of the rich (2:5-6, 15; 5:4), while others are likely suffering from serious illness (5:14-15). Perhaps some are suffering because they are targets of slander, judgment, discrimination, grumbling, envy, anger, and other community sins (2:1-4; 3:9-10, 14; 4:1-2, 11-12; 5:9). Since the rich *blaspheme the . . . name* of the one to whom they belong (2:7), some could be suffering because they follow Jesus. The prophets too suffered because they spoke in the *name of the Lord* (5:10). James began the letter by encouraging his readers to consider trials as a path to endurance, maturity, and ultimately blessing (1:2-4, 12). Now at the end of the letter, he addresses how they experience such trials—as suffering. What is the appropriate response to such experiences? James's answer is prayer.

James also addresses the experience of those who are *cheerful* (5:13 NRSVue) or *happy* (NIV). It is difficult to know what James has in mind here. He could simply be naming the two extremes of misery and happiness to imply that the whole range of human experience can and should be brought before God (just as "young and old" can mean the whole spectrum of ages). On the other hand, James might have in mind something that better fits the immediate context.

The word for *cheerful* or *happy* (*euthymeō*) appears elsewhere in the New Testament only in Acts 27:22, 25, where it means "keep up courage" in the midst of danger. Here it is sandwiched between two words related to suffering and illness, suggesting that James could be speaking to Christians who remain positive and cheerful despite hardships. To them, James says, *Sing songs of praise*. This phrase translates a single verb (*psallō*), from which our word "psalm" comes. Although originally referring to music played on a stringed instrument, by the time of the New Testament it included vocal music (1 Cor 14:15; Eph 5:19). James encourages those who are of good cheer to sing praises to the One who sustains them in trouble and gives good gifts.

In verse 14 James becomes more specific about the nature of their suffering and anticipates (or knows) that some are seriously ill. The word he uses here (*astheneō*) simply means "weak" and could refer to mental, spiritual, or emotional affliction as well as physical. In the Gospels it tends to be used for physical illness (Luke 4:40; John 5:3). Paul uses it to refer to other weaknesses (Rom 14:1; 1 Cor 8:12). Given its immediate context, James is probably speaking about people who are physically unwell. That the illness is serious is suggested by the fact that the sick should ask the elders of the church to come and *pray over them*, perhaps because they are too sick to pray themselves, and anointing with oil is called for.

This is the first and only time in the letter that James uses the word *ekklēsia,* usually translated *church.* The word *ekklēsia* was not originally a religious term. It appears in Greek literature to refer to a political or social "assembly." In Greco-Roman cities, the assembly was similar to a city council in which elders met to discuss and manage the affairs of the *polis* (city). In the Septuagint, *ekklēsia* usually translates the Hebrew *qāhāl,* referring to the "assembly" of the people of God. In 2:2, James used the word "synagogue" for their physical meeting space, but in 5:14 he uses *ekklēsia* for the body of people who gather for worship and fellowship. They have a corporate identity as the renewed people of God, forged together by Jesus' name (2:7). This *ekklēsia* exists as a new sociopolitical reality, a countercultural alternative to the Greek *polis.*

The word *ekklēsia* is one of the most important words in the letter even though it is used only once. Although individuals sin against each other and individual bodies get sick, these are not individual problems. These issues belong to the whole church. The corporate body engages in prayer and confession and receives gifts of healing, forgiveness, and salvation. Lutheran scholar Frederick Gaiser tells the story of how once, while visiting his dangerously ill daughter in the hospital, a nurse shooed him out, saying, "She needs to learn to get well on her own." Both he and other nurses were appalled. As Gaiser says, "No one can be well on their own" (Gaiser 2015: 245). Indeed, the *ekklēsia* that gathers around Jesus Messiah consists of brothers and sisters who need each other and help each other to do and be what they cannot be on their own. Therefore, James instructs the sick to call on the church elders.

Who are these *elders of the church*? Like *ekklēsia,* "elder" (*presbyteros*) is not a uniquely Christian word and did not originally refer to a specific office in the church. Greco-Roman cities and towns had "elders" who functioned as local leaders. In the Gospels and Acts, the Jewish elders are important community leaders and often members of the Jewish council (Matt 21:23; Mark 15:1; Acts 4:5). It is not surprising, then, that Christian assemblies also had elders. Some of the later letters of the New Testament speak of elders as having designated leadership roles in the church (1 Tim 5:17-19; Titus 1:5; 1 Pet 5:1-5). There is no evidence that James had such an office in mind. Although he refers to teachers in 3:1, there are no references to bishops, deacons, or other official positions. If James is dated early, the church would likely not yet have formal structures in place, as it did later. As Scot McKnight concludes, "The balance of evidence favors an informal term designating the senior males in a community to whom honor and respect were given because of wisdom and prestige" (437).

James enjoins the sick to call on elders, the respected leaders of the Christian communities. Presumably the elders are to pray for healing, though prayers for courage, comfort, and peace amid suffering cannot be excluded. There is nothing to indicate that the elders have special gifts of healing. Rather, they are *brothers and sisters* who act on behalf of the entire church family to support and intercede for the weak and ill in their midst. They are like the friends who brought a paralyzed man to Jesus for healing (Mark 2:1-12). When Jesus observes "their faith," not the man's own faith, he declares the latter's sins forgiven and physically heals him (2:5, 11). In Paul's reflections on the body in 1 Corinthians 12, he reminds the church that when "one member suffers, all suffer together" (12:26). So also the church in James 5:13-14 is a mutually dependent body, which holds its sick members up to God in prayer.

James recommends that the elders *anoint [the sick] with oil in the name of the Lord.* The Roman Catholic sacrament of "extreme unction," anointing people on their deathbed, developed from this verse. Today many denominations practice anointing of the sick in services for healing and wholeness (see TLC below). It is unclear precisely why the sick were to be anointed with oil. Was it primarily medicinal, to promote physical healing? Or was its significance more symbolic and ritual? Or both?

On the one hand, there is evidence that olive oil was used for healing purposes in the ancient world. Isaiah 1:6 refers to wounds being softened with oil. Josephus recounts how Herod was put in a bath of oil when he was ill (*Jewish War* 1:657–58). Celsus recommended rubbing oil on people with fevers or stomach problems (*De medicina* 2.14; 3.6). In the Gospels, oil is used for healing of diseases and wounds (Mark 6:13; Luke 10:34).

On the other hand, the immediate context of James suggests that anointing the sick with oil had more of a ritual significance: It accompanies prayer and is done *in the name of the Lord.* Elsewhere in the New Testament, when this Greek word for "anointing" (*aleiphō*) is used, it is almost always in the context of rituals, for example, during fasting (Matt 6:17), when anointing a dead body (Mark 16:1), to show hospitality (Luke 7:46), and when expressing devotion (Luke 7:38; John 12:3).

Anointing in James 5:14 may thus be primarily symbolic rather than medicinal. It may have been a tangible representation of the community upholding the sick person in prayer and a sign of God's power to heal, mediating comfort and peace. Perhaps neither James nor his churches had a tidy theory about how anointing and prayer promoted healing. As W. F. Brosend said, "Asking if the anointing with oil was intended medicinally, pastorally, symbolically, or sacramentally is to begin in the wrong place, assuming distinctions simply not present in the ancient Mediterranean world" (quoted in Allison 2013: 759, n. 105). In any case, the source of the healing was always God, who worked through the prayers of the people and the anointing ritual to bring physical and spiritual relief to those who suffered.

James says that the sick should be anointed with oil *in the name of the Lord*. This does not mean that *the name* itself was infused with magical power. Rather, the name represented the person. To do something "in the name of" the Lord was to call on the power and the authority of the Lord. Interpreters disagree whether *Lord* here is a reference to God or to Jesus, since *kyrios* (Lord) is used for both in the letter (God in 4:10; 5:10-11; Jesus in 1:1; 2:1; 5:7-8). Also, *the excellent name* (2:7) is most likely that of Jesus, and in 5:10 *the name* refers to God. The manuscript tradition also reflects this ambiguity: one important codex omits *of the Lord* altogether, and some later manuscripts insert *Jesus*, presumably for clarification. Elsewhere in the New Testament, the disciples heal and cast out demons "in the name of" the Lord Jesus (Matt 7:22; Luke 10:17; Acts 3:6).

James's original audience may not have thought to ask the question. Perhaps the fact that "Lord" is used interchangeably for Jesus and God throughout the letter is a clue that we should understand the work and the power of the one as the work and power of the other—as no doubt the early church also did.

Communal Prayer and Confession 5:15-16

These verses continue the theme of prayer for the sick but add confession of sin. Both sickness of body and sickness of soul affect the church's health. The way James blends language of sickness and sin, healing and salvation, might seem strange to modern readers, for he speaks of the *sick* being *saved* (v. 15a) and those who confess their *sins* as being *healed* (v. 16a). Many today would think of the sinful being saved and the sick being healed. In James, as in the New Testament as a whole, the physical and spiritual dimensions of human experience cannot be sundered. Verse 15 begins by considering the sick individual and moves in verse 16 to the health of the community, with acknowledgment of sin being part of both.

James confidently asserts that *the prayer of faith will save the sick, and the Lord will raise them up.* Interpreters debate whether this refers to physical healing in the present or to future resurrection of the dead. On the one hand, the verb "to save" (*sōzein*) is used elsewhere in James with reference to spiritual matters, not physical healing (1:21; 2:14; 4:12; 5:20). Moreover, understanding the verse in reference to eschatological salvation avoids the tension between what it seems to promise and the reality that the sick do not *always* rise up healed, despite many faithful prayers.

On the other hand, Jesus' ministry of salvation in the Gospels is holistic. *Sōzein* often refers to physical and not just spiritual healing (Matt 9:22; Luke 18:42). The sick are literally "raised" (Mark 1:31; Luke 7:14; John 12:1; Acts 3:6-7). In context the verse seems to refer to present physical healing, but James may have been deliberately ambiguous. Luke Timothy Johnson sums this up well: "James' language shares this polyvalence, so that his reassurance can be read at two levels simultaneously: the Lord is able to 'raise him up' from sickness, and thus 'save him' by physical healing, *and* is able to 'raise him up by resurrection' even if he should die and 'save his life/soul' in the resurrection life" (Johnson 1995: 333; cf. Hartin 2009a: 268–69; McCartney 2009: 256).

James moves immediately to topics of sin, confession, and forgiveness, perhaps implying that sickness and sin have a causal relationship. The notion that the two are connected was common in the ancient world and has roots in the biblical tradition (Deut 28:58-62; Ps 38:3; 1 Cor 11:29-30; Sir 38:9-10). Yet the Bible also challenges this conventional wisdom. Job contests the claim that his misfortune is the consequence of sin (Job 9:13-24), and in John 9:3 Jesus tells his disciples that a man's blindness is the result of neither his own nor his parents' sin. Although sickness and sin are not unrelated, James does not endorse the erroneous and dangerous belief that sickness is God's punishment for sin. Verse 15b is conditional in Greek: "*if* someone has committed sins."

At the same time, this text suggests that physical, spiritual, emotional, and mental well-being are all intertwined. Human beings are not compartmentalized creatures: speaking of sin in the context of sickness acknowledges that. In Mark 2:1-12 forgiveness and healing of a paralyzed man are deeply intertwined. Confession of sin, reconciliation, and forgiveness may thus indeed be vital for personal or communal healing.

This is not the first time James has mentioned sin in the letter (1:15; 2:9; 4:8, 17). Although he uses the nouns "sin" and "sinner," he does not use the verb "to sin." Rather, he talks about "doing" or "working out" sin. Paul tends to speak about sin as a power that enslaves, but James refers to sin in terms of behavior and action or inaction. Sin results from disordered desires and leads to hostility, destruction, and death (1:15; 4:1-3). Sin is thus relational in that it hurts others.

The point of bringing up sin in 5:15 is that it will be forgiven. As elsewhere in the New Testament, the passive voice implies that God is the one forgiving the sin. Even before James says people in the church should confess their sins and pray for each other, he assures them of God's forgiveness. An integral part of healing is the forgiveness that awaits sinners before they even ask for it, a forgiveness that comes from a God *who gives to all generously and ungrudgingly* (1:5, 17).

Although the Greek verbs and pronouns are singular in verse 15 (not pl., as in some versions), they become plural in verse 16. Not only do individuals in the church suffer from sickness and sin, but also the whole body needs healing. James does not use the metaphor of the church as a body, as in 1 Corinthians 12, but the corporate identity of these *brothers and sisters* is deeply embedded in his letter (15× in NRSVue). He urges them, *Therefore, confess [pl.] your sins to one another and pray [pl.] for one another, so that you [pl.] may be healed.* The church as a whole is sick. Why? Because they are sinning against each other. Their sins of slander, judgmentalism, selfishness, envy, favoritism, arrogance, and disordered desire are tearing at the seams, creating conflicts that are figuratively "killing" them as a community (4:1-3, *commit murder*). The body of the church aches for healing.

To receive God's healing power, they must begin by confessing their sins *to one another*. Important as private confession of sin to God may be, James is addressing the reciprocal confession of sin in community. The repetition of *one another* in 5:16 emphasizes this. Sometimes individual believers must acknowledge their wrongdoing to another and give and receive forgiveness. However, if the body as a whole needs healing, confession must also be part of its corporate gathering. As Dan McCartney aptly states, "Corporate confession is appropriate for corporate sin" (2009: 258).

The same is true of corporate prayer, which is why James says they should *pray for one another*. The circumstances of each community will guide its praying. In James's churches, prayer could include petitions that God might heal the wounds they have inflicted on each other, that God might imbue them with wisdom and patience (1:5; 3:17-18; 5:7-8), and that they might act with compassion toward the poor and vulnerable (1:27; 2:15). How to incorporate confession into worship services today will no doubt differ from James's time, but it must always be guided by love. Public confessions that are coerced, that shame or demean, that target some sins as more egregious than others, and that air other people's dirty laundry—such have no place in corporate worship.

Using synonyms, this subunit (5:15-16) begins and ends with parallel statements about the efficacy of prayer:

> *The prayer of faith will save the sick.* (v. 15a)
> *The plea of the righteous has much power.* (v. 16c AT)

What is a *prayer of faith?* Who are *the righteous*? The *prayer of faith* arises out of a relationship with God and is characterized by trust in and commitment to God. To quote McCartney again, "It is not the 'prayer that really, really thinks that it will get what is asked for' that will rescue the sick person, but the 'prayer that flows from trust and faithful commitment'" (2009: 260). Likewise, the righteous person is not someone who is sinless or perfect but someone who is right with God and does God's will. Abraham and Rahab were righteous because they acted on their trust in God (2:20-26). In 5:17-18 James offers Elijah as an example of someone whose prayers are *powerful and effective*—not because he was perfect, for he was a *human like us*, but because he trusted in God and acted on it.

These assertions about the efficacy of prayer (vv. 15a, 16c) surround words about confession, forgiveness, and healing (vv. 15bc-16ab). When people of faith confess their sins to each other and know themselves to be forgiven, they can more effectively pray for healing, both for sick individuals and for the community in pain. For James and for the church in all ages, prayers for healing and confession of sin belong together.

Elijah, the Prayer Warrior 5:17-18

James offers Elijah as an example of someone whose praying brought results. To communicate that Elijah prayed with intense fervor, James uses a Semitic idiom that pairs a noun with its cognate verb (lit., *with prayer he prayed*). Elijah was a biblical hero of faith, a prophet second in importance only to Moses. He was expected to return and prepare Israel for the day of the Lord (Mal 3:1-4; 4:5). In the Gospels he appears with Jesus at his transfiguration (Mark 9:4).

James assumes that his Jewish Christian readers will be familiar with the stories about Elijah in 1 Kings 17–19.

In these chapters Elijah vows, "as the LORD the God of Israel lives, . . . there shall be neither dew nor rain these years, except by my word" (17:1). After accusing King Ahab of forsaking Yahweh and after challenging and defeating the prophets of Baal, Elijah predicts rain will come and bows down in a posture of prayer (18:41-45). The references to prayer in this narrative are direct (18:36-37; 19:4, 10, 14) and indirect (18:42). Knowing these stories, James lifts up Elijah as a prayer warrior. Likely he remembers other dramatic outcomes of Elijah's praying, such as those sandwiched in the Baal-Yahweh contest (16:31–19:21): Elijah prayed, a widow's oil and grain miraculously did not run out, and her dead son was raised to life (17:8-24). In the contest with the prophets of Baal, fire rained down from heaven to consume the sacrifice to the Lord and the entire altar, all of which had been thoroughly doused with water (in a drought, no less!). These tales of Elijah gave him a reputation in later Jewish tradition of being a prophet whose prayers produced impressive results (Sir 48:1-11; 2 Esd 7:109 = 4 Ezra 7:39). Tradition also set the time of the drought as three years and six months, even though the text does not specify the exact time (cf. Luke 4:25). This could be because the number (half of seven years) symbolizes a period of judgment in apocalyptic writings (e.g., Dan 7:25; 12:7; Rev 11:2; Hartin 2009a: 272).

Many interpreters find it puzzling that James recalls the story of Elijah and the rains instead of, for example, the story of him raising the widow's son. The latter is more explicit about Elijah praying for health and would seem to be a more cogent example of the healing power of prayer. Perhaps James introduces Elijah here because of the many ways he connects to the previous unit (5:7-12). Elijah functions not only as an example of fervent prayer but also of patience and suffering while waiting for God to act. In 5:7, James noted that farmers must wait patiently for their harvest, which depends on the early and late rains. Elijah too had to wait patiently for the rain and sent his servant out seven times to look at the horizon before even a small cloud appeared (1 Kings 18:42-45). In 5:10 James names *the prophets* as examples of patient suffering, one of whom was surely Elijah (1 Kings 19:1-10).

Finally, this reference to Elijah, the anticipated precursor of the Messiah (Mal 4:5; Matt 17:10-12), reminds James's Jewish Christian readers of their eschatological hope (5:7-8). Although we cannot know for certain why James used this story of Elijah as an example of effective prayer, his purpose to encourage the church is clear, since they too must pray fervently and patiently in their suffering, even as they wait in hope.

Lest readers think Elijah too grand a hero to emulate, James assures them that he was a *human like us*. The Greek word here means "experiencing similarity in feelings or circumstances, *with the same nature*" (BDAG, *homoiopathēs*), and is used elsewhere in the New Testament only in Acts 14:15. Elijah did not float above the challenges of life, godlike, but experienced them like an ordinary mortal. After the dramatic prayer "highs" in 1 Kings 17–18, he had to flee for his life and was so despondent that he wished to die. As one scholar says, "If he can pray like that, then we can too" (Moore-Keish: 195).

So what was it about the prayer of this *human like us* that the church should and can emulate? James names Elijah because he wants to encourage his church to keep on praying even and especially in times of suffering and sickness and not to give up. Elijah prayed with confidence and trust, and his prayer was effective because he was aligned with God's purposes and had discerned God's ways (Gaiser 2015: 248). The church too can pray with trust in God, *who gives to all generously and ungrudgingly* (1:5) and is the giver of every perfect gift (1:17). James wants his audience to believe that God hears the prayers of ordinary people and that prayer changes things, even when the outcome is veiled in mystery (see TLC below).

Restoring a Believer Who Has Strayed 5:19-20

The last two verses of the letter both conclude this unit (5:13-20) and wrap up the entire letter. As the former, they continue the theme of dealing with sin in the church (vv. 15-16). As the latter, they return to James's earlier words about sin, death, and truth (1:15-18). They are his final exhortations about repentance, restoration, and living with integrity as followers of Jesus. The subjects of healing and restoring the wayward are connected in several Jewish and early Christian writings; thus some scholars have posited that James is drawing on ancient liturgical traditions in 5:13-20 (Allison 2013: 747–48, 780–81).

Verses 19-20 begin with the familiar words, *My brothers and sisters*. Throughout the letter, this address has often (though not always) marked a new topic or unit (1:2, 19; 2:1, 14; 3:1; 4:11; 5:7). It sets verses 19-20 off slightly from the previous verses, not so much as a new topic but as an intake of breath before some parting words. This address also reminds James's readers that they are family, in a relationship of mutual accountability rather than hierarchical submission (Hartin 2009a: 286).

James says, *If someone among you is led astray* and *if someone turns that person around . . .* (AT). Two things are significant about this wording. First, James is talking about people inside the faith community, not outsiders, and about what could happen, not what has happened. Second, the whole church is responsible for restoring a sinner, not only church leaders. His concern is mutual accountability and admonition, as in the Community Discourse of Matthew 18. The faithfulness of individuals matters, of course, but throughout the letter, James is concerned about *communal* faithfulness. This is different from a Westernized private faith, which assumes that someone's sin is nobody's business but their own. James's vision of the church is of a body knit together by mutual concern and mutual accountability, where the well-being of the one is essential to the well-being of the whole. In a letter so full of direct admonition to its readers about how to live and how not to live, it is striking that the focus in these verses is not on the wrongdoing itself or on the sinner but almost entirely on the responsibility of the church to restore the sinner to right relationship with others and with God.

English translations sometimes obscure how often the words "wander," "bring back," and "sinner/sin" recur in the Greek of these verses: their repetition adds emphasis. James does not specify what constitutes wandering or being led astray from the truth. That it is equivalent to sinning is evident from the fact that "one who wanders" and "sinner" are both direct objects of "bring back" in verses 19 and 20. Is he referring to apostasy or false teaching, as in some other New Testament letters (Col 2:4; 2 Tim 2:14-19)? The two prior references to "truth" (1:18; 3:14) imply that truth is *not* a set of correct doctrines, but rather the word of salvation and wisdom that manifests itself in good works. When James refers to straying from the truth, he could have both belief and practice in mind, for the two are intertwined for him. However, given his concern for lived faith and integrity of word and deed, it is likely that James's concern is more orthopraxy than orthodoxy. Believing the right thing is virtually useless if one does not also live the right way (2:19-20).

James does not specify whether the cause of being led astray is internal or external (Painter and deSilva: 170). Nowhere does he mention external stumbling blocks, such as false teachers (though he does say, *Resist the devil*, 4:7). At the beginning of the letter, James used similar vocabulary of *sin, death*, and being *led astray* (AT) or *deceived* (1:13-16), which sheds light on his meaning here. Sin is the result of disordered desires, which find expression in the kinds of sinful behavior James addresses throughout the letter. Cravings and coveting give birth to disputes and violence (4:1-3). Misguided esteem for status and wealth bears fruit in favoritism and discrimination (2:1-13). Envy and selfish ambition give rise to wicked deeds (3:14-16). At the end of the letter, James admonishes the church to hold each other accountable and correct those who engage in such sinful behavior.

The words of 1:15-16 also shed light on how restoring a sinner *will save [their] soul from death* (v. 20). According to James, death is the inevitable outcome of sin. It is not only physical death but also eschatological, eternal death. On the other hand, God is the source of life: the giver of *every good and perfect gift* (1:17, cf. NIV) and of wisdom that leads to *righteousness* and *peace* (3:17-18). Turning a sinner away from death means turning someone who has strayed back to God and God's desires. In his commentary Dan McCartney suggests the following analogy: "It is not unlike the experience of getting lost in the woods. When hikers leave the path, they can get entangled and lost, but if a park ranger leads them back to the path, the lost hikers have been saved from grief and possibly from death" (2009: 263).

The language James uses here of wandering from the truth or straying off the path is related to the imagery of the "two ways" found in Jewish wisdom literature and early Christian teaching (Deut 11:26-28; Ps 1; Jer 21:8; Didache 1–7; see comments on 4:4). People can only follow one of two ways: the way of life or the way of death. The way of life is the way of wisdom, righteousness, and truth; it is the way to God. It is a narrow path, though, and many do not find it. If they do, they wander away from it (Matt 7:13-14) when they are lured away by disordered desire and sin (James 1:14-15). Warnings not to stray from the path of truth and life are common in Jewish literature, especially in Wisdom writings (Prov 21:16; Wisd of Sol 5:6; 12:24).

In many biblical texts, as in James, the verb *to turn* (NRSVue, "brings back"; Gk., *epistrephō*) has a moral or spiritual sense of turning someone away from sinful conduct or belief and toward God (1 Kings 8:33; Isa 45:22; Luke 1:16; Acts 3:19; 26:18; 1 Thess 1:9; BDAG). How does the church do this? James does not say. One might think of Matthew 18:15-20, where Jesus briefly sketches a process for holding others in the community accountable (see TBC below). The broader context of James's letter provides clues about the manner in which the church should admonish those who stray: by speaking and acting with gentle wisdom (3:17-18), by modeling what it means to live out one's faith with integrity (2:20-26), and by praying for each other (5:15-16).

Any involved in the work of restoring wanderers must themselves avoid the sins James warns against (cf. Matt 7:1-5). They should not judge believers who have strayed, avoid gossiping about them and maligning them (4:11-12), and remember that people who sin are still *made in the likeness of God* (3:9). They must be *quick to listen, slow to speak, slow to anger* (1:19). Restoring any fellow believer who *wanders from the truth* means treating them with love, as we ourselves would want to be treated (2:8), instead of distancing ourselves. The motive must always be the healing and strengthening of individuals and communities, not arrogance, judgment, or self-righteousness.

Whose soul is saved from death and whose sins are covered? The Greek pronouns in verse 20 are ambiguous. The Greek has *his* (*autou*), not "the sinner's," as in NRSVue. It could be the one doing the restoring or the one being brought back. Interpreters who think the restorer is saved and has their own sins covered sometimes cite Ezekiel 3:18-21 as support, since the prophet's "soul" is delivered when he warns the righteous person not to sin (KJV). The idea that restoring a sinner benefits oneself is also found in early church writings such as 2 Clement 17.2, "Let us help one another to restore those who are weak with respect to goodness, so that we may all be saved."

Some interpreters (e.g., Laws: 239) understand the person whose soul is saved from death as referring to the *sinner* who returns, while the person who brings the sinner back is the one whose *sins* are covered. This switch in referent between the first and second half of the verse, however, is confusing and grammatically unwarranted (Hartin 2009a: 286). It is most straightforward to understand verses 19-20 as saying that the soul of a *sinner* who repents will be saved and that this person's sins will be covered (see also, e.g., Johnson 1995: 339; Hartin 2009a: 286–87). Such a meaning parallels verse 15, where the prayer of the faithful is efficacious in saving the one who is sick. Still, as Martha Moore-Keish says, "It is worth lingering over the ambiguity" since in a community the sins of one affect the whole, and the rescue of an individual might indeed mean salvation for many (202).

James says that one who turns around a sinner *will cover a multitude of sins.* Similar words appear in 1 Peter 4:8, except that there "love covers a multitude of sins." To be sure, helping someone who has stumbled can indeed be an act of love. Both resemble Proverbs 10:12, but James's wording is different enough from the Septuagint that he either has the Hebrew text in mind or an oral tradition.

What does it mean to *cover . . . sins*? Synonymous parallelism in Psalms 32:1 and 85:2 suggests that covering sin is equivalent to forgiving sin. Covering sin does not mean hiding it and letting it continue to fester. Rather, covering sin is like putting a lid on a fire so that it cannot get oxygen and thus dies out. Forgiving or covering sin removes its power to harm and provides space for healing from the consequences of wrongdoing (Moore-Keish: 202).

Although James does not spell this out, he implies that bringing back a sinner from wandering involves a process of repentance, reparation, and healing. We would expect God to be the one to *save . . . from death* and *cover . . . sins*, not the one who brings the errant one back. Ultimately, of course, it is God who saves and forgives, as James well knows (1:12, 21; 2:12-13; 4:12; 5:15). However, the church is the arena in which followers of Jesus live out their faith. Through prayer, acts of mercy and hospitality, and the work of mutual accountability, the church functions as God's agent of healing, forgiveness, and salvation.

Compared with Paul's letters, verses 19-20 seem like an abrupt ending. Absent are any greetings to fellow Christians, final words of blessing, future plans, or a doxology. The letter simply ends with this statement about helping a fellow believer get back on track. Though not typical in the New Testament, such an ending is not unprecedented, for 1 John also ends abruptly with an exhortation: "Little children, keep yourselves from idols" (5:21).

Fred O. Frances has argued that James's ending fits the epistolary pattern of many other Hellenistic letters, citing 1 Maccabees 10:25-45 as an example (110–26). Other commentators note that James 5:7-20 pulls together themes found throughout the letter and addresses topics one would expect to see at the end of a literary epistle (Davids 1982: 181). On the other hand, Ben Witherington argues that this is "not how ancient letters normally ended" and that what James has produced is a sermon that follows rhetorical conventions by concluding with these "stirring words" (2007: 533).

Regardless of whether or not they fit epistolary conventions, the final two verses are a fitting way to conclude this letter. What James advocates here is what he himself has been doing throughout the letter: chastening, admonishing, and encouraging his faith family to live with integrity and to turn from sins of favoritism, bad-mouthing others, selfish ambition, and envy. The task is not his alone, of course; it belongs to the whole church. As it engages in mutual admonition and support, the community of brothers and sisters in Christ will become more whole, more "perfect." It will be healed of its divisions and suffering, becoming more authentically the *first fruits of [God's] creatures* (1:18). As Patrick Hartin notes in his commentary, James is realistic about the fact that believers are tempted and inevitably sin, but in these final verses he expresses confidence that when the church engages in its work of being the church, "the errant brother/sister will be reclaimed by and for the community" (2009a: 288). James's vision of the church is of a body of brothers and sisters who take responsibility for each other, who pray for each other, and who together live with integrity as faithful followers of *our glorious Lord Jesus Christ* (2:1 NRSV).

THE TEXT IN BIBLICAL CONTEXT

When a Brother or Sister Sins . . .

Paul writes that those who have died with Christ are freed from sin and its power (Rom 6:6-7, 14). The writer of 1 John says that those who are born of God do not and cannot sin (1 John 3:9). The reality is that people sanctified and redeemed by Christ do still sin, as even 1 John recognizes (1:8). James 5:19-20 is one of many New Testament texts that address the problem of sin in the church and yet are positive about the outcome of confronting an errant believer. The Gospels and epistles give clues about the kinds of problems that warranted discipline in the early church, as well as how it should be done.

The early church did not invent the practice of disciplining community members, for it was also part of Jewish tradition in the first century. Indeed, the process outlined in Matthew 18 is similar to procedures described in literature of the Qumran community (1QS 5.25–6.1; CD 7.2-3; 9.2-8, 16-22), even though it has significant differences (for a helpful comparison, see Garland: 194–95; Carmody).

Jesus said, "If a brother or sister sins, you must rebuke the offender, and if there is repentance, you must forgive" (Luke 17:3). This brief instruction for dealing with sin in the church is expanded in Matthew 18:15-17. First, the one sinned against should confront the offender in private. The words "against you" are absent from some of the best manuscripts. If omitted, the implication is that anyone in the church might confront the sinner. The goal is clearly to "regain" the sinner. If the person remains unmoved, a group of two or three should speak to the sinner, thereby fulfilling the Jewish requirement for witnesses. If that too fails to convince, the matter is brought before the whole church. No further details about the process are provided, such as how or where the interaction should take place or how many times they should meet. In other words, this is not necessarily a "three strikes, you're out" procedure.

The wider context of Matthew 18 is essential for understanding this process of restoration. The needy and humble (not those who want to be "right") are the greatest in God's reign (vv. 1-5). Disciples must not cause others to stumble and must take drastic measures to get rid of sin in their own lives (vv. 6-9). Great effort must be taken to seek out those who stray, since God does not want even one "sheep" to be lost (vv. 10-14). They must not be "despised" or written off as insignificant. Immediately after verses 15-17, Jesus talks about extravagant forgiveness, which is part of the process of restoration to community (vv. 21-35).

If someone who has strayed refuses to listen to counsel, that "offender" takes on the status of "a gentile and a tax collector" (v. 17). In other words, the person becomes someone who does not yet understand the ways of Jesus' kingdom and is not ready to follow Jesus in the company of other disciples. As David Garland notes, when a believer refuses to listen, "the church is not so much breaking off fellowship with an offender as recognizing that there is no fellowship to break" (195). The relationship is radically redefined, and the work of calling the person to follow Christ begins again.

What gives the church the authority to do this? In Matthew 18:18, Jesus says that the church has the authority to bind and to loose, that is, to make judgments about what is sin and what is not sin, and to release, or forgive, people when they do sin (cf. John 20:23). When the church forgives sin, it releases people to move forward. When the church retains sin, it exposes sin and holds people accountable for it so that they might change (Koester: 159–60).

The New Testament letters depict the church as striving to deal faithfully with sin in its midst. Although they do not outline church practices explicitly or in detail, what we see is generally consistent with Matthew 18. Sometimes the disciplinary actions have to do with false teaching or beliefs (e.g., Rom 16:17; Titus 3:9-11); sometimes the problem is moral or ethical (e.g., 1 Cor 5).

As in the Letter of James, belief and behavior cannot be neatly separated.

The church should pray for those who stray (1 John 5:16). Correction and restoration must be done with a spirit of gentleness, patience, and kindness (Gal 6:1-2; 2 Tim 2:24-26). Christians must guard against sin themselves, avoiding temptation and not being deceived (Gal 6:1; Titus 3:9-11). Although one-on-one admonition may sometimes be appropriate, the letters also acknowledge the importance of "witnesses." That is, they must avoid groundless accusations and engage in communal discernment and correction (2 Cor 13:1-2; 1 Tim 5:19). Leaders like Paul gave multiple admonitions before taking more serious disciplinary action (2 Cor 13:1-2; Titus 3:10). Sometimes the whole church was involved in restoring a wanderer, and sometimes it was only church leaders.

Several texts speak about avoiding or expelling a person who persists in sin and refuses to heed the church's admonition, but this was a last resort (1 Cor 5:5, 13; 2 Thess 3:14-15; 1 Tim 1:18-20; Titus 3:10-11; 2 John 10-11). This could include refusal even to eat with the person, perhaps at eucharistic meals (1 Cor 5:11). References to "hand[ing]" someone "over to Satan" (1 Cor 5:5; 1 Tim 1:20) are not about eternal damnation but a way of talking about separation from the church, since anything that was not of God was of Satan (cf. Hays 1997: 85). Disciplinary action was not punitive but intended to restore the sinner to right relationship with God and fellow believers (see the "so that" even in 1 Cor 5:5; 1 Tim 1:20). Finally, just as Matthew 18 concludes with an emphasis on forgiveness, so the epistles also lift up the centrality of forgiveness in the church (2 Cor 2:5-11; Eph 4:32; 1 John 1:9; 2:1-2).

According to the New Testament, to be a Christian is to be inextricably tied to other members of the body of Christ. When an individual strays or sins, it is not just a private issue but a matter of concern to the entire community. When an unrepentant sinner was excommunicated from the early church, it meant the loss of social, economic, and spiritual support not available elsewhere. It meant being severed from the people of God and a change in identity. This is something we can hardly fathom in our individualistic Western society, where the church is but one of many communities to which someone might belong, and where a desire to avoid intolerance and judgmentalism prevents us from ever speaking out about sin. The church today will need to reimagine what it means to confront sin and to hold each other accountable in this radically different context.

Health and Healing

Readers of the Bible today inevitably bring their assumptions and knowledge about modern medicine to ancient texts about health and healing. However, ancient cultural values and perceptions about illness differ significantly from those of contemporary Western society. The modern world approaches illness from within a framework of biomedical diagnoses and therapies for individual diseased bodies. But in biblical times, sickness and health concerned not only individuals but also the well-being of people in networks of relationships and within the cosmic order of things (Green: 332–33). People "were not self-sufficient individuals" but "experienced both illness and health communally" (Gaiser 2010: 240). A good example is the case of leprosy in the Bible. The term could refer to a variety of skin conditions, not necessarily serious from a biomedical perspective. However, those who were diagnosed as lepers were excluded from the community because of ritual impurity. Healing therefore involved not only physical cure but also religious and social restoration as well.

From a biblical perspective, all healing comes from God, the great Healer (Exod 15:26; Job 5:18). Thus, humans cry out to God when they suffer and offer prayers of thanks for divine healing (Num 12:13; 2 Kings 20:1-11; Ps 6; Jer 17:14). In the New Testament, Jesus becomes the channel of God's healing power, and his healing deeds are signs of the inbreaking reign of God (Luke 11:20). Jesus anointed people with mud, touched impure bodies, and healed with only a word. His healings were holistic in that he not only cured bodies of physical ailments but also restored people to community, delivered them from evil, and healed them from sin (Mark 2:1-12; 5:25-34; Luke 17:11-19).

Jesus sent his disciples to heal and proclaim the kingdom of God during his earthly ministry (Luke 9:1-6; 10:8-9), and the early church continued to do powerful deeds of healing in Jesus' name (Acts 3:1-10; 5:12-16; 9:32-35; 14:8-10). Paul recognized healing as one of the gifts that the Holy Spirit gives to the body of Christ (1 Cor 12:28). Sociologist Rodney Stark describes how the early church grew rapidly, in part because of how the first Christians cared for the sick and the weak during plagues and in horrific urban conditions.

The biblical conviction that God is the source of healing does not mean that people did not or should not use traditional healing methods or consult practitioners (Gaiser 2010: 241). God's healing power could happen through natural means or in unexpected and unexplainable ways (miracles). God created bodies "fearfully and wonderfully" (Ps 139:14), many times able to mend on their own when hurt or sick. To be sure, the Bible is wary of healers who use magic and warns against turning to other gods for healing. Moreover, some physicians took advantage of the sick and did more harm than good (Mark 5:26).

However, the Bible is not inherently opposed to medical practice or physicians, and Jesus himself employed traditional first-century healing methods (like saliva and mud). A remarkable text praising the work of physicians in Sirach 38:1-15 begins, "Honor physicians for their services, for the Lord created them; for their gift of healing comes from the Most High." It also says, "The Lord created medicines out of the earth, and the sensible will not despise them" (v. 4). Biblical writers were not as concerned about *how* people were healed as what the healings *meant*, namely, that God desires the flourishing of all and is actively bringing that about.

The New Testament shows a close relationship between healing and faith, and between communal worship and wellness. Although Jesus healed people because they needed help, not only when they could profess faith (Luke 7:11-17; John 5:2-9), there is a reciprocal relationship between faith and healing. Sometimes expressions of faith result in healing (Matt 15:21-28; Mark 2:1-12; Luke 8:43-48; John 4:46-54), and sometimes healing kindles or enlivens faith (Luke 8:34-39; Acts 9:40-42). Sometimes an individual asks for healing (Mark 10:46-52), and sometimes the community intercedes (Mark 2:1-12). In Philippians, the illness of a beloved brother is the cause of communal concern, and his recovery stimulates communal joy (2:25-30). The Holy Spirit's gift of healing occurs so that the whole body may be built up (1 Cor 12). More explicitly than any other New Testament writer, James connects healing with corporate prayer. As Gaiser so aptly says, "My healing is never mine alone. It cries out to be shared and is fulfilled in that sharing" (2010: 244).

Of course, in the Bible, as today, not all people are cured of their diseases. Even when healing does occur, it is always temporary, for bodies are finite and eventually die. To see health and wholeness as the norm for what it means to be human implies that the chronically ill, those living with a disability, or the elderly cannot be fully human. Furthermore, the Christian life was never guaranteed to be free of pain and suffering. In fact, Jesus warns his disciples that they *will* suffer (e.g., Matt 24:21). That does not mean God wills the suffering, for God is a God of life, who consistently works for the shalom and salvation of all.

Nevertheless, when illness, pain, and deterioration of the body occur, as they do for everyone, God is present. God is with people amid vulnerability, illness, and death, sometimes even more clearly than when everything is going well, and God is able to bring good even out of suffering. The apostle Paul repeatedly prayed that his affliction might be taken from him, . . . but apparently it was not. He came to see that God was working for good even through his suffering and that Christ's power was present in his weakness (2 Cor 12:7b-10).

Genuine healing occurs already, now, but full, eternal healing and wholeness is possible only in the new creation (Gaiser 2010: 243). Jesus' healings and the healing God grants today are temporary glimpses of the restoration that God will bring about for all creation on the last day.

THE TEXT IN THE LIFE OF THE CHURCH

Does Prayer for Healing "Work"?

Many Christians have had the experience of praying fervently and persistently for the healing of a loved one, only to have that person die too young and too soon. Sometimes such experiences create a crisis of faith for the ones who are praying. Why does God seem deaf to the pleas of God's faithful children? Does prayer actually "work," and if so, how? The aching question of God's silence in the face of dire need is not a new one. Centuries ago, the psalmist exclaimed, "O my God, I cry by day, but you do not answer; and by night but find no rest" (Ps 22:2).

Prayer is more than just asking God for help in time of need, of course. At its most basic, prayer is communication with the Divine. It involves listening as well as speaking to God and can be spoken or wordless. Prayer includes praise, thanksgiving, confession, intercession, lament, and petition. In James 5:13-18, the focus is primarily on petitionary prayer, especially prayer for those who are sick and suffering. Such prayer generates more difficulties for people than do prayers of gratitude, lament, or confession, which do not usually expect a tangible outcome or raise questions about whether prayer "works." Confident assertions like *The prayer of faith will save the sick* (James 5:15) and *The prayer of the righteous is powerful and effective* (v. 16) collide with the reality that prayers of faith do not always save the sick and do not always seem effective. This has troubled more than just a few Christians.

Interpreters find various ways to live with the tension these verses create. Perhaps James is promising that the sick will experience salvation and resurrection on the last day. Or perhaps he is not talking about physical healing, but spiritual sickness resulting from unconfessed sin, since he also addresses confession and forgiveness in this same context. Perhaps it is easier to believe that prayers for spiritual healing will be answered than prayers for physical healing. Interpretations such as these are possible but leave one with the uneasy suspicion that they are attempts to squirm away from what the text seems to be saying plainly: prayers of faith will heal the sick in body and mind, not only on the last day but even now.

Perhaps James himself wrestled with how prayer "works," for at times he implies that certain conditions must be met if prayer is to be effective. The one who asks for wisdom must not doubt or vacillate, says James (1:6-8). People who pray must not ask wrongly, selfishly, simply to get what they desire (4:2-3). What we pray for must be within God's will (4:15). Since unresolved sin can handicap prayer, requests for healing must be accompanied by confession of sin (5:15-16). Other New Testament writers suggest similar conditions for prayer (1 John 3:21-23; 5:14). These requirements for effective prayer are valid. Selfishness, lack of trust, and sin can indeed interfere with a person's relationship with God and can hinder prayer. Yet one cannot infer that if prayers for healing are *not* answered, the individual or the community must not have enough faith or must have false motives. Even when prayers for healing are unselfish and offered with complete trust in God, and even when death seems contrary to God's will, some sick people still die.

Intellectually, we understand why prayers for healing cannot always have the desired result. We live in a world where all people experience death, suffering, and brokenness. We are not yet in the new creation, the reign of God has not yet come in full, and the last enemy, death, has not yet been destroyed. To be human is to be mortal and finite, needy and vulnerable, so sick people sometimes are not healed, even with fervent, faithful prayer. This reality must be held in tension with texts such as James 5:14-15 that promise healing for righteous people who pray with faith. It is a reality at times difficult to accept.

Unanswered prayer is especially difficult for moderns to accept. Richard Bauckham's reflections on prayer in the modern world are worth quoting at length:

> The fundamental reason why prayer became difficult in the modern period was humanity's modern self-image as those who, especially

> through technology, have gained control over the world. . . . Whereas petitionary prayer is recognition of the limits of human abilities, the modern age has encouraged the sense that all problems have human solutions and that all human desires may in the end be realizable by human means, especially through the unlimited potentialities of technology. (Bauckham 1999: 207)

But prayer is not technology. James's words in 5:15-16 must not be read instrumentally, "as though prayer were a powerful means which qualified people can use to achieve things. That way of thinking ends by making God himself a means to human ends" (Bauckham 1999: 207). There is no cause-and-effect relationship between prayer and its outcome, and God is not a commodity or a strategy to be manipulated. Saying all the right words and doing all the right things do not guarantee that God will act the way we think God should act. Ultimately, how prayer "works" lies shrouded in mystery—as it should, if prayer is indeed relationship with the great mystery of the Divine.

What, then, can those who pray for healing in the church today draw from James? First, we pray because God is abundantly *compassionate and merciful* (James 5:11), *gives . . . generously and ungrudgingly* (1:5), as the Giver of *every good and perfect gift* (1:17 NIV). God is not capricious, waiting for an opportunity to trip people up, but is *always* on our side (Rom 8:31-39; 2 Cor 1:20), desiring shalom for all God's creatures. James is confident that God hears the prayers of those who cry out to God and that God cares (5:4).

Second, prayer for healing occurs in the context of the church. Those who are sick call on the church to pray over them, to touch their hurting bodies with the oil of God's comfort. The implications of this are that sick people are not sick alone. Their well-being is integral to the health of the whole body. When the church gathers around its sick, the walls of loneliness, fear, and isolation that often surround those who are gravely ill are torn down. In that action there is social and spiritual healing, even if physical illness remains.

Third, petitionary and intercessory prayer is an acknowledgment of our need for God and our inability to be masters of our own destiny. As J. Ramsey Michaels so aptly says, "Intercessory prayer for James . . . is simply a matter of placing things where they belong—that is, in the hands of the Lord" (240).

Fourth, *the prayer of faith* (James 5:15), by definition, is a prayer of trust that although God's ways and God's will may sometimes be hidden from human eyes, God nevertheless hears and attends to

God's children. When people begin from a place of such trust, openness to an answer that is different from what one expected or hoped for becomes more possible. Just as the farmer must wait patiently for the crop after the rain comes (5:7), so also those who intercede for the sick must wait patiently for God to act, for God's timeline is not necessarily ours. Sometimes healing comes only in the new creation. A person may receive healing even when illness remains. God responds to what humans need, even if not always what they want.

Fifth, James invites believers to pray with confidence and hope. Because petitionary and intercessory prayer is not a magic formula with predictable outcomes, Christians sometimes pray with caution, erecting a hedge around themselves lest they be disappointed. James invites believers to pray boldly, as Elijah did. *Elijah was a human like us* (5:17). He got depressed, he got angry, he had to wait for God to act, but he prayed boldly for rain to come. Prayer can change God's mind and move God to do new things, as various stories in Scripture attest (Exod 32:12-14; Amos 7:3-6; Jon 3:9-10). True, sick people are not always healed, even when prayers of faith pound on heaven's gates. James calls on the church to pray anyhow. James calls the church to petition God boldly, knowing that a good and generous God hears their prayers and is constantly acting for the salvation and well-being of God's people. Perhaps James would agree with the following quip (source unknown): "I do not believe in the power of prayer; I believe in the goodness of God" (cf. Ps 27:13).

Anointing with Oil

The reference to anointing the sick with (olive) oil is only a small part of one verse in James, yet it has received an inordinate amount of attention in the history of the church. Although anointing has been used at the coronation of kings, for the consecration of priests, and in rites such as baptism, the focus here is on anointing of the sick. Anointing was practiced both by the Eastern and Western church from the early centuries of the church's existence. Patristic and medieval writers often connected it to James 5:14. Over time, the practice of anointing in the Western church became so closely associated with repentance that it developed into the sacrament of extreme unction, that is, the anointing of someone at the end of life in conjunction with confession and absolution. Timothy George reports that the "most frequently quoted text from the epistle [during the millennium between Augustine and Luther] was James 5:14, which became the classic proof text for the sacrament of extreme unction" (370). The Council of Trent, Session XIV, in 1551, stated the following: "This holy anointing of the sick was instituted as a true and proper sacrament of the New Testament by Christ our Lord. While implied in the Gospel of Mark (cf. 6:13), it was commended and promulgated to the faithful by James, the Apostle and brother of the Lord" (quoted in Hartin 2009a: 279). After the Second Vatican Council in the 1960s, anointing again became a sacrament of healing and prayer for the seriously ill, even when death was not imminent. Modern Catholic scholars are more cautious about basing "last rites" on James 5, even though they see the text as laying the foundation for the church's later sacramental practice.

Protestant Reformers such as Calvin and Luther rejected the sacrament of extreme unction as part of their critique of the medieval church's sacramental system. Although they continued to pray for the sick and sometimes anoint them with oil, they argued that James 5:14 had nothing to do with last rites, since James clearly anticipated these rituals to promote healing.

For sixteenth-century Anabaptists, the practice of anointing with oil was not much of an issue. According to one study, "references to anointing from the sixteenth century to the nineteenth century are extremely rare" in Anabaptist and Mennonite writings (M. Wenger: 20). Where it is mentioned as a practice, the Anabaptists seemed to concur with the Reformers: anointing the sick with oil was a practice enjoined by James, but as a sacrament administered to the dying, it was to be repudiated. The words of Michael Sattler at his trial in 1527 are illustrative: "We have not rejected the oil [of extreme unction]. For it is a creature of God, and what God has made is good and not to be refused, but that the pope, bishops, monks, and priests can make it better[,] we do not believe. . . . That of which the Epistle of James [5:14] speaks is not the pope's oil" (Williams: 140). Some Anabaptist writers seem to have understood the reference to anointing in symbolic rather than literal terms. For example, in "Letter to the Church of God at Rattenberg" (1527), Leonard Schiemer interpreted the oil of anointing in James 5:14 as referring to the gift of the Holy Spirit (cf. Snyder 2001: 80).

The practice of anointing the sick has varied among groups descended from the sixteenth-century Anabaptists. There is little documentary evidence for anointing among Brethren and Mennonite groups in North America before the nineteenth century. That is not to say it was never practiced, but it was not common enough to be addressed by church leaders.

Questions about anointing arose in the Church of the Brethren in the early nineteenth century and in Mennonite writings later that century, perhaps influenced by revivalist movements in America. Should James 5:14 be understood literally or spiritually or both? Was anointing only for physical sickness? How many times could someone be anointed? What kind of oil should be used? Who was qualified to anoint a sick person?

By the late 1800s some Mennonite leaders included anointing among the seven ordinances of the church. For example, in 1891 evangelist John S. Coffman published a "pamphlet entitled *Fundamental Bible References*, the earliest compilation of Mennonite ordinances that specifically included anointing with oil" (M. Wenger: 30). In 1921 the General Conference of the Mennonite Church formally included anointing as an official ordinance of the church in a statement called "Fundamentals of the Christian Faith" (M. Wenger: 26–27). From 1887 onward, the Brethren in Christ endorsed the anointing of the sick with oil along with offering a prayer for their physical healing (Wittlinger: 71–73). The practice of anointing the sick continued to expand in Mennonite denominations, but not among all and not with any uniformity. For example, the "General Conference Mennonite Church group did not observe this practice" (J. Wenger). In all cases, the oil was seen as symbolic and not having healing power in itself. The focus was on God's power to heal and on encouraging the sick person's faith.

Today many Mennonite and Brethren churches practice anointing with oil. They see themselves as continuing Jesus' ministry of healing not only souls, but also bodies, minds, and emotions. In addition to anointing in times of illness, people may request anointing before surgery, when they are in a time of discernment, or when relationships are fragile. Anointing may take place in a private setting with family and friends or in a public worship service.

The oil is not seen as having magical properties nor is it a replacement for medical care. The service of anointing is not a "faith healing," and there is no guarantee of physical recovery, even though that may happen. The emphasis is on God, who heals and desires shalom for all. The oil symbolizes the comfort and presence of God with the person receiving anointing. The church's ministry of anointing is an expression of trust that God will hear the prayers of God's people and will grant what is needed for that time of illness. It is a way for individuals and congregations to open themselves to God's healing work in a broad sense. The ritual of anointing with oil is usually accompanied by prayer and laying on of hands. Often James 5:14-15 is read. Because unresolved sin and hurt can affect overall health, sometimes a service of anointing might include confession of sin and forgiveness, as in James 5:13-20.

Outline of James

Essays

AUTHORSHIP AND DATE The Letter of James identifies its author as *James, a servant of God and of the Lord Jesus Christ* (1:1) but provides no other explicit information about this person's identity. Attempts to fill out this identification must depend on what can be inferred from the rest of the New Testament, historical factors, and the character of the letter itself. Because questions of authorship are inextricably tied to the date of the letter, the two will be considered together in what follows.

Evidently the author was well known enough that the recipients did not require further identification. The New Testament mentions several people named "James":

1. James the son of Alphaeus, one of the twelve apostles (Matt 10:3; Mark 3:18; Luke 6:15; Acts 1:13).
2. James the son of Mary, sometimes called "James the Younger or Lesser" (Matt 27:56; Mark 15:40; 16:1; Luke 24:10).
3. James the father of Judas, one of the Twelve but not Iscariot (Luke 6:16; Acts 1:13).
4. James the son of Zebedee, brother of John and one of the Twelve (Mark 1:19; 3:17; Luke 6:14; Acts 1:13).
5. James, Jesus' brother, who became a leader in the early church (Mark 6:3; Matt 13:55; Acts 12:17; 15:13; 21:18; Gal 1:19; 2:9, 12).

Of the above options, only the last two men were prominent enough in the early church to be the James of this letter. James the son of Zebedee was part of the inner circle of Jesus' disciples, but according to Acts 12:2, he was killed by Herod Agrippa I, perhaps early in 44 CE. Since the letter was likely not written earlier than that and since there is nothing in church tradition to connect this letter to James the son of Zebedee, he is probably not responsible for this letter.

Church tradition has most consistently associated the letter with James the brother of Jesus. This association, however, is not without problems. Some early church leaders voiced doubts about the brother of Jesus being the author (Allison 2013: 18–19). Two main alternatives exist: (a) The letter is pseudepigraphical, written by someone who lived considerably later than James but attributed the letter to him, wishing to honor and pass on the legacy of this eminent church leader; (b) the letter was written in two stages, with substantial content going back to James, but it was edited and received final form after his death. Scholars who deem the letter to be pseudepigraphical argue that the practice of attributing writings to renowned people in the past was widespread in the ancient world and would not have been considered deceptive or fraudulent. Others are less convinced that such writings, while in existence, would have been considered for inclusion in a sacred canon.

In what follows, we examine various factors that must be considered in assessing authorship. The date of the letter is entangled with these factors because if the brother of Jesus was the author, it must have been written before 62 CE, when James was martyred, according to Josephus (*Jewish Antiquities* 20.9.1). Features of the letter that suggest an early date argue for traditional authorship since it is unlikely that someone else would have attached James's name to a letter when he was still alive. Characteristics that point to a later date imply the author was someone other than the brother of Jesus.

One of the most significant factors is that the letter was written in excellent literary Greek by someone who must have been fluent in the language. In addition to many vocabulary words that appear only here in the New Testament, it incorporates Hellenistic literary themes, motifs, patterns of thought, rhetorical devices, and arguments used by Greek moralist writers. Given that literacy rates were low in the first century and that Greek would not have been the native language of most Jews in Galilee, many scholars consider it unlikely that a Galilean peasant could have penned such a letter.

On the other hand, scholarship in recent decades has shown the influence of Hellenism in Palestine to be far-reaching. Greek would have been the language of trade and commerce in Galilee, especially in towns such as Sepphoris, only a few kilometers north of Nazareth. Acts 6:1-6 suggests that there was a significant Hellenistic element in the Jerusalem church, where James was the leader for about thirty years after Jesus' death. Martin Hengel estimates that "10–20% of the population in Jerusalem were Jews whose vernacular or mother tongues was Greek" (Bauckham 1999: 24). It is not impossible that James would have become proficient in Greek. Even if he was not fluent at the level of Greek reflected in the letter, he could have employed a scribe or amanuensis to help him compose or polish it. Such a practice was common, with scribes doing everything from transcribing a letter dictated by the author to composing it with the author's input and final approval. Additionally, some scholars maintain that it "lacks certain characteristics typical of pseudonymous literature" (McCartney 2009: 30). In short, the argument against Jacobean authorship based on the quality of Greek is not as insurmountable as sometimes claimed.

Another factor in considering authorship is how well the letter was known by ancient writers and how it fared in the canonization process. The evidence here is primarily against the brother of Jesus being the author. The letter seems to have been relatively unknown in the early church, at least, in the literary works those church leaders left behind, and it took a long time for it to be considered canonical. One would think something written by Jesus' brother and a leader in the Jerusalem church would have been valued and oft cited. The oldest extant manuscripts containing pieces of James date from the mid- to late-third and early fourth century ($\mathfrak{P}^{20}$, $\mathfrak{P}^{23}$, $\mathfrak{P}^{100}$). Irenaeus, bishop of Lyons, seems to quote James in *Against Heresies* (around 180 CE), but he does not explicitly cite James. The first extant references to the Letter of James as Scripture and to the brother of Jesus as author appear in the writings of Origen (185–253), who drew from the book extensively. The Shepherd of Hermas, a postapostolic writing from the early second century, contains many striking parallels to the Letter of James (e.g., cf. Herm. Mandate 9.1-4 and James 1:5-8; Herm. Mandate 8.2 and James 4:17) and extensive use of *dipsychos*, a word not found elsewhere in the New Testament or in Greek literature before James (1:8; 4:8). Luke Timothy Johnson argues persuasively that Shepherd of Hermas must have used James as a source even though he does not explicitly refer to it (2004e: 56–60). Similarities between James and 1 Clement (an epistle to the Corinthians attributed to the bishop Clement of Rome in the late first century) might also suggest that the latter used James, though other explanations are possible. The Muratorian Canon (an early canon list that may date from the late second century or possibly the fourth) does not seem to include James (though the text is damaged) nor do several later canonical lists. By the time the bishop Athanasius wrote his Easter letter to the churches in 367 CE, however, James was on the list of the twenty-seven New Testament books considered to be inspired Scripture. The letter was also accepted at the late fourth-century church councils (e.g., Hippo, Carthage) and by Western church theologians such as Augustine and Jerome. Although space does not permit a fuller discussion of the church's reception of James here, Luke Timothy Johnson has written several essays telling this fascinating story (2004a). The upshot is that use and recognition of James as Scripture was sluggish for the first two or three centuries of the church. This could be because it was written late by a pseudonymous author. Or perhaps this short letter's intensely practical nature made it less useful for the great christological debates that preoccupied the early church.

A third factor to consider in determining authorship and date is the letter's relationship to the Pauline epistles *[James and Paul on Faith and Works, p. 348]*. If James 2:14-26 was written as a direct challenge to Paul's teaching on justification by grace through faith, James's letter must have been written after Romans—that is, after 55–57 CE. The vocabulary about faith and works, the reference to Abraham, and the citation of Genesis 15:6 are so similar in these two writings that it is impossible for some scholars to believe that James wrote without knowledge of Romans (e.g., Allison 2013: 445–54). However, James and Paul seem to be speaking about entirely different problems as they address faith and works. Consequently, some argue that such a serious misconstrual of Paul's theology could only have arisen decades after Paul wrote Romans and thus after James's death in 62 CE, eliminating the possibility of him as author. Still, some people were apparently misunderstanding Paul's theology of justification by grace already during his lifetime (e.g., Rom 6). And Paul also taught that redeemed lives must bear fruit in good deeds. If so, James could well have written against a misunderstanding of Paul early on, before 62 CE.

Some scholars are not convinced that James's letter was written with any knowledge of Paul's theology of faith and works in Romans. James could have been addressing a different problem in a different part of the church entirely distinct from Paul's concern in Romans. James's usage of Genesis 15:6 and Abraham need not have depended on Paul (e.g., McCartney 2009: 16). If so, the letter could have been written early by the brother of Jesus. The relationship between the letters of Paul and James's letter is complex, and no argument about authorship based on this relationship is without problems.

The three factors discussed above are the weightiest in assessing whether James the brother of Jesus wrote the letter, but there are other relevant considerations. Again, the date of writing figures prominently. Characteristics that point to an early date and Palestinian provenance increase the likelihood of James's authorship. Features shared with second-century writings or theological tendencies of the later church tip the argument toward pseudepigraphy.

The Letter of James resonates strongly with the teachings of Jesus in the synoptic gospels, especially in the Sermon on the Mount *[James and the Jesus Tradition, p. 353]*. Nowhere does it directly quote the Gospels, however, or show signs of direct dependence. Instead, it seems to incorporate pre-synoptic Jesus traditions. This points to an early date for the letter near the events of Jesus' life. If the letter were written by someone at the end of the first century or in the second, one would expect to see closer correspondence to the written Gospel tradition. For W. G. Kümmel, one of only two points in favor of James as author is "the close but probably not literary contacts with important parts of the gospel tradition" (Kümmel: 412).

James 2:2 refers to someone entering "your synagogue" (Gk.; NRSVue: "assembly"). This suggests that the letter may have been written early, when Jewish followers of Jesus were still gathering with those who did not confess him as Messiah and before the parting of the ways for Judaism and Christianity. On the other hand, a reference to meeting in synagogues does not necessitate an early date, since the separation between Jews and Christians happened in different ways at different times and places, and Jesus' followers continued to attend synagogues even in the fourth century (Allison 2013: 12).

Some interpreters argue that the content of the letter reflects an early date, making Jacobean authorship more plausible. The letter lacks any reference to the death and resurrection of Jesus or the atonement. There is no developed Christology, no sign of later debates about the nature of Christ, and no trinitarian thinking. References to the parousia suggest an imminent expectation rather than the reality of a delay. Absent are references to Gentiles joining the church and related issues of circumcision and ritual observance of the law. Despite its distinctly Jewish character, the letter never mentions the temple and deals with ethical matters more than ritual worship.

All these characteristics fit the picture of the church in the early stages of its life and theology. At the same time, none of these factors conclusively point to the brother of Jesus as author. Some streams of later Jewish Christianity, such as the Ebionites, were not characterized by the soteriological and christological concerns that preoccupied the Western church (McKnight: 36). Perhaps issues related to Gentile inclusion are missing because these had long since been resolved. The temple is not mentioned, perhaps because the letter was written after its destruction in 70 CE.

The significance of the Jewish character of the letter for questions of authorship and date is ambiguous (on the Jewish character of the letter, cf. the Introduction above). The early church was born and flourished within first-century Judaism, eventually becoming more Gentile as it spread throughout the Mediterranean world. Some interpreters thus view the Jewish character of the letter as evidence of an early date. Others note that Christians in the second century continued to practice circumcision, keep the Sabbath, and attend synagogue. As Scot McKnight concludes, "What we find in James could have been written . . . anytime from the middle 40s of the first century into the middle of the second century" (35). The fact that the letter is concerned only with moral/ethical law (love of neighbor, care for the poor) and not with ritual law (sacrifice, circumcision, ritual purity) is also ambiguous evidence. Some argue that this emphasis is not consistent with the portrayal of James in Acts, Paul's letters, and church tradition: a conservative, pious Jewish leader who upholds the ritual law (Acts 21:18-26; Gal. 2:11-13). Thus he is unlikely to be the author. Conversely, the fact that the letter focuses on moral aspects of law (as Jesus also did), does not mean the writer was unconcerned about other aspects of Torah observance. It just means that these were not issues in the church to which he was writing.

Other minor factors add nothing compelling to the argument for or against the brother of Jesus as author. Some interpreters have pointed to similarities between the Letter of James and James's speech and letter in Acts 15 to argue in favor of Jacobean authorship. Although some interesting parallels in wording do exist, this argument does not sufficiently consider Luke's influence in shaping the language and speeches of Acts. Some argue that if James the brother of Jesus had written the letter, he would surely have made his relationship to Jesus explicit. On the other hand, James may not have mentioned his relationship to Jesus because it was stating the obvious and because his authority rested not on his blood ties but on his call from God and his leadership in the church.

In the end, the evidence regarding authorship is inconclusive. As K. Jason Coker notes, "The debate between authentic, composite, and pseudonymous authorship relies on cumulative data rather than any single factor" (67). My inclination is to see James the brother of Jesus as the author of the letter or, at least, the source of its contents even if transcribed by someone else. There seems much to commend this position and no compelling reasons not to. However, I hold this opinion lightly and interpretation of the letter in this commentary does not depend on it.

Does it matter who the author of the letter was? Perhaps not. For at least eighteen hundred years, the church has deemed this short epistle to be Scripture. Because of this alone, it is worthy of our attention and instructive for a life of faith. Although the question of authorship played a role in canonization, the letter's ongoing authority for the church does not depend on resolving this intractable question. Knowing who wrote it would satisfy our historical curiosity and contribute to a fuller understanding of the history and theology of the early church; but in the end, it is the message of this ancient letter and how faith is lived out that is of lasting value.

JAMES AND PAUL ON FAITH AND WORKS Many contemporary scholars rightly insist on the importance of reading James "on his own terms" rather than through the lens of Paul. Nevertheless, few readers of Scripture, past or present, can resist the temptation to compare James with Paul when they read James 2:14-26. The reason for this is that James and Paul seem clearly to contradict each other on the question of faith and works. The following verses epitomize the problem:

James 2:24	"A person is justified by works and not by faith alone."
Romans 3:28	"A person is justified by faith apart from works."
Galatians 2:16	"so that we might be justified by faith in Christ, and not by doing the works of the law" (NRSV)

In addition, both use the example of Abraham and quote Genesis 15:6—James to argue that a person is "justified by works" (2:21-23) and Paul to argue that a person is "justified by faith" (Rom 4:3; Gal 3:6). James's message that faith without works cannot save also rubs against Ephesians 2:8-10 and Titus 3:5. If one takes intracanonical conversation seriously, we cannot exclude Paul's letters from a discussion about James. As Margaret Mitchell has said, "'To read James on his own terms' *must include grappling with Paul if Paul was one of those terms*" (75, italics original).

The questions surrounding these seemingly divergent perspectives are both historical and canonical (Bauckham 1999: 119; A. Chester: 50). Historically, what was the relationship between James and Paul? To use Mitchell's words, was Paul really one of James's "terms"? Was 2:14-26 intended to challenge Paul (or a misinterpretation of him)? Or did Paul write in response to James? Perhaps James wrote without knowledge of Paul's letters? Regardless of their historical relationship, both are in the canon, and people ancient and modern experience them in conversation with each other. Canonically, then, do James and Paul represent incompatible views on the relationship of faith and works or can their perspectives be reconciled?

The amount of scholarly debate about these questions seems out of proportion to the simple conclusion: both James and Paul believe that genuine faith in Jesus Christ must be evident in the way one lives. Their comments about faith and works contrast because they are speaking into different problems and contexts. Despite this straightforward consensus, some discussion of these issues seems warranted.

Historical Questions Questions about the historical relationship between the letters of James and Paul are complicated by uncertainties about authorship and date of writing *[Authorship and Date, p. 343]*. If Jesus' brother wrote the Letter of James, it was written before James's martyrdom (62 CE?). Romans was likely penned between 55 and 58 CE and Galatians before that. From other writings of the New Testament, we know that James and Paul were acquainted and that they discussed matters of faith and law observance (Acts 15; 21:17-26; Gal 1:19-24; 2:1-10). While these accounts portray James as a Torah-abiding leader of the primarily Jewish church in Jerusalem, nothing in these texts (including Gal 2) suggests that he was opposed to Paul's mission to the Gentiles or to his theology of salvation by grace through faith *[James the Brother of Jesus, p. 357]*. And yet the letters of these two church leaders sound so different on the topic of faith and works.

Of the three possibilities mentioned above (Paul was challenging James, James was challenging Paul, or the two were not addressing each other), the idea that Paul was responding to James is highly improbable. Paul's perspective on faith and works was animated by the inclusion of Gentiles in the church, whereas the Letter of James contains no hint of this Jew-Gentile issue. James's argument about faith needing to bear fruit in good works is not something with which Paul would disagree, and what Paul says about being saved by faith and not by works of the law makes no sense as a rebuttal of James. If Paul were responding to James's letter, then James would have had to be written very early indeed.

The other two options are both possibilities. Some scholars argue that there is no reason to think James had read Paul's letters or that he wrote deliberately to refute Paul's theology (e.g., Witherington 2007: 470–71; Bauckham 1999: 129; Davids 1982: 20–21; Blomberg and Kamell: 140). If James *had* been writing to counter Paul, he either seriously misunderstood Paul or was responding to a distortion of Paul's teaching. As Davids says, "To argue that James directly attacks Paul is to argue that James is a consummate blunderer, for he fails to meet Paul's arguments at all and instead produces a work with which Paul would have agreed!" (Davids 1982: 21).

These scholars think James was addressing an issue entirely different from what bothered Paul. In his Jewish messianic communities, James perceived a tendency to give intellectual assent to beliefs, such as monotheism, but a dearth of good deeds, such as caring for the poor. The question of whether Gentiles could be saved without doing works of the law was not on his horizon. James and Paul both appealed to Abraham and Genesis 15 because they were drawing from a common well of Jewish traditions about Abraham's great faith. First Maccabees 2:52 also links Genesis 15:6 and the near-sacrifice of Isaac. James sounds like he is arguing with Paul only because he used a standard rhetorical device, the diatribe, to enliven his teaching. "Such an interlocutor is not imagined as a [real] opponent, but as a student slow to grasp his teacher's point" (Bauckham 1999: 125).

Other scholars contend that James sounds like he is arguing against Paul because he is. Based on literary evidence alone, it seems unlikely that James was unaware of Paul's thinking on justification by faith and not works of the law. Dale Allison has shown how the Greek phrases translated "by works," "by faith," "a person is justified," and "without works" are either rare or nonexistent in this combination before Paul, but they appear together densely in Paul and James (see Allison 2013: 445–46 for a detailed examination of the data). He says, "One would be hard pressed to find a similar concatenation of rare expressions in two texts that are not directly related" (446). If one is going to argue that James knew and incorporated the Jesus tradition preserved in Matthew *[James and the Jesus Tradition, p. 353]*, despite few verbal parallels, one cannot easily argue that James was unaware of Paul's discussion of faith and works, where there *are* such close and distinctive verbal parallels. According to Allison, it seems unlikely that James would have chosen Genesis 15:6, a text about faith, to defend the importance of works if Paul had not already used the text to argue that Abraham was justified by faith (2013: 450). In fact, Genesis 15:6 is quoted only in James, Romans, and Galatians in the New Testament.

It also seems strange that James would distinguish between faith and works only to argue that they cannot be separated if he were not aware of someone who had indeed separated them. Rather than arguing against and completely misrepresenting Paul, it is possible that James was polemicizing against a misinterpretation of Paul circulating among some churches. Paul himself recognizes the possibility that some will distort his message, when he says, "What then are we to say? Should we continue in sin in order that grace may abound? By no means! How can we who died to sin go on living in it?" (Rom 6:1-2; cf. Rom 3:8; Gal 1:7). Even though Paul strongly refutes lawless behavior in his letters, he might have been wrongly heard to condone lawless behavior (Allison 2013: 452–54).

The arguments for both positions are strong. Although certainty is not possible, the vocabulary, use of Abraham as an exemplar, and quotation of Genesis 15:6 are too similar to dismiss the idea that James knew of Paul's message of justification by faith. However, that does not mean he was picking a quarrel with Paul in James 2:14-26. The contexts in which these two church leaders were writing were completely different (see further below). What James is saying must be understood *first* in the context of his letter and not first as a hypothetical response to Paul. In Acts and in his letters, Paul was adamantly arguing for the salvation of Gentiles and their incorporation into the people of God based on faith in Christ and not on keeping Jewish ritual law. This was not James's concern. His target was the church—specifically, Jewish followers of Jesus who were not loving their neighbors, who were eroding community with angry words, and who were neglecting the poor while pandering to the rich. Much of the modern discussion about faith and works in James and Paul seems to be motivated by a post-Reformation worry that the Letter of James jeopardizes the doctrine of forensic justification by grace apart from human merit. This is not James's agenda. He simply wants the church to live as though they indeed have been given birth by God's word of truth and are the first fruits of God's creatures (1:18). To do this, James intentionally or unintentionally appropriates Paul's language to argue his point, without addressing Paul's concerns.

Canonical Questions Although James and Paul *sound* contradictory within the canon, they are not as theologically at odds as they seem. They use the same words differently, appeal to Scripture in different ways, and are writing in different contexts.

The key words in the passage are *faith*, *justify*, and *works*. In understanding true faith as not only belief, but even more trust, commitment, and fidelity, James and Paul do not disagree. Like James, Paul would not recognize mere intellectual assent as genuine faith.

Both James and Paul believe that justification—being brought into right relationship with God and becoming part of God's people—is a gift from God, not a human achievement. James says, *Every good gift and perfect gift is coming down from above, from the Father of lights. . . . Because [God] willed it, [God] gave birth to us by the word of truth, in order that we might be a kind of first fruits of his creatures* (1:17-18 AT). Paul declares that all "are now justified by [God's] grace as a gift, through the redemption that is in Christ Jesus" (Rom 3:24); "By grace you have been saved through faith, and this is not your own doing; it is the gift of God" (Eph 2:8).

However, James and Paul use the verb "justify" somewhat differently. Two primary definitions of *dikaioō* are "to declare righteous" and "to prove to be in the right" (BDAG 249; McCartney 2009: 162). Paul uses it in the former way and James primarily in the latter. Paul means that God declared Abraham to be righteous because Abraham trusted in God's promise and was faithful to God. That is, Abraham was justified on the basis of his faith. James means that Abraham was proven to be righteous in God's eyes when his trust in God was demonstrated by his actions, especially his radical readiness even to give up the son of promise. Even though God deemed Abraham to be righteous because of his trust in God (Gen 15:6), it was only through his deeds that his righteousness was clearly demonstrated. His works completed, or perfected, his faith, resulting in synergy between the two. The Greek verb *synergeō* is used in James 2:22: *Faith was working together with his works* (AT).

David Maxwell has argued that both of these uses of *dikaioō* appear close together in the letter 1 Clement (32.4). As in Paul, "justify" is used in the sense of "declare righteous" when the contrast is between faith and works. And, as in James, it means to "prove to be righteous" when the contrast is between words and works (1 Clement 30.3; Maxwell: 377–78).

James and Paul also use the word "works" differently. In James's letter, *works* refers to deeds of mercy, justice, and compassion (2:16-17). In Romans and Galatians, the word refers mostly to works of the Mosaic law, especially circumcision, Sabbath observance, and purity laws, which set Jews apart from Gentiles. Paul is adamant that all people, Jews *and* Gentiles, are set right with God not by meeting the ritual requirements or by becoming Jewish or by any human achievement, but by the grace of God, through the death and resurrection of Jesus the Messiah (Rom 3:20, 28; 4:6; Gal 2:16; 3:10). That Paul also believes in the necessity of "doing good" or "good work" is evident throughout his letters (Rom 2:6-10; 1 Cor 15:58; 2 Cor 9:8; Gal 5:6; Phil 2:12-13; Eph 2:10; Titus 1:6). In Galatians he argues vehemently against circumcision (5:2-6; 6:12), but not against good works (Gal 6:9-10). In Romans, Paul uses the phrase "obedience of faith" as a statement of his mission, which he uses to frame the letter as a whole (Rom 1:5; 16:26).

Both ancient and modern scholars have articulated the different contexts of James and Paul as follows (Hartin 2009a: 166–67). In Romans and Galatians, Paul addresses the situation of the believer *before* justification and speaks to how redemption through Christ is first received: by faith (Rom 3:24-26; 6:1-11; Gal 2:20). James, on the other hand, addresses the question of how to live as followers of Christ *after* being given new *birth* (1:18) and after confessing faith *in our Lord Jesus Christ* (2:1 NRSV). Although potentially helpful, this perspective still severs faith and works in a way that James would find strange. To be justified *is*, by definition, to live differently; without the fruit of good works, there is no evidence that a person is in right relationship with God.

In addition, both James and Paul focus less on the individual believer and more on the church, the redeemed and recreated people of God. Paul was convinced that the life, death, and resurrection of Jesus made one part of a peoplehood, the body of Christ. As such, Gentiles could be part of the church—not by adhering to Jewish ritual laws like circumcision, but by trusting in what God had done in and through Christ Jesus. At stake for James was not how God could declare sinners "just/righteous" or how one became part of God's covenant people, but rather the integrity of the church's confession that Jesus is Lord. The church was not living as though that were true. They were slandering each other, honoring the rich over the poor, envying others, and not loving their neighbors.

James was speaking to a church that behaved as though it could have faith without deeds of mercy and love. Paul was speaking to a church that wrestled with whether belonging to a people in right relationship with God required doing all the works of the Mosaic law. If we could put James and Paul in the same room today, they might wonder what all the fuss was about.

JAMES AND THE JESUS TRADITION The near absence of Jesus in the Letter of James is striking. Not once does James refer to any events of Jesus' life, such as his baptism or miracles, nor does he mention Jesus' death and resurrection. In fact, the letter's failure to "preach Christ" was one of the main reasons Martin Luther considered James to be of little value. The name "Jesus" appears only twice (1:1; 2:1), although *the excellent name* (2:7) and "the Lord" (5:7, 8) likely also refer to Jesus. Scholars disagree about these indirect references. Some maintain that even the explicit references to Jesus are later insertions. One interpreter finds it incomprehensible that a Christian author would use Job rather than Jesus as the prime example of a righteous sufferer (5:7-11; Shillington: 86).

Despite the scarcity of direct references to Jesus, the letter abounds with echoes of Jesus' teachings. To be sure, nowhere does James quote the Gospels, nor does he attribute any sayings to Jesus. Yet the cumulative weight of the similarities suggests some kind of dependence. In his dissertation, Dean B. Deppe surveyed sixty commentators between 1833 and 1985 who made correlations between James and the synoptic gospels. The number ranged from only four or five resemblances to sixty-five, with an overall average of eighteen parallels. Almost every verse in James was at some point cited as a parallel (Batten 2009: 73; Bauckham 2019: 9–10). One reason for the range in number of parallels scholars find is the difficulty of knowing what constitutes an allusion. The following list represents the most notable connections to the synoptic sayings of Jesus, with the first eight being what Deppe considered "conscious" or "deliberate allusions":

- James 1:5 and Matthew 7:7//Luke 11:9 (Ask and you will receive.)
- James 2:5 and Matthew 5:3//Luke 6:20b (The poor will inherit the kingdom.)
- James 4:2 and Matthew 7:7//Luke 11:9 (Ask and you will receive.)
- James 4:9 and Luke 6:21, 25b (Those who laugh will mourn.)
- James 4:10 and Matthew 23:12//Luke 14:11//18:14b (The humble are exalted.)
- James 5:1 and Luke 6:24 (Woe to the rich.)
- James 5:2-3a and Matthew 6:19-20; Luke 12:33b (Do not store up wealth.)
- James 5:12 and Matthew 5:33-37 (Oaths are prohibited.)
- James 1:2 and Matthew 5:10-12//Luke 6:22-23 (Rejoice in suffering.)
- James 1:4 and Matthew 5:48 (Be perfect.)
- James 1:19-20 and Matthew 5:22 (Refrain from anger.)
- James 1:22-23 and Matthew 7:24-26//Luke 6:47-49 (Hearing and doing are important.)
- James 2:10 and Matthew 5:18-19 (Keep the whole law.)

- James 3:12 and Matthew 7:16 (Trees bear their kind of fruit.)
- James 3:18 and Matthew 5:9 (Make peace.)
- James 4:4 and Matthew 6:24//Luke 16:13 (Choose between two loyalties.)
- James 4:11-12; 5:9 and Matthew 7:1-2//Luke 6:37 (Do not judge others.)

The closest parallel is the prohibition of oaths, found only in James and Matthew. It does not seem to have roots in earlier Jewish tradition, suggesting that it originated with Jesus. Notably, most of the parallels are to Jesus' teachings in the Sermon on the Mount (fifteen of the above seventeen examples) or to material that Luke and Matthew have in common.

Even though James rarely if ever uses the same wording as the Gospels, the thematic and theological parallels with the Jesus tradition are evident. Both Jesus and James speak of God upsetting power imbalances between rich and poor. Both highlight the moral requirements of the Jewish law rather than ritual purity. Both understand God to be a generous Giver of good gifts. And both urge people to choose between the way of good and the way of evil. Dale Allison notes that James also shows the influence of the Jesus tradition in his use of certain linguistic idioms (e.g., "Who among you . . . ?"; 2014a: 70–73).

How best to explain the similarities between James and the Jesus tradition in the synoptic gospels is a matter of considerable debate. Despite many variations, the proposals can be categorized into three main groups, with the last one dominating current discussion. (The following paragraph relies heavily on John Kloppenborg's survey, although he groups the models into six different categories.)

First, some interpreters do not believe there is any direct relationship between James and the Jesus tradition. This view is represented by older scholars such as Friedrich Spitta (1896) and Arnold Meyer (1930) and more recently by George Shillington (2015), who maintains that "the search for echoes and parallels between the epistle of James and the sayings of Jesus is less than profitable" (87). According to these writers, any similarities exist because they both drew from common Jewish wisdom traditions or Hellenistic moral teaching. In his influential mid-twentieth-century commentary on James, Dibelius acknowledged similarities between James and the sayings of Jesus and even some dependence, but he attributed their commonalities to the fact that they both belong to the literary genre of paraenesis, which involves advice or exhortation (17; Kloppenborg 2009: 73–74).

A second possibility is that James was literarily dependent on the written Gospels, especially the Gospel of Matthew. This view assumes that the letter was written by an anonymous Christian in the late first or early second century, decades after the Gospels. One scholar who exemplifies this view is Massey Shepherd (1956), who argued that the letter lacks exact verbal parallels because the author did not have a copy of Matthew's gospel but only heard it read in liturgical settings. Dale Allison is inclined to think James was dependent on Matthew (perhaps also on Luke) for reasons such as the appearance of the same Greek words (*poor, kingdom,* and *inherit*) in close succession in James 2:5 and Matthew 5:3-5 (2014a: 66). According to Allison, James did not attribute his teachings to Jesus, nor did he expect his readers to recognize them as such, since he was writing for a nonmessianic Jewish audience.

Third, the most common view currently is that the writer of James drew on a prewritten form of the Jesus traditions. A minority, who believe the brother of Jesus wrote the letter, attribute the similarities to James remembering and internalizing the teachings he personally heard from Jesus (Mayor; Adamson). This seems unlikely since the Gospels suggest that James was not a follower of Jesus during his lifetime (Mark 3:20-21; John 7:3-5). More likely, James drew on oral traditions of Jesus' teachings that circulated freely in the early church and were available to the authors of the synoptic gospels. This accounts for the similarities between the Letter of James and the Jesus traditions while also explaining the lack of verbal correspondence. Peter Davids exemplifies this perspective as he comments on the saying about oaths (James 5:12; Matt 5:33-37): "The structural variety would indicate that the saying circulated in more than one form in the church with James having a shorter, more classical form and Matthew a longer, more Semitic one. Priority cannot be established, especially since mixed forms were also known" (1982: 190). Some have suggested that the earliest stages of the oral tradition did not have Jesus' name attached, which could be why James did not credit Jesus (Schröter: 238).

Some scholars argue that James's sources included written traditions, "a form of the Jesus tradition prior to its incorporation into the gospel narratives," perhaps a version of Q (for the German term *Quelle*), the hypothetical "source" of Jesus' sayings used by Matthew and Luke but not Mark or John (Batten 2011: 382). This would explain the letter's similarity to Matthew and Luke but not Mark. Since the letter has so many parallels with the Sermon on the Mount, James may have known a form of Q that was circulating in the Matthean community (Q^{Matt}) and that had been influenced by traditions unique to Matthew, such as the saying about oaths. This theory has been argued in detail by Patrick Hartin but is embraced by others as well (2009b; e.g., Kloppenborg 2009). Although the connection with Matthew's Sermon on the Mount is strong, some scholars caution that in some matters James is closer to the Gospel of Luke, as with some vocabulary and his hostility toward the rich (Davids 1982: 49).

If James deliberately used or was heavily shaped by pre-synoptic Jesus traditions, the question still remains as to *how* he used these teachings. In general, he seems to have reformulated and adapted them for his own context. Since ancient societies did not understand intellectual property as we do today, this kind of paraphrasing would not have been considered plagiarism. In fact, reformulating a respected teacher's work was a way to honor them. The letter already exemplifies such paraphrasing in its use of Septuagint texts. For example, in 1:9-11 James echoes Isaiah 40:6-8, but in his own words, rather than as a recognizable quotation. Allison argues that James 3:7-9 alludes to Genesis 1:26 and is a "clear illustration of its author turning scripture into his own words" (2014a: 63). At times James may be reformulating Jewish wisdom aphorisms (cf. James 1:19; Prov 16:32; Sir 5:11; Bauckham 1999: 83).

What follows are two different understandings of how James incorporated and reshaped the Jesus traditions. First, some scholars have argued that James intentionally adapted his written sources using the practice of *aemulatio* taught in ancient Greco-Roman rhetorical handbooks (e.g., Wachob; Kloppenborg 2009). Students learning the art of rhetorical argumentation were taught not to copy their sources verbatim but to "perform the sources in new ways" by augmenting, clarifying, and paraphrasing them to address the needs of a different audience (Hartin 2009b: 58–59). The purpose was to adapt the source to be as persuasive as possible for a new situation. Listeners/readers were expected to recognize the source of the reformulation, since that would elicit appreciation and give the new rendering authority.

Second, Richard Bauckham's proposal draws less from Greek rhetorical education and more from Jewish wisdom. He compares James's use of the Jesus traditions to the way the second-century BCE sage Ben Sira (Sirach) depended on Proverbs for creating his own aphorisms. Ben Sira never quotes Proverbs directly but reproduces ideas in fresh ways, sometimes supplementing them, sometimes tweaking them. He states, "When intelligent people hear a wise saying, they praise it and add to it" (Sir 21:15; cf. 39:1, 6). Thus, where Proverbs says, "A stone is heavy, and sand is weighty, but a fool's provocation is heavier than both" (Prov 27:3), Ben Sira reformulates: "Sand, salt, and a piece of iron are easier to bear than a stupid person" (Sir 22:15).

What this ancient sage did with Proverbs, James did with the Jesus tradition. Bauckham insists that James's sayings are not intentional allusions to the Jesus tradition (contrary to the model that envisions James adapting written sources using Greek rhetorical methods), nor is it "possible to pin down his knowledge of the tradition of Jesus' sayings to particular Gospels or Gospel sources" (1999: 31). Rather, James was a teacher who drew on Jewish wisdom tradition and especially on the wisdom of Jesus. He was so immersed in the teachings of Jesus that they became his own. He did not repeat them but was inspired by them (14).

The one saying that could be a deliberate allusion is James 5:12, but even here James expands Matthew's version to include a motive clause. James's readers may have recognized his indebtedness to Jesus, but this is irrelevant since it was not his intent to make allusions. Bauckham also notes that neither Jesus nor James incorporated all features of traditional Jewish wisdom (e.g., warnings against idleness, advice on raising children). Rather, like Jesus' distinctive wisdom, James's teaching calls for uncompromising obedience. It aims at the formation of a countercultural community that overturns dominant values. It is conscious of eschatological judgment and worships a God who is extravagantly compassionate, generous, and merciful. And it contrasts the priorities of God with those of the world (Bauckham 2019: 24).

We cannot know for certain whether the writer of the Letter of James had access to a written source or oral traditions about Jesus, nor can we prove that James expected his readers to recognize allusions to Jesus' teachings. However, given the sheer number of similarities, especially to the Sermon on the Mount, it is difficult not to conclude that James knew and intended to pass on the teachings of his Lord. He was so thoroughly soaked in these teachings that he did not need to or attempt to attribute them to Jesus but simply used them to exhort the struggling Jewish messianic communities in the Diaspora to align themselves more closely with the vision of Christian discipleship present in those teachings.

JAMES THE BROTHER OF JESUS Scholars disagree about whether the Letter of James was written by the brother of Jesus or a later anonymous Christian *[Authorship and Date, p. 343]*. Nevertheless, there is a consensus that the name refers to Jesus' brother and that the author was claiming to stand in Jesus' tradition and pass on his teachings. Given James's stature in the early church, it is perhaps surprising that the New Testament contains only eleven clear references to him, three of them in Acts of the Apostles. Traditions about James also developed outside the canon; studies in the last few decades suggest that he was "a towering figure in the earliest church" (Painter 1999: 1).

Sources about James The earliest canonical references to James are in Paul's letters, where he appears as an apostle, church leader, and one of the people to whom Jesus appeared after his resurrection (Gal 1:18-19; 2:9, 11-14; 1 Cor 15:7). In 1 Corinthians 9:5-6, Paul says that "the brothers of the Lord" took their wives on missionary journeys. We know nothing about James's wife, however, and there is no indication elsewhere that James traveled beyond Judea with the gospel message. Apart from general references to Jesus' brothers in the Gospels (Matt 12:46-50//Mark 3:21-35//Luke 8:19-21; John 2:12; 7:3-10), James is explicitly named as part of Jesus' family in Mark 6:3//Matt 13:55. Acts describes the birth of the church in Jerusalem, where James became a prominent leader, but the book foregrounds the roles of Peter and Paul in the mission of the church. James is mentioned only in 12:17; 15:13-21; 21:18 ("brothers" in 1:14). Finally, the Letter of Jude names its author as the brother of James, presumably Jesus' brother.

Evidence about James in noncanonical writings is varied and complex and requires careful sifting. The Jewish historian Josephus (37–100 CE) confirms the prominence of James by reporting on the death of "the brother of Jesus, who was called Christ, whose name was James" (*Jewish Antiquities* 20.9.1). Early Christian writers in the second to fourth centuries contain traditions about James's character and his death (e.g., Eusebius, Clement of Alexandria, Jerome). Various noncanonical and apocryphal writings contain legends about the death of James (e.g., the Pseudo-Clementine Recognitions), claim to be written by James (e.g., Protevangelium of James), or relay Jesus' instructions to or about James (e.g., First Apocalypse of James; Coptic Gospel of Thomas). Such writings, while not providing reliable historical information, offer fascinating glimpses into how James was perceived in the early centuries of the church.

James's Biological Relationship to Jesus According to Mark 6:3//Matt 13:55-56, Jesus' siblings included not only James but also Joses, Judas, Simon, and some unnamed sisters. Paul calls James "the brother of the Lord" in Galatians 1:19. The question of whether James and his siblings were biologically related to Jesus arose within a few centuries of the early church and has continued throughout history. The primary reason is the tradition of the perpetual virginity of Mary. In short, if Mary remained a virgin both before and after Jesus' birth, then James could not have been Jesus' actual brother. Two traditions dominate church teaching on this. According to the Protevangelium of James, Joseph had several children, including James, and was an older widower before he was betrothed to Mary. Joseph died sometime after Jesus was born and fathered no more children with Mary, explaining his absence in the Gospels. This became the dominant view in the Eastern church. The other position, found in Eusebius and Jerome, was that James was a cousin or other near relative of Jesus. Proponents argue that the word "brother" in Aramaic and Hebrew can mean kinsman or even neighbor. Thus, James was purportedly the son of Joseph's brother Clopus and/or another Mary who was the sister of Mary the mother of Jesus (John 19:25). This tradition has been dominant in Western Christianity.

Both views have problems. The Protevangelium of James is an imaginative, apocryphal story about Mary, not reliable historical writing. Moreover, if James had been a cousin, Gospel writers would presumably have used Greek words for "cousin," not "brother." Eusebius makes a clear distinction between Jesus' brother James, the first bishop of Jerusalem, and Symeon, the second bishop and Jesus' cousin. In short, there is no compelling reason to believe that James was not the biological son of Mary and Joseph and the brother of Jesus. This is the position of most Protestants today and also most biblical scholars.

James during Jesus' Earthly Ministry The question of whether James was a follower of Jesus during his earthly ministry is difficult to answer with certainty, but Mark 3:20-21 and John 7:3-5 suggest he was not. Some scholars argue differently, however (e.g., Shillington, Painter). Painter argues that the people who try to restrain Jesus in Mark 3:21 are his disciples, not his family, since the Greek is ambiguous (2019: 241). Even though the Gospel of John explicitly says, "For not even his brothers believed in him" (7:5), Painter counters that the Johannine disciples also do not fully understand or believe until after the resurrection (John 16:31-32; Painter 2019: 242). Shillington believes James would not have risen to prominence in the Jerusalem church so soon after Jesus' resurrection if he had not been a follower during Jesus' lifetime (50). Even though James was probably not counted among Jesus' disciples during Jesus' earthly ministry, he was an early witness to the resurrected Christ (1 Cor 15:7) and gathered with other believers after the ascension (Acts 1:14).

James's Character, Status, and Role in the Early Church The New Testament does not say how James became the leader of the church in Jerusalem. According to Acts and Galatians, however, he appears to have risen to that stature quickly after Jesus' resurrection. By the time James the son of Zebedee was killed by King Herod, perhaps early in 44 CE, James's position was such that Peter asked for the news of his own release from prison to be conveyed to "James and to the brothers and sisters" (Acts 12:17). Paul says that on his first visit to Jerusalem after meeting the risen Christ, he conferred only with Peter and James (Gal 1:19), implying that these were the two key leaders. Early church writers such as Eusebius, Clement, and Hegesippus offer inconsistent reports, sometimes saying that Jesus himself appointed James leader and apostle and other times suggesting that his authority derived from the other apostles (Johnson 1995: 100–101).

James played an important role in negotiating the relationships between Jewish and Gentile Christianity. Although James and Paul have sometimes been pitted against each other, several New Testament texts portray James as a mediator who fully supported Paul's mission to the Gentiles. In his Letter to the Galatians, Paul sounds bristly and defensive when he speaks about the other leaders of the church (2:6) because he is facing challenges from Jewish believers who insist that Gentiles must adhere fully to Jewish law. Yet Paul does not question the other apostles' authority. Instead, he goes to Jerusalem to seek approval for his mission (2:2). Paul calls James one of the "acknowledged pillars" of the Jerusalem church and lists him before Cephas and John (2:9). In contrast to the "false brothers and sisters" challenging Paul (2:4), James approves of Paul's mission to the "uncircumcised" (2:7) and extends to him and Barnabas "the right hand of fellowship" (2:9). The only condition James sets, that Paul's team "remember the poor" (2:10), is consistent with the Letter of James's concern for the poor.

At the so-called Jerusalem Council in Acts 15 (which may or may not be the same meeting that Gal 2 describes) the outcome is similar. As leader of the Jerusalem church, James mediates a conflict stirred up in Antioch by some who argue that Gentile believers must be circumcised to be saved. After listening to testimony from Peter, Paul, and Barnabas and quoting Scripture, James offers a compromise: Gentiles need not be circumcised but must follow laws that guard against idolatrous practices (Acts 15:13-21).

In Galatians 2:11-14 Paul recounts another run-in with the leaders of the Jerusalem church. "Certain people [who] came from James" prompted Peter and other Jews to withdraw from table fellowship with Gentiles. These are not the same people as the "false believers" in 2:4, but it is unclear who they were, what they said, or if they even represented James's views. Paul only says that, as a result of their coming, Peter and the other Jews acted hypocritically out of fear of the "circumcision party." Because Paul says "certain people came from James" (2:12), readers of Galatians often assume James was responsible for their behavior even though this was not necessarily the case.

Acts 21 also highlights James's negotiating skills. After Paul's third missionary journey, he pays an official visit to James and the elders in Jerusalem. The Jerusalem leaders "glorify God" when they hear of Paul's work among the Gentiles and reciprocate with reports of God's work among the Jewish believers. To squelch false rumors that Paul is teaching Jews in the Diaspora to abandon the Mosaic law, James counsels Paul to demonstrate his Torah loyalty by participating in purification rites with four men who had taken a vow and to pay the expenses for these rituals, which he does.

In short, in both Galatians and Acts, James appears as a conflict mediator, negotiating between those who insist on full observance of Jewish law for believing Gentiles, including circumcision, and those who advocate for inclusion of Gentiles without demanding adherence to Jewish ritual law. He is depicted as a devout observer of the Torah, adept at listening to both sides and arriving at a compromise acceptable to both.

Church tradition after the New Testament amplifies this portrayal of James. For example, the following quotation from Eusebius (325 CE) illustrates the esteem in which James was held:

> Then James, whom the ancients surnamed the Just on account of the excellence of his virtue, is recorded to have been the first to occupy the throne of bishop of the church of Jerusalem. . . . Clement [of Alexandria] . . . writes thus: "For they say that Peter and James and John after the ascension of our Savior, as if also preferred by our Lord, strove not after honor, but chose James the Just bishop of Jerusalem." (*Ecclesiastical History* 2.1.2–3)

Other stories and sayings about James "the Just" or "the Righteous" (Greek *dikaios*) highlight his piety and asceticism. Eusebius and Jerome portray him as a Nazirite, although they do not use the term (Eusebius, *Ecclesiastical History* 2.23.5; Shillington: 133). Jerome quotes Hegesippus as saying that James "also went alone into the temple and prayed in behalf of the people insomuch that his knees were reputed to have acquired the hardness of camels' knees" (*Illustrious Men* 2; cited in Van Voorst: 187). In the Coptic gnostic Gospel of Thomas, Jesus instructs his disciples to go to James the Righteous as their leader, "for whose sake heaven and earth came into being" (5.12). Although most of these traditions are exaggerated and of questionable historicity, they point to the reputation that James had in the early church.

James's Death The New Testament contains no record of James's death. Josephus reports that he was stoned to death when Ananias ("Ananus") was high priest, in the interim period between Roman procurators Festus and Albinus (*Jewish Antiquities* 20.9.1). That would set his death in 62 CE, which is generally taken to be historically reliable. Beyond the date, the circumstances surrounding James's death vary according to the motives of the sources, and accounts are likely fictionalized (Johnson

1995: 100). In Josephus's account, the high priest, a Sadducee, accuses James and some others of breaking the law and orders them to be stoned, but the Pharisees protest. According to Eusebius, Clement of Alexandria said James was thrown off the pinnacle of the temple and beaten to death (*Ecclesiastical History* 2.1.4). Hegesippus reports that it was the scribes and Pharisees, not the Sadducees, who threw James down from the temple and began stoning him when he declared his allegiance to Jesus as Messiah and refused to persuade the crowds otherwise.

Like Jesus, James prayed, "Forgive them, for they know not what they do" (Luke 23:34 KJV) before he was clubbed to death (*Eccl. Hist.* 2.23). The Pseudo-Clementine Recognitions recounts an altercation between James and the high priest on the steps of the temple in which James argued that the Law and the Prophets point to Jesus as Messiah. This led to a riot in which James was thrown from the steps and beaten (1.66–70). Other apocryphal writings continue this idealizing, martyrologic tradition, always lauding James's great righteousness. In the end, all that can be said with some confidence is that James died a violent death around 62 CE, probably at the hands of Jewish leaders opposed to the messianic movement.

The "James Ossuary" In 2002, *Biblical Archaeology Review* reported a discovery that drew widespread attention. An ancient ossuary with the Aramaic inscription "James, son of Joseph, brother of Jesus" had been found in a private collection (Lemaire). In the Second Temple period, Jewish burial customs prescribed that a dead body be interred in a sepulchre until it decomposed. The bones were then removed and placed into an ossuary, a box or container often made of limestone, which was kept in a family tomb (McCane). Although the "James ossuary" has been confirmed as dating from the first century, considerable controversy surrounds the inscription. The Israeli Antiquities Authority deemed it to be a forgery in 2003, but in 2012 the owner, the antiquities collector Oded Golan, was acquitted of forgery charges. Further analyses of the artifact have continued over the years. Even if the inscription is genuine, the names would have been common enough that one cannot say for certain that they refer to the Jesus and James of the New Testament. However, the identification of the deceased as not only a son, but also a brother, suggests that the brother may have been important. The authenticity and historical value of the ossuary continues to be debated and to intrigue many.

James in the New Testament and Today According to the New Testament, after Jesus' resurrection, James became a respected leader of the primarily Jewish church in Jerusalem. He was a follower of the Messiah Jesus after the latter's resurrection and possibly before. In terms of Jewish law, he seems to have played a mediating role between groups that urged a more conservative stance toward Gentiles and the Pauline mission, which advocated open acceptance of Gentiles. He (or someone who wished to pass on his teachings) wrote a letter to several churches about faith that is lived out in compassion for the poor, love of neighbor, patience in suffering, and nonjudgmental speech. In this letter, he not only reflected the Hebrew Scriptures but also the teachings of Jesus. Extracanonical sources suggest that he died a violent death in 62 CE.

Given James's stature in the Jerusalem church, it is puzzling that relatively little remains about him in the New Testament writings. Perhaps it was because the early church, wishing to emphasize Jesus' divine origins, distanced him from his biological siblings and minimized James's role. Perhaps it was because the Gospels and Acts were written after the Jewish war and destruction of the temple (66–70 CE), when the Jewish Christian community centered on James's leadership had dispersed (Shillington: 53). For whatever reason, we catch only glimpses of the stature, character, and life of James. Still, his practical letter to Jewish believers scattered around the Mediterranean continues to be cherished by the church today.

READING JAMES THROUGH THE CENTURIES The Letter of James is a short and arguably insignificant book in comparison with New Testament giants such as the Gospel of John or Paul's Letter to the Romans. Yet the history of how it has been used and interpreted through the centuries is fascinating, illuminating its distinctiveness, its potential for controversy, and its broad appeal. Attentiveness to reception history guards against myopic interpretations of Scripture and reveals that sometimes contemporary "new" solutions to exegetical problems really are not so new after all (Allison 2000).

Because a thorough survey of the history of interpretation is impossible here, we briefly comment on emphases and issues in certain periods of history and in some sample contexts. Unfortunately, such a study must rely largely on what has been written about James in scholarly contexts. Missing is the use of the letter in sermons, liturgy, letters, family devotions, hymns, and poetry, all of which would give a more fulsome understanding of how Christians throughout history have appreciated James.

A foray into reception history quickly illuminates how social location and religious context affect interpretation and reveals the "plasticity of texts" (Allison 2000: 12). Doctrinal disputes in the patristic era influenced which verses received attention. Martin Luther's personal religious experience and consequent theological developments have had an enormous influence on the history of the letter's interpretation. Preoccupation with historical-critical questions in the Enlightenment meant that James's moral teachings and practical wisdom were often sidelined. Reading James in the global South and in contexts of oppression does just the opposite. People who are suffering tend to care more about loving neighbors than about date and authorship. Reading James with people of other faiths provides yet another interpretive lens and opens possibilities for dialogue and mutual understanding. Recognizing how context shapes interpretation reminds readers today to consider how their own circumstances govern what they see in James and suggests a stance of humility rather than insistence that *my* reading is the only valid one.

Early Church and Medieval Period By the end of the fourth century, James was firmly established in the New Testament canon. Until then its status as authoritative Scripture was on less solid ground, at least in some parts of the church.

On the whole, the Greek church in the East was quicker to accept James than the Western Latin church. The first explicit reference to the Letter of James as Scripture is in the writings of Origen (ca. 184–251), who was the head of the catechetical school in Alexandria, Egypt, and quoted James frequently. The letter may have been known before then, but evidence is unclear. Eusebius says that Clement of Alexandria (d. ca. 211–15), Origen's predecessor, wrote a commentary on the Catholic epistles, but it is not extant; although knowledge of James is implicit in his writings, Clement never cites the letter directly. Patristic writers after Origen also used the Letter of James, no doubt because of his influence. Didymus the Blind (313–98), another head of the Alexandrian school, wrote the first extant commentary on James. Athanasius (296–373) included James in the canonical list that comprises the New Testament as we have it today. Cyril of Alexandria (d. 444) "used James more extensively than any other Greek writer," quoting from 39 verses about 124 times (Johnson 1995: 130).

Acceptance and use of James was slower in the Western, Latin church. First Clement (late first century) and Shepherd of Hermas (second century) exhibit some remarkable similarities to James in language and content. For example, Shepherd of Hermas uses a form of the word "double-minded" some fifty-five times, a word that does not appear in Greek literature before James. First Clement 10.1-7 contains ideas and vocabulary found in James 2:21-25 (Lockett 2019: 257–61). Luke Timothy Johnson argues that 1 Clement and Shepherd of Hermas drew from the letter even if they did not explicitly quote it (1995: 72–79). However, without explicit citations, it is difficult to ascertain whether there was literary dependence or whether these hortatory writings (writings intending to exhort) all drew from common Christian tradition and stock themes.

James is absent from the Muratorian Canon (late second century or perhaps fourth century). The letter is rarely, if ever, alluded to by North African church fathers such as Tertullian (160–215) and Cyprian (d. 258), or by Ambrose of Milan (339–97). Allusions or direct references to James in the writings of the Roman church in the third and fourth centuries, while not plentiful, do exist (Johnson 1995: 136). According to Johnson, "James came into general use in the West through the influence of three scholars closely associated with Rome and devoted to Origen: Rufinus, Jerome, and Augustine" (1995: 137). Jerome included James in the Vulgate, which became the most widely used Latin version. Augustine's consideration of the letter as authoritative Scripture and written by the brother of Jesus also ensured its acceptance.

By the end of the fourth century, James was widely received as canonical and was in the canon lists of various church councils. Its use varied in different parts of the church, however. The Cappadocians' use of James was sparse, for example, whereas "monks in every region made enthusiastic use of James," finding the practical ethical teaching appealing (Johnson 1995: 131–32). Although major lengthy commentaries were scarce before the Reformation (Allison 2013: 100), one of the most influential was by the Venerable Bede in England in the eighth century.

Issues that preoccupied later interpreters were not the concerns of theologians in this era. Although differences in emphasis between Paul and James on faith and works were noted, the hermeneutical impulse was always to harmonize. For example, Paul had people not yet baptized in mind, and James was instructing Christians after baptism. Hotter on the ecclesiastical agenda were the immutability of God and the divinity of Christ, and for this James 1:17-18 proved to be a favorite text. A passage that challenged ancient interpreters was 1:12-15 because of its perceived tension with "Lead us not into temptation" in the Lord's Prayer (Matt 6:13 KJV) and stories of God testing people. Interpretation in these early writings tended to be somewhat atomistic rather than sustained theological reflection.

Reformation and Enlightenment Period Although James received scant attention in the centuries after Augustine, that changed in the Reformation era, especially with Martin Luther. In his preface to the letter in his 1522 German translation of the New Testament, Luther notoriously described James as "a right strawy epistle . . . for it has nothing of the nature of the gospel about it" (George: 372). Initially he did not view James and Paul as contradictory, but as his theology of justification "by faith alone" developed and hardened, so did his perspective on James. Luther's objection to the letter was based on two factors: (1) its failure to "preach Christ," since it contains nothing about Christ's atoning death or resurrection; and (2) its message of justification by faith *and* works, which Luther deemed to be incompatible with Paul's gospel of salvation *sola fide*. Luther concluded that James could not be apostolic and that the unknown second-generation author "[threw] things together chaotically" (quoted in Allison 2013: 102).

Even though Luther did preach from James and said it included many worthwhile teachings, he relegated it to the end of the New Testament, along with Hebrews, Jude, and Revelation. For Luther, the doctrine of justification by faith alone was the "article by which the church either stands or falls" (George: 373). By implication, the church would surely fall if it relied on the message of James.

Other Reformers did not share Luther's radical views on James even though they too believed that salvation was by divine grace and not human works. Calvin wrote a major commentary on the letter in 1550 and considered it authoritative even if its authorship was in doubt. He and other Reformers like Zwingli understood Paul and James to be complementary, not contradictory, and addressing different concerns.

According to Calvin, "We must remember not to expect everyone to go over the same ground" (quoted in S. Chester 2019: 283). He also emphasized, with James, that true faith must result in good deeds and that the rich should not be greedy but help the poor. Again, context is significant since Calvin was writing at a time when many refugees had come to Geneva, fleeing persecution in France.

The Catholic church reacted vigorously to Luther's reading of James. In various debates, at the Council of Trent (1546), and in polemical writings post-Trent, church leaders asserted the letter's apostolic authorship and authority and drew heavily on James to refute Protestant theological claims. They often cited James 2:14-26 to support the traditional teaching on the necessity of good works for justification, harmonizing Paul and James. Also significant was the use of 5:14 to support the doctrine of extreme unction, which Reformers consistently opposed.

In the radical wing of the Reformation, Anabaptists and Mennonites insisted that faith and works could not be separated, even as they too believed salvation to be the gift of God rather than the result of human effort. To be a Christian meant to follow Jesus in all of life and even to death. The Sermon on the Mount encapsuled what discipleship should look like; since James echoed many of Jesus' teachings in Matthew 5–7, they regarded the letter highly.

Although Anabaptists did not all read Scripture the same way, and there was diversity in Anabaptist theology and practice, some verses and themes in James stand out in writings of the early Anabaptists. They found strength in James's words about enduring trials and suffering with patience during times of persecution and economic hardship (1:2-4; 5:7-11). Anabaptists believed strongly that God effects real change in people through new birth and that this transformation is reflected in obedience and holy living. Thus, they quoted James 1:18 with some frequency. Keeping unstained from the world (1:27) and not being friends with the world (4:4) fit nicely into an ecclesiology of being a visible church separate from the world. Anabaptists supported their refusal to swear oaths of allegiance by citing James 5:12. Undergirding all their belief and practice was the conviction that "true evangelical faith cannot be dormant" but must bear fruit in deeds of service, compassion, and peace (Menno Simons, *CWMS*: 307; see the TLC sections through the commentary for how James resonates with the Anabaptist tradition of faith and practice.)

Luther's quarrel with James subsided for a time but erupted again with new vigor in historical-critical scholarship of the eighteenth century and beyond. As William Baker aptly summarizes, "Efforts to resolve the issue of authorship and the related issue of James's relationship to early Christianity occupied nearly all scholarly resources from the mid-1800s to the late twentieth century" (Baker 2005: 348). In short, James was valued more as a source for historical reconstruction than a practical guide for Christian living. Like Luther, many scholars perceived James and Paul to be incompatible on the question of justification, and

James 2:14-26 dominated interpretation. Like Luther, many believed the letter was written by a pseudonymous, second-century Jewish Christian.

One reconstruction primarily (but not solely) associated with the Tübingen School in the nineteenth century pitted Jewish Christianity, represented by James, and the dominant Pauline Gentile Christianity against each other. Adolf Jülicher, anticipating the work of Dibelius, deemed James to have no coherence of thought and to be "the least Christian book of the New Testament" (quoted in Johnson 1995: 150).

Of course, traditional views on apostolic authorship and the relationship of James and Paul continued as well. Ordinary Christians continued to read James and listen to sermons that were edifying for daily life, providing them help to manage their tongues, encouraging them in times of hardship, and inspiring them to care for widows and orphans. A substantial and influential commentary by Puritan clergyman Thomas Manton in the 1600s exemplifies this approach.

A significant voice challenging the Enlightenment's historical-critical approach to James was the nineteenth-century Danish philosopher and theologian Søren Kierkegaard. James was his favorite book of the Bible. It deeply influenced his thought, writings, and even personal life. Kierkegaard was not an exegete nor did he attend to the community-shaping orientation of the letter. Still, his work offers a perspective on James that still rings true for many today. He was disdainful of those who were Christians in name only and for whom the doctrine of justification by faith had become justification for a comfortable lifestyle barren of good works (Bauckham 1999: 162–63). Although he did not explicitly refer to James 2:14-26 often, he insisted that salvation by God's grace must be held in dialectical tension with a vigorous and practical ethic of love. The following three samples exemplify the significance of James for Kierkegaard's theology and draw heavily on Richard Bauckham's work on the topic.

In *For Self-Examination*, Kierkegaard uses the metaphor of a mirror in James 1:22-25 to reflect on biblical hermeneutics. He critiques academic biblical scholars who study Scripture objectively (look *at* the mirror), but never see themselves reflected *in* it. He argues for subjective personal reading that leads to self-knowledge, encounter with God, and transformation (Bauckham 1999: 2–3). In Kierkegaard's *Purity of Heart Is to Will One Thing*, James 4:8 prompts reflection on wholeness and perfection (versus double-mindedness) as the coherent center of the letter. Purity of heart is single-minded devotion to God and God's will, and it is only this that can make people whole or perfect. Such purity is "not inactive inwardness" but is expressed in concrete acts of love (Bauckham 1999: 167).

Kierkegaard's most beloved passage, on which he wrote four discourses, was 1:17-20. He called verse 17 "my first love" and "a commemorative coin more magnificent than all the world's treasures, but also a small coin that is usable in the daily affairs of life" (quoted in Bauckham 1999: 160). Characterizing God as the unchangeable Giver of all good gifts, this verse was the theological foundation of the letter. For

Kierkegaard, it implied that "everything that comes to one in life [even hardship] is a good and perfect gift so long as one accepts it with receptivity to God and trust in God" (Bauckham 2016: 45–46).

Contemporary Threads

Scholarship Scholarship on James in the last century is too voluminous to survey, but a few general observations can be made. Hugely influential has been the Hermeneia commentary by Martin Dibelius (German, 1921; English, 1976). His critical assessment was that James is not an actual letter addressed to a specific audience but paraenesis, "a text which strings together admonitions of general ethical content" (3). Moreover, it has no coherent structure and is virtually devoid of theological content.

Few scholars on James would agree with this assessment today. As one writer notes, "Nearly all twentieth-century study has attempted to breathe life into James after Dibelius's near deathblow to it" (Baker 2005: 348). In fact, the last forty years have shown a revival of interest in James, with many new commentaries, monographs, and articles published. Current scholarship gives attention to historical and literary questions and to insights gained from comparing James with contemporary Jewish and Greco-Roman literature. Instead of using James to promulgate negative anti-Jewish stereotypes, as often happened in the past, efforts are made to show James's positive indebtedness to his Jewish tradition. Questions about the relationship of Paul and James have not disappeared, and little consensus exists about critical questions such as structure, author and date, audience, or unifying theme.

Reading for Liberation James denounces the rich who live opulently and oppress the poor (5:1-6), and he warns against privileging those who enter the assembly with fine clothes and gold rings (2:1-9). Throughout the history of the church, Christians with privilege, power, and wealth have found ways to soften James's words and squirm out from under their condemnation. As just one example, the annotator of James in the sixteenth-century *Rhemes New Testament* says the following: "The Apostle means not . . . that there should be no difference . . . [between] the free man and the bond, the rich and the poor, between one degree and another. For God and nature, and the necessity of man, have made such distinctions, and men are bound to observe them" (quoted in S. Chester 2019: 286–87). Such an interpretation contrasts sharply with the way James has been read in social locations of poverty and injustice in the last century or two.

Frederick Douglass (1818–95) was an African American who escaped slavery and became an ardent abolitionist and orator. Margaret Aymer's book *First Pure, Then Peaceable: Frederick Douglass Reads James* illuminates how the Letter of James figured prominently in Douglass's arguments for the abolition of slavery. Especially significant for him was 3:17, which he used in ten extant sermons between 1845 and 1860 (Aymer: 27). Douglass read Scripture through the "darkness" of slavery, says Aymer. Even though the Bible was often "inhospitable" because of how it was used to justify slavery, African American readers "consistently read the Bible against the culture in which they found themselves" and "established rhetorical-imaginary 'homes' within the 'scriptures' of their captors," from which they could draw strength, courage, and comfort (Aymer: 29). James 3:17 became such a "home" for Douglass and most fully defined true Christianity for him. In a speech he gave in London in 1846, titled "American Slavery, American Religion, and the Free Church of Scotland," he talked about the religion he loved as opposed to the false religion of chattel slavery: "I love the religion of our blessed Saviour. I love that religion that comes from above, in the 'wisdom of God, which is first pure, then peaceable, gentle, and easy to be entreated, full of mercy and good fruits, without partiality and without hypocrisy'" (quoted in Aymer: 36). Given his context, it is not surprising that another text Douglass frequently used in his speeches was James 1:27. Social location shapes reading.

Cain Hope Felder (1943–2019), an African American professor and leader in the black Methodist church, also exemplifies the liberationist perspective on James: "For readers today James contains a harvest of good things for those seeking an alternative to the comfortable kind of civil religion that tolerates injustices of the status quo" (Felder 1998: 1786).

Elsa Tamez is a Mexican liberation theologian and biblical scholar who for many years taught in the Latin American Biblical University in Costa Rica. The opening line in her book *The Scandalous Message of James* is this: "If the Letter of James were sent to the Christian communities of certain countries that suffer from violence and exploitation, it would very possibly be intercepted by government security agencies. The document would be branded as subversive" (2002: 1). She notes efforts to "intercept" the letter throughout history. Because Western academia has privileged abstract thought, the practical ethical teachings of James have often been sidelined. Even more, James has been ignored by rich Christians who find its radical critique of wealth and injustice unpalatable. Tamez reads the letter through the lens of immigrant (diasporic) communities who suffer from economic deprivation and persecution and who might find the values of patronage seductive (2011). For them, James offers a liberating message of hope that commends solidarity with the poor, militant patience, and faith grounded in praxis.

The popularity of James extends to Africa and Asia as well. According to one scholar, "James may be the single biblical book that best encapsulates the issues facing global South churches today" (Jenkins: 60). A study of West African churches in the 1960s reported, "James was the most-cited work in sermons" (61). The letter appeals to many African Christians because of its wisdom character, practical advice about daily living, and strong Old Testament connections. Additionally, it resonates with people who find themselves in socioeconomic situations of suffering, poverty, and disparity, similar to James's original readers. The letter has been used to inspire resistance movements against injustice and oppression. African churches that emphasize physical and spiritual healing ministries rely heavily on James 5:13-18. And James 1:27 offers valuable teaching about the church's care for vulnerable widows and orphans (Jenkins: 174–75).

The need for healing and deliverance from oppression comes in many forms. One of those is addiction. The Letter of James was one of the "absolutely essential" New Testament writings for the founders of Alcoholics Anonymous, who met together regularly for Bible study and prayer. In fact, they valued James so highly that they considered calling their fellowship "The James Club" ("*Pass It On*": 147). Especially important was James's emphasis that "faith without works is dead," a line that appears several times in *Alcoholics Anonymous* (often called *The Big Book*) and influenced some of the "twelve steps" that urge people to act on what they believe and know. James's exhortation "Confess your sins to one another . . . so that you may be healed" (5:16) was incorporated into the practice of sharing honestly about one's failings in meeting circles. Other themes appear in the organization's literature, even when James is not explicitly quoted, such as patience, temptation and trials, seeking wisdom, and controlling the tongue.

From this cursory survey, it is evident that Christians in social locations of poverty, sickness, and oppression are much less concerned about whether James and Paul contradict each other or whether the apostle James authored the letter than were European scholars in the Enlightenment or North American scholars in the late twentieth century. For them, James is about practical, everyday faith, lived out in concrete deeds of compassion, solidarity with the poor, and spiritual practices such as prayer and healing.

Interreligious Dialogue In the last few decades, the potential of James for interreligious dialogue has become apparent. The reasons for this are twofold: (1) Because James does not speak about Jesus as divine Son of God nor mention his death and resurrection, adherents of faiths that find such ideas objectionable are more amenable to James. (2) James's emphasis on moral living, conveyed through aphorisms and short, practical teachings, also makes the letter attractive to non-Christian faiths. Although examples could be drawn from numerous traditions, we highlight two.

Kōsuke Koyama draws on his experiences as a missionary in Thailand to explore how James can bridge Christianity and Buddhism. In a chapter of *Waterbuffalo Theology*, he imagines welcoming the apostle to Thailand. Again, we see how context influences reading. Koyama says that Asian Buddhists value detachment, for it leads to tranquility. James's claim that possessions decay (1:9-11; 5:1-3) expresses "the basic sentiment in Thai religious life" (119). If possessions are transient and life itself is a mist that will vanish (4:14), one learns the value of detachment. God is detached from the material world and does not change or "heat up" (1:17). According to James, evil desire and passions are the source of conflicts and quarrels (4:1) and eventually lead to death (1:14-15); therefore, people must remain cool and detached. Since anger is "a state of a hot heart" (Koyama: 120), James's counsel to slow down, take time, and listen resonates (1:19). One cannot get to nirvana (heaven) with a "hot" tongue. Koyama maintains that 4:4 expresses James's "'detachment theology' in a nutshell: 'Don't you know that to be the world's friend means to be God's enemy?'" (122). Some attachment is nevertheless necessary, especially commitment to Jesus Christ (2:1) and involvement with the world in caring for widows and orphans.

Others have noted resonance between Buddhism and James. The Dalai Lama, in a collection of reflections on the Bible, introduced James thus: "I am struck by the similarities between this beautiful letter in the Bible and some of the texts in my own Buddhist tradition" (359). He notes the following similarities between James and his own faith: single-minded commitment, being slow to speak and anger, the transience of life, respect for the poor, and the importance of translating faith into action (360–64).

James also contains much that is attractive to Muslims. His admonition to make plans according to what "God wills" (cf. 4:15) is very close to the Muslim "*Inshallah*." Additionally, in 5:11 James describes God as compassionate and merciful, which is how Muslims characterize God (Jenkins: 88). Mustafa Akyol, author of *The Islamic Jesus* (2017), begins his book by recounting how he was given a New Testament in his hometown of Istanbul. He began underlining passages that he liked in blue and those he found objectional to his Muslim faith in red. When he got to the book of James, all his underlining was in blue. Not only did the letter not contradict his faith, but many passages were similar to teachings in the Qur'an. In addition to those noted above, he says that, in Islam, believers are also "those who have faith and do right actions," an expression that is used in some forty-five different verses in the Qur'an (Akyol: 66). Muslims understand Jesus as a prophet and teacher. This is compatible with James, where Jesus is most evident in the teachings that James passes on and where Jesus' divine status is muted. Finally, the eschatology of James overlaps with eschatology in Islam: both believe in a final judgment of God and the return of Jesus.

This survey of some representative ways that James has been read and used through the centuries illuminates how different aspects of the letter receive attention, depending on the political, economic, religious, and intellectual landscape of the time. Although historical and literary questions, such as the relationship between Paul and James, will undoubtedly occupy scholars for the foreseeable future, the greatest impact of this short letter will continue to be, as it always has been, James's practical teachings about how to live as followers of Jesus.

THE TONGUE One of the most memorable and provocative parts of the Letter of James is its discourse on the tongue in 3:2-12. This unit is loaded with figurative language, demonstrating James's skill as a literary artist. Less often noticed is how the physical structure of the tongue is uniquely suited to the comparisons the author makes.

Figurative Language about the Tongue Human speech is a common topic in wisdom literature; the book of Proverbs contains many succinct, often colorful sayings about its positive and negative potential. Nowhere is the topic developed as extensively as in James 3:2-12, however, nor with such rhetorical impact. The language is almost entirely figurative, with only verses 2 and 9 containing words explicitly about speech. Because the figures of speech draw on common, everyday experiences, the down-to-earth message of the passage is easily grasped.

The main literary feature of the text is *metonymy*, which is "calling a thing by the name of something typically associated with it" (Caird: 136). Referring to a queen as "the crown" or the film industry as "Hollywood" are examples of metonymy. Since the tongue is necessary for the formation of words, it is easily associated with speech. This metonymy is so commonplace that we do not even think about the fact that "the power of the tongue" (cf. James 3:5) does not refer literally to a muscle in the body.

Most of the figures of speech in 3:2-12 are *metaphors* or *similes*, which connect two different things to make a comparison. As G. B. Caird says, in metonymy "the link between the two referents is one of contiguity and in metaphor it is one of comparison" (137). These literary figures use something known to prompt a listener to perceive something else in fresh ways. Similes make the comparison explicit, usually with "like" or "as." Metaphors make implicit and nonliteral comparisons by substituting the name of one thing for the name of the other (152). "Her hands were as cold as ice" is a simile. "Her feet were blocks of ice" is a metaphor.

In James's discourse on the tongue, 3:3-5a are similes even though the writer does not use "like" or "as." After describing the effects of a bit on a horse and a rudder on a ship, James says, *So also the tongue is a small member* (v. 5a). The words *so also* make the comparison explicit. In 3:10-12 James juxtaposes the mouth that both blesses and curses with a spring that gives both fresh and brackish water. A mouth is *like* a spring in that it is impossible for two opposite things to come out of the same opening. Similarly, a mouth that both blesses and curses is *like* a fig tree that yields olives or a grapevine producing figs. These comparisons take the form of rhetorical questions, not similes, but the analogy is nonetheless clear.

The sentence *the tongue is a fire* is a metaphor. Of course, the tongue is not literally a fire, but it has elements in common with fire, thereby helping James to sharpen the point. In every metaphor there is correspondence between some aspects of the tenor (the thing described) and the vehicle (the figurative language describing it) but not all. That is, there is always an "is" and an "is not." Irrelevant features of the analogy must thus be ignored. For example, it is not fruitful to wonder about the "oxygen" that keeps the tongue burning. When James compares the tongue (that is, speech) to fire, the primary point of comparison is the *effect* each can have—what G. B. Caird calls a "pragmatic comparison" (147–48). Speech and fire can cause both pain and widespread destruction when not controlled. They can both "burn" people.

The second key point of comparison is that each begins small relative to the extent of damage it can cause. A small spark from a tossed cigarette can ignite a huge forest fire, just as a few words can inflict pain with lasting consequences. (Consider the potential consequences of words like "I don't love you anymore" or "Stupid!")

A third key point of comparison is that both fire and speech are difficult to control and can quickly get out of hand. Finally, in 3:6 James says the tongue *is itself set on fire by hell* (Gehenna), implying that the source of the tongue's destructive power is external to itself, like a match that lights a fire. Metaphors that have a high degree of correspondence between vehicle and tenor, such as this one, often become popular since the comparison they make is quite obvious (Caird: 155). Not surprisingly, the metaphor of speech as fire appears elsewhere in Jewish wisdom and prophetic literature (Prov 16:27; 26:21; Isa 30:27; Jer 5:14; Sir 28:11, 22; Psalms of Solomon 12.2). James's skillful hand prevents the metaphor from being simply a stock metaphor that ceases to be effective by developing it further and piling on even more metaphors.

The use of parallel metaphors helps the reader focus on key points of comparison, instead of getting sidetracked by inconsequential characteristics (Caird: 150). Initial references to horses being guided by bits and ships by rudders (vv. 3-4) draw attention to how small things have power to effect great change. The fact that ships and horses can be steered contrasts with the uncontrollability of the tongue. Subsequent metaphors then turn to the tongue's destructive capacity.

In another metaphor, James juxtaposes *restless evil* and *deadly poison* (v. 8), evoking the image of a poisonous snake's "restless" tongue (cf. Ps 140:3). The word *stain* or *pollute* (v. 6 NET) is a metaphor that evokes a visual image for a verbal phenomenon. When James contrasts the tongue with animals that can be tamed (vv. 7-8), he depicts the tongue as a wild animal. Ironically, the human species can tame other species, but not its own members.

Although most of the literary devices in 3:2-12 are those which elicit comparison (metonymy, simile, metaphor), other figures of speech also animate this section. *Rhetorical questions*, such as those in verses 11-12, do not seek an answer but are often used in persuasive discourse for their expressive force (Abrams: 183). James also utilizes *hyperbole* to make his point. For example, claiming that the tongue *sets on fire the cycle of life* (v. 6) and is *a restless evil, full of deadly poison* (v. 8), is exaggeration, since the tongue can also be comforting and kind. Saying that every species can be tamed and has been tamed (v. 7) is another hyperbole. The text is full of *alliteration*, although it is difficult to represent this feature of the Greek well in English translations. Someone once suggested that *mikros melos . . . megalē* might be captured by "a minuscule member [with] massive boasts" (v. 5), *polla ptaiomen* by "substantial stumbling" (v. 2), and *hēlikon pyr hēlikēn hylēn anaptei* by "a wee fire a wide woods ignites" (v. 5).

An example of *onomatopoeia*, in which the sound of words corresponds to their meaning, is the Greek *akatastaton kakon* (*restless evil*, v. 8);

the words not only *mean* something harsh but also *sound* harsh. Finally, *parallelism* of clauses contributes to the rhythmic flow of the text, as in verses 6 and 9.

It is ironic that in a discourse on the destructive power of the tongue, James exemplifies the delights of speech and the ability to craft words that enchant and persuade. Precisely with his literary artistry, he proves his point: the tongue is powerful. The vivid metaphors and clever figures of speech appeal to the imagination, prompt reflection, and lodge firmly in the memory. The more they stick in the mind, the greater the likelihood that they will affect behavior for the good.

The Physical Tongue Although James's words about the tongue in 3:2-12 are entirely metaphorical, attention to the anatomical features of the tongue reveal that it is uncannily suited to the qualities of speech that he highlights. Primary among these are the tongue's agility and strength, especially in relation to its size, and the need to control it. The ability of speech to persuade, delight, and provoke corresponds to the tongue's physical flexibility. The following comments about the relevance of the anatomy and physiology of the tongue for James 3 are heavily indebted to Dr. Denny M. Smith, longtime professor of dentistry at the University of Manitoba.

The human tongue is part of an intricate and complex group of muscles. It consists of four paired intrinsic muscles, which run in different directions (vertical, lateral, etc.), enabling the tongue to change its shape from long and narrow to short and thick. Whereas most human muscles pull in only one direction and change shape mostly by contracting, the tongue has no such limitations (Smith). It can change its height, length, width, and thickness. The intrinsic muscles that make up the tongue are surrounded and supported by four other extrinsic muscle groups, some of which are attached to the lower jaw and some of which are attached to a bone loosely connected to the neck. These muscle groups allow the tongue to move in almost all directions. The unique combination of intrinsic and extrinsic muscles allows us to move food around in our mouths and to swallow. They also enable us to make a variety of sounds that we put together to form words. Attention to what the tongue does when one makes a hard "g" sound (touches the palate) and "d" sound (touches the teeth) illustrates how important the tongue is for the formation of words.

Notable for our purposes is the "high degree to which the tongue is free from [physical] restraints. . . . While the human body contains other muscles that lack secure bony attachments (the heart and the intestines, for example), there is no muscular tissue comparable to the human tongue" (Smith). In contrast to other skeletal muscles, the tongue is attached at only one end, while the other end flaps around freely.

> It is [thus] freer to change shape and to move than is any other human muscle complex. With reduced skeletal restraints, control of the tongue is dependent upon nerves, a highly complex

> element itself. The nerves that control the tongue (cranial nerves) are connected directly to the brain, and thus provide the fastest, and the least disturbed, means for interacting with human thought and emotions. The tongue . . . functions in great part by way of patterned responses (habits). (Smith)

This remarkable lack of anatomical restraint corresponds to the metaphorical lack of restraint that the tongue exhibits when it speaks. Idiomatic expressions like "wagging tongues" or to be "loose-tongued" capture this relationship between the physical and metaphorical. Since nerves connected to the brain control the tongue, awareness of one's emotions, careful thought, and the development of habits of self-discipline become important for controlling the tongue. Nevertheless, humans will always struggle with the tongue's lack of restraint. Physically and metaphorically, this lack of restraint is a gift—but only if the tongue is being directed from "above."

The tongue is dangerous because of the damage speech can do. The tongue also lives in a physically dangerous environment. To quote Dr. Smith again,

> It is subject to abrasion and to laceration from sharp tooth surfaces and sharp [or hot] foodstuffs. It resides in a bacteria-laden cavity. It has the responsibility of moving food back onto tooth surfaces during each chewing cycle. This function places the tongue between the teeth as the jaws begin to close, moving away to safety only a fraction of a second before the teeth close with a force of several hundred pounds per square inch. It is surprising that we do not bite our tongue in each chewing cycle.

Just as the tongue's agility and quickness can prevent it from getting crushed by the teeth, so also it is metaphorically agile and can extricate us from sticky situations, saving us from harm. Although living in a physically dangerous environment, the tongue nevertheless allows us to taste delicious food and lick our lips. In a metaphorically dangerous environment, it enables us to make jokes, speak kind words to our neighbor, and praise God. The tongue is a powerful muscle in our bodies and a powerful instrument of speech. It is a gift of God to be nurtured, guarded, and disciplined.

WISDOM IN THE APOCRYPHA The Apocrypha, the deuterocanonical books, are not in the Hebrew Bible but are part of the Septuagint (LXX), the Greek version of the Hebrew Bible prepared in the third and second centuries BCE. Consisting mostly of translations of the Hebrew Bible, it also contains some additional writings that do not appear in the Hebrew Bible as well as additional material in books that do, such as Esther and Daniel. Since the Septuagint functioned as the Scriptures of the early church, these additional writings were considered authoritative for centuries and were included in Jerome's influential Latin translation, the

Vulgate (late 4th c.). The Protestant Reformers of the sixteenth century did not consider them part of the canon since they were not in the Hebrew Bible, but they continued to see them as useful. The Roman Catholic church retained their canonical status, however, and continues to include these books in the Bible, as does the Orthodox church.

The two writings of the Apocrypha that are most significant for a study of the Letter of James are the Wisdom of Solomon and the Wisdom of Jesus, Ben (son of) Sira (also referred to as Sirach or Ecclesiasticus). Both fall into the category of wisdom literature.

The Wisdom of Solomon, though written in the name of King Solomon, is an anonymous work dating from the first century BCE or early first century CE. It was probably written in Greek by a Hellenistic Jew in Alexandria, Egypt. Unlike the ancient Israelite wisdom, the Wisdom of Solomon has an eschatological outlook and refers to events from Israel's history, such as the exodus (10:14-21; 19:1-12). It contains a striking personification of Wisdom as a woman (chaps. 7–8), who is co-existent with God, "a spotless mirror of the working of God and an image of God's goodness" (7:26).

Sirach was written in Hebrew in the 180s BCE and translated into Greek in Alexandria by Ben Sira's grandson after 132 BCE (R. Clifford 1998: 116). In structure, content, and style, Sirach was influenced by the book of Proverbs (Bauckham 1999). Like Proverbs, the book contains aphorisms and instructions about life, but it also contains other literary material, such as prayers (36:1-17) and a panegyric about heroes of Israel's past (chaps. 44–50). According to some scholars, "the author's major theological step is the identification of the figure of Wisdom with the Torah" (Dell: 874). Like Proverbs and the Wisdom of Solomon, it contains a hymn of praise to personified Wisdom (chap. 24).

Much in the Letter of James resonates with these two deuterocanonical writings. James does not quote them directly, but the resemblances suggest that he was influenced by them. This is especially true of Sirach. Like James, Sirach sees wisdom as a gift from God (1:1-10), warns against the dangers of the tongue (19:7-12; 20:5-8, 18-20; 28:13-26), urges patience in times of testing (2:1-5), and speaks of silver rusting (29:10). At times the two writers even use similar wording (cf. James 1:12-14//Sir 15:11-17; James 1:19//Sir 5:11; McCartney 2009: 46).

James also echoes themes and perspectives of the Wisdom of Solomon, though they do not share as many verbal similarities. Like James, the Wisdom of Solomon speaks about wisdom as a divine gift to those who ask in faith (7:7); the oppression of the righteous (2:10-20); the brevity of life, especially of the arrogant (5:8-14); and the problem of grumbling and slander (1:10).

Some Protestant Christians may wonder why they should pay attention to the similarities between James and wisdom books that are not part of their Bible. For one thing, these writings *were* religiously authoritative writings for the first Christians, and the author of James would not only have been familiar with them but also was influenced by them. They would especially have resonated with his Hellenistic Jewish Christian readers as they used the Septuagint, with those apocryphal books. We gain a better understanding of and appreciation for James and his church when we consider the impact of Sirach and the Wisdom of Solomon. Second, the Deuterocanon continues to be read and esteemed by many Christians today—certainly the Roman Catholic and Orthodox church, yet also others, including descendants of the Anabaptists, such as the Hutterites. The Apocrypha was part of the Bible of the early Anabaptists and is quoted in their writings. The Scripture index of *Martyrs Mirror*, for example, includes more references to Sirach and the Wisdom of Solomon than any other book in the Apocrypha. It can be instructive to read the Bible together with the worldwide communion of churches throughout time, including those parts that are often neglected.

THE WISDOM TRADITION AND JAMES In biblical studies, the word "wisdom" characterizes a particular genre of literature as well as the tradition or theology embedded in such literature. The Letter of James has sometimes been called the wisdom book of the New Testament (Conzelmann: 960; Kovalishyn 2021: 173). Of the sixty-seven words that appear only in James in the New Testament, thirty-four occur in the wisdom literature of the LXX; of the twenty-one words that appear only once in the New Testament outside of James, nineteen are common in wisdom literature (McCartney 2009: 281). On the basis of vocabulary alone, James clearly draws on the wisdom tradition, if not also wisdom literature itself.

The biblical books considered to be "wisdom literature" are Proverbs, Job, and Ecclesiastes, and in the Apocrypha, the Wisdom of Solomon and Sirach (Wisdom of Ben Sira or Ecclesiasticus) *[Wisdom in the Apocrypha, p. 374]*. Elements of the wisdom tradition also appear in various other writings, including Genesis (e.g., the Joseph narrative), Song of Songs, Daniel, and several Psalms (e.g., 1, 25, 34, 37, 39, 49, 73, 111, 112, and 128). Biblical wisdom literature has similarities to and may have been influenced by ancient Egyptian and Mesopotamian wisdom texts (cf. Proverbs 22:17–24:22//the Egyptian Instruction of Amenemope; Woman Wisdom in Proverbs 8//*Maʿat* of Egyptian wisdom).

The wisdom traditions of Israel probably originated in the family and tribe and were passed on orally from generation to generation. At some point, though, proverbs were written down and collected and other wisdom writings were created. This could have happened only in educated circles in school or court settings or among professional scribes and sages who were political and social advisers to the king (Dell: 870; R. Clifford 1997: 6–7).

It is difficult to define "wisdom tradition" because it is so broad. Wisdom writers used some common literary forms, but not all are present in all wisdom literature. Likewise, wisdom shares a certain perspective on life, and themes and topics recur, but not all are universally present. Both literary forms and typical wisdom content appear in the Letter of James, leading to the perception of James as "wisdom literature of the New Testament."

In terms of literary forms and genres, much wisdom literature in the Ancient Near East consisted of instruction, such as the Egyptian wisdom text Instruction of Amenemope. Such instruction included exhortations and aphorisms and sometimes collections of proverbs (R. Clifford 1997: 8). Wisdom literature also incorporated dialogues, poetry, longer discourses, autobiographical elements, short fables, beatitudes, and analogies. The Letter of James contains many of these literary forms. The aphoristic style and numerous short proverbs (e.g., James 2:13; 3:18; 4:4b, 17) give the letter a disjointed style and encourage comparison with the book of Proverbs. The letter also contains dialogues (James 2:18-20) and some longer discourses (e.g., 2:14-26; 3:2-12). Like other wisdom literature, James makes liberal use of similes (e.g., 1:6), metaphors (e.g., 4:14), and observations from nature (1:11; 3:11-12).

An underlying conviction of the wisdom tradition is that a divinely ordained order in creation encompasses both the natural and the human world (R. Clifford 1997: 9). In the biblical worldview, the universe's structure is ordained by God. Humans must learn to fit within this order if they want to live well and successfully. Wisdom is not knowledge for its own sake; it is practical. It "is the reasoned search for specific ways to assure well-being and the implementation of those discoveries in daily existence" (Crenshaw: 15). Because creation has an inherent order, wisdom can be acquired by careful observation of nature and the way the world works, as in James 3:11-12. Its theology is thus creational rather than covenantal. It generally does not consider key salvation-historical events, such as God's promise to Abraham and Sarah, the exodus, Sinai covenant, or kingship. This is true for the Letter of James as well, which does not mention the deeds, death, or resurrection of Jesus so central to Christian faith.

Wisdom literature draws lessons for life from human experience, reason, and observation (cf. James 2:1-4; 3:3-5). It "entails knowledge of and appropriate action with reference to *particular* circumstances" (Van Leeuwen: 849). Wisdom pays attention to consequences of deeds and to cause and effect. Often it embodies an ethical dualism, identifying two ways of living. The way of righteousness leads to blessing, and the way of the wicked brings curses (cf. Ps 1; James 4:4). Some wisdom literature wrestles with the question of unjust suffering and the problem of evil, and some is critical or skeptical of conventional wisdom (Job, Ecclesiastes).

The following topics, common in wisdom literature, also appear in James: riches and poverty, speech, anger, suffering, planning for the future, patience, pride, and envy. Often wisdom literature reflects on the nature of wisdom itself (Sir 24; James 3:13-18). Even though biblical wisdom draws insights from human experience and nature, it is nevertheless rooted in God, the source of all true wisdom (Prov 9:10; James 1:5; 3:17).

Although early forms of Israelite wisdom (e.g., Proverbs) interacted little with God's revelation to Israel, law, and prophecy, this changed by the second century BCE. Wisdom in the Second Temple period "assumes the authority of the law for Jewish life and bases some of its instruction on the law" (Bauckham 1999: 33). After Sirach, wisdom "views the world in an eschatological perspective and attaches eschatological sanctions to its precepts" (33). This is evident in James, which views the law as authoritative and has a clear eschatological orientation (1:12; 2:8-12; 4:11-12; 5:7-9).

All of the above explains why the Letter of James is sometimes understood as wisdom literature. That it draws on the wisdom tradition seems clear. However, some scholars argue that although James *incorporates* many features of wisdom, it is not a wisdom book *per se* (McCartney 2000: 55). James shows significant differences from Jewish wisdom literature.

First and most compelling is that James seems to address real situations (e.g., 2:1-9; 5:13-16). He is not merely a sage offering arm's-length, generic advice on how to live well. As McCartney aptly states, "He is a pastor concerned for his people" (2000: 55).

Second, the letter envisions a horizontal relationship of mutuality between James and his *brothers and sisters*, rather than a hierarchical one of teacher and student or parent and child, as in much wisdom instruction.

Third, much of traditional wisdom is absent from James, such as advice about working hard, raising children, human friendship, and being a good wife, as in Proverbs. In fact, "like the teaching of Jesus, that of James lacks the moderation, practical compromise, and alignment with social convention that are often characteristic of the Jewish wisdom tradition" (Bauckham 1999: 100). For example, the prohibition of oaths radicalizes Jewish practice (5:12); also, in his castigation of the rich, James resembles the prophets more than wisdom (5:1-6).

Fourth, although the letter incorporates various literary forms used in wisdom literature, they are only tools and not constitutive of the writing as a genre (McCartney 2000: 55). Finally, James's Christian presuppositions make it distinct from the Jewish wisdom tradition. References to God giving us birth by the word of truth (1:18), the church as a body that prays and confesses sin (5:13-20), the coming of the Lord (5:7-9), and both true faith and true wisdom being evident in deeds (2:14-26; 3:13-18) are some of the things that set James apart from traditional wisdom.

Bibliography

Abrams, M. H.

1993 *A Glossary of Literary Terms*. 6th ed. Fort Worth: Harcourt Brace. College Publishers, 1993.

Achtemeier, Paul J.

1985 *Romans*. Interpretation, a Bible Commentary. Louisville: John Knox.

Adamson, James B.

1976 *The Epistle of James*. New International Commentary on the New Testament. Grand Rapids: Eerdmans.

Akyol, Mustafa

2017 *The Islamic Jesus: How the King of the Jews Became a Prophet of the Muslims*. New York: St. Martins Press.

Alcoholics Anonymous

1984 *"Pass It On": The Story of Bill Wilson and How the A.A. Message Reached the World*. New York: Alcoholics Anonymous World Services.

Allison, Dale C.

1999 *The Sermon on the Mount: Inspiring the Moral Imagination*. Companions to the New Testament. New York: Crossroad Publishing Co.

2000 "Exegetical Amnesia in James." *Ephemerides theologicae Lovanienses* 76 (2000): 162–66.

2013 *A Critical and Exegetical Commentary on the Epistle of James*. New York: Bloomsbury.

2014a "The Audience of James and the Sayings of Jesus." In *James, 1 & 2 Peter, and Early Jesus Traditions*, edited by Alicia Batten and John Kloppenborg, 58–77. Library of New Testament Studies 478. London: Bloomsbury T&T Clark.

2014b "James Through the Centuries." *American Theological Inquiry* 7, no. 1 (January): 11–23.

2015 "The Jewish Setting of the Epistle of James." *In die Skriflig/In Luce Verbi* [online] 49, no. 1 (May 8). doi: https://doi.org/10.4102/ids.v49i1.1897.

Anderson, Bernhard W.
1988 "Abraham, the Friend of God." *Interpretation* 42.4 (October): 353–66.

Autero, Esa
2017 "Reading the Epistle of James with Socioeconomically Marginalized Immigrants in the Southern United States." *Pneuma* 39:504–35.

Aymer, Margaret P.
2007 *First Pure, Then Peaceable: Frederick Douglass Reads James*. Library of New Testament Studies 379. London: T&T Clark.

Baker, William R.
2005 "James, Book of." In *Dictionary for Theological Interpretation of the Bible*, edited by Kevin J. Vanhoozer, 347–51. Grand Rapids: Baker Academic.
2008 "Searching for the Holy Spirit in the Epistle of James: Is 'Wisdom' Equivalent?" *Tyndale Bulletin* 59.2:293–315.
2011 "Slander." In *Dictionary of Scripture and Ethics*, edited by Joel B. Green, Jacqueline E. Lapsley, Rebekah Miles, and Allen Verhey, 735–36. Grand Rapids: Baker Academic.

Balentine, Samuel E.
2002 *Leviticus*. Interpretation, a Bible Commentary. Louisville: John Knox.

Balko, Radley
2020 "There's Overwhelming Evidence That the Criminal Justice System Is Racist. Here's the Proof." *Washington Post*, June 10. https://www.washingtonpost.com/graphics/2020/opinions/systemic-racism-police-evidence-criminal-justice-system/.

Bartchy, S. S.
1997 "Slave, Slavery." *Dictionary of Later New Testament and Its Developments*, edited by Ralph P. Martin and Peter H. Davids, 1098–102. Downers Grove, IL: InterVarsity.

Batten, Alicia J.
2009 *What Are They Saying about the Letter of James?* New York: Paulist Press.
2011 "The Jesus Tradition and the Letter of James." *Review and Expositor* 108 (Summer): 381–90.
2014 "The Urbanization of Jesus Traditions in James." In *James, 1 and 2 Peter, and Early Jesus Traditions*, 78–96. Edited by Alicia J. Batten and John S. Kloppenborg. Library of New Testament Studies 478. New York: T&T Clark.
2017a "Early Anabaptist Interpretation of the Letter of James." *Annali di Storia dell'Esegesi* 34.2 (July–December): 537–51.
2017b *Friendship and Benefaction in James*. Emory Studies in Early Christianity 15. Atlanta: SBL Press.
2019 "Reading James with the Social Sciences." In *Reading the Epistle of James: A Resource for Students*, edited by Eric F. Mason and Darian R. Lockett, 177–91. Atlanta: SBL Press.

Bauckham, Richard
1999 *James: Wisdom of James, Disciple of Jesus the Sage*. New Testament Readings. London: Routledge.
2016 "Kierkegaard and the Epistle of James." In *Kierkegaard and Christian Faith*, edited by Paul Martens and C. Stephen Evans, 39–54. Waco: Baylor University Press.

2019 "James and Jesus Traditions." In *Reading the Epistle of James: A Resource for Students*, edited by Eric F. Mason and Darian R. Lockett, 9–26. Atlanta: SBL Press.

Bird, Michael F., and Preston M. Sprinkle, eds.

2009 *The Faith of Jesus Christ: Exegetical, Biblical, and Theological Studies.* Peabody, MA: Hendrickson.

Bird, Phyllis

1999 "The Harlot as Heroine: Narrative Art and Social Presupposition in Three Old Testament Texts." In *Women in the Hebrew Bible*, edited by Alice Bach, 99–117. New York: Routledge.

Block, Daniel I.

2012 *The Gospel according to Moses: Theological and Ethical Reflections on the Book of Deuteronomy.* Eugene, OR: Cascade Books.

Blomberg, Craig L.

1999 *Neither Poverty nor Riches. A Biblical Theology of Possessions.* New Studies in Biblical Theology. Downers Grove, IL: InterVarsity.

Blomberg, Craig L., and Mariam J. Kamell

2008 *James.* Exegetical Commentary on the New Testament. Grand Rapids: Zondervan.

Bonhoeffer, Dietrich

1954 *Life Together: The Classic Exploration of Christian Community.* Translated by John W. Doberstein. New York: Harper & Row.

1959 *The Cost of Discipleship.* Translated from the German *Nachfolge.* London: SCM. First published 1937.

Boyd, Gregory A.

2013 *Benefit of the Doubt. Breaking the Idol of Certainty.* Grand Rapids: Baker Books.

Braght, Thieleman J. van

1886 *The Bloody Theatre or Martyrs Mirror. The Story of Seventeen Centuries of Christian Martyrdom, from the Time of Christ to A.D. 1660.* 3rd English ed. Translated by Joseph Sohm from the 1660 Dutch ed. Elkhart, IN: Mennonite Publishing. https://archive.org/details/MartyrsMirror.

Bratcher, Robert G.

1980 "The Meaning of *Kosmos*, 'World,' in the New Testament." *Bible Translator* 31.4 (October): 430–34.

Bray, Gerald, ed.

2000 *James, 1–2 Peter, 1–3 John, Jude.* Ancient Christian Commentary on Scripture, New Testament: vol. 11. Downers Grove, IL.: InterVarsity.

Brueggemann, Walter

2016 *Money and Possessions.* Interpretation: Resources for the Use of Scripture in the Church. Louisville: Westminster John Knox.

Byron, Gay L.

2007 "James." In *True to Our Native Land: An African American New Testament Commentary*, edited by Brian K. Blount, 461–75. Minneapolis: Fortress.

Caird, G. B.

1980 *The Language and Imagery of the Bible.* Grand Rapids: Eerdmans.

Carey, James W.

1989 *Communication as Culture. Essays on Media and Society.* Boston: Unwin Hyman.

Carmody, T. R.

1989 "Matthew 18:15-17 in Relation to Three Texts from Qumran Literature (CD 9:2-8, 16-22; 1QS 5:25-6:1)." In *To Touch the Text*, edited by M. P. Horgan and P. J. Kobelski, 141–58. New York: Crossroad.

Chester, A.

1994 "The Theology of James." In *The Theology of the Letters of James, Peter, and Jude*, edited by A. Chester and R. P. Martin, 6–62. New Testament Theology. Cambridge: Cambridge University Press.

Chester, Stephen J.

2019 "Salvation, the Church, and Social Teaching: The Epistle of James in Exegesis of the Reformation Era." In *Reading the Epistle of James: A Resource for Students*, edited by Eric F. Mason and Darian R. Lockett, 273–89. Atlanta: SBL Press.

Cheung, Luke L., and Kelvin C. L. Yu

2019 "The Genre of James: Diaspora Letter, Wisdom Instruction, or Both?" In *Reading the Epistle of James: A Resource for Students*, edited by Eric F. Mason and Darian R. Lockett, 87–98. Atlanta: SBL Press.

Claassens, L. Juliana M.

2012 *Mourner, Mother, Midwife. Reimagining God's Delivering Presence in the Old Testament*. Louisville: Westminster John Knox.

Clifford, Anne M.

2001 *Introducing Feminist Theology.* Maryknoll, NY: Orbis Books.

Clifford, Richard J.

1997 "Introduction to Wisdom Literature." In *The New Interpreter's Bible*, vol. 5. Nashville: Abingdon.

1998 *The Wisdom Literature*. Interpreting Biblical Texts. Nashville: Abingdon.

Coker, K. Jason

2015 *James in Postcolonial Perspective: The Letter as Nativist Discourse.* Minneapolis: Fortress.

Conrad, Edgar W.

2009 "Satan." In *The New Interpreter's Dictionary of the Bible*, edited by Katharine Doob Sakenfeld, 5:112–16. Nashville: Abingdon.

Conzelmann, H.

1976 "Wisdom in the NT." In *The Interpreter's Dictionary of the Bible: An Illustrated Encyclopedia; Supplementary Volume*, edited by Keith Crim, 956–60. Nashville: Abingdon.

Creach, Jerome F. D.

2003 *Joshua*. Interpretation, a Bible Commentary. Louisville: John Knox.

Crenshaw, James L.

1998 *Old Testament Wisdom: An Introduction*. Revised and enlarged. Louisville: Westminster John Knox.

Culpepper, R. Alan

1986 "The Power of Words and the Tests of Two Wisdoms: James 3." *Review and Expositor* 83.3 (Summer): 405–17.

Dalai Lama

2005 "The General Epistle of James." In *Revelations: Personal Responses to the Books of the Bible*, edited by Richard Holloway, 359–64. Toronto: Viking Canada.

Davids, Peter H.
1982 *The Epistle of James. A Commentary on the Greek Text.* New International Greek Testament Commentary. Grand Rapids: Eerdmans.
2005 "The Test of Wealth." In *The Missions of James, Peter, and Paul: Tensions in Early Christianity*, edited by Bruce Chilton and Craig Evans, 355–84. Supplements to Novum Testamentum 115. Leiden: Brill, 2005.
2019 "The Good God and the Reigning Lord: Theology of the Epistle of James." In *Reading the Epistle of James. A Resource for Students*, edited by Eric F. Mason and Darian R. Lockett, 117–28. Atlanta: SBL Press.

Davis, Ellen F.
2000 "Critical Traditioning: Seeking an Inner Biblical Hermeneutic." *Anglican Theological Review* 82.4 (Fall): 733–51.

Dell, Katharine J.
2009 "Wisdom in the OT." In *The New Interpreter's Dictionary of the Bible*, edited by Katharine Doob Sakenfeld, 869–75. Nashville: Abingdon.

Deppe, Dean B.
The Sayings of Jesus in the Epistle of James. Doctoral dissertation. Chelsea, MI: Bookcrafters.

Dibelius, Martin
1976 *James.* Revised by H. Greeven. Translated by M. A. Williams. Edited by H. Koester. Hermeneia . . . Commentary. Philadelphia: Fortress.

Doerksen, Paul
2024 "Extravagant Hope, Urgent Patience: The Uncontrollability of Renewal." *Direction* 53.1 (Spring): 24–38. https://directionjournal.org/53/1/extravagant-hope-urgent-patience.html.

Dordrecht Confession of Faith
1632 https://gameo.org/index.php?title=Dordrecht_Confession_of_Faith_(Mennonite,_1632).

Downs, David J.
2013 "Economics, Taxes, and Tithes." In *The World of the New Testament: Cultural, Social, and Historical Contexts*, edited by Joel B. Green and Lee Martin McDonald, 156–68. Grand Rapids: Baker Academic.

Dyck, Cornelius J.
1985 "The Suffering Church in Anabaptism." *Mennonite Quarterly Review* 59.1 (January): 5–23.
1995 *Spiritual Life in Anabaptism.* Scottdale, PA: Herald Press.

Edgar, David H.
2001 *Has God Not Chosen the Poor? The Social Setting of the Epistle of James.* JSNTSup 206. Sheffield: Sheffield Academic.

Elkins, Kathleen Gallagher, and Thomas M. Bolin
2020 "Boundaries, Intersections, and the Parting of the Ways in the Letter of James." *Interpretation: A Journal of Bible and Theology* 74.4 (2020): 335–43. https://www.scribd.com/document/557388214/Boundaries-Intersections-and-the-Parting-of-the-Ways-in-the-Letter-of-James-Elkins.

Elliott, John Hall
1993 "The Epistle of James in Rhetorical Social Scientific Perspective: Holiness-Wholeness and Patterns of Replication." *Biblical Theology Bulletin* 23.2 (Summer): 71–81.

2007 "Envy, Jealousy, and Zeal in the Bible: Sorting Out the Social Differences and Theological Implications—No Envy for YHWH." In *To Break Every Yoke: Essays in Honor of Marvin L. Chaney*, edited by Norman K. Gottwald and Robert B. Coote, 344–64. Sheffield: Sheffield Phoenix.

Ellul, Jacques

2014 *On Being Rich and Poor. Christianity in a Time of Economic Globalization.* Compiled, edited, and translated by Willem H. Vanderburg. Toronto: University of Toronto Press.

Evans, M. J.

1983 "The Law in James." *Vox evangelica* 13:29–40.

Felder, Cain Hope

1982–83 "Partiality and God's Law: An Exegesis of James 2:1-13." *The Journal of Religious Thought* 39.2 (Fall–Winter): 51–69.

1998 "James." In *The International Bible Commentary: A Catholic and Ecumenical Commentary for the Twenty-First Century*, edited by William Reuben Farmer, 1786–1813. Collegeville, MN: Liturgical Press.

Finger, Reta Halteman

2007 *Of Widows and Meals. Communal Meals in the Book of Acts.* Grand Rapids: Eerdmans.

Finger, Thomas N.

2004 *A Contemporary Anabaptist Theology. Biblical, Historical, Constructive.* Downers Grove, IL: InterVarsity.

2006 "Salvation: Contrasting Concepts and Church Conflicts." *Vision: A Journal for Church and Theology* 7.1 (Spring): 22–31.

Francis, F. O.

2970 "Form and Function of the Opening and Closing Paragraphs of James and 1 John." *Zeitschrift für die neutestamentliche Wissenschaft* 61:110–26.

Freyne, Seán.

2014 *The Jesus Movement and Its Expansion: Meaning and Mission.* Grand Rapids: Eerdmans.

Friedmann, Robert

1955 "*Gelassenheit.*" In *Global Anabaptist Mennonite Encyclopedia Online (GAMEO)*. 1955. Rev. 2018 by Sam Steiner. https://gameo.org/index.php?title=Gelassenheit&oldid=162946.

Furcha, E. J.

1989 *Selected Writings of Hans Denck, 1500–1527.* Texts and Studies in Religion 44. Lewiston, NY: Mellen.

Furnish, Victor P.

1972 *The Love Command in the New Testament*. Nashville: Abingdon.

Gaiser, Frederick J.

2010 *Healing in the Bible: Theological Insight for Christian Ministry*. Grand Rapids: Baker Academic.

2015 "'Are any among you sick?': The Church's Healing Mandate (James 5:13-20)." *Word & World* 35.3 (Summer): 241–50.

Gardner, Richard B.

1991 *Matthew*. Believers Church Bible Commentary. Scottdale, PA: Herald Press.

Garland, David E.
2001 *Reading Matthew: A Literary and Theological Commentary*. Macon, GA: Smyth & Helwys.

Gench, Frances Taylor
2015 *Encountering God in Tyrannical Texts: Reflections on Paul, Women, and the Authority of Scripture*. Louisville: Westminster John Knox.

George, Timothy
1986 "'A Right Strawy Epistle': Reformation Perspectives on James." *Review and Expositor* 83.3 (Summer): 369–82.

Gerbrandt, Gerald E.
2015 *Deuteronomy*. Believers Church Bible Commentary. Harrisonburg, VA: Herald Press.

Gibbs, Jeffrey A.
2006 *Matthew 1:1—11:1*. Concordia Commentary. Saint Louis: Concordia.
2015 "The Myth of 'Righteous Anger': What the Bible Says About Human Anger." *Concordia Theology*. October 19. https://concordiatheology.org/2015/10/the-myth-of-righteous-anger-what-the-bible-says-about-human-anger/.

Goldingay, John
2006 "Anger." In *A–C*, vol. 1 of *The New Interpreter's Dictionary of the Bible*, edited by Katharine Doob Sakenfeld, 156–68. Nashville: Abingdon.

Gorman, Michael J.
2008 *Reading Paul*. Eugene, OR: Cascade Books.

Gowan, Donald E.
1987 "Wealth and Poverty in the Old Testament: The Case of the Widow, the Orphan, and the Sojourner." *Interpretation* 41.4 (October): 341–53.

Gowler, David B.
2014 *James through the Centuries*. Wiley Blackwell Bible Commentaries. Chichester, West Sussex: Wiley Blackwell.

Green, Joel
2013 "Healing and Healthcare." In *The World of the New Testament: Cultural, Social, and Historical Contexts*, edited by Joel B. Green and Lee Martin McDonald, 330–41. Grand Rapids: Baker Academic.

Gwyn, Douglas, George Hunsinger, Eugene F. Roop, and John H. Yoder
1991 *A Declaration on Peace: In God's People the World's Renewal Has Begun*. Scottdale, PA: Herald Press.

Harder, Leland, ed.
1985 *The Sources of Swiss Anabaptism*. Classics of the Radical Reformation. Scottdale, PA: Herald Press.

Harrill, J. Albert
2009 "Slavery." In *S–Z*, vol. 5 of *The New Interpreter's Dictionary of the Bible*, edited by Katharine Doob Sakenfeld, 288–308. Nashville: Abingdon.

Hartin, Patrick J.
2007 "The Religious Context of the Letter of James." In *Jewish Christianity Reconsidered*, edited by M. Jackson-McCabe, 203–31. Minneapolis: Fortress.
2009a *James*. Sacra Pagina. Updated ed. Collegeville, MN: Liturgical Press.

2009b "James and the Jesus Tradition: Some Theological Reflections and Implications." In *The Catholic Epistles and Apostolic Tradition*, edited by Karl-Wilhelm Niebuhr and Robert W. Wall, 55–70. Waco: Baylor University Press.

Hauerwas, Stanley, and William H. Willimon
1989 *Resident Aliens.* Nashville: Abingdon.

Hays, Richard B.
1997 *First Corinthians.* Interpretation, a Bible Commentary. Louisville: John Knox.
1999 "Wisdom according to Paul." In *Where Shall Wisdom Be Found? Wisdom in the Bible, the Church, and the Contemporary World*, edited by Stephen C. Barton, 111–23. Edinburgh: T&T Clark.

Hearon, Holly
2020 "The Storied World of James." *Interpretation* 74.4 (2020): 353–62.

Hengel, Martin
1989 *The 'Hellenization' of Judaea in the First Century after Christ.* Translated by J. Bowden. London: SCM Press.

Holmes, Michael, ed.
2007 *The Apostolic Fathers: Greek Texts and English Translations.* 3rd ed. Grand Rapids: Baker Academic.

Hubmaier, Balthasar, H. Wayne Pipkin, and John Howard Yoder
1989 *Balthasar Hubmaier: Theologian of Anabaptism.* Classics of the Radical Reformation 5. Scottdale, PA: Herald Press.

Hus, Jan
1972 *The Letters of Jan Hus.* Translated by Matthew Spinka. Manchester: Manchester University Press.

Hylen, Susan E.
2019a "Widows in the New Testament Period." The Bible and Interpretation. Universities of Wyoming, Arizona, and Evansville. February. https://bibleinterp.arizona.edu/articles/widows-new-testament-period.
2019b *Women in the New Testament World.* New York: Oxford University Press.

Jackson-McCabe, Matt
2019 "The Letter of James and Hellenistic Philosophy." In *Reading the Epistle of James: A Resource for Students*, edited by Eric F. Mason and Darian R. Lockett, 45–71. Atlanta: SBL Press.

Jacobson, Rolf A., and Karl N. Jacobson
2017 "The Old Testament and the Neighbor." *Word and World* 37.1 (2017): 16–26.

Janzen, Waldemar
2000 *Exodus.* Believers Church Bible Commentary. Waterloo, ON: Herald Press.

Jenkins, Philip
2006 *The New Faces of Christianity: Believing the Bible in the Global South.* Oxford: Oxford University Press.

Jobling, David
2009 "Wealth." In *S–Z*, vol. 5 of *The New Interpreter's Dictionary of the Bible*, edited by Katharine Doob Sakenfeld, 825–28. Nashville: Abingdon.

Johnson, Luke Timothy
1982 "The Use of Leviticus 19 in the Letter of James." *Journal of Biblical Literature* 101 (1982): 341–401.
1985 "Friendship with the World—Friendship with God: A Study of Discipleship in James." In *Discipleship in the New Testament*, edited by Fernando Segovia, 166–83. Philadelphia: Fortress.
1995 *The Letter of James.* Anchor Bible Commentary. New Haven: Yale University Press.
1998 "James." In vol. 12 of *The New Interpreter's Bible: Hebrews–Revelation.* Nashville: Abingdon.
2002 "God Ever New, Ever the Same: The Witness of James and Peter." In *The Forgotten God: Perspectives in Biblical Theology*, edited by A. Andrew Das and Frank J. Matera, 211–27. Louisville: Westminster John Knox.
2004a *Brother of Jesus, Friend of God: Studies in the Letter of James.* Grand Rapids: Eerdmans.
2004b "James 3:13–4:10 and the *Topos* **περὶ φθόνου**." In *Brother of Jesus, Friend of God: Studies in the Letter of James*, 182–201. Grand Rapids: Eerdmans.
2004c "The Mirror of Remembrance: James 1:22-25." In *Brother of Jesus, Friend of God: Studies in the Letter of James*, 168–81. Grand Rapids: Eerdmans.
2004d "Taciturnity and True Religion: James 1:26-27." In *Brother of Jesus, Friend of God: Studies in the Letter of James*, 155–67. Grand Rapids: Eerdmans.
2004e "The Reception of James in the Early Church." In *Brother of Jesus, Friend of God: Studies in the Letter of James*, 45–60. Grand Rapids: Eerdmans.

Keenan, James P.
2005 *The Wisdom of James: Parallels with Mahāyāna Buddhism.* New York: Newman, 2005.

Kettering-Lane, Denise D.
2015 "Anointing for Healing: Critical Analysis of a Brethren Practice." *Brethren Life and Thought* 60.2 (Fall): 61–74.

Kierkegaard, Søren
1940 *For Self-Examination. Recommended for the Times.* Translated from the Danish by Edna and Howard Hong. Originally published in 1851. Minneapolis: Augsburg.
1956 *Purity of Heart Is to Will One Thing.* Translated from the Danish by Douglas V. Steere. Originally published in 1847. New York: Harper.

Kirk, J. A.
1969 "The Meaning of Wisdom in James: Examination of a Hypothesis." *New Testament Studies* 16 (October): 24–38.

Klaassen, Walter
1991 "'Gelassenheit' and Creation." *The Conrad Grebel Review* 9.1 (Winter): 23–35.

Klaassen, Walter, ed.
1981 *Anabaptism in Outline: Selected Primary Sources.* Classics of the Radical Reformation. Kitchener, ON: Herald Press.

Klassen-Wiebe, Sheila

2011 "In the World but Not of the World: A Johannine Perspective on the Church-World Relationship." In *The Church Made Strange for the Nations: Essays in Ecclesiology and Political Theology*, edited by Paul G. Doerksen and Karl Koop, 9–20. Eugene, OR: Pickwick.

Kloppenborg, John S.

2008 "Love in the New Testament." In *I–Ma*, vol. 3 of *The New Interpreter's Dictionary of the Bible*, edited by Katharine Doob Sakenfeld, 703–13. Nashville: Abingdon.

2009 "The Reception of the Jesus Tradition in James." In *The Catholic Epistles and Apostolic Tradition*, edited by Karl-Wilhelm Niebuhr and Robert W. Wall, 71–100. Waco: Baylor University Press.

Koester, Craig R.

2008 *The Word of Life. A Theology of John's Gospel*. Grand Rapids: Eerdmans.

Kovalishyn, Mariam Kamell

2011 "The Implications of Grace for the Ethics of James." *Biblica* 92.2:274–87.

2021 "Wisdom in the New Testament." In *The Oxford Handbook of Wisdom and the Bible*, edited by Will Kynes, 173–86. New York: Oxford University Press.

Koyama, Kōsuke

1999 *Waterbuffalo Theology*. 25th Anniversary ed. Maryknoll, NY: Orbis Books. First ed., Singapore: Distributed by SPCK, 1974.

Krall, Ruth E.

1996 "Anger and an Anabaptist Feminist Hermeneutic." *Conrad Grebel Review* 14.2 (Spring): 145–63.

Kraybill, Donald B.

2010 *Concise Encyclopedia of Amish, Brethren, Hutterites, and Mennonites*. Baltimore: Johns Hopkins University Press.

Kraybill, Donald B., Steven M. Nolt, and David Weaver-Zercher

2007 *Amish Grace: How Forgiveness Transcended Tragedy*. San Francisco: Jossey-Bass.

Kümmel, Werner Georg

1975 *Introduction to the New Testament*. 17th rev. ed. Translated by Howard Clark Kee. Nashville: Abingdon.

Laws, Sophie

1980 *The Epistle of James*. Black's New Testament Commentary. Peabody, MA: Hendrickson.

Lemaire, André

2002 "Burial Box of James the Brother of Jesus." *Biblical Archaeology Review* 28.6 (November–December): 24–33.

Lewis, Simon, and Heather Timmons

2020 "Trump Seeks to Shore Up Evangelical Support at 'Prosperity Gospel' Church." Reuters, January 3. https://www.reuters.com/article/world/trump-seeks-to-shore-up-evangelical-support-at-prosperity-gospel-church-idUSKBN1Z21JU/.

Liechty, Daniel, trans. and ed.

1994 *Early Anabaptist Spirituality: Selected Writings*. New York: Paulist Press.

Lockett, Darian R.

2007 "'Unstained by the World': Purity and Pollution as an Indicator of Cultural Interaction in the Letter of James." In *Reading James with New Eyes. Methodological Reassessments of the Letter of James*, edited by Robert L. Webb and John S. Kloppenborg, 49–74. Library of New Testament Studies. London: T&T Clark.

2019 "Use, Authority, and Canonical Status of James in the Earliest Church." In *Reading the Epistle of James: A Resource for Students* edited by Eric F. Mason and Darian R. Lockett, 253–71. Atlanta: SBL Press.

2020 "What Do James, Peter, John, and Jude Have in Common? Arguing for the Canonical Collection of the Catholic Epistles." *Southern Baptist Journal of Theology* 24.3: 119–41.

Loewen, Howard John

1994 "An Analysis of the Use of Scripture in the Churches' Documents on Peace." In *The Church's Peace Witness*, edited by Marlin E. Miller and Barbara Nelson Gingerich, 15–69. Grand Rapids: Eerdmans, 1994.

Longenecker, Richard N.

1990 *Galatians*. Word Biblical Commentary 41. Dallas: Word Books.

Lowe, Bruce A.

2009 "James 2:1 in the **Πίστις Χριστοῦ** Debate: Irrelevant or Indispensable?" In *The Faith of Jesus Christ: Exegetical, Biblical, and Theological Studies*, edited by Michael F. Bird and Preston M. Sprinkle, 239–57. Peabody, MA: Hendrickson.

Luther, Martin

1529 Large Catechism. https://bookofconcord.org/large-catechism/.

Malina, Bruce J.

1987 "Wealth and Poverty in the New Testament and Its World." *Interpretation* 41 (October): 354–67.

1993 *The New Testament World: Insights from Cultural Anthropology*. Rev. ed. Louisville: Westminster John Knox.

Manton, Thomas

1840 *A Practical Commentary, or an Exposition with Notes on the Epistle of James*. London: R. Gladding et al. https://archive.org/details/apracticalcomme01mantgoog/page/n9/mode/1up.

Martens, Elmer A.

2002 "How Is the Christian to Construe Old Testament Law?" *Bulletin for Biblical Research* 12.2: 199–216.

Martin, Ralph P.

1988 *James*. Word Biblical Commentary. Waco: Word Books.

Mason, Eric F.

2019 "Use of Biblical and Other Jewish Traditions in James." In *Reading the Epistle of James: A Resource for Students*, edited by Eric F. Mason and Darian R. Lockett, 27–43. Atlanta: SBL Press.

Matties, Gordon H.

2012 *Joshua*. Believers Church Bible Commentary. Harrisonburg, VA: Herald Press.

Maxwell, David R.

2007 "Justified by Works and Not by Faith Alone: Reconciling Paul and James." *Concordia Journal* 33.4 (October): 375–78.

Maynard-Reid, Pedrito U.
1987 *Poverty and Wealth in James*. Maryknoll, NY: Orbis Books.

Mayor, Joseph B.
1954 *The Epistle of St. James: The Greek Text with Introduction, Notes and Comments, and Further Studies in the Epistle of St. James*. Original, 1892. Reprint, Grand Rapids: Zondervan.

McCane, Byron R.
n.d. "Burial Practices in First Century Palestine." *Bible Odyssey* (newsletter). https://www.bibleodyssey.org/articles/burial-practices-in-first-century-palestine/.

McCartney, Dan G.
2000 "The Wisdom of James the Just." *Southern Baptist Journal of Theology* 4.3 (Fall): 52–64.
2009 *James*. Baker Exegetical Commentary on the New Testament. Grand Rapids: Baker Academic.

McKnight, Scot
2011 *The Letter of James*. New International Commentary on the New Testament. Grand Rapids: Eerdmans.

McNutt, Jennifer Powell
2014 "James, 'The Book of Straw,' in Reformation Biblical Exegesis: A Comparison of Luther and the Radicals." In *Reconsidering the Relationship between Biblical and Systematic Theology in the New Testament*, edited by Benjamin E. Reynolds, Brian Lugioyo, and Kevin J. Vanhoozer, 157–76. Tübingen: Mohr Siebeck.

Melcher, Sarah J.
2015 "Rahab and Esther in Distress: A Feminist Biblical Theology of Moral Agency." In *After Exegesis. Feminist Biblical Theology*, edited by Patricia K. Tull and Jacqueline E. Lapsley, pp. 155–69. Essays in Honor of Carol A. Newsom. Waco: Baylor University Press.

Menno Simons
1539 "Why I Do Not Cease Teaching and Writing." *CWMS*: 292–320, esp. 307 on "true evangelical faith." https://stauffer-scribbler.blogspot.com/2015/08/true-evangelical-faith.html.
1956 *CWMS: The Complete Writings of Menno Simons, c. 1496–1561*. Translated by Leonard Verduin. Edited by John C. Wenger. Scottdale, PA: Herald Press.

Meyer, Arnold
1930 *Das Rätsel des Jacobusbriefs*. Beihefte zur Zeitschrift für die neutestamentliche Wissenschaft 10. Giessen: Töpelmann.

Michaels, J. Ramsey
2001 "Finding Yourself an Intercessor: New Testament Prayer from Hebrews to Jude." In *Into God's Presence: Prayer in the New Testament*, edited by Richard N. Longenecker, 228–51. McMaster New Testament Studies. Grand Rapids: Eerdmans.

Milgrom, Jacob
2000 *Leviticus 17–22*. Anchor Bible 3A. New York: Doubleday.

Miller, John W.
2004 *Proverbs*. Believers Church Bible Commentary. Scottdale, PA: Herald Press.

Miller, Steven P.
2008 Review of *Diaspora in the Countryside: Two Mennonite Communities and Mid-Twentieth Century Rural Disjuncture*, by Royden Loewen. *Mennonite Quarterly Review* 82.1 (January): 203–5.

Mitchell, Margaret M.
2007 "The Letter of James as a Document of Paulinism?" In *Reading James with New Eyes: Methodological Reassessments of the Letter of James*, edited by Robert L. Webb and John S. Kloppenborg, 75–98. Library of New Testament Studies. London: T&T Clark.

Moo, Douglas J.
2009 *James: An Introduction and Commentary*. Tyndale New Testament Commentaries. Nottingham, UK: IVP Academic.

Moore-Keish, Martha L.
2019 *James*. Belief: A Theological Commentary on the Bible. Louisville: Westminster John Knox.

Moule, C. F. D.
1959 *An Idiom Book of New Testament Greek*. 2nd ed. Cambridge: Cambridge University Press.

Murray, Stuart
2000 *Biblical Interpretation in the Anabaptist Tradition*. Studies in the Believers Church Tradition. Kitchener, ON: Pandora.

Neff, Christian, Harold S. Bender, and William Klassen
1958 "Oath." *Global Anabaptist Mennonite Encyclopedia Online*. 1958. http://www.gameo.org/encyclopedia/contents/O358.html.

Nouwen, Henri
1981 *The Way of the Heart*. New York: Seabury.

Ollenburger, Ben C.
1984 "The Hermeneutics of Obedience: Reflections on Anabaptist Hermeneutics." In *Essays on Biblical Interpretation: Anabaptist-Mennonite Perspectives*, edited by Willard M. Swartley, 45–61. Text-Reader Series No. 1. Elkhart, IN: Institute of Mennonite Studies.

Painter, John
1999 *Just James: The Brother of Jesus in History and Tradition*. Minneapolis: Fortress Press.
2019 "James 'the Brother of the Lord' and the Epistle of James." In *Reading the Epistle of James. A Resource for Students*, edited by Eric F. Mason and Darian R. Lockett, 231–51. Atlanta: SBL Press.

Painter, John, and David A. deSilva
2012 *James and Jude*. Paideia Commentaries on the New Testament. Grand Rapids: Baker Academic.

Perkins, Pheme
1995 *First and Second Peter, James, and Jude*. Interpretation, a Bible Commentary. Louisville: John Knox.

Philips, Dirk, Cornelius J. Dyck, William E. Keeney, and Alvin J. Beachy
1992 *The Writings of Dirk Philips, 1504–1568*. Classics of the Radical Reformation 6. Scottdale, PA: Herald Press.

Philo
1929 *Legum allegoriae* [*Allegorical Interpretation*] III.223–24. In *Philo*, vol. 1, translated by F. H. Colson and G. H. Whitaker. Loeb Classical Library. Cambridge: Harvard University Press, 1929.

Pietersz, Pieter
1625 *Wegh na Vreden-stadt* (*The Way to the City of Peace*). From the 1715 ed. of his *Opera*, 1–53. In *Spiritual Life in Anabaptism*, translated from the Dutch and edited by C. J. Dyck, 231–83. Scottdale, PA: Herald Press, 1995. Cf. https://www.goshen.edu/mqr/2004/10/october-2004-harder/.
1638 *Spiegel der Gierigheydt* (*Mirror of Greed*). Cf. https://www.academia.edu/62746328/Dangers_of_Superabundance_Pieter_Pietersz_Mennonites_and_Greed_during_the_Dutch_Golden_Age.
Powell, Mark Allan
2009 *Introducing the New Testament. A Historical, Literary, and Theological Survey*. Grand Rapids: Baker Academic.
Pries, Edmund
1992 "Oath Refusal in Zurich from 1525 to 1527: The Erratic Emergence of Anabaptist Practice." In *Anabaptism Revisited*, edited by W. Klaassen, 65–84. Scottdale, PA: Herald Press.
Reformed/Calvinistic churches
1563 Heidelberg Catechism. https://www.crcna.org/welcome/beliefs/confessions/heidelberg-catechism.
Ris, Cornelis
1766 Mennonite Articles of Faith by Cornelis Ris (1776) https://anabaptistwiki.org/mediawiki/index.php/Mennonite_Articles_of_Faith_by_Cornelis_Ris_(1766).
Ropes, James H.
1916 *A Critical and Exegetical Commentary on the Epistle of St. James*. International Critical Commentary. Edinburgh: T&T Clark.
Sanders, E. P.
1990 *The Question of Uniqueness in the Teaching of Jesus*. The Ethel M. Wood Lecture 15. London: University of London.
Sattler, Michael
1527 The Schleitheim Confession of Faith. Available at https://courses.washington.edu/hist112/SCHLEITHEIM CONFESSION OF FAITH.htm
Schleitheim Confession
1527 *See* Sattler
Schmitt, John J.
1986 "You Adulteresses! The Image in James 4:4." *Novum Testamentum* 28.4 (January 1): 327–37.
Schröter, Jens
2008 "Jesus Tradition in Matthew, James, and the Didache: Searching for Characteristic Emphases." In *Matthew, James, and Didache: Three Related Documents in Their Jewish and Christian Settings*, edited by Huub van de Sandt and Jürgen K. Zangenberg, 233–55. SBL Symposium Series 45. Atlanta: Society of Biblical Literature.
Schüssler Fiorenza, Elisabeth
1983 *In Memory of Her: A Feminist Theological Reconstruction of Christian Origins*. New York: Crossroad.
Shepherd, Massey H.
1956 "The Epistle of James and the Gospel of Matthew." *Journal of Biblical Literature* 75.1 (March): 40–51.

Shillington, V. George
2015 *James and Paul. The Politics of Identity at the Turn of the Ages.* Minneapolis: Fortress.

Sider, Ronald J.
1997 *Rich Christians in an Age of Hunger*. 4th ed. Dallas: Word Publishing. First published, 1978. 6th ed. Rev. and expanded. Nashville: Nelson, 2015.

Silva, Moises
2014 *New International Dictionary of New Testament Theology and Exegesis.* 2nd ed. Grand Rapids: Zondervan.

Simons, Menno. *See* Menno Simons

Skarsaune, Oskar
2007 "The History of Jewish Believers in the Early Centuries—Perspectives and Framework." In *Jewish Believers in Jesus: The Early Centuries*, edited by Oskar Skarsaune and Reidar Hvalvik, 745–81. Peabody, MA: Hendrickson, 2007.

Sleeper, Freeman
1998 *James.* Abingdon New Testament Commentaries. Nashville: Abingdon.

Smit, D. J.
1990 "Exegesis and Proclamation: 'Show No Partiality . . .' (James 2:1-13)." *Journal of Theology for Southern Africa* 71 (June): 59–68.

Snodgrass, Klyne
1992 "Matthew's Understanding of the Law." *Interpretation* 46 (October): 368–77.

Snyder, C. Arnold
1995 *Anabaptist History and Theology: An Introduction.* Kitchener, ON: Pandora.
2004 *Following in the Footsteps of Christ: The Anabaptist Tradition.* Traditions of Christian Spirituality Series. Maryknoll: Orbis Books.

Snyder, C. Arnold, ed.
2001 *Sources of South German/Austrian Anabaptism.* Classics of the Radical Reformation. Translated by Walter Klaassen, Frank Friesen, and Werner O. Packull. Kitchener, ON: Pandora.

Spitaler, Peter
2009 "James 1:5-8: A Dispute with God." *Catholic Biblical Quarterly* 71.3 (July): 560–79.

Spitta, Friedrich
1896 *Der Brief des Jakobus.* Göttingen: Vandenhoeck & Ruprecht.

Stark, Rodney
1996 *The Rise of Christianity: A Sociologist Reconsiders History.* Princeton, NJ: Princeton University Press.

Stokes, Ryan E.
2019 "The Devil and Demons in the Epistle of James." In *Reading the Epistle of James: A Resource for Students*, edited by Eric F. Mason and Darian R. Lockett, 145–59. Atlanta: SBL Press.

Streett, Daniel R.
2011 "Food, Fellowship, and Favoritism: Early Christian Meals as the Setting for James 2:1–9." Unpublished paper presented at the Society of Biblical Literature Annual Meeting, San Francisco, November 19.

Stulac, George M.
1993 *James*. IVP New Testament Commentary 16. Downers Grove, IL: InterVarsity.

Suderman, Derek
2004 "A Goring Ox and a Wealthy Man." *Canadian Mennonite* 8.10 (May 17): 6–8. https://canadianmennonite.org/wp-content/uploads/past-issues/8-10small.pdf.

Swartley, Willard M., ed.
1988 *Essays on Spiritual Bondage and Deliverance*. Occasional Papers 11. Elkhart, IN: Institute of Mennonite Studies.

Tamez, Elsa
1982 *Bible of the Oppressed*. Translated by Matthew J. O'Connell. Maryknoll, NY: Orbis Books.
2002 *The Scandalous Message of James: Faith without Works Is Dead*. Rev. ed. New York: Crossroad.
2011 "James: A Circular Letter for Immigrants." *Review and Expositor* 108 (Summer): 369–80.

Tannehill, Robert C.
1996 *Luke*. Abingdon New Testament Commentaries. Nashville: Abingdon.

Thurston, Bonnie Bowman
1989 *The Widows: A Women's Ministry in the Early Church*. Minneapolis: Fortress.
2009 "Widow." In *S–Z*, vol. 5 of *New Interpreter's Dictionary of the Bible*, edited by Katharine Doob Sakenfeld, 846–47. Nashville: Abingdon.

Toews, John E.
2004 *Romans*. Believers Church Bible Commentary. Harrisonburg, VA: Herald Press.

Townsend, Michael J.
1976 "James 4:1-4: A Warning against Zealotry?" *Expository Times* 87 (April): 211–13.

Van Leeuwen, Raymond C.
2005 "Wisdom Literature." In *Dictionary for Theological Interpretation of the Bible*, edited by Kevin J. Vanhoozer, 847–50. Grand Rapids: Baker Academic.

Van Voorst, Robert E.
2009 "James." In *I–Ma*, vol. 3 of *The New Interpreter's Dictionary of the Bible*, edited by Katharine Doob Sakenfeld, 183–88. Nashville: Abingdon.

Verseput, Donald
2000 "Genre and Story: The Community Setting of the Epistle of James." *Catholic Biblical Quarterly* 62 (January): 96–110.

Vlachos, Chris A.
2013 *James*. Exegetical Guide to the Greek New Testament. Edited by Murray J. Harris and Andreas J. Köstenberger. Nashville: Broadman & Holman.

Wachob, Wesley H.
2000 *The Voice of Jesus in the Social Rhetoric of James*. Society for New Testament Studies Monograph Series 106. Cambridge: Cambridge University Press.

Wall, Robert W.
1997 *Community of the Wise: The Letter of James*. The New Testament in Context. Valley Forge, PA: Trinity Press International.

Wallace, Daniel B.
1996 *Greek Grammar Beyond the Basics: An Exegetical Syntax of the New Testament*. Grand Rapids: Zondervan.

Ward, Roy Bowen
1969 "Partiality in the Assembly: James 2:2-4." *Harvard Theological Review* 62.1 (January): 87–97.

Watson, Troy
2020 "The Power of Paradox." *Canadian Mennonite* 24, no. 9 (April 22): 12. https://canadianmennonite.org/power-paradox/.

Wenger, John C.
1953 "Anointing with Oil." *Global Anabaptist Mennonite Encyclopedia Online*. http://gameo.org/index.php?title=Anointing_with_Oil&oldid=103729.

Wenger, Mark R.
2005 "The Origins and Development of Anointing Among Nineteenth-Century Mennonites." *Mennonite Quarterly Review* 79.1 (January): 19–50.

Williams, George H., and Angel M. Mergal
1957 *Spiritual and Anabaptist Writers*. Library of Christian Classics. Philadelphia: Westminster.

Wink, Walter
1984 *Naming the Powers: The Language of Power in the New Testament*. Philadelphia: Fortress.
1992 *Engaging the Powers*. Minneapolis: Fortress.
1998 *The Powers That Be: Theology for a New Millennium*. New York: Doubleday.

Witherington, Ben, III
2007 *Letters and Homilies for Jewish Christians*. Downers Grove, IL: InterVarsity.
2010 *Jesus and Money: A Guide for Times of Financial Crisis*. Grand Rapids: Brazos.

Wittlinger, Carlton O.
1978 *The Quest for Piety and Obedience: The Story of the Brethren in Christ*. Nappanee, IN: Evangel.

Yoder, Perry B.
1987 *Shalom: The Bible's Word for Salvation, Justice, and Peace*. Newton: Faith and Life.
2017 *Leviticus*. Believers Church Bible Commentary. Harrisonburg, VA: Herald Press.

Yoder Neufeld, Thomas R.
2002 *Ephesians*. Believers Church Bible Commentary. Waterloo, ON: Herald Press.
2011 *Killing Enmity: Violence and the New Testament*. Grand Rapids: Baker Academic.

Zerwick, Max, and Mary Grosvenor.
1981 *A Grammatical Analysis of the Greek New Testament*. Unabridged, revised edition. Rome: Biblical Institute Press.

Selected Resources

Commentaries

Allison, Dale C. *A Critical and Exegetical Commentary on the Epistle of James*. New York: Bloomsbury, 2013. A massive and thorough commentary, with detailed discussion of exegetical issues. Distinctive for its attention to the history of interpretation and reception of the text throughout history.

Blomberg, Craig L., and Mariam J. Kamell. *James*. Exegetical Commentary on the New Testament. Grand Rapids: Zondervan, 2008. A commentary for pastors and teachers, written by two evangelical scholars. It pays careful attention to the literary structure of the text and provides theological and practical insights into the letter.

Davids, Peter H. *The Epistle of James: A Commentary on the Greek Text*. New International Greek Testament Commentary. Grand Rapids: Eerdmans, 1982. A solid commentary, providing careful exegetical insights into the text.

Hartin, Patrick J. *James*. Sacra Pagina. Updated ed. Collegeville, MN: Liturgical Press, 2009a. An excellent commentary by a Roman Catholic scholar, with helpful excursuses on various topics important for understanding the letter. Contains verse-by-verse notes as well as broader theological interpretation of each section.

Johnson, Luke Timothy. *The Letter of James*. Anchor Bible Commentary. New Haven: Yale University Press, 1995. Notable for its attention to James's literary relationships with Greco-Roman moralists, the Old Testament, Jewish literature, and noncanonical Christian literature. The introduction comprises almost half the book and offers a wealth of background information on the letter.

McCartney, Dan G. *James*. Baker Exegetical Commentary on the New Testament. Grand Rapids: Baker Academic, 2009. An outstanding commentary, thorough in its exposition of the text, and theologically rich. It argues that James is a book about true faith.

McKnight, Scot. *The Letter of James.* New International Commentary on the New Testament. Grand Rapids: Eerdmans, 2011. A solid commentary that focuses on a literary and theological reading of the letter.

Moore-Keish, Martha L. *James.* Belief: A Theological Commentary on the Bible. Louisville: Westminster John Knox, 2019. An excellent contribution to a commentary series written by theologians instead of biblical scholars. Moore-Keish offers theologically rich interpretation of James and thought-provoking, creative engagement with contemporary concerns.

Witherington, Ben, III. *Letters and Homilies for Jewish Christians.* Downers Grove, IL: InterVarsity, 2007. A commentary attentive to social setting and rhetorical strategies of the author, within a Jewish context. Includes commentary on Hebrews and Jude in addition to James.

Other Resources of Interest

Baker, William R. "James, Book of." In *Dictionary for Theological Interpretation of the Bible.* Edited by Kevin J. Vanhoozer. Grand Rapids: Baker Academic, 2005. An introduction to the Letter of James with attention to theological interpretation in history.

Batten, Alicia J. "Early Anabaptist Interpretation of the Letter of James." *Annali di Storia dell'Esegesi*, 34.2 (July–December, 2017): 537–51. An excellent survey of how early Anabaptists used James and which verses and themes were favorites.

———. *Friendship and Benefaction in James.* Emory Studies in Early Christianity 15. Atlanta: SBL Press, 2017b. A scholarly treatment of James that uses social-scientific methods and rhetorical analysis to consider how the author used language and concepts related to friendship in ancient Greek and Roman literature.

Bauckham, Richard. *James: Wisdom of James, Disciple of Jesus the Sage.* New Testament Readings. London: Routledge, 1999. Argues that James, like Jesus, was a wisdom teacher and that James passed on Jesus' wisdom by reformulating it and making it his own.

Hartin, Patrick. *A Spirituality of Perfection: Faith in Action in the Letter of James.* Collegeville, MN: Liturgical Press, 1999. An engaging study of James that argues for "perfection" or "wholeness" as the key to understanding the message of the letter.

Johnson, Luke Timothy. *Brother of Jesus, Friend of God: Studies in the Letter of James.* Grand Rapids: Eerdmans, 2004. A collection of essays that Johnson has written over the years on various topics, including the history of interpretation, reception of the letter, gender in the Letter of James, and studies of specific texts in their Hellenistic context.

Mason, Eric F., and Darian R. Lockett, eds. *Reading the Epistle of James: A Resource for Students.* Atlanta: SBL Press, 2019. A wonderful and diverse collection of essays, scholarly yet accessible, on topics and themes related to study of the Letter of James.

Tamez, Elsa. *The Scandalous Message of James: Faith without Works Is Dead.* Rev. ed. New York: Crossroad, 2002. A short study of James by a Latin American scholar reading James from the angles of oppression, hope, and praxis.

Index of Ancient Sources

Mark

The Author

Sheila Klassen-Wiebe is associate professor of New Testament at Canadian Mennonite University, where she teaches New Testament and Bible courses at both the undergraduate and graduate level. She has degrees from Canadian Mennonite Bible College, the University of Manitoba, Associated Mennonite Biblical Seminary, and Union Theological Seminary. Klassen-Wiebe is enthusiastic about making the Bible come alive for people, both in university and church settings.

Klassen-Wiebe's home congregation in Winnipeg is Charleswood Mennonite Church, where she is actively involved. She and her husband Vern have three adult daughters. When she is not working, Klassen-Wiebe finds joy in getting her hands dirty in the garden, walking in the forest, making decadent desserts, and spending time with family and friends.